Policy and Politics in
West Germany

Policy and Politics in Industrial States

A series edited by Douglas E. Ashford, Peter J. Katzenstein, and T. J. Pempel

Peter J. Katzenstein

Policy and Politics in
West Germany

The Growth of a Semisovereign State

Temple University Press
Philadelphia

Temple University Press, Philadelphia 19122
Copyright © 1987 by Temple University. All rights reserved
Published 1987
Printed in the United States of America

Library of Congress Cataloging-in-Publication Data

Katzenstein, Peter J.
  Policy and politics in West Germany.

  (Policy and politics in industrial states)
  Bibliography: p.
  Includes index.
  1. Germany (West)—Politics and government.
I. Title. II. Series.
DD258.75.K37   1987   320.943   87-1909
ISBN 0-87722-263-0 (alk. paper)
ISBN 0-87722-264-9 (pbk. : alk. paper)

For
Tai and Suzanne

Contents

Acronyms

BDA	Federation of German Employers' Associations
BDI	Federation of German Industry
CDU	Christian Democratic Union
CSU	Christian Social Union
DAG	Union for Employees
DBV	German Farmers' Union
DGB	Federation of German Trade Unions
DIHT	Diet of German Industry and Commerce
EC	European Community
EMS	European Monetary System
FDP	Free Democratic party
KMK	Standing Conference of Ministers of Culture
KV	Association of Doctors for Statutory Health Insurance
NATO	North Atlantic Treaty Organization
NDP	National Democratic party
NSDAP	Nazi party
OECD	Organization for Economic Cooperation and Development
SPD	Social Democratic party

Tables

Figures

Editors' Preface

All industrial states face a tension between bureaucracy and democracy. Modern governments have found it increasingly difficult to formulate policies adequate to the complex tasks they undertake. At the same time the growing specialization and widening scope of government have led many to question whether it can still be controlled democratically. Policy and Politics in Industrial States explores how some of the major democracies have dealt with this dilemma.

Policy is a pattern of purposive action by which political institutions shape society. It typically involves a wide variety of efforts to address certain societal problems. Politics is also a much broader concept, involving the conflict and choices linking individuals and social forces to the political institutions that make policy. Comparative analysis of the interaction between policy and politics is an essential beginning in understanding how and why industrial states differ or converge in their responses to common problems.

The fact that the advanced industrial states are pursuing many similar aims such as increasing social well-being, reducing social conflict, and achieving higher levels of employment and economic productivity means neither that they will all do so in the same way nor that the relevance of politics to such behavior will always be the same. In looking at an array of problems common to all industrial states, the books in this series argue that policies are shaped primarily by the manner in which power is organized within each country. Thus, Britain, Japan, the United States, West Germany, Sweden, and France set distinctive priorities and follow distinctive policies designed to achieve them. In this respect, the series dissents from the view that the nature of the problem faced is the most important feature in determining the politics surrounding efforts at its resolution. Taken to its logical extreme, this view supports the expectation that all states will pursue broadly similar goals in politically similar ways. Though this series will illustrate some important similarities among the policies of different countries, one of the key conclusions to which it points is the distinctive approach that each state takes in managing the problems it confronts.

A second important feature of the series is its sensitivity to the difficulties involved in evaluating policy success or failure. Goals are ambiguous and often contradictory from one area of policy to another; past precedents often shape present options. Conversely, adhering to choices made at an earlier time is often impossible or undesirable at a later period. Hence evaluation must transcend the application of simple economic or managerial criteria of rationality, efficiency, or effectiveness. What appears from such perspectives as irrational, inefficient, or ineffective is often, from a political standpoint, quite intelligible.

To facilitate comparison, the books in the series follow a common format. In each book, the first chapter introduces the reader to the country's political institutions and social forces, spells out how these are linked to form that country's distinctive configuration of power, and explores how that configuration can be expected to influence policy. A concluding chapter seeks to integrate the country argument developed in the first chapter with the subsequent policy analysis and provides more general observations about the ways in which the specific country findings fit into current debates about policy and politics.

The intervening six chapters provide policy cases designed to illustrate, extend, and refine the country argument. Each of the six policy analyses follows a common format. The first section analyzes the *context* of the policy problem: its historical roots, competing perceptions of the problem by major political and social groups, and its interdependence with other problems facing the country. The second section deals with the *agenda* set out for the problem: the pressures generating action and the explicit and implicit motives of important political actors, including the government's objectives. The third section deals with *process:* the formulation of the issue, its attempted resolution, and the instruments involved in policy implementation. The fourth and final section of analysis traces the *consequences* of policy for official objectives, for the power distribution in the issue area, for other policies, and for the country's capacity to make policy choices in the future. The element of arbitrariness such a schema introduces into the discussion of policy and politics is a price the series gladly pays in the interest of facilitating comparative analysis of policy and politics.

An important feature of these cases is the inclusion, for each policy problem, of selected readings drawn primarily from official policy documents, interpretations, or critiques of policy by different actors, and politically informed analysis. We have become persuaded that the actual language used in policy debates within each country provides an important clue to the relationship between that country's policy and its politics. Since appropriate readings are more widely available for Britain and the United States than for the non-English-speaking countries in the series, we have included somewhat more policy materials for these countries. In all instances, the readings are selected as illustration, rather than confirmation, of each book's argument.

Also distinctive of the series, and essential to its comparative approach, is the selection of common policy cases. Each volume analyzes at least one case involving intergovernmental problems: reform of the national bureaucracy or the interaction among national, regional, and local governments. Each also includes two cases dealing with economic problems: economic policy and labor-management relations. Lastly, each book includes at least two cases focusing on the relationship of individual citizens to the state, among them social welfare. Our choice is designed to provide a basis for cross-national and cross-issue comparison while being sufficiently flexible to make allowance for the idiosyncrasies of the countries (and the authors). By using such a framework, we hope that these books will convey the richness and diversity of each country's efforts to solve major problems, as well as the similarities of the interaction between policy and politics in industrial states.

D. E. A.
P. J. K.
T. J. P.

Preface

This book's subtitle, *The Growth of a Semisovereign State,* summarizes its main argument. West German politics is distinguished by an intricate web of relations among different political actors. As a result, the power of state officials is both severely circumscribed and widely diffused. This organization of power shapes West German policy. The evidence that I present in six case studies emphasizes the great difficulties that the Federal Republic faces in formulating and implementing large-scale policy changes. The German state no longer exists; but its power has not been eclipsed altogether. Instead, since 1945 the power of the West German state has been tamed.

Although in this book I focus exclusively on West Germany, my approach is comparative. For a decade I have resisted the temptation of writing about a country I feared I knew too well. Although it has provided intellectual nourishment to German specialists, the preoccupation with "the German problem" and the past has often diverted attention from the present. I thus chose to learn more about the politics of other large and small industrial states in order to comprehend better the political possibilities and limitations of the Federal Republic. The costs of imposing such intellectual distance are many, but my perspective on West German politics may offer an alternative to that of scholars who experience West Germany at close range.

My interest in the state as an important organizing concept of political analysis dates back more than a decade. I still remember vividly the mixture of barely suspended disbelief and good-natured derision which greeted my first lecture on this subject at Cornell in the mid-1970s. A number of friends and colleagues now share my interest and have helped reduce my confusion somewhat. Discussions with Bruce Cumings, Peter Evans, Albert Hirschman, Ira Katznelson, Stephen Krasner, Dietrich Rueschemeyer, Theda Skocpol, and Charles Tilly, all members of the Committee on States and Social Structures of the Social Science Research Council, have helped me greatly to articulate my ideas.

I owe a special debt of gratitude to Douglas Ashford and T. J. Pempel. They taught me much about comparative policy studies through their individual writings, our collaborative teaching, and our joint editorship of this book series. Their generous patience while waiting for a long overdue manuscript and their insightful criticisms of its first draft have made this a better book.

In writing this book I have benefited from the help of many friends and colleagues. My greatest intellectual debt is to those who commented critically on a full draft of the manuscript: Joachim Jens Hesse, Herbert Kitschelt, Gerhard Lehmbruch, Stephan Leibfried, Wolf-Dieter Narr, Fritz Scharpf, and Manfred Schmidt. Too often, I fear, I disagreed with their views. But without their critical comments I could not have sharpened my own ideas. I have also received many helpful criticisms and suggestions from those who read one or several chapters: Chris Allen, Bernhard Badura, Knut Dohse, Wolfgang Fach, Michael Greve, Jost Halfmann, Arnold Heidenheimer, Sheila Jasanoff, Gerd Junne, Ulrich Karpen, Gregg Kvistad, David Laitin, Andrei Markovits, John Meyer, Jonas Pontusson, Ray Rist, Dietrich Rueschemeyer, Gebhard Schweigler, Martin Shefter, Wolfgang Streeck, Ulrich Teichler, and Manfred Zuleeg.

My work has also been supported generously by many other people. Over the years a number of Cornell students have helped me in my research for this book. I would like to thank in particular Jean-Louis Amann, Marcia Carpentier, Bernd Decker, Elizabeth Newton, Udo Staber, and Rhonda Wassermann. David Armstrong, Arline Blaker, Michael Busch, and Delores Robinson did much more, and in good humor, than merely type and retype several drafts of the manuscript. For years Michael Ames of Temple University Press kept encouraging me to write this book, while I kept disappointing him. I think we were both equally surprised when I managed to meet even one deadline. In her careful editing of this manuscript Emily Wheeler patiently taught me some elementary rules of English grammar and persistently queried my inconsistencies. Without her tactful interference this book about West Germany would have been marred by a Teutonic prose style.

I am grateful for the financial support of the German Marshall Fund

of the United States (grant no. 3-51025), which permitted me to draft
the book's initial prospectus.

Portions of Chapters 1, 2, and 8 have been previously published and
are used here with permission: "Problem or Model? West Germany in
the 1980s," *World Politics* 32 (July 1980):577–99; "West Germany as
Number Two: Reflections on the German Model," in Andrei S. Markovits, ed., *The Political Economy of West Germany: Modell Deutschland* (New York: Praeger, 1982), pp. 199–215; and "Economic Management in the Federal Republic of Germany," *German Studies News-
letter,* no. 8 (July 1986):3–10.

I dedicate this book to Tai and Suzanne. Over the past several years
they have taught me in daily life the deeper meaning of the concept of
semisovereignty.

Policy and Politics in
West Germany

1 The Taming of Power: West Germany's Semisovereign State

For the last thirty years political analyses of German history have focused on two questions: Why World War I and World War II? Why Hitler and Auschwitz? These questions have invited what by now are familiar answers. Delayed political unification and late but rapid industrialization in the second half of the nineteenth century led to a combination of extreme military aggressiveness abroad and extreme political illiberalism at home. Such has been the conventional depiction of the German Question. Fears are receding of a revival of German militarism and authoritarianism feeding on the sore of national reunification and reinforced by a downturn in the economic fortunes of the Bonn Republic. In the eyes of many, West Germany has successfully combined Anglo-Saxon liberalism with continental statism and corporatism in a modern social welfare state. The result appears to be a prosperous society that is also a stable democracy.

The twin pressures of a global economic crisis and national political disappointments have led to sweeping changes in some major democratic states and surprising policy continuities in others. The United States and Britain have moved resolutely away from long-standing social welfare programs and toward private-sector initiatives. France, on the other hand, attempted in 1981–83 to solve its problems with a socialist program that eventually ran up against the constraints imposed by the international economy. In Sweden, as in France, the government changed in the mid-1970s and early 1980s, but policy did not. A conservative coalition government that held office between 1976 and 1982 found itself prisoner of the "hegemony" of Social Democratic policies (Heclo and Madsen, 1987). And in Japan, a conservative party that has held office uninterruptedly since 1955 has continued its export offensive on world markets to pay for the oil and other raw materials on which its economy depends so crucially. At the same time Japan's conservative political leaders are making subtle adjustments in domestic policies that outflank their opponents.

If viewed comparatively, West Germany is striking for its lack of new policy initiatives (as distinct from political rhetoric) despite the 1983 triumph of a new conservative coalition government over a left-of-center coalition. The continuation of previous policy is particularly surprising since neoconservatism has struck a very responsive ideological chord in West Germany. As in Sweden, the conservatives' victory changed the composition of the government but not the basic policy approach. But in contrast to their Swedish counterparts, West German conservatives did not confront hegemonic Social Democratic policies. West Germany's SPD had in fact been quite conservative in the 1970s, eschewing both French-style socialism and Swedish-style social democracy. Similarly, since 1983 the more conservative CDU has avoided breaking sharply with the past in favor of changing well-tested policies incrementally. This situation bears some resemblance to the failed political reforms introduced by the SPD-FDP government in 1969 after it succeeded two decades of CDU-led governments. In West Germany "alternation leads to small policy changes" (von Beyme, 1985, p. 21). The version of the German Question that I pose here asks how we can account for the absence of large-scale policy change in the face of changes in the composition of government. As in the United States, Britain, and France, the parties in power have changed: however, in the Federal Republic, policy changes do not mirror these shifts in power. Policies remain constant, as they do in Japan and Sweden. Unlike Japan, however, political parties in the Federal Republic have been voted out of office; and in contrast to Sweden, no party has successfully imposed hegemonic policies. I hope to identify the elements in West Germany's political structure that act as shackles and to elucidate how such shackles shape policy.

Whether new or old, policy solutions always create new problems which in turn require new solutions. The American tax cut of 1981 and a simultaneous military build-up have accelerated the arms race and are threatening the stability of the international financial and trade system. Britain's strong dose of deflationary policy has instilled an ugly note of class confrontation into politics and has accelerated the process of deindustrialization. French industrial policy for high technology may require a European-wide collaboration that will probably not be feasible considering the current state of the European Community (EC). Seeking to renew international competitiveness for Swedish products, that country's Social Democratic party and its unions are weakening the social consensus on which their strength depends. And in the 1970s and 1980s Japan's commercial offensive reinforced European protectionism and created a serious political backlash in the U.S. Congress.

After 1973 foreign observers celebrated West Germany as a model for how to deal with the effects of the first oil shock (Edinger, 1986; Markovits, 1982; Paterson and Smith, 1981). But after the second oil shock of 1979 the Federal Republic was viewed either caustically—the sick man of Europe—or condescendingly—part of dusty old Europe, unable to compete any longer in high technology sectors with either the United States or Japan (Kahn and Redepenning, 1982; Nussbaum, 1983). It is quite improbable that West Germany's politics and policy have changed so greatly in less than a decade. But it is possible that the incremental policy changes which have resulted from West Germany's political structures may, for a variety of reasons, have been more appropriate to the economic and social conditions of the 1970s than of the 1980s. We should study West German policy not merely to learn what we can borrow, for foreign lessons are rarely well suited to fit a different national context. Instead, through the analysis of public policy we can illuminate the distinctive strengths and limitations of foreign political structures and thus, by inference, of our own.

1. Policy and Politics in West Germany

It is one of the peculiarities of German language that, like other continental languages, it fails to differentiate between the two concepts of policy and politics. This lack of differentiation reinforces Mark Twain's indictment of linguistic complexity in his essay "The Awful German Language." Twain recommended that German "ought to be gently and reverently set aside among the dead languages, for only the dead have time to learn it" (Twain [1880], 1961, p. 454). Arnold Heidenheimer has suggested that in German the lack of conceptual differentiation may have been the result of a historical evolution of strong states. The evolution was complex because in the eighteenth century Germany was in fact the first country to develop the academic discipline of "police science" which tried to mobilize the resources of the state and calibrate state interest with citizen welfare. In any case, Heidenheimer, an American political scientist of German origin, concludes (1985, p. 24; 1986) that the development of particular political arenas, expressed in the aphorism "policies determine politics," holds "much less well in European systems with their older bureaucratic traditions and weaker legislatures." In a similar vein Claus Offe, a West German sociologist, has pointed (1975, p. 45) to the imprecision of the German language which conceals the dual character of political processes by failing to distinguish between the primacy of politics over policy, of the struggle for power over the production of order. The slightly old-fashioned term "state activity" is perhaps the closest German translation of the American concept of policy.

Relating policy to politics is the purpose of this book. It examines in detail how in West Germany policy and politics interrelate in six problem areas common to all advanced industrial states—economic management, industrial relations, social welfare, migrant workers, administrative reform, and university reform. The editors' preface to this volume justifies the choice of cases. Plausibility rather than representativeness is the main criterion for selection. The six cases include two that deal with economic policy (economic management and industrial relations); two that address social issues (social welfare and migrant labor); one that deals with the organization of the state (administrative reform); and finally, one that examines the link between individuals and a particular state institution (university reform). In West Germany, as in all of the countries examined in this series, social forces and political institutions shape political power in a distinctive manner. Policy analysis should appreciate more than the obvious, the important components of the political system—for example, legislature, parties, the courts, or the bureaucracy—which are common to all industrial democracies. It should also determine the relative weight of these components and the distinctive way in which they fit together. The West German model reveals particular capacities and strengths according to the policy problem under consideration. Analyzing a range of policy cases has two advantages. It protects us from the vice of uncritical admiration. And it has the virtue of raising perhaps the most puzzling question in the whole field of comparative public policy.

That question provides the organizing framework for each of the country studies issued in this series: are public policies shaped primarily by the way a country organizes political power, or are these policies shaped instead primarily by the functional imperatives of particular problems? The implicit premise of much writing on public policy is that the political logic of the problem is more important than the political logic of the country. This book, as well as the entire series that comprises it, attempts to make the opposite case. The interaction between policy and politics is affected primarily by the institutional organization of power in West German politics rather than by the imperatives for action inherent in particular policy problems. Although the particular capacities and incapacities of West German politics explain much of West German policy, they do not explain everything. In some instances examined in this volume, the particular features of policy problems have an undeniable and visible effect on policy and politics. But these cases tend to be the exception rather than the rule. They are instructive because they help us, in an indirect way, to appreciate more fully some distinctive features of West German politics.

Before analyzing in greater detail the institutional structures of state and society which shape West Germany's incremental policy changes, it may be worthwhile to take a step back and to view the caution of the present within the context of the recklessness of the past. The key to an understanding of modern German politics lies in the interaction of the national and the social questions. The national question concerned the integration of regions. Which Central European regions should be included and which excluded from a united German state? The social question concerned the integration of classes. How should peasants, workers, the middle class, and the aristocracy be ranked in a modernizing society?

Both questions posed profound political challenges. The political fragmentation of Central Europe spawned a nationalism and an imperialism that pushed Prussia and the German states to war three times in the 1860s. And in the twentieth century German nationalism and imperialism were a profound cause of both world wars. But the Germans were divided not only by state boundaries. In their social structure and political organization they were a people set apart from one another. The dream of social harmony and the quest for national community were equally arresting to them.

The nature of Germany's key political problem, naturally, has influenced the tools of foreign and domestic policy. German political discourse has coined two contrasting imperatives that describe these tools in summary fashion. The first imperative is derivative of *Realpolitik* theory and has been utilized by the political Right. The second imperative stems from what might be called *Sozialpolitik* theory and has been used by the political Left. The Right has interpreted the country's needs and history from the perspective of the primacy of foreign policy. The Left has viewed those needs and history from the vantage point of the primacy of domestic policy. Both imperatives are partial truths best seen in the context of the historical relation between the country's national and the social questions.

The primacy of foreign policy doctrine was a result of Germany's geostrategic position. According to the Right, the primacy of foreign policy should lead to the subordination of all domestic policy goals to the goal of national security in foreign policy. It should elevate considerations of diplomatic strategy above the valley of domestic dissent. The primacy of domestic policy doctrine, by way of contrast, focused on the key place Germany occupied in Europe's capitalist order. That place, the Left argued, linked considerations of national security and diplomatic strategy to the instabilities of Germany's capitalistic structure. Crisis abroad, advocates of the primacy of foreign policy doctrine insisted, requires continuity at home. Continuity at home, advocates of the primacy of domestic policy doctrine argued, requires crisis abroad.

Germany's past political experience has been distinguished by the manner in which the country's political problems have shaped the choice of policy, how the targets of policy have determined the tools of policy. Over the last century, Germany's most notable and notorious political leaders—men such as Bismarck, Stresemann, Hitler, and Adenauer—succeeded in putting their individual stamp on entire generations of German political life because their expert use of foreign policy could be brought to bear on the national question. There have been, on the other hand, no great reformers of Germany's domestic political life, men in the mold of Franklin Roosevelt. Subordinated as it was, the social question in Germany simply did not offer potential champions the opportunities that would have made likely their political success in German domestic politics.

On the other hand, the choice of policy has shaped the country's problems; the tools of policy have determined the targets of policy. The individual successes Germany's famous political leaders may have gained from their attention to the national question entailed a collective failure with regard to the social question. Frequently the social question was manipulated in the service of particular foreign policies. Rarely was it managed. Never did it become the focus of a broad and sustained state

effort to furnish solutions. Germany's peculiar political pathology resulted, in part, from this lack of political attention to the divisions within German society.

Defeat in World War II, partition, and the Allied Occupation transformed foreign and domestic policy. And they assigned the Federal Republic special political status. State sovereignty is incomplete (Schlotter, 1985). Students of West German foreign policy have concluded that
West Germany is a political system that is peculiarly "penetrated" by
international forces (Hanrieder, 1967). A brief visit to the Wall that
divides Berlin will convince even the novice that this label describes the
international position of West Germany more aptly than that of other
advanced industrial state. Furthermore, conquered and divided, the
Federal Republic more than any other medium-sized state relied for political and military support on the United States and its West European
neighbors. With the entire West German army under the command of
NATO (the North Atlantic Treaty Organization) and firmly committed
to staying nonnuclear, central questions of military offense and defense
have been removed from the sole jurisdiction of West German state
actors. Moreover, because the country is deeply enmeshed with multilateral economic institutions such as the EC, its officials can no longer
decide alone to pursue aggressive export offensives or protectionist de-
fenses (Bulmer and Paterson, 1987; Schwarz, 1985). Finally, for a host
of reasons too complicated to review here, political efforts of state elites
to foster an intense nationalism are no longer plausible (Schweigler,
1975, 1984). West Germany has depended since 1945 on the United
States for military deterrence and the liberalization of international markets. Thus stability in Central Europe was created largely by external
forces. In short, since 1945 traditionally central issues of foreign policy
have been dramatically transformed. Lower stakes have weakened the
role of the German state in international politics. Semisovereignty is an
external condition of West German politics.

This change in West Germany's external setting brings to full view
the internal organization of state power. In the era of absolutism state
sovereignty offered the prospect of unity by embracing and ordering
older status groups. These were often internally decentralized and held
together by traditional or charismatic leadership. As the juridical expression of the king's supreme power, sovereignty was the principal
embodiment of the state as constituted by law. It became "the formal
juristic synthesis of a highly complex system of legal and political rela-

tionships" (Emerson, 1928, p. 254). The dramatic change in the external condition of the Federal Republic thus highlights its traditional organizational decentralization; the distinction between state and society is blurred. We find state institutions, norms, and practices diffused throughout civil society. Conversely social forces have also gained access to state institutions. This institutional interpenetration has moderated political power and encouraged cautious policies and incremental changes. Semisovereignty, as I shall argue at greater length in this book, is thus also an internal condition of West German politics.

Some twenty-five years ago Elmer Schattschneider published *The Semisovereign People* (1960), in which he offered a critique of pluralist interpretations of American democracy. In this book I criticize the notion that the state should be interpreted as an actor, such as the West German chancellor, or as particular agencies of the executive branch of government. Such a view ascribes to the modern state both too much and too little power. It runs the risk of crediting state actions for political outcomes often brought about equally by the structural incentives and constraints of capitalism. But at the same time it also tends to underemphasize the importance of the modern state whose broad presence is diffused throughout society, shaping social forces, institutions, norms, and practices far removed from the direct intervention of the executive branch of government. The taming of power and the preference for incremental policy change are not aspects of contemporary politics unique to the Federal Republic. We find similar tendencies in other states including the United States, Britain, or France, which have attempted large-scale policy changes in the 1980s. But because of the historical changes that have transformed its international position so dramatically, West Germany illustrates particularly well the domestic capacities of the modern industrial state. The subtitle of this book, *The Growth of a Semisovereign State,* conveys the idea that the power of the West German state has been tamed rather than broken.

2. Germany as a Latecomer

When Konrad Adenauer was elected with a one-vote majority, admittedly his own, the first chancellor of the Federal Republic in 1949, nobody could have guessed the eventual shape of West Germany's semisovereign state. But at the time it was apparent to many that the loss of World War II, the division of the country, and the Cold War would change West German politics in significant ways. Compared to Britain and France, Germany's industrialization and national unification had occurred late (Dahrendorf, 1979, pp. 31–60). The social strains and national passions that accompanied Germany's belated arrival as an industrial society and a modern nation-state favored the growth of political authoritarianism, and eventually Nazi dictatorship, at home and an expansionist military policy abroad. An entrenched bureaucracy and a powerful military flourished as the twin pillars of Germany's strong state.

Although the transformation of German industry in the mid-1800s was neither as late nor as rapid as in Japan, the cometlike ascendance of German power after the unification of the German Empire in 1871 gave a powerful impetus to bourgeois society (Blackbourn and Eley, 1984; Eley, 1986). But left in place was an aristocracy that viewed with suspicion the threat of competition to its economic base in the wheat-growing parts of Eastern Prussia. Britain's repeal of the Corn Law (1846), by way of contrast, undermined the political position of agriculture. And Japan's Meiji Restoration (1868) helped eliminate feudalism. Germany, on the other hand, was marked by the heterogeneity of the political alliances, especially after the onset of the Great Depression of 1873–96. In fact, social historians have described the political alliance between "iron" and "rye" in 1879, a protectionist coalition of large agriculture in the East and heavy industry in the West, as the second foundation of the German Empire. Heterogeneity and fragmentation also marked the opposition to this conservative coalition. The numerous divisions within the socialist, liberal, and center factions prevented the articulation of a political vision of Germany's role in the modern world which could have effectively challenged the forces of conservatism.

Germany's national unification also occurred late. Like Italy, it became a nation-state; it experienced the processes of economic, social, and cultural integration before the imposition of one set of state institutions. Britain, France, and Japan, on the other hand, were state-nations: the state came first, the nation later. This characteristic feature of Germany's historical evolution profoundly affected German politics. The tide of German nationalism rose with its defeat in the Napoleonic Wars, the failed revolution of 1848, and the wars Prussia fought leading to unification (with Denmark in 1864, with Austria-Hungary in 1866, and with France in 1870–71). What was initially a yearning later became a passion sufficiently powerful to convert German Liberals from opponents to supporters of the forces of conservatism. Bismarck's aggressive military policy succeeded in bringing about the unification that had eluded the Liberals in 1848–49. In short German liberals became "national liberals." But the force of German nationalism had powerful effects as well on other quarters in German politics. German conservatism drew strength from it while confronting an increasingly powerful labor movement and Socialist party. The pan-German nationalist movement of the late nineteenth century, in retrospect, was not only a partner in a marriage of convenience for German conservatives but the creator of a climate of opinion about the German nation which eventually made possible the gas chambers of Auschwitz. Finally, in the hysteria and elation that surrounded the outbreak of World War I, even the German Left succumbed to the force of German nationalism. In short nationalism provided an integrative force that helped organize the political relations among actors deeply divided in politics.

The result of Germany's late arrival as a modern industrial society and a unified state-nation had fundamental consequences for its foreign and domestic affairs (Calleo, 1978). The growing speed of industrialization gave the German conservatives dominating state institutions the power to achieve often vaguely defined objectives that an intense nationalism legitimated. In foreign policy the conservatives' aim eventually became nothing less than a bid for world power. The naval arms race between Germany and Britain preceding World War I emerged from the dynamics of interstate rivalry. But it also resulted from the political dynamics of the aforementioned coalition between "iron and rye." Hitler's second attempt to construct a continental and eventual world empire carried Germany's nationalist illusions to their logical conclusion, their ultimate destruction. Within the country the heterogeneous social forces and political alliances increasingly immobilized the conservative regime of Imperial Germany. The main pillars of that regime—bureaucracy, judiciary, and army—viewed with deep suspicion the democratic institutions of the Weimar Republic and were ready to experiment with the new social and political order that the Nazis promised and that the traditional Right erroneously thought it could control. Totalitarian rule and genocide were not predetermined by prior developments. But we can safely conclude that the historical foundations on which the Weimar Republic was built favored an authoriarian politics rather than a democratic politics.

The cumulative effect of defeat in World War II, the Occupation, and partition was to reduce sharply the heterogeneity of society and the passion for nationalism which had tormented German, European, and world politics so much during the preceding century (von Beyme, 1983, pp. 47–51). Any potential appeal that communism or socialism might have had in the Federal Republic was soon contained by the Cold War, Soviet policy, and the barbed wire with which the East German government fenced in its state. The force of the nationalist Right in all its guises was finally spent. During the 1950s the CDU/CSU followed a deliberate policy of courting and eventually absorbing the remnants of the Nazi Right and of revanchist parties that spoke for the more than 10 million ethnic German refugees from Eastern Europe. In 1966–67, during West Germany's first serious postwar recession, a neo-Nazi party gained close to 10 percent of the vote in several state elections. That party barely missed election to the Bundestag in 1969. During subsequent recessions (1974–75 and 1981–83) rightist parties have been conspicuous by their absence, in striking contrast, for example, to France. A new West German national consciousness has gradually, though not completely, replaced traditional German nationalism. Its trademark is a state of mind rather than the military projection of German values (Schweigler, 1975, 1984).

What has emerged is a West German society that has tamed the drive for power. The landed aristocracy in Eastern Prussia, which had been so important to the bureaucracy, army, and the forces of conservatism, ended up in the Soviet Union, Poland, and the Soviet zone of occupation where its property was soon nationalized. Agricultural interests were integrated into the CDU and the FDP. The conflict between Protestants and Catholics was bridged by the CDU which opened itself deliberately to both major religions. And regional disparities declined with the demise of Prussia. With the exception of Bavaria and the Hanseatic city-states, the West German states are largely postwar creations.

As in Japan, military defeat and occupation deeply affected the structure of the West German state. Unlike Japan, Germany was divided. The Western Allies adopted what one might call a policy of the "4 d's": demilitarization, democratization, de-Nazification, and decartelization (Montgomery, 1957; Wolfe, 1984). On balance they came closer to achieving the first two objectives than the last two. That political life emerged first in local and state politics, well before the creation of the Federal Republic in 1949, proved decisive for the structure of the West German state. Consequently, federal officials could not take national initiatives in many policy sectors already appropriated by local and state elites.

Although the heterogeneity of German society has diminished since

1945, it has not disappeared. The major political parties in the Federal Republic express different social interests which push for different policies. The policies of the center-right governments representing a broad social alliance led by the CDU/CSU were informed by the models of "social capitalism." Center-left governments representing workers and a segment of the professional middle class led by the SPD sought to expand a "Keynesian capitalism" (Schmidt, 1983). In the 1950s CDU policies aimed at reconstructing and consolidating a capitalist market economy, thus strengthening the position of higher-income employees, property owners, and the traditional middle class. Free enterprise mitigated by social welfare was coupled to a strict anticommunism and antisocialism. And the dominant mode of policymaking was distributive, lacked coordination, eschewed medium- and long-term planning, and opposed Keynesian aggregate demand management. In the 1970s SPD policies favored more state intervention in the economy, organized labor, and more collectivist welfare policies for the disadvantaged. Because it was left of center, the SPD was mistakenly charged with being the instrument of Soviet and East German policy. And the prevalent mode of policymaking aimed at coordination and medium- and long-term planning, and favored Keynesian aggregate demand management.

The FDP as the third, though much smaller, national political party has primarily represented the self-employed middle class and small business; salaried, white-collar employees representing the new middle class; and in some states, farmers. Its social constituency embraces a middle-class ideology of individual self-help and civil liberty, a belief in market competition, and a secular world view. In the late 1960s the relative importance of the social-liberal wing of the party increased at the expense of the national-liberal wing. And in the early 1980s economic liberals gained the upper hand over the social liberals. As a result of these changes in the internal balance of power, the FDP moved to form a coalition government with the SPD in 1969 and with the CDU/CSU in 1982. But the FDP retains an identity that contrasts with both that of the CDU/CSU and that of the SPD. The FDP lacks the ties that both of the major parties have with the labor movement as well as with the clientele of the welfare bureaucracy. In contrast to the CDU/CSU, its concerns are secular. Unlike the SPD, it consistently champions issues involving civil liberties. And unlike either of the large parties, its political, financial, and policy ties with the business community are close.

Compared to earlier German regimes, the range of social interests represented in politics is narrow in the Federal Republic. But conflicts of interest between "social capitalism" and "Keynesian capitalism" do exist. They are not politically more manageable simply because the underlying diversity of social interests has been narrowed. In politics as in other spheres of social life it is often true that the smaller the objective differences the greater the need for political differentiation. To stop inquiry at the level of social interests would short-circuit the analysis of the interplay of institutions and policy which informs the character and consequence of West Germany's semisovereign state.

3. Decentralized State, Centralized Society

The institutional structure that has proved compatible with the relative homogeneity of West Germany's political forces since 1945 comprises a decentralized state and a centralized society. The dispersion of state power among competing institutions contrasts sharply with the concentration of private power in large social groups. In this section I shall discuss the major components of state and society; in section 4 I shall analyze the political mechanisms that connect them.

Decentralized State

The decentralization of the West German state combines its own tradition, American political precepts (a strong federalism and judicial review) and the emerging political properties of the Federal Republic (the growing importance of the Bundesrat, or Federal Council, and increasing judicial activism in policymaking). Countervailing tendencies, to be sure, did exist. Bonn's "Chancellor democracy" offers great power to the person at the top who has the instinct and talent to exploit fully the advantages of the office. And the legal norms and political practices that guide a complex system of intergovernmental relations can provide a measure of effective policy coordination. Notwithstanding these countervailing tendencies, the decentralization of the state contributes to the political predisposition for incremental policy change.

Federalism. Compared to federalism in Japan, Britain, France, and Sweden, West German federalism is remarkably strong (Blair, 1981; Johnson, 1973, pp. 98–137; Laufer, 1974; Lehmbruch, 1976, 1978; Merkl, 1959; Pinney, 1963). Only the United States has a federal system that accords to the individual states the prominence granted to the eleven states in the Federal Republic. This is not surprising given the convergence of the preferences of the victorious Allied powers after 1945 and the legacy of German history. Although American, British, and French authorities disagreed on the degree and type of political decentralization that they preferred, they strongly agreed that a territorial decentralization of the Federal Republic would shield democratic institutions from the possible reemergence of centralizing, totalitarian political movements. Since West Germany included the traditionally strongest centers of anti-Prussian sentiment—Bavaria and the Rhineland, Hanover and the Hanseatic city-states—in their constitutional deliberations in 1948–49, the country's political leaders were divided not on the principle of federalism but on the size of the states and on what type of federalism to adopt. This was in fact the most controversial and contested of all the constitutional issues that had to be resolved.

The Basic Law, West Germany's Constitution, assigns the states two important roles. First, states, rather than the federal government, have primary powers in important areas, most notably education, cultural affairs, radio, television, law enforcement, the environment, the organization of the bureaucracy, and the regulation of local government. Second, West Germany has a field system of administration with only a very small number of bureaucrats in the federal capital, Bonn. The effect of these constitutional provisions on West German policymaking is readily apparent. The federal government has no choice but to negotiate and cooperate with centers of state power over which it has no control.

This lack of control is very apparent in the growing importance of the Bundesrat. This institution is a hybrid between the American Senate, which accords each state an equal number of representatives (favored by the SPD and FDP in 1948–49), and the Federal Council of Bismarck's empire, which allotted the number of representatives according to the size of each state (favored by the CDU, CSU, and some smaller parties). The Bundesrat reflects in attenuated form differences in size. Large states such as North Rhine-Westphalia have 5 votes; small ones such as Bremen have 3 votes; and medium-sized states have 4 votes. The Bundesrat is not a proper parliamentary body. The precedents for its particular form of organization can be found in the German Confederation before 1866 and in the Standing Imperial Diet after 1648. Its forty-one representatives are delegates that vote as instructed by their respective state governments. Although attendance of prominent state politicians may have been the intention of the constitutional design, the proceedings are dominated by the senior civil servants delegated to attend Bundesrat sessions. Bureaucrats also predominate in the Bundesrat's numerous committees. The Bundesrat rarely initiates legislation. Although it participates in the nomination of the federal attorney general, in the election of members of the Constitutional Court, and in the selection of the managers of some public corporations, the power of concurrent legislation is the real source of the Bundesrat's strength. On matters that affect the "material interests" of the states the Bundesrat needs to approve Bundestag legislation. Because the states administer most federal programs, this veto power extends far beyond the issues that the Basic Law specifies as the political domains of the states.

Since the early 1950s more than half of all of the bills passed by the Bundestag have required Bundesrat approval. Although the political importance of the Bundesrat increased especially after 1969, a decision of the Constitutional Court in 1974 somewhat circumscribed its importance. Still the Bundesrat considers and comments on draft legislation submitted by the cabinet; it approves bills that have passed the Bundestag; it exercises its right of an absolute or suspensive veto; and in the case of a veto it seeks to resolve its differences with Bundestag representatives in a conference committee that normally succeeds in redrafting controversial legislation. In short, as an expression of West German federalism, the Bundesrat is a powerful institution in a decentralized state.

Constitutional Court. The same is true of the Constitutional Court, the most political and institutionally autonomous component of West Germany's decentralized judicial structure (Blair, 1978, 1981; Dyson, 1979; Kommers, 1976; Landfried, 1984, 1985; Massing, 1974). With the exception of seven federal courts of appeal, all regular courts operate at the local or state level. Within the guidelines of federal law, the court system is administered by the statutes of the eleven states. West Germany also has a well-developed system of specialized courts dealing with administrative. social, labor, and fiscal matters. The number of levels at which the courts are organized varies: four for civil and criminal cases, three or less for the specialized courts. All told there exist about nine hundred courts with about fifteen thousand judges.

Politically most visible is the Federal Constitutional Court. Unlike the American Supreme Court, which served as its model, it is not a court of appeal in civil or criminal cases. Instead, the Constitutional Court is a watchdog for the Basic Law. Its mission is not only to defend individual liberty and civil rights but to protect the legislature from the courts applying laws incorrectly. The Court is the final arbiter of disputes between the federal executive and the Bundestag, between the federal government and the states, between the different states, and between other courts. It may consider complaints by individuals or organizations charging that their constitutional rights have been impaired. And on two occasions, in 1952 and 1956, it outlawed neo-Nazi and Communist parties that in its eyes espoused principles undermining West Germany's Basic Law.

Not only is the scope of the Court's jurisdiction remarkably broad; the Court is also largely autonomous. This de jure provision the court won de facto in political struggles with the Ministry of Justice in the 1950s. Its judges are exempt from the administrative regulations that apply to all other judges. There exists no provision for parliamentary impeachment of individual judges. Only in extreme cases can the Court request the president to remove a sitting judge. But normally the Court does all of its hiring and firing, draws up its own budget, and negotiates independently with the Ministry of Finance. The Court's First Senate deals with civil rights, constitutional complaints involving the substantive rights of individuals, and the judicial review of legislation. The Second Senate addresses questions of constitutional law and decides complaints involving the procedural rights of individuals. Between 1951 and 1980 both senates decided more than three-quarters of the 44,238 cases that were filed (von Beyme, 1983, p. 182). Ninety percent of all cases were constitutional complaints of individuals, many of which are declined for a variety of reasons or decided by a committee composed of members of both senates. Deciding the remaining cases, the Court has interpreted about half of the articles of the Basic Law (Conradt, 1982, p. 199).

But from the perspective of public policy the matter is not merely one of the quantity of decisions. The Constitutional Court has developed an active stance that puts it center stage in some of the most controversial political issues that have faced the Federal Republic. In 1961, for example, it blocked Chancellor Adenauer's attempt to create a second nationwide television network under federal control. The Court found in favor of multiple centers of programming, persuaded by the states' argument that a federal network would encroach on their exclusive jurisdiction over cultural policy. In 1966 the Court ruled on the issue of party financing. Relying on its power of judicial review, in 1972 the Court suspended litigation in a lower court since it judged as unconstitutional a norm relevant to the restricted admission to university (*numerus clausus*) (see Chapter 7). In 1973 the Court upheld the constitutionality of the basic treaty with East Germany which Chancellor Brandt had negotiated. However, it imposed clear limits on any future move toward formal recognition of a sovereign East German state. In the same year the Court ruled that tenured professors must have at least one half of the votes in any board governing university affairs (see Chapter 7). In 1974 it ruled as unconstitutional the liberal abortion reform of the SPD-FDP coalition government, citing the Nazi legacy as a major reason why the right to life needed to be defended more strongly in West Germany than in some of its Western European neighbors. In 1975 the Court ruled on the constitutionality of government decrees prohibiting the admission of "political radicals" into the civil service (see Chapter 6). And in 1979 it ruled that the revised Codetermination Act of 1976 was legal (see Chapter 3). Despite its politically active stance, the support from public opinion enjoyed by the Court is stronger than that enjoyed by the Bundestag, the churches, or the universities. The Constitutional Court has established itself as an important actor in West Germany's decentralized state.

Bureaucracy. In contrast to Japan, France, and Sweden, decentralization is also the hallmark of the West German system of public administration. Significantly, that decentralization occurs within a hierarchical structure. West German bureaucracy concentrates authority at successive levels and encourages direct contact between superiors and subordinates. This system of bureaucratic organization is the "institutional reflection of a highly personalized and functionally restricted conception of executive control" (Mayntz and Scharpf, 1975, p. 86; Brecht and Glaser, 1940). Even a casual visitor riding West Germany's trains or buying some stamps in the local post office cannot help discovering that she is dealing with the personification of concentrated rather than diluted state power. West Germany thus has its own distinctive version of a "bureaucratic phenomenon" (Crozier, 1967).

The federal bureaucracy is a steep hierarchy in which the top has little control over lower levels (Jacob, 1963; Johnson, 1973; Hesse, 1982; König, Oertzen, and Wagener, 1983; Mayntz and Scharpf, 1975). Although the sixteen federal ministries differ in size—the largest ministry, Finance, has just under 2,000 employees, the smallest, Relations with

East Germany, has only 300—they all have the same four-tiered organizational structure. The executive level, the minister, and one or two state secretaries, preside at the top of the pyramid. The second and third levels are organized as divisions and subdivisions. Sections with typically between three and five members make up the fourth level. There are about sixteen hundred sections in the federal bureaucracy. The working capacity and expertise of the federal bureaucracy are almost entirely concentrated at this fourth and lowest level. In 1980 among the 1,700 top bureaucrats in Bonn, 2 percent belonged to the first tier, 19 percent to the second and third tiers, and 79 percent to the fourth tier. Together this top group of the federal bureaucracy accounted for less than 2 percent of the civil service employed by the federal administration (Mayntz, 1984, p. 180). The small size of bureaucratic sections creates a predisposition to work intensively on areas of limited subtance. Fragmented responsibilities are not counteracted by coordination at the top of the ministry. The relations between different ministries experience similar problems of coordination. Significantly, what coordination exists does not derive from central staff functions performed at the level of the federal cabinet. Instead, coordination is provided by the "cross-sectional responsibilities" assigned to the classical Ministries of Finance, Foreign Affairs, Justice, and the Interior (Mayntz and Scharpf, 1975, p. 64). Thus one of the main studies of the West German federal bureaucracy concludes that "a major feature of the policy-making process in the federal departments is its considerable decentralization" (Mayntz and Scharpf, 1975, p. 67).

The West German system of "field administration" is a second reason bureaucracy is decentralized. The federal bureaucracy accounts for less than 10 percent of the total number of civil servants. Federal ministries typically leave policy implementation to the states, which act "on behalf of the Federation." Only foreign affairs, defense, railways, customs, postal services, aviation, and waterways have a federal bureaucratic infrastructure of their own. Civil servants at the state or local level, on the other hand, are in charge of education, all social services, tax collection, regional economic policy, hospitals, environmental protection, energy, agriculture and forestry, roads, public housing, rent rebates, and other administrative matters. They act on the basis of statutes and delegated legislation. Figure 1-1 summarizes the structure of West Germany's bureaucracy.

A final structural feature of West German bureaucracy are the numer-

FIGURE 1-1   West Germany's Administrative Structure

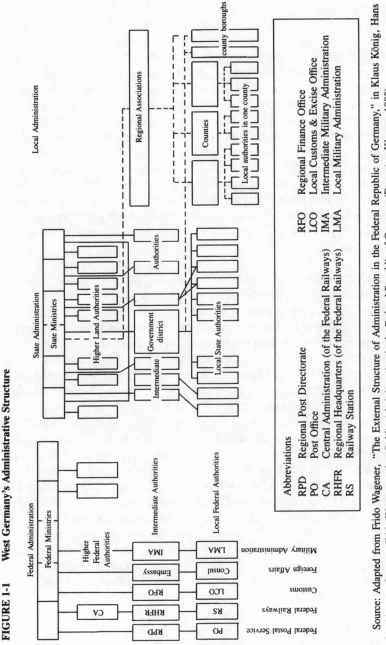

Source: Adapted from Frido Wagener, "The External Structure of Administration in the Federal Republic of Germany," in Klaus König, Hans Joachim von Oertzen, Frido Wagener, eds., *Public Administration in the Federal Republic of Germany* (Deventer: Kluwer, 1983).

ous organizations that count as part of the nonministerial federal administration. These organizations are under the direct or indirect control of a federal ministry but have different legal standing. Already before 1945 federal ministries favored handing over business to subordinate bureaus that were "detached from the department as separate units but subject to their orders and supervision" (Brecht and Glaser, 1940, p. 6). In 1974 a government report counted 497 such organizations. Half of these were health and accident insurance funds, which fall in the domain of the Ministry of Labor and Social Welfare. This peculiarity of administrative structure illustrates the decentralization of the West German system of public administration. It also points to the fact that, without a bureaucratic substructure of their own, federal ministries lack experience in the details of policy implementation and tend to focus more on policy formulation.

Chancellory. One might think that federalism, the Constitutional Court, and the fragmented character of the bureaucracy would be held in check by the office of the chancellor (Dyson 1974; Mayntz, 1980; Paterson, 1981). The Basic Law gives clear priority to the chancellor as the head of government rather than the president as the head of state. Once the chancellor is elected it is in fact extremely difficult to unseat her. Because they wanted to avoid the negative majorities that had crippled the exercise of democratic leadership in the Weimar Republic, the drafters of the Basic Law included Article 67 which describes the "constructive vote of no confidence." Parliamentary majorities can vote a chancellor out of office only if at the same time they agree on a successor. Since 1945 this has occurred only twice. It was attempted unsuccessfully on April 27, 1972, when the bid by the CDU/CSU to replace Chancellor Brandt failed by two votes. And on October 1, 1982, Helmut Schmidt of the SPD was replaced as chancellor by Helmut Kohl of the CDU. Secure in her office, the chancellor also enjoys the constitutional prerogatives (Article 65) of nominating her ministers, determining the internal organization of government, coordinating the work of the cabinet through the chancellor's office, and, most important, formulating the general policy guidelines of her government. The notion of West Germany's "chancellor democracy" is rooted in these formidable constitutional powers and in the exercise of leadership by Konrad Adenauer in the 1950s.

Since then, however, the chancellor's capacity to unify a decentralized state has been small for several reasons. First, within the policy guidelines ministers have full autonomy to run their departments without interference from the chancellor. This constitutional right reinforces the bureaucratic fragmentation (*Ressortprinzip*) inherent in the federal bureaucracy. Furthermore, the cabinet shares power with the chancellor. The prevalence of government by coalition has made it virtually impossible for the chancellor to ride roughshod over the ministers of the minor coalition partner. In fact, the guidelines of policy have been subject to detailed and complex negotiations between coalition partners. Rather than setting these guidelines, the chancellor manages them. The tenures of Ludwig Erhard (1963–66), Kurt Georg Kiesinger (1966–69), Willy Brandt (1969–74), and Helmut Schmidt (1974–82) illustrate that the chancellor remains a political hostage of changes in political climate that she does not control.

On balance the formal powers of the office are less important than the informal political restraints. On particular issues, the chancellor may attempt to impose unity on West Germany's decentralized state. In the field of foreign policy Adenauer in the early 1950s and Brandt in the early 1970s did just that. And during their terms in office Erhard and Schmidt exercised great influence over economic policy. But even when the issues are as central as foreign and economic policy, the chancellor is rarely able to parlay her political authority onto a decentralized state structure. "Government in the Federal Republic of Germany," Renate Mayntz argues (1980, p. 139), "seems characterized by a considerable dispersion of executive power."

Centralized Society

In sharp contrast to the decentralization of power in the public sector, the organization of West Germany's private sector is thoroughly centralized and very encompassing (Heinze, 1981). The business community, for example, founded its first peak association in the 1870s, some ninety years before a similar institution finally emerged in Britain. And after 1945 West Germany's unions decided on a united, industrywide form of organization which, though less centralized than Sweden's, stands in striking contrast to the decentralization of America's and Britain's industrial unions, France's syndicalist labor movement, and Japan's enterprise unions. And West Germany's integrated financial structures give the large private banks, rather than the federal government, access to the command posts of the economy. Britain, by way of contrast, lacks West Germany's large-scale and effective investment banks; and unlike in the Federal Republic, large public investment banks in France are instruments in the hands of the state bureaucracy. Furthermore, as I shall argue in section 4, West Germany's social professions and to some extent its powerful churches illustrate that the centralization of power in the private sector characterizes not only economic institutions but West German politics in general.

Klaus von Beyme has shown (1983, pp. 87, 90) the value of distinguishing between two kinds of interest groups. Class-based groups have a mass membership and face strong counterorganizations. In contrast, small status groups such as farmers or physicians often do not face an institutionalized opposition. I shall discuss business and labor as examples of class groups and farmers and physicians as examples of status groups. The interests of business, for example, are represented by about five thousand associations employing a staff estimated, at a minimum, at fifty thousand and commanding an income estimated in the late 1960s at between 0.8 and 1.5 billion deutschmarks. The interests of labor are represented by seventeen industrial unions, employing a staff of about ten thousand and disposing of an income of about 0.7 billion deutschmarks (*Der Spiegel*, Nov. 15, 1976, pp. 82–89). Neither farmers nor physicians control even a fraction of such resources. Yet over prolonged periods they have enjoyed an important position in the policy process which affects their substantive interests.

Employers. The political foundations of West Germany's business community date far back into the nineteenth century and are inextricable from international developments. In the interest of furthering economic integration, segments of German business organized on a national scale before the unification of 1871. The effect of international competition during the Great Depression of 1873–96 as well as the growing strength of the German labor movement prompted the organization of two types of peak associations, one for collective bargaining, the other for political lobbying and other matters. Since 1945 the fortune of West German business has depended largely on that of the Federal Republic. Like the military in Latin America or the state bureaucracy in Japan, business (rather than labor, the state or fortuitous circumstances) has been credited for the "economic miracle" of the 1950s which has provided it with a pervasive legitimizing myth. As a result, irrespective of which party holds the reins of power, business enjoys a preeminent place in West

Germany's political life. The West German public was thus dismayed when the largest political corruption scandal in the history of the Federal Republic unfolded in the early 1980s, revealing how far business had penetrated West German political parties.

West Germany's business community has three major associations. The Federation of German Industry (Bundesverband der Deutschen Industrie, or BDI) is the central organization representing the overall economic policy objectives of West German business (Braunthal, 1965; Berghahn, 1985; Simon, 1976; Streeck, 1983b; Webber, 1983). It has 39 associations which themselves are organized into 370 branch and 188 regional associations. These associations organize about 95,000 firms, or between 80 and 90 percent of all firms, totaling about 8 million employees. In addition to its national headquarters in Cologne, the BDI has regional offices in each state; and it maintains branch offices as well in New York, London, and Brussels representing the interests of West German business abroad. In the 1950s and 1960s the leadership of the BDI was typically recruited from industry located in the Ruhr area. But the most colorful and political of its former presidents was Hanns Martin Schleyer, a member of the board of directors of Daimler Benz. Schleyer had established himself in 1963 with his hard-nosed bargaining strategy for business and the introduction of regionwide lock-outs in the metal workers strike in Baden-Württemberg. In the 1970s he advocated a political offensive against the program of political reforms proposed by the SPD-FDP coalition government. He was assassinated by West German terrorists in 1977.

Among other of Schleyer's distinctive achievements was the unification for a brief period of the BDI with the Federation of German Employers' Associations (Bundesvereinigung der Deutschen Arbeitgeberverbände, or BDA), which coordinates the collective bargaining strategy of West German employers, administers a strike fund, gives legal advice, and deals with questions of social policy. Its 44 branch and 13 territorial organizations are themselves subdivided, respectively, into 366 regional branch organizations and 471 general regional associations. At least 80 percent of all employers are organized by the BDA, and many firms belong to both the branch and the general organization in their regions.

Finally, the Diet of German Industry and Commerce (Deutscher Industrie-und Handelstag, or DIHT) represents the interests of small business and the crafts on a regional basis (Groser, 1985). It organizes under one roof West Germany's Chambers of Commerce, which are public law bodies that help organize West Germany's highly touted vocational training program, run the stock exchanges, grant licenses, and help formulate regional economic policy. The DIHT has 69 domestic and 35 foreign chambers organized along regional lines. Membership for business in the regional organizations is compulsory. Because economic interests in a given region may be so divergent, arriving at a political consensus in the DIHT is very difficult.

On matters of public policy these and many other business organizations seek to influence legislation at all stages (Groser, 1983b; Hilbert, 1984; Weber, 1984). Since the late 1960s they have criticized government for increasing unduly the fringe benefits that employers have to pay above the working wage; they have opposed increasing worker participation in management (see Chapter 3); and they have strongly resisted plans for compulsory profit sharing which were debated by the left-wing of the SPD in the early 1970s. However, the prominent public role business played in the 1972 election was a fiasco that it has not been eager to repeat.

Unions. Although only 40 percent of West German workers are organized, as opposed to 80–90 percent of business, West Germany emerged from World War II with a relatively centralized labor organization. Even before World War I the bulk of German workers rejected the syndicalist model of a strict division between political parties of the Left and the union movement. And organization by industry rather than by craft unions as in Britain was also quite widely accepted before 1933. The crushing of the labor movement after 1933 and the Nazis' organization of an all-encompassing Labor Front prepared the West German labor movement after 1945 for imposing a more unified structure on itself than it had ever had before. Today seventeen unions organize about 7.5 million workers along industry lines under the umbrella of the Federation of German Trade Unions (Deutscher Gewerkschaftsbund, or DGB) (Markovits, 1986; Markovits and Allen, 1984; Streeck, 1982; Willey, 1974). In addition, there exist independent unions for white-collar employees (0.5 million members) and for civil servants (0.8 million members). Although the DGB formally keeps equal distance from all political parties, its natural inclination is to side with the SPD with which it shares a similar ideological outlook and programmatic commitment. But it is important to remember that the DGB also has a wing of Christian-Democratic trade unions which, traditionally, is represented at the very top of the organization. Since the CDU has a sizable labor wing and since the DGB feels that it must be able to deal with whatever party controls the levers of power in Bonn, it stops far short of formally endorsing all SPD positions.

Although the DGB is a political umbrella, the real power rests with the seventeen industrial unions. They act independently in collective bargaining, develop their own political strategies, and control the strike funds. Most important among them is the metal workers' union. Composed of roughly 2.5 million members, it is the largest industrial union in any Western democratic state. Traditionally controlled by the top, it has allowed little room for spontaneous action or dissenting opinions by the rank and file. It sets the trend for West German labor both in collective bargaining and in articulating demands that deviate from American- or Japanese-style "enterprise unionism." These demands have included further extending codetermination to achieve substantive equality with business in the running of large corporations, humanizing working conditions, and since the late 1970s reducing the workweek to 35 hours as the most promising way of combating mass unemployment. This demand was at stake in a prolonged strike in 1984 from which I.G. Metall emerged more or less successful. Although the unions' projections of the employment effects of the new contract may be unrealistic, few observers doubt that the strike served its purpose—drawing a clear political line that business and the CDU/CSU-FDP coalition government is unlikely to cross in the near future. Deregulation, deindustrialization, and privatization with mass unemployment is not a political solution that a West German government can impose on labor.

The programmatic commitment of the union movement to socialist doctrine, long superceded by political pragmatism, was finally discarded in its Düsseldorf Program of 1963, four years after the SPD had made a similar, drastic change in its party platform. Although union demands for nationalization of key industries and economic planning have virtually vanished, West German labor retains a strong interest in the extension of codetermination, that is, joint decision making both at the workplace and in the corporate boardroom (see Chapter 5). The unions favor a liberal market economy and a strategy of export-led growth. But they also stress the need for an active labor market policy and generous welfare programs. An important ally of the SPD, the unions contribute a substantial proportion of the SPD's income. Although their primary affiliation is to their party, many SPD members in the Bundestag have ties to the DGB. Chancellor Schmidt included five union members in his first cabinet (1974–76). And the candidacy of three leading trade unionists on the SPD ticket for the European Parliament election of 1979 fueled suspicion among business leaders and conservative party politicians that the Federal Republic was well on its way to becoming a union state.

Then as now such fears seem misplaced. West German unions have been on the defensive both politically and economically. In the 1970s they had to settle for a reform, initiated and implemented by the SPD-FDP coalition, which extended codetermination but which the labor movement found highly unsatisfactory (see Chapter 3). And since 1974 the DGB has watched unemployment increase to 2 million, about 9 percent of the West German workforce, despite efforts by both SPD- and CDU-led governments. An increasing membership in a shrinking workforce shows that in its organizational structure and political presence West German labor is a model of strength for the unions in all of the major industrial societies, except for Sweden. Despite what appear to be growing disparities among different groups of workers, the labor movement is accepted as an organization that legitimately represents the interests of organized and unorganized workers.

Agriculture. The German farmers' union (Deutscher Bauernverband, or DBV) is much smaller than the DGB but organizes a much larger proportion of this sector of society. With a membership of about one million, the DBV organizes about 90 percent of all farmers (Ackermann, 1970; Averyt, 1976, pp. 53–88; Heinze, 1976). The organization of agricultural interests originated in the depression of the late nineteenth century. As part of the coalition of iron and rye, agriculture was in an excellent position not only to defend its economic interests but to articulate a broader, traditional social vision of what Germany should stand for in an industrial era. The end of World War II witnessed the breakdown of the centralized Reich Food Estate (Reichsnährstand), compulsory membership in which the Nazis had imposed on all groups engaged in food production. As an interest group with a single focus, the DBV has not only successfully maintained political protection for West Germany's agriculture but also helped create prices in Europe well above world market level. The DBV is a conglomeration of regional organizations which themselves represent local constituencies. Its decision-making procedures are dominated by full-time, large-scale farmers.

The cohesion of the DBV is the result of a number of factors. Individual interests are tied closely to the collective interest of agricultural producers in maintaining high prices. Furthermore, at the local level the DBV provides many indispensable services including technical information on agricultural production, advice on financial and legal issues, and access to agricultural cooperatives that help finance machinery and market products. In several states West German farmers are legally obligated to join the local Chamber of Agriculture which is in turn under the de facto control of the farmers' union. But the union's greatest source of strength derives from the crucial core of electoral support it offers, especially to smaller parties such as the CSU and the FDP (Andrlik, 1981; Bulmer and Paterson, 1987). In addition, the DBV has traditionally developed very close relations to the CDU. And its formal and informal access to the Ministry of Agriculture is arguably greater than that of any other West German interest group in Bonn.

Although the DBV could not stem the sharp decline in the agricultural population (from 25 percent of the working population in 1949 to 7 percent in 1978), it did succeed with the agricultural law of 1955 and subsequent subsidies in stopping a growing gap between agricultural and industrial incomes. In fact, through control of all levels of the Ministry for Agriculture and its strong political base in the CDU/CSU, the FDP, and the Bundestag Committee on Food and Agriculture, the "Green Front" maintained an exceptionally strong position in West German politics throughout the 1960s. The strength of that coalition has eroded with the adoption of the EC's Common Agricultural Policy in 1967. Still, for almost two decades the DBV has resisted all attempts to adjust the prices of European agricultural products to the much lower levels of the world market. That resistance has helped push the EC to the brink of bankruptcy and has caused serious conflicts over agricultural trade with the United States, West Germany's most important military ally.

Doctors. Like the farmers, physicians are a small professional group representing a fairly narrow interest. Around the turn of the century, after the introduction of health insurance in 1883 and in reaction to the growing power of the labor movement, doctors began to organize. At stake was who would eventually control the policies of the health insurance funds, doctors or unions. Dominated by the unions, the funds favored a fixed doctor's fee per patient, no choice of patients among doctors, and an expansion of the insured population. It was in the doctors' professional interest, on the other hand, to ask for a fee for service, free patient choice of doctors, and no expansion of the insured population. This bitter conflict lasted until after 1933 when the Nazis eliminated the funds—an odious source of strength of the labor movement in their eyes—and converted many doctors to their pronatalist and racist policies.

After 1945 West Germany's physicians regrouped. The Federal Chamber of Physicians (Bundesärztekammer) acts as their peak association (Leichter, 1979; Safran, 1967; Stone, 1980). At the state level regional physician chambers have compulsory membership. The federal chamber is dominated by specialists who keep their distance from the general practitioners. Of equal importance is the Association of Doctors for Statutory Health Insurance (Kassenärztliche Vereinigung, or KV) which has eighteen regional offices and federal headquarters in Cologne right next door to the federal chamber. Created by emergency decree in 1931, it distributes to the doctors the moneys it receives from the insurance funds, according to the services rendered. Finally four interest groups also exist to organize different groups of doctors.

The politics of class confrontation which had marked health insurance policy before 1933 has not reappeared since 1945. One important reason is the fact that the social insurance funds are no longer a countervailing power resisting the professional claims of doctors. As discussed in section 4, the role the unions play in the insurance funds has diminished since 1945. A conservative, professional orientation favoring a maximum of discretion by the doctors has been the hallmark of West German health insurance policy. It stems from a variety of factors not typically distinctive of the Federal Republic: the lack of organizations representing the interests of patients; the ambivalent position of government; physician chambers with compulsory membership run by older doctors; and voluntary interest groups such as the Hartmann Federation which represent private physicians rather than those in hospitals. But in the structure of their comprehensive organizations, physicians, like farmers, workers, and businessmen feature a high degree of centralization.

Policy Consequences

What connects West Germany's decentralized state to its centralized society? Drawing on a few policy episodes in the areas of environmental and health policy, I would like to illustrate how the West German policy process bridges the gap between public and private and the strength of the links between state and society (von Beyme and Schmidt, 1985).

In the area of environmental policy, for example, regulation remains a distinctive aspect of West German policy. But in sharp contrast to the United States, such regulation does not pit government against business in a public, adversary relation marked by widespread litigation. The regulatory agency forcing the issue of social change so common in Washington does not exist in the Federal Republic. Instead cooperation between business and government is formalized. Rather than delegating broad discretion to independent regulatory agencies, as in the United States, West German legislation confers restricted powers on public authorities, to be exercised only in consultation with major societal interests. Leigh Hancher and Matthias Ruete have thus characterized (1985, p. 13) West German administration as a "formalised regulatory or legal culture" which they contrast with Britain's "flexible bargaining culture."

The control of carcinogens as a specific aspect of environmental and health policy is a good example (Brickman, Jasanoff, and Ilgen, 1985). West Germany's chemical industry tried for a long time to deal with the problem on the strength of its past record of civic-mindedness. But when it became clear that the established system of self-control was politically no longer acceptable, business insisted on precise bureaucratic guidelines that are applied inflexibly thus limiting the discretion of the state, narrowing the scope of the issue, reducing public discussion, and keeping out of the policy process a broader political constituency favoring environmental protection. Since West German policymakers were unencumbered by the inexperience of U.S. regulatory agencies, congressional mistrust, and the unrestricted access to the legal system characteristic of the United States, they were able to recalibrate a relatively stable compromise between business and the government which kept intact the tradition of consultation behind closed doors and avoided polarization among conflicting viewpoints.

The coordination of federal, state, and local policy is in fact more difficult than the creation of a consensus between government, business, and labor (Hucke, 1982; 1985; Mangun, 1979; Mayntz, 1978; Müller, 1986; Watkins, 1984). The Federal Emission Control Act of 1974 was adopted without much controversy only because the states had underestimated the political importance of air pollution. On the issue of water pollution their determined opposition subsequently kept the federal government from passing any legislation. Because the federal government lacks any equivalent to the American Environmental Protection Agency, federal law is administered by state and local governments. "The predominant control pattern . . . is a kind of 'management by exception' " (Mayntz, 1978, p. 204). Differences in administrative approach and the extent of business opposition, as well as local environmental political mobilization and technical competence, create multiple conflicts that must be solved intergovernmentally. Air pollution policy is often implemented by state trade inspection authorities (Gewerbeaufsichtsämter) that lack the legal enforcement powers often exercised by general administrative agencies. These inspectorates are in close contact with business. The act of licensing a plant is in fact often little more than a ratification of prior, secret negotiations.

How West Germany dealt with the control of exposure of workers to vinyl chloride illustrates similar tendencies (Badaracco, 1985). West Germany does not have an Occupational Safety and Health Administration. Instead one finds a dual system for supervising health issues at the workplace. First, like thirty-four other major branches of industry, the chemical industry has the Industry Injuries Insurance Institute (Berufsgenossenschaft Chemie) with a substantial budget, research staff, and inspectors. These inspectors visit plants and supervise the implementation of industry standards which have state support and are thus binding. A second hierarchy of inspectors, under the jurisdiction of the Labor Ministry, enforces the government's own guidelines. Characteristically, government involvement has not led, as it would have in the United States, either to jurisdictional conflicts over administrative turf or to a public clash between government and business. Instead the Industry Injuries Insurance Institute specifies and makes operational the guidelines of the federal government. Cooperation is close. The style of discourse is technical. And a broader political constituency is kept at bay.

But it would be a mistake to infer that only bureaucrats and businessmen are involved in this cozy bilateral relation. The inspectors visiting individual plants cooperate closely and fully with the works councils, whose members are overwhelmingly union members (see Chapter 3). On questions of health West German business and labor practice total cooperation. All industrial accidents or potential health hazards are thus reported. Furthermore, regulatory decisions of the federal government are made by the appropriate ministries acting upon the advice of one or several technical agencies which in turn have links to business, labor, universities, and independent research institutes. Under this system, for example, responsibility for regulating pesticides lies with the Ministry of Agriculture, the policy advocate of large-scale producers most heavily reliant on pesticides. Partisan considerations and political parties also have access to the machinery of regulation. Although on the issues of industrial accidents and health hazards they are secondary players, labor unions and political parties are thus part of the policy network.

West German health insurance policy is also characterized by a network that bridges state and society and is at the same time both accessible to organized groups and closed to other social actors. In 1977 the Bundestag passed a health cost containment law with the truly untranslatable title of Krankenversicherungskostendämpfungsgesetz. (Landsberger, 1981; Murswieck, 1985; Stone, 1979; Wiesenthal, 1981). As elsewhere the cost of providing health care services had become a major problem. Between 1965 and 1975 health costs increased by 300 percent, and compared to 1965–70, by the mid-1970s the annual rate of health inflation had doubled to 17 percent. The proximate cause, however, was the fiscal crisis in West Germany's pension fund. Three billion deutschmarks were subsequently cut from its subsidy of health insurance funds. The law established changes in average wages and salaries as a benchmark for evaluating cost changes in the health care sector. For the first time the medical profession was thus forced to take general economic conditions into consideration. The law also provided for procedures by which to impose negotiated cost ceilings on doctors, dentists, and druggists. And it formalized cost containment measures that had already existed on an ad hoc basis.

The modalities of implementation emerged from discussions in the Bundesrat which sought to bridge the gap separating the physicians from almost all other important actors—government, insurance funds, and employers—who strongly opposed inflation. Modeled after an experiment in economic policy which ended in 1977 (see Chapter 2), the "concerted action" (Konzertierte Aktion) brought around one table from sixty to seventy players representing the different organizations active in this policy sector: doctors and dentists, insurance funds, the pharmaceutical industry, employers, unions, and the representatives of federal, state, and local government. In case this round table failed to implement cost containment measures, the federal government provided a sequence of further steps: direct negotiations between the health insurance funds and the doctors, binding arbitration, and an amendment to the 1977 legislation, scheduled for 1981. To the dismay of the Ministry for Labor, which wanted to create a durable, centralized institution in the health sector, the two peak associations representing the health insurance funds and the physicians settled on cost increases even before the concerted action convened in 1979. As a result the ministry simply ratified a decision reached voluntarily by the two main organizations.

Concerted action was successful for some time. The inflation rate in the health sector declined by about one half. But the coordination of health insurance policy in the late 1970s did nothing to address underlying structural problems in this policy sector, such as the numbers of doctors, the research in the pharmaceutical industry, and the role of hospitals. For example, the exclusion from reimbursement of a list of drugs treating trivial ailments went into effect only after six years of political bargaining (MacMillan and Turner, 1985, pp. 21–25). When health care costs accelerated in the early 1980s, the federal government proposed thirty-two revisions of the original legislation. Of these only two were eventually passed by the Bundestag. Cost increases abated for a few years. But by 1985 it was clear that more intervention was needed. Yet for reasons of electoral strategy, the CDU/CSU-FDP coalition government decided not to do anything before the next election. In less than a decade the policy cycle thus had repeated itself three times.

Health care and insurance policy involve more than bargaining among peak associations. West Germany's system of health administration reserves broad legislative powers for the federal government. And in the 1970s the federal government has used its financial muscle to expand its role in policymaking. But as in most other areas of policy, the federal government lacks the bureaucratic infrastructure for implementing its policies. Instead state governments and local health insurance funds make contacts with the individual citizens. Detailed analysis has identified the complex patterns that link this system of intergovernmental relations to professional associations (Altenstetter, 1974, 1978, 1980, 1982a, 1982b, 1982c; Murswieck, 1983).

The policy consequences of West Germany's decentralized state and centralized society should thus not be gauged by a reduction in the level of toxic substances or the inflation rate of health care services. What matters for purpose of this argument is how the interaction between policy and politics is shaped by specific West German institutions that in linking state and society as well as different levels of government encompass political opponents in a tight policy network. Such interdependence makes large-scale departures from established policies an improbable occurrence. If we uncover the crucial institutional nodes that are central to West German policy and politics, we should come closer to understanding why incremental policy change is so pervasive in the Federal Republic.

4. Three Nodes of the Policy Network

I have in mind three institutional nodes. The structure of West German party competition at the federal level imposes a centripetal politics that narrows differences in the process of policy formulation. In the process of policy implementation, West German politics is characterized by an interlocking grid representing territorial interests. Federal politics and policy link up with state and local levels in a West German version of "cooperative federalism." And a wide range of parapublic institutions typically are open to West Germany's centralized economic and social interest groups, party politicians, and the senior civil service. Parapublic institutions can be both political actors and policy arenas facilitating the process of policy implementation. Political parties, an interlocking politics between different levels of government, and parapublic institutions are the three nodes of such a tightly integrated policy network that major changes in policy stand little chance of success.

Political Parties

Political parties are an important institutional arena where a decentralized public and a centralized private sector converge in the formulation of public policy. With the exception of the years 1949–53, 1969–74, and the mid-1980s, the major parties have agreed on most matters of political substance. The ideological intensification of the debate between the SPD-FDP government and the CDU/CSU opposition in the 1970s stemmed in part from the necessity to emphasize differences in political style in order to mobilize electorates. To some it betrayed the increasing irresponsibility of partisan politics in the Federal

Republic, to others its growing irrelevance. Whatever the merits of such views, the balance of conflict and cooperation among West Germany's parties has created new political opponents. Social movements that question the consensus among leaders of major parties have in the Greens a party able to articulate new issues. But opposition movements are not likely to become in the foreseeable future a dominant political force that will shape West German policies.

Political parties have a predominant influence in the West German policy process (Döring and Smith, 1982; Kirchheimer, 1957, 1966; Schmidt, 1985). After 1945 virtually all Nazi institutions were discredited in the public eye. The mainstays of the German state, the military and the bureaucracy, had been defeated in war and were weakened by the Occupation. With the strong encouragement of the Allied powers, political life in the Federal Republic was rebuilt from the local level with the leaders of the democratic parties filling the void.

The CDU is a novel factor in German politics (Haungs, 1983; Irving, 1979; Layton-Henry, 1982; Pridham, 1977). For the first time one party united all of the center-right forces that in the Weimar Republic and before had been organized by different political parties: conservatives, nationalists, liberals, Catholic social reformers, conservative Protestants, entrepreneurs, and Catholic workers. The CDU became West Germany's first catch-all party, sacrificing ideological purity for mass appeal. Furthermore, its cooptation of a succession of smaller parties representing millions of refugees from the East and regionalist movements reduced the threat of a revanchist mass party appearing on its right and extended the CDU's predominance over West German politics in the 1960s. The internal organization of the CDU has traditionally been decentralized. It is a federation of regional party organizations headed at times by powerful "chieftains." It is also a federation of interest groups. The labor wing is close to the trade union movement. The business wing speaks for the interests of industry and finance. In addition various groups represent among others small businessmen, refugees, students, churches, and women. Far-reaching decentralization forces the formulation of political compromises inside the CDU which more generally typify the structure of the West German party system.

The SPD has been the second largest party in the Federal Republic since 1945 (Braunthal, 1983; Drummond, 1982). Some Marxist and socialist currents still ran strong in that party after 1945. Representing the West German working class, it demanded the nationalization of major industries. But the political restoration of West Germany under CDU auspices eventually impressed upon a new generation of SPD leaders the need also to move from a party based on class to one based on mass support. The SPD thus prevented Japanese-style one-party dominance from establishing itself in West Germany. In Bad Godesberg in 1959 the SPD gave itself a new party program which ratified a fundamental change, namely adoption of a pragmatic style of politics. At the same time the party accepted as irreversible Chancellor Adenauer's policy of Western integration which it had opposed so strongly in the 1950s. The political success of this policy of "embracement" was undeniable. By 1966 the SPD had entered a coalition government with the CDU, and in 1969 it seized the reins of power in a coalition with the FDP. That coalition was voted out of office in 1982 by a new CDU-led coalition that then formed a government.

West Germany's party system was simplified in the 1950s. The small parties which existed in 1949, representing particular movements on the far right or left, pressure groups such as the refugees, or particular provinces such as Bavaria were all by 1961 effectively eliminated from West German politics. Mindful of the splintered party system of the Weimar Republic, West Germany's political elite has legislated that representation in the Bundestag requires garnering 5 percent of the total vote or the direct election of three candidates in West Germany's hybrid system of proportional representation. These were formidable barriers that between 1961 and 1983 have kept all but three small parties out of the Bundestag.

The Christian Social Union (CSU) is the Bavarian wing of the CDU (Carl-Sime, 1979; Mintzel, 1978). The CSU is a modern, conservative party. Since 1949 the alliance between CDU and CSU has taken the form of a joint parliamentary party in the Bundestag. But the CSU is an autonomous party with its own organization, a separate program, its own party congress, and an independent caucus of CSU Bundestag deputies. Although the CSU and the CDU believe in the principles of Christian democracy, on most issues of public policy the CSU stands to the right of the CDU. Throughout the 1970s its leader, Franz-Josef Strauss, argued that regaining an absolute CDU/CSU majority in the Bundestag required the mobilization of voters on the far right of the electoral spectrum.

The Free Democratic party (FDP) represents West German liberals (Albertin et al., 1980; Broughton and Kirchner, 1984; Verheugen,

1984). The party's identity has fluctuated between the business orientation that it shares with the CDU/CSU and its support of many of the domestic reforms championed by the SPD. The FDP's strong commitment to civil liberties issues remains distinctive, however. Finally, there are the Greens, a political party that emerged from the environmental movement of the 1970s. Campaigning on a platform of ecology and peace, it proved successful enough to win representation in the Bundestag in 1983. In the 1980s it became the major critic of the political practices of both government and the opposition (see Chapter 8). Illustrating the concentration in the number of West German parties, Table 1-1 gives an overview of the results of West German elections since 1949.

Since 1949 the importance of West Germany's parties in relation to other institutions has increased (Frye, 1965). In the 1950s, for example, the tactics particular groups used to influence the outcomes of elections were very evident. Among others, refugees, farmers, and opponents of rearmament directly pressured political parties to embrace their cause. The major parties partly consolidated their political position by incorporating some of these groups. And the concentration of the party system also made it increasingly difficult for such groups to exert direct pressure. Disaffected social sectors thus had little choice but to become political parties themselves and to enter the electoral arena. Political parties in the 1970s have also made great inroads in local politics. A long tradition of nonpartisan "citizen lists" was replaced by contested elections that newly created local party cells organized. And party

TABLE 1-1   Elections to the Bundestag, 1949–83 (percentage of list vote)

	1949	1953	1957	1961	1965	1969	1972	1976	1980	1983
CDU/CSU	31.0	45.2	50.2	45.3	47.6	46.1	44.9	48.6	44.5	48.8
SPD	29.2	28.8	31.8	36.2	39.3	42.7	45.8	45.6	42.9	38.2
FDP	11.9	9.5	7.7	12.8	9.5	5.8	8.4	7.9	10.6	6.9
Greens	—	—	—	—	—	—	—	—	1.5	5.6
Refugee parties	4.0	9.1	8.0	2.8	—	0.1	—	—	—	—
Communist parties	5.7	2.2	—	1.9	1.3	0.6	0.3	0.4	0.2	0.2
Neo-Nazi parties	1.8	1.1	1.0	0.8	2.0	4.3	0.6	0.3	0.2	0.2
Other parties	16.4	4.1	1.3	0.2	0.3	0.4	—	0.2	0.1	0.1

Source: *Statistisches Jahrbuch für die Bundesrepublik Deutschland* (Stuttgart: Kohlhammer, various years).

membership soared. By 1984 the CDU had 680,000 members; the CSU, 170,000; the FDP, 85,000; and membership in the SPD topped 1 million.

The structure of West German parties has profoundly influenced the formulation of policy (Lehmbruch, 1968; Müller-Rommel, 1982; Pulzer, 1978; Schönbohm, 1979; Smith, 1976, 1979). For a variety of reasons, that structure encourages centrist political solutions. First, each of the two main parties (the CDU/CSU and the SPD) contains strong wings that prevent much movement away from the political center. The rightist tendency of some segments of the CDU and the CSU toward American-style conservatism in both foreign and domestic policy is held in check by a substantial left wing of social reformers representing reform-minded Catholics and Catholic workers. How far the SPD can move to the left is constrained by the presence of a solid block of parliamentarians who represent union interests and the orthodoxy of the reformist Bad Godesberg program and who are deeply suspicious of the issues—ecology and peace—being raised especially by the younger generation.

The pivotal role of the FDP is the second reason why West German politics has been so centrist. The FDP knows that its survival depends on maintaining its middle ground between the two major parties (Norpoth, 1982). Throughout the 1970s, for example, the SPD-FDP coalition gave crucial portfolios including foreign affairs, economic affairs, and the interior to the FDP. Using its pivotal power, the FDP articulated the view of the 10–15 percent of the white-collar employees whose attachment to either of the large parties is not particularly deep and whose "floating vote" thus shapes electoral outcomes decisively. By the late 1960s and early 1970s the preference of that segment of the voting public had moved from the CDU/CSU to the reform program of the SPD-FDP. During the 1970s the FDP obstructed several Social Democratic reforms. And by the late 1970s, in West Germany as in other industrial states, the public mood had turned conservative. Sensing this social change and feeling compelled to accommodate it or face extinction, the FDP leadership prepared to switch alliances to form the 1982 coalition. Significantly, once it had formed the government with the CDU/CSU, the FDP began to articulate its own political position to the left of the CDU/CSU on questions of foreign policy and civil liberties, to the right on many economic and social issues. In its shifting alliances with the major parties as well as in day-to-day politics, the FDP's pivotal position reinforces the centrist political tendencies inherent in the composition of the two large parties.

Government by coalition defines the structure of West Germany's party system. The prevalence of government by coalition encourages incremental policy change (Schmidt, 1985). Table 1-2 gives a statistical summary of different types of governments in federal and state politics between 1949 and 1982. The data point to three conclusions. First, coalition governments led by the two major parties are about twice as frequent as single-party governments (columns 1 plus 3, columns 2 plus 4, respectively). Second, both of the major parties have held executive power for the same amount of time (columns 1 plus 2, columns 3 plus 4, respectively). Finally, oversized coalitions such as the Great Coalition of the CDU/CSU and the SPD in Bonn between 1966 and 1969 have occurred frequently at the state level. However. a closer inspection of the data reveals that their incidence was far greater in the early years of the Federal Republic than in later years.

TABLE 1-2   Political Composition of West German Federal and State Governments, 1949–82, by Months

	CDU/CSU Coalitions[a]	CDU/CSU Governments[b]	SPD Coalitions[a]	SPD Governments[b]	Oversized Coalitions[c]
Federal government	213	0	154	2	34
Baden-Württemberg	49	129	18	31	146
Bavaria	112	73	40	0	112
Berlin, West	17	19	173	49	156
Bremen	0	47	177	133	97
Hamburg	48	0	240	151	14
Hesse	0	0	288	99	64
Lower Saxony	60	56	141	48	135
North Rhine-Westphalia	123	49	194	31	43
Rhineland-Palatine	240	142	0	0	55
Saar	185	77	0	0	62
Schleswig-Holstein	252	140	0	37	9
Total	1,299	732	1,425	581	927

Source: Manfred G. Schmidt, "Two Logics of Coalition Policy: The West German Case," in Vernon Bogdanor, ed., *Coalition Government in Western Europe* (London: Heinemann), pp. 41–43.
a. Coalitions with smaller parties.
b. Single-party governments.
c. Coalitions involving the CDU/CSU and the SPD, the CDU and the SPD, or the CSU and the SPD.

At the federal level since 1949 minimum winning coalitions have predominated in ten of the thirteen governments led either by the CDU or by the SPD. Table 1-3 summarizes on a left-right scale the party positions on some of the major policy issues. The SPD is on the left on 14 out of 15 issues, while the CDU/CSU is on the right on 9 out of 15 issues. The FDP's policy position varies between right (6 issues), center (8 issues), and left (1 issue). In his probing analysis Manfred Schmidt concludes (1985, p. 44) that "one could plausibly argue that the bargaining process within coalitions tends to exclude extreme policy

TABLE 1-3   Party Position on Issues

Issue	Rank order on Left-Right scale[a]
Nationalisation and control of means of production	1) SPD 2) CDU/CSU and FDP
Government role in economic planning	1) SPD 2) CDU/CSU and FDP
Pubic debt	1) SPD 2) CDU/CSU and FDP
Distribution of wealth	1) SPD 2) CDU/CSU 3) FDP
Collective provision of social welfare	1) SPD 2) CDU/CSU 3) FDP
Protection and support of trade unions	1) SPD 2) CDU/CSU 3) FDP
Extension of non-class political participation	1) SPD and FDP 2) CDU/CSU
Centralisation/decentralisation of state	1) SPD 2) FDP 3) CDU/CSU
Equal opportunity	1) SPD 2) FDP 3) CDU/CSU
Protection of environment	1) SPD and FDP 2) CDU/CSU
Strict law and order policy	1) SPD and FDP 2) CDU/CSU
Degree of political tolerance towards new political movements	1) SPD and FDP 2) CDU/CSU
Secularisation of society	1) FDP 2) SPD 3) CDU/CSU
Foreign policy: cooperation with Eastern countries	1) SPD 2) FDP 3) CDU/CSU
Development aid	1) SPD 2) FDP 3) CDU/CSU

Source: Manfred G. Schmidt, "Two Logics of Coalition Policy: The West German Case," in Vernon Bogdanor, ed., *Coalition Government in Western Europe* (London: Heinemann), p. 45.

a. The rank order is based on a summary of data from the 1960s and 1970s. John Clayton Thomas, *The Decline of Ideology in Western Political Parties: A Comparative Analysis of Changing Policy Orientations* (Sage Professional Papers, Contemporary Political Sociology Series, 1975) and Lawrence C. Dodd, *Coalitions in Parliamentary Government* (Princeton: Princeton University Press, 1976), and common sense on the part of good journalists were particularly helpful in constructing this table. The entries have also been successfully checked with data on the preferences and attitudes of elites in the FRG in the late 1970s (Rudolph Wildemann, *Linkage Problems: Positional Elites and Party System in the FRG,* IPSA World Congress, Rio de Janeiro, 1982).

stances and issues which are highly controversial between the partners, and therefore that conditions are conducive to the diminution of policy differences." The policies of all coalition governments have clearly aimed to combine a capitalist economy with the welfare state. Since the late 1950s the two major parties have favored political, economic, and military integration with the West. And both CDU- and SPD-led governments have been tough defenders of West German democracy against what they and the state bureaucracy have considered "political radicals" (see Chapter 6).

At different levels of government partisan disagreement is also less evident than one might expect at first. At the federal level less than 10 percent of all legislation is contested by the major parties in the Bundestag (Rose, 1982, p. 21). In a careful analysis of the public policies adopted by the eleven states, Schmidt identified four issues on which state governments had maintained the greatest amount of autonomy from federal intervention. In three of the four issues (public-sector employment, internal security, and the treatment of the handicapped) Schmidt found remarkably few differences separating the CDU/CSU from the SPD. Only on questions of educational policy do partisan differences noticeably effect policy choice (Schmidt, 1980, 1983, pp. 50–51). And in his statistical analysis of urban government in West Germany, Robert Fried concludes similarly that party was not necessarily the most important factor shaping municipal policy. Specifically, in contrast to the CDU, Social Democratic control over municipal government had no uniform impact on the direction of government activism, its size, and its collective qualities (Fried, 1976; Otte and Zuelch, 1977).

Although the composition of government matters in policy and politics, incremental policy changes are the parties' typical response to the constraints of coalition governments as well as to their own internal organization. Only one exception to this generalization exists. During the years 1966–69 the CDU/CSU and the SPD joined forces to form the Great Coalition. This permitted major innovations in economic and budgetary policy and in a number of other institutions linking federal and state governments. Otherwise the CDU's limited push for "social capitalism" and the SPD's limited attempts to extend "Keynesian capitalism" was shaped largely by the economic context (Schmidt, 1985, p. 55). Economic growth in the 1950s facilitated the work of CDU-led coalition governments and resulted in the "overproduction" of policy changes. Conversely, economic crisis in the 1970s stalled SPD-led coalition governments and resulted in the "underproduction" of policy changes. In sum, for a variety of reasons government by coalition creates a centrist politics and incremental policy change.

The Bundestag reinforces these tendencies. Political parties are the chief determinant of the distribution of power in the Bundestag (Loewenberg, 1967, p. 217). Yet the institutional rules of the Bundestag tend to produce consensual political outcomes, as the high proportion of unanimously passed bills illustrates. In the first legislative period (1949–53), for example, the CDU/CSU and the SPD differed substantially over major issues including foreign policy, economic management, industrial relations, and social welfare. Nonetheless, 86 percent of all bills were passed with the votes of both major parties. That proportion rose to 93 percent in the sixth legislative session (1969–72), which was also marked by deep partisan divisions. A more refined typology of voting results on important distributive, participatory, protective, regulative, and repressive issues before the Bundestag between 1949 and 1976 has concluded that about two-thirds of the 519 votes were carried either unanimously or with very large majorities (von Beyme, 1986, p. 164). In the Federal Republic party opposition within the Bundestag seeks to exercise control through cooperation in legislation rather than confrontation in debate.

How and why the Bundestag produces legislative agreements that accommodate the divergent preferences of the major political parties requires analysis that would lead us too far afield from the argument I wish to develop here. But one important factor is the fact that the Bundestag is a "working" rather than a "debating" parliament, in contrast to the British House of Commons. Most of its work is carried out in committees whose structure largely corresponds to that of the ministerial bureaucracy. Except for the party leadership, parliamentarians quickly become policy specialists. Their high degree of professional expertise enjoins against partisan politicization of issues. Between 1949 and 1980 only 292 of the 22,133 committee sessions, or little more than 1 percent, were open to the public (von Beyme, 1983, p. 123). And as early as the 1950s and 1960s informal, unanimous consent procedures had replaced formal rules for organizing the work of the Bundestag (Loewenberg, 1967, pp. 206–18). In short, on matters of both substance and procedure the West German Bundestag reinforces the tendencies toward a centrist politics and incremental policy change which characterize West Germany's political parties and party system.

West Germany's parliamentary procedures also reinforce the tendency toward incremental policy change when the major parties begin increasingly to diverge, as they arguably did in the 1970s. Indeed, one could argue that West Germany's party system has become a system of party blocs in which, given the closeness of federal elections, the FDP determines which bloc will prevail. Public rhetoric separating government from opposition was intense in the 1950s, which were dominated by the CDU/CSU, and in the 1970s, dominated by the SPD. But such rhetoric was often less important for policy formulation than the intense political struggles within each bloc. The 1957 reform of West Germany's pension system and the 1976 revision of codetermination legislation are excellent examples of this process (see Chapters 3 and 4).

The effect of the Greens on this party-bloc system during the 1980s and 1990s will be interesting to note. Whatever the future electoral success of that party may be, the Greens have clearly accelerated political change in the Federal Republic by articulating issues that the established parties were not eager to raise. Since 1983 the SPD has moved cautiously in some states toward collaboration with the Greens by deliberately trying to link issues of ecology and peace to the concern over unemployment and other economic and social issues. This strategy may succeed in permanently enlarging the SPD's electoral base; or may deeply divide the right wing of the SPD from the rest of the party; or it may permit complex alliances between the Greens, the SPD, the FDP, and the CDU/CSU in local, provincial, and federal politics. We simply do not know. But we do know that, like the social movements of the 1970s, the Greens have substantially broadened the range of issues addressed in politics and that the process of political bargaining within and between blocs has become more fluid and complex.

Conceptual distinctions such as "active-passive" or "interventionist-noninterventionist" do not capture adequately the role West Germany's political parties play in the process of policy formulation. They are better viewed as an essential institutional node linking state and society. The significance of their political position in relation to other institutions has grown since World War II. And the dynamics of a coalition government that allots to the smaller party, the FDP, disproportionate influence create substantial problems for the chancellor within her own party. Chancellor Kohl must defend himself constantly against criticism from the right wing of the CDU/CSU that he is depending too much on the cooperation of the liberal FDP. Similarly, in the 1970s Chancellor

Schmidt's estrangement from his own party was a partial result of the strains that government by coalition imposed on his political base in the SPD. Both cases illustrate how the centrist dynamics of the structure of party competition create strong inducements for incremental policy change.

Cooperative Federalism

A second node of the West German policy network vertically links the political actors in West Germany's federal system. Considerable variety exists between policy sectors that are centrally administered, such as the railway system or the payment of benefits to individuals; sectors that remain largely under the domain of state and local government, such as education; and policy sectors in which federal, state, and local competencies overlap. Most instructive for the analysis of intergovernmental relations is this third group of sectors. The West Germans describe the structural features of their system of intergovernmental relations with terms such as "cooperative federalism" or "interlocking politics" (*Politikverflechtung*). In the West German system of intergovernmental relations, divergent interests are brought together through a policy process that resists central reform initiatives and defies sustained attempts to steer policy developments. Yet far-reaching political initiatives in the United States which would place more responsibility back in the hands of state governments would not be possible in the Federal Republic. At the same time West German federalism is sufficiently flexible to accommodate important social change. Tight links between conflict and consensus as well as centralization and decentralization forestall total blockages and intermittent social and political eruptions so characteristic of the pattern of change in French politics.

The German term "self-administration" (*Selbstverwaltung*) dates back to the nineteenth century (Heffter, 1950; Thränhardt, 1981). Napoleon's defeat of Prussia in 1806 led to large-scale institutional and political reforms masterminded by state ministers Stein and Hardenberg. They reformed the bureaucracy of Prussia's absolutist monarchy by adapting the British principle of self-government to Prussian realities. Although the reforms enhanced the political role of the middle classes at the local and provincial level, they stopped far short of threatening Prussian authoritarianism. The Prussian system of self-administration, conceived of as a part of civil society rather than the state, was decidedly a matter of "low" politics rather than "high" politics. The bureaucracy was an area reserved for minor functionaries and notables. Municipalities, like other corporate sectors of German life, excelled in meeting their technical tasks. But they did little to encourage citizens to actively shape local politics. The idea of self-administration was implemented primarily in Prussia's communes, and it spread widely through the various principalities prior to Germany's unification in 1871. In the late nineteenth century a conservative, Rudolf von Gneist, reformulated that idea in order to firmly attach Germany's liberal middle class to a state founded and dominated by Prussia's conservative landowners. Previously a sphere of influence for the bourgeoisie that was shielded from an absolutist state bureaucracy, Germany's municipalities have increasingly since the late nineteenth century lost their importance. The Industrial Revolution, political developments during the Weimar Republic, and the "artificial revolution" by which the Allied powers implanted democratic institutions after World War II (Montgomery, 1957) have fully integrated today's 8,800 communes into West Germany's system of intergovernmental relations.

West German federalism has an institutional particularity that sets it apart from its American analogue. "Responsibilities are not divided by policy areas, but by functions in the policy-making process" (Reissert and Schaefer, 1985, p. 106). In the United States the exercise of power by the federal government is formally independent of the powers of the American states. Functions of state government taken over by the federal government are sometimes centrally administered. In contrast to the United States, in West Germany the Bundestag must reach agreement with the states represented in the Bundesrat on all major policy initiatives. Furthermore, the federal government relies on the eleven state bureaucracies to administer most federal programs. But federal tax legislation in turn constrains the realm of action of state and local governments. Power in intergovernmental relations is thus shared horizontally among different states (as in education); hierarchically between the federal government and state as well as among local politicians (in the few policy sectors such as labor market administration where the federal government commands its own bureaucracy for policy implementation); or, most typically, in bilateral or multilateral policy networks linking federal, state, and local governments.

On questions of education, including university reform, the constitutional prerogative of state autonomy has left the federal government without a mandate and a bureaucratic structure for implementing policy. Instead the eleven West German states have sought to coordinate their activities. As early as 1948, even before the founding of the Federal Republic, the states laid the foundation for creating West Germany's cooperative federalism by establishing the Standing Conference of Ministers of Culture (Ständige Konferenz der Kultusminister, or KMK). The KMK coordinates cultural policy that affects all states. Endowed with its own secretariat, the conference has four permanent subcommittees, staffed by the relevant section heads of the education ministries in the eleven states. And there exist a number of subcommittees. Since 1948 it has issued more than 500 nonbinding recommendations. Because confidentiality and unanimity are its operational principles, it avoids politically divisive issues. Over time, however, the role of the federal government has grown even in this highly decentralized sector of policy. The individual states simply could not mobilize the financial resources necessary to cope with the dramatic expansion in the West German university system (see Chapter 7).

As a result of some important constitutional revisions in 1969, the prior growth of the federal government's financial involvement in university expansion was given a firm constitutional basis. The federal government also acquired the competence to issue the framework legislation to which the university laws of the individual states had to conform. Furthermore, a planning commission of federal and state governments was formed to oversee the new construction or enlargement of universities. The Joint Commission for Educational Planning was also set up. But instead of developing long-term plans for the educational system, an openly partisan conflict over the principle of comprehensive school education led to a deadlock between the federal government and a majority of the states on the one hand and the CDU/CSU opposition and a minority of states on the other. Since the decisions of the Joint Commission have binding power only under rare circumstances, the commission de facto failed in its task of coordinating policy. Significantly, in its first plan the Commission for the Construction of New Universities took account of this failure. "It became clear that 'redistributive policies' could not be promoted within the institutional framework of cooperative federalism . . . though formally the concept of a 'comprehensive university' (*Gesamthochschule*) was taken as a basis, all sorts of variations were permitted, even those that were 'comprehensive' only nominally. This semantic compromise permitted the commission to concentrate its attention on clearly 'distributive' issues" (Lehmbruch, 1978, p. 173). By the late 1970s influence had shifted back to the KMK.

That the federal government does not command its own bureaucracy for implementing its policies is a crucial feature of the West German system of intergovernmental relations. The area of labor market policy illustrates this feature well, for it is one of the few policy sectors in which the federal government sits on top of a bureaucratic chain of command, at the bottom of which are 538 branch employment offices— also part of the state administration (see below pp. 69–71). Employment programs passed by the SPD-FDP coalition in the 1970s could be implemented fairly quickly. Vocational training, on the other hand, does not fall under the jurisdiction of this bureaucratic chain but is organized instead by employers' associations, unions, Chambers of Industry and Commerce, special schools, and the training centers of large corporations. When the SPD-FDP coalition revamped its labor market policy in 1969, it could do so with ease for the programs that were administered by the employment offices (see Chapter 4). But since it lacked jurisdiction over the decentralized structure of vocational training, passage of federal reform legislation in this sector was delayed by six years. The final bill was robbed of many of the key provisions discussed in the late 1960s (Blankenburg, Schmid, and Treiber, 1975, pp. 26–30; Briese, 1972; Offe, 1975; Streeck, 1983a).

In the 1960s West Germany's cooperative federalism spawned a growing number of consultative arrangements intended to link the different levels of government in traditional as well as emerging policy sectors. By 1962 eleven permanent ministerial conferences existed for "horizontal" coordination. State governments consulted frequently with one another on most of the major policy sectors for which they were responsible. "Vertical" coordination existed in the form of extra-constitutional federal grants programs in such areas as housing, agriculture, and aid to economically depressed regions. One study reports that in the mid-1960s over 400 federal-state administrative committees existed whose main task it was to prevent the decisions of one level of government from negatively affecting other levels (Johnson, 1973, p. 116).

Public expenditures are one way of measuring the changing role of different levels of government (Gunlicks, 1985; Hunter, 1973; Johnson, 1973, pp. 120–26; Knott, 1981; Spahn, 1978; Zimmermann, 1981). As a share of national income, the expenditures of all levels of government, including the social security funds, increased from 15 percent before World War I, to 25 percent during the interwar period, to 35 percent around 1960, and about 48 percent in 1975. During the same period the share of central government expenditures rose sharply at the expense of local government. In 1975 the ratio of expenditures of the three levels of government was 40:35:25. The Basic Law divides the responsibilities between the federal and the state levels more explicitly than those between state and local governments. Federal and state legislation defines the scope of local functions, for example, by transferring traditionally local functions to other levels of government (such as teachers' salaries) or by mandating that local governments assume certain tasks (for example, providing for waste-water treatment and land-use planning). Local governments spend most of their funds on health care, welfare, education, sewage treatment, and road construction. Education and police are the largest items in the budget of state governments. The two largest items in the federal budget are social welfare and defense. Government expenditures differ not only by policy sector but by type. Transfer payments loom largest in federal expenditures, salary payments in state budgets, and public investment in the budgets of local government; local governments fund two-thirds of total public investment in West Germany.

Since 1951 "horizontal" transfers from rich to poor states and supplementary financial support for some states from the federal government have been used to equalize states' financial positions. A constitutional amendment in 1969 extended the principle of "vertical" tax-sharing among different levels of government. Revenue quotas for federal, state, and local governments are either fixed by law, as in the case of income taxes, or left to periodic renegotiation, as in the case of the value-added tax. In 1980 revenues derived from this system of shared taxation accounted for more than 80 percent of total taxes. Since 1951 fiscal equalization among states and between different levels of government has been a contentious issue with the rich states resisting the pressures of poorer ones, as well as of the federal government, for a redistributive system of equalization. But compromise proved possible and the system of shared taxation has raised the revenues of the poorest state from 88 percent of average state tax revenue in the 1950s to 95 percent in 1969 (Reissert and Schaefer, 1985, p. 113). But in the 1970s progress toward further equalization halted, and five states filed suits with the Constitutional Court asking for different revisions of the tax code. Although the 1969 reforms have also tended to increase fiscal equalization among local governments, the primary guarantors of general revenue sharing among local governments are the states that rely on complex formulas for allocating revenues.

The influence of the federal government increased gradually in the

1960s. In the eyes of the two major parties, pressing policy problems required the powers of the federal and state governments to be revamped, which gave the federal government the constitutional basis to help formulate policy in a number of areas previously reserved exclusively for the states. In 1969 by constitutional amendment Articles 91a and 91b of the Basic Law provided for "Joint Tasks" whereby federal and state governments shared responsibility for the planning and financing of new construction in higher education, regional industrial policy, structural policy affecting agriculture and environmental protection of coast lines, and educational planning. At the same time Article 104a/IV permitted the federal government to grant investment subsidies to the states. Legislation subsequently adopted made these subsidies available in a number of policy sectors including urban renewal, urban transport, hospital construction, social housing programs, and environmental protection. Finally the federal government won the right to help plan both the primary and secondary education systems and jointly financing research institutes (Article 91b). Table 1-4 summarizes these changes in intergovernmental relations. Between 1969 and 1975 the direct investments and investment subsidies of the federal government almost doubled. Most of the increase occurred in the "Joint Tasks" and in investment subsidies. By the end of the 1970s the proportion of the federal budget designated for "Joint Task" financing was more than 10 percent and thus roughly comparable to the American figure (Gunlicks, 1985, p. 20). The political decisions leading up to the reforms of 1969 were made by the Great Coalition after tough negotiations with the states. The reform program of the SPD-FDP coalition government after 1969 appeared likely to be enacted because it combined the financial powers of the federal government with the administrative expertise and information resources of the states.

The hopes for initiating major substantive policy changes so apparent in the late 1960s were defeated by West Germany's system of "interlocking politics." Numerous case studies have illustrated in detail the failure of the attempt to impose central political direction on West Germany's cooperative federalism (Bruder and Ellwein, 1979; Hanf and Scharpf, 1978; Hesse, 1978, 1982; Scharpf, Reissert, and Schnabel, 1976, 1977; Schreckenberger, 1983; Waterkamp, 1974). Political bargaining between the specialists in the federal bureaucracy and among the state governments has led to three characteristic types of behavior (Garlichs and Hull, 1978, p. 145). First, financial resources are dis-

TABLE 1-4 Constitutional Provisions for West Germany's Cooperative Federalism

Criterion	Joint Tasks (Article 91a GG)	Joint Tasks (Article 91b GG)	Grants-in-Aid (Article 104a(4) GG)
Degree of Generality	*Programs* (a) Expansion and construction of institutions of higher education (b) Improvements of regional economic structures (c) Improvement of agrarian structure and of coast preservation	*Programs* (a) Educational planning (b) Scientific research	*Programs* Important investments
General and Economic Conditions	Provided they are important for society as a whole or for the improvement of living conditions.	Supraregional importance	Provided they are necessary: (a) to avert a disturbance of the overall economic equilibrium, or (b) to equalize differences in economic capacity, or (c) to promote economic growth
Degree of Commitment	The federal government *shall* participate.	The federal government and the states *may* cooperate.	The federal government *may* grant financial assistance.
Form of Cooperation	*Procedure* and *institutions* for *joint overall planning* defined by *federal legislation*.	No specific procedure and institutions. No specific requirements on joint planning. Details by *agreement*.	No specific requirements about procedure. Details by *federal legislation*.
Cost Sharing	Fixed proportions (the federal government meets one-half of the costs for items (a) and (b), at least one-half for item (c)).	Apportionment of costs by agreement.	No details.

Source: P. Bernd Spahn, *Financing Federalism: West German Constitutional Issues and Proposals for Reform* (Canberra: The Australian National University, Centre for Research on Federal Financial Relations, n.d.), p. 19.

51

tributed on a per capita basis, which favors the equal treatment of different states. Second, the relative shares of the different states de facto cannot be altered. In the few instances when the federal government has tried to impose its own political priorities, it had to make available additional financial resources. Existing resources can not in fact be redistributed. Third, policy programs lack specificity. Objectives are vague. A large number of measures qualify for assistance. Moreover, the federal government often lacks the necessary information to evaluate programs. These three types of behavior result from the deliberate attempts of political actors to avoid conflict. The dynamics of intergovernmental relations thus established a unanimity rule even before the Constitutional Court for all practical purposes made unanimity mandatory for joint decisions. Gone is the discretionary power to award extraconstitutional categorical grants to state and local governments that the federal government enjoyed in the 1960s. Although the federal government could fund more programs in the new era of block grants, it had less to say about how the funds could be spent. "Any attempt by the federal government (or by the state governments) to force through changes in priorities and thus in the distribution of resources would necessarily cause the system to stall" (Garlichs and Hull, 1978, p. 145).

The waning of the reform program of the SPD-FDP coalition government—for example, in education—and a growing awareness of the political blockages in the system of intergovernmental relations coincided. Four criticisms heard with increasing frequency pointed to the inefficiency and inflexibility, as well as the lack of urgency and democratic character of many of the joint programs (Scharpf, 1985). The allocation of resources was inefficient because of a tendency to overspend. For example, since West Germany's health insurance system permits hospitals to charge their operating costs to the insurance funds, hospitals had every incentive to expand their capacities once the joint programs reimbursed them fully for their investments. Similarly, the states had no desire to forfeit investment subsidies for which they were eligible under the informal quota system of allocating resources. As a result, this new program created an excess number of hospital beds while inflation in the health sector accelerated sharply. The need for the cost control measures adopted in 1977 (see above pp. 33–34) was in part prompted by the cost escalating effects of the system of intergovernmental relations.

In the areas of agriculture and regional industrial policy, the rules regarding decisionmaking by which the joint programs were administered were too inflexible to accommodate changing economic conditions. For example, under conditions of joint decisionmaking, traditional agricultural subsidies that had favored the big farms in northern Germany over the smaller and less efficient farms in southern Germany could not be changed. Federal subsidies thus contradicted the program's intention, namely to meet actual need as specified by a planning and evaluation group set up by the state ministries of agriculture. Similarly, with unemployment rising in the mid-1970s, the federal government's fiscal policy measures were frustrated by the inflexibility of the joint program for regional industrial policy and of public investment in infrastructure. Despite a growing scarcity of funds, it proved to be impossible to funnel resources away from the underpopulated, rural periphery to the centers of unemployment in West Germany's industrial core. And other policy sectors, including local transport and housing, by the late 1960s no longer needed the federal grants that had been critical when the Federal Republic confronted the task of physical reconstruction after World War II.

A fourth and final criticism points to the undemocratic character of joint decisionmaking in West Germany's system of intergovernmental relations. The availability of federal funding reduces the opportunity costs of particular projects at lower levels of government, encourages overspending, and distorts political preferences. Specialists in the federal and state bureaucracies are interested in the growth of particular program areas and take an offensive approach to the system of intergovernmental relations in the hope of receiving funds otherwise unobtainable. By contrast, the generalists at different levels of government view West Germany's cooperative federalism defensively. They see it as an important mechanism for containing political pressure to achieve the most advanced condition in a given policy sector in their particular locality (Scharpf, Reissert, and Schnabel, 1976, pp. 236–43).

Although West Germany's cooperative federalism initially appeared to be a further attempt to centralize power in the hands of the federal government, it has in fact reinforced the ties among political elites in different institutions (Benz, 1985, pp. 34–35; Bruder and Ellwein, 1979). Strategies of consensus formation through problem solving, persuasion, bargaining or coercion are in fact less typical than strategies of conflict avoidance (Scharpf, Reissert, and Schnabel, 1978, pp. 100–106). The complexity of policy issues is reduced through a process of sequential decisionmaking that divides issues into smaller decision segments in which agreement can be reached more easily. Similarly, the practice of negative coordination minimizes conflict by leaving functionally related policy decisions politicallv unconnected. Finally, the substantive purposes of policies that can be pursued in intergovernmental relations are also limited. Specifically, the federal government cannot pursue redistributive programs intended to discriminate among individual states. The politics of West Germany's intergovernmental relations transforms redistributive intent into a log-rolling style of policy.

The limitations imposed on federal policy initiatives are evident even in sectors such as highway planning which are under the sole jurisdiction of the federal government and fully financed by federal funds (Dunn 1981, pp. 57–72; Garlichs and Hull, 1978; Yago, 1984). Even in this policy sector the federal government is so dependent on the information and technical expertise provided by the states that it has virtually no control over lower levels of government. States participate directly in the policy process at the federal level. The style of political bargaining is thus no different from that in other sectors where the formal consent of the states is a constitutional requirement. Fritz Scharpf, Bernd Reissert, and Fritz Schnabel (1978, pp. 106–7) thus arrive at a pessimistic conclusion. "If problem loads do not exceed moderate levels the established practices and habits of incremental learning through limited problem solving and persuasion are likely to remain viable, even though the general tendency toward policy-making by conflict avoidance will continue to block reform strategies. . . . If, however, problem loads should increase much beyond present levels, political processes in the Federal Republic are more likely to be immobilized by conditions of overload then would be the case in political systems with either less need for consensus or greater consensus building capacity."

This conclusion raises the obvious question of how West Germany's cooperative federalism has managed to avoid total stagnation and immobility. A plausible answer has been suggested by West German scholars who emphasize that cooperative federalism is not only creating blockages but also providing political mechanisms for partially unfreezing them. Specifically, West Germany's local governments are conduits for transferring social and political changes into the West German system of intergovernmental relations (Benz, 1985; Fürst, Hesse, Richter, 1984; Hesse, 1978, 1985; Hesse et al., 1983; Konukiewitz and Wollmann, 1985; Nelles and Oppermann, 1980).

Since the mid-1970s West German cities in particular have regained some of the political leverage which had disappeared in the previous two decades. Their growing importance mirrors a change in the issues confronting West German policymakers. The concern with economic growth, jobs, and international competitiveness which dominated West German politics in the 1950s and 1960s has not disappeared. But it has been complemented by new issues such as the quality of urban life and environmental protection. Put starkly, the politics of production must now be balanced with the politics of consumption.

Cities and local governments in general have become the political stage that displays and articulates the new politics. In the system of intergovernmental relations, they act as transmission belts for new demands, forcing a change in the established political strategies of governments at the federal and at the state level. Persuasion and cooperative bargaining have far less effect on this change than do the political vulnerabilities of local and regional officials. On questions of affordable housing and a clean environment, urban political activists can count on broad support spanning the political spectrum. Peaceful demonstrations, illegal occupations of empty apartment buildings, and at times violent clashes between small bands of youth and the police make local office holders hostages of political crises that can upset their electoral prospects. In an era of shrinking resources, cooperation among local governments has become more important. The political importance of cities manifests itself not only in the various peak associations of local government but in the coalition strategies of groups of mayors acting independently. The process of political bargaining between different levels of government has also changed. Top-down regulation has become less important than bargaining by persuasion.

The growing importance of the West German cities is evident in the reorientation of West Germany's regional planning policy (Benz, 1985; Fürst and Hesse, 1981; Hoffman 1981; Scharpf, Reissert, and Schnabel, 1976). By most accounts the efforts of federal planners have failed. The political objective of achieving equivalent economic opportunities and life chances in all parts of the Federal Republic had until the mid-1970s focused political attention on rural and economically depressed regions. But during the last decade attention has shifted to issues concerning the quality of life in West Germany's metropolitan areas and its declining industrial regions. Questions of urban renewal and housing are replacing issues of macroregional equality. The rapid shift of centers of economic growth to the southern part of the country and the growing electoral importance of the Greens in the major cities also tends to increase the prominence of West German cities.

Such changes are also evident in the area of regional industrial policy. Problems of implementing West Germany's labor market policy often derive from objectives that are not tailored to the specific situations in local or regional labor markets. Increased decentralization of particular programs would permit "policy outreach" and an "active implementation" of policy. The specific social groups for whom the programs were intended might thus be reached. An ambitious program of regional industrial policy funded by North Rhine-Westphalia to the tune of 6.9 billion deutschmarks between 1979 and 1984 relied heavily on the cooperation of local government and, in particular, cities to achieve its programmatic objectives.

Similar developments are evident in West German housing policy (Konukiewitz and Wollman, 1982, 1985). The Urban Renewal and Development Act of 1971 provided a legal framework for allocating federal funds to local government. The federal government hoped that it would be able to steer the selection of projects to fit with its regional industrial policy. But as in other policy sectors, the need for compromise with the states stymied the reformist zeal of the federal bureaucracy and left the allocation of funds in the hands of the states. The waning of political enthusiasm for federal grants and a growing scarcity of funds have diminished the weight of federal and state influence. "Market failures" of the 1960s brought skyrocketing housing prices. "Policy failures" of the 1970s were revealed in a far-reaching scandal involving West Germany's largest housing corporation.

In the 1980s local governments are developing new approaches that incorporate independent groups into public policy. Cost reductions in new construction, self-help initiatives, or the conversion of empty office space for residential use require a policy orientation that seeks to identify local groups. The major cities have moved rapidly to funnel money to disadvantaged groups. Between 1979 and 1982, while cities and local governments were experiencing their most severe fiscal crisis since 1949, housing expenditures in sixty-two cities with more than 100,000 inhabitants increased by 75 percent. Significantly, this development in local politics is not tied strongly to partisan preference. Although in the 1980s the CDU government was advocating a lower public profile in housing policy at the federal and state level, local representatives of the same party, including big city mayors, were at the forefront of developing a new style of local interventionism.

This difference points to an important aspect of West German politics. State and local politics are important for the recruitment of political elites. The father figures governing some of the West German states in the 1950s—Karl Arnold in North Rhine-Westphalia, Max Brauer in Hamburg, Wilhelm Kaisen in Bremen, and Georg-August Zinn in Hesse—have been succeeded by a new generation of regional activists and leaders. In the CDU, for example, it is very important to build a strong base of support in one of the West German states, as did Gerhard Stoltenberg and Kurt Biedenkopf. And in the SPD the territorial base of elites leads at times to the advancement of a whole cohort. In the 1970s the SPD from Hamburg was represented in top leadership positions in Bonn by Chancellor Helmut Schmidt, Defense Minister Hans Apel, and the SPD's Bundestag leader Herbert Wehner. When they are in opposition in Bonn, both CDU and SPD have looked to state and local politicians to rebuild the party. In the 1970s prominent CDU politicians emerged in Hesse (Alfred Dregger), Baden-Württemberg (Lothar Späth), and Lower Saxony (Ernst Albrecht). And in the 1980s the SPD is similarly testing and training in state politics its next generation of leaders such as Johannes Rau, Oskar Lafontaine, Volker Hauff, and Klaus von Dohnanyi. Chancellor Kohl himself best exemplifies this aspect of West German politics. A former governor of Rhineland-Palatine, he became leader of the CDU/CSU and its chancellor candidate in 1976 without any experience in Bonn save for his membership in the Bundesrat.

West Germany's interlocking politics prevents the kind of substantial reorganization in intergovernmental relation which has occurred in the United States since 1981. The swings in West German policy are narrower and more constrained by the tight grip of West German institutions and the organizing principles of the Basic Law. Nonetheless, West German federalism appears sufficiently flexible to respond to the economic, social, and political changes that have occurred in the last decade. In contrast to France, the blockages in the system of intergovernmental relations have not been total. In the last decade the growing political importance of local governments, particularly in urban areas, and a greater emphasis on political decentralization have gone hand in hand. Policymakers in a number of sectors rely less on centralized control and top-down regulation and more on a consensual bargaining process that takes account of the growing political vulnerabilities of central decisionmakers. In sum, the change that West Germany's system of intergovernmental relations permits is incremental.

Parapublic Institutions

The third node of the West German policy network is a heterogeneous set of parapublic institutions, such as the Federal Reserve, the Federal Employment Office, or the social welfare funds, that bridge the gap between public and private (Groser, 1983a). These institutions provide the key to a relatively quiet and harmonious process of formulating and implementing policy, the controversies of partisan politics notwithstanding. Some of these institutions, such as the self-administered social welfare funds, date back to the nineteenth century. Others, such as the Federal Reserve, are the creation of Allied policies after 1945. Some are active in only one area, others are concerned with a whole range of policy problems. But all of them link the public and private sectors firmly together. They have helped to reinforce the peace that has prevailed between the social forces of the Left and the Right since 1945. These institutions have worked relatively smoothly, especially in the management of economic and social welfare issues. Parapublic institutions act like political shock-absorbers. They induce political stability both directly and indirectly. They tend to limit political controversies in the process of policy implementation. And they limit the scope of policy initiatives.

West Germany's political life has a peculiarity that is often overlooked by foreigners. Numerous institutions—corporate bodies, foundations, institutes—are organized under public law and carry out important policy functions. Chambers of Industry and Commerce as well as Agriculture, professional associations, public radio and television stations, and various university bodies among many others express a general principle of organization: the independent governance by the representatives of social sectors at the behest of or under the general supervision of the state (Breuer, 1977; Huber, 1958). State administration is thus mediated by the self-government of many social sectors. Public administration and policy implementation, it is hoped, will consequently become politically less oppressive and technically more informed. The diversity of these institutions is great. They include, for example, state institutions that wield substantial power virtually unchecked by the federal government. And they encompass efforts to increase group participation in state institutions, in corporate hierarchies, and in large insurance funds. But this diversity notwithstanding, most of these efforts are part of an institutional design that seeks to link the responsibilities and jurisdiction of the state bureaucracy to well-organized social sectors.

The untranslatable German term "subsidiary right" (*Subsidaritäts-prinzip*) expresses the political intent of marshaling the expertise and initiative of the main social sectors under the auspices of state administration. Put briefly, West Germany's parapublic institutions merge public and private bureaucracies. Although some of these institutions— for example, the corporations of some of the professions—date back to the guilds of the preindustrial era, most point to historical roots in the nineteenth century. The Industrial Revolution created social problems so severe that more than a territorial reorganization of the state bureaucracy was required. Bismarck's social legislation of the 1880s established insurance funds in the form of cooperative societies under the protection and supervision of the state. The health insurance funds, for example, became a stronghold of Germany's labor movement, while the accident insurance fund was run by the employers. But even though, in contrast to the situation after 1945, parity representation of major social groups was not adopted, the principle of self-administration under state auspices was adapted by corporative societies from municipalities. Part of the early beginnings of the modern German welfare state, parapublic institutions now permeate the functional organization of German politics.

In the remainder of this section I shall describe West Germany's most important social and economic parapublic institutions. The columns in Table 1-5 list parapublic institutions that are important actors or arenas in the five different policy sectors that I analyze in greater detail in Chapters 2–5 and 7. Only on questions of the administrative reform of state institutions (Chapter 6) are parapublic institutions conspicuous by their absence. This table reminds us of the variegated character of West Germany's parapublic institutions. The Bundesbank and the Council of Economic Experts help to neutralize a policy sector that the West Germans think requires a particularly high degree of substantive knowledge uncontaminated by partisan politics. The system of codetermination and factory councils and the de facto mediation rather than adjudication of many plant-level conflicts by labor courts go beyond private-sector conflicts between business and labor. Because of its power to define and

TABLE 1-5   **Parapublic Institutions in Different Policy Sectors**

Policy Sector	Type of Parapublic Institution
Economic management	Bundesbank
	Council of Economic Experts
Industrial relations	Codetermination
	Labor courts
Social welfare	Social security funds
	Federal Employment Office
	Private welfare associations
	Churches
Migrant labor	Federal Employment Office
	Private welfare associations
	Churches
University reform	West German Conference of University Presidents
	Science Council
	German Educational Council

enforce legal norms, the West German state is deeply enmeshed in regulating industrial relations. The parapublic institutions that are active on questions of social welfare and migrant labor carry out important policy functions irrespective of whether or not they have standing under public law. And in university reform issues parapublic institutions center on West Germany's federal structure.

Economic Management. The Bundesbank is the parapublic institution that plays the most important role in protecting West Germany's low inflation rate (Duwendag, 1973; Faber, 1969; Könneker, 1973; Lampe, 1971; Müller, 1969; Schnitzer, 1972; Wadbrook. 1972). As part of the executive branch of government, it enjoys a degree of autonomy from the federal government and private interest groups which is more far-reaching than comparable institutional arrangements in the United States, Britain, France, Japan, and Sweden. The bank's president in the early 1980s, Karl-Otto Pöhl views the bank as "a very political institution. It really makes policy, unlike most other central banks" (Norman and Gumbel, 1984). In 1984 the bank's total international reserves, without gold, stood at 41 billion dollars, compared to 27 billion for Japan, 24 billion for the United States, 21 billion for France, 10 billion for Britain, and 4 billion dollars for Sweden. Between 1982 and 1986 the Bundesbank transferred profits from the interest it had earned on its dollar assets, roughly 48 billion deutschmarks, to the coffers of the finance minister, thus alleviating the deficits of the federal government (*Der Spiegel*, April 28, 1986, pp. 56–59).

Two disastrous inflationary periods in the twentieth century are responsible for the far-reaching autonomy of the Bundesbank. The Directorate and the Central Bank Council are its governing bodies. They have the legal status of a central federal office (Oberste Bundesbehörde). The Bundesbank has branches in each state. Its headquarters in Frankfurt is generally acknowledged to have more economic expertise and better economic information than all of the federal ministries in Bonn combined. Unlike other parapublic institutions, such as the Federal Employment Office, the Bundesbank is not subject to the supervision of any federal ministry. In fact, it is exempted even from the guidelines by which the chancellor defines the general political objectives of his government. And the Bundesbank is not accountable to the Bundestag. It is true that the president appoints to eight-year terms the candidates for membership of the Directorate recommended by the federal government. Although the Central Bank Council must be consulted before the federal government recommends its preferred candidates to the president, it has no control over the government's ultimate choice. The Central Bank Council, in turn, is dominated by the presidents of the regional branches of the Bundesbank who are appointed by the Bundesrat acting on the de facto binding suggestions of the state governments. The appointees of the federal government are thus in a minority position. In fact, for a variety of reasons, since its establishment in 1957 the governing bodies of the Bundesbank have been free of political factions. That the six members of the Bundesbank's Directorate do not include a single supporter of the CDU years after the election of CDU Chancellor Kohl is thus relatively unimportant.

The appointment of the president of the Bundesbank is one of the most important decisions a chancellor makes, and not only because at the equivalent of $200,000 it is the best paid public office in West Germany. It was the intent of Chancellors Brandt and Schmidt, for example, to choose candidates who would be acceptable to both the banking community and responsive to the economic objectives of the SPD. Like his predecessors, Brandt chose in 1970 a prominent private banker, Karl Klasen, who over many years had developed close links with the SPD in Hamburg. In 1980 Chancellor Schmidt broke with tradition by choosing

Pöhl, a former journalist. Pöhl had once worked as head of public relations for the Federation of German Banks and was also a high-ranking SPD bureaucrat who in the 1970s had occupied several key economic policy positions in the federal bureaucracy. Many speculated at the time that Schmidt's choice was based on the hope of reaching a better informal understanding with the Bundesbank about West Germany's economic policy.

But as it quickly turned out, both Klasen and Pöhl were coopted by the institutional culture of the Bundesbank. Although the Bundesbank must support the government's overall economic policy, it is bound to do so only as long as that policy does not interfere with the overriding aim of "safeguarding the currency." Cabinet members have the right to attend meetings of the Central Bank Council. And the president of the Bundesbank has the right to attend cabinet meetings dealing with important monetary issues. The bank must satisfy the federal government's request for information. But the government can do no more than to veto for only two weeks any decision by the Central Bank Council to which it objects strongly. In fact, this has rarely happened. Over the years both the federal government and the Bundesbank have chosen to defend the stability of the deutschmark.

What public controversy has existed has concerned how to defend that stability in volatile international markets that curtail the autonomy of the Bundesbank. In the system of fixed exchange rates which finally collapsed in 1973, the decision about revaluation or devaluation of national currencies rested with national governments. Like other central banks, the influence of the Bundesbank was greatly enhanced after 1973 when that decision was transferred to market forces under a system of flexible exchange rates. Throughout the 1960s controversy centered on the revaluation of the deutschmark and on how to stem the inflow of unwanted foreign capital that inflated the domestic money supply. In the late 1970s controversy between the federal government and the Bundesbank arose over Chancellor Schmidt's policy of linking the deutschmark to the European Monetary System (EMS) in which inflation-prone France and Italy, among others, were also members. Since member states of the EMS relinquished some monetary sovereignty, the Bundesbank was openly opposed to a political initiative that tied it to West Germany's less stability-conscious neighbors. But Chancellor Schmidt pushed ahead for reasons both of foreign policy and domestic politics. In the area of foreign policy he hoped for a partial decoupling of European currencies from a volatile and weak dollar; domestically, he hoped to weaken the Bundesbank's commitment to price stability in times of sharply rising unemployment. These episodes illustrate that the Bundesbank has the ability to constrain large-scale policy change. But the autonomy of the bank is not unlimited.

In West Germany, as in other industrial states, expert commissions have proliferated. In 1969, 264 commissions existed to advise the federal administration. By 1977 that number had increased to at least 358 with a total membership of more than three thousand (von Beyme, 1984, pp. 5, 10). Created by the state, these commissions serve both technical and political purposes and are not easily controlled. In the narrower area of economic research, the five main economics research institutes in Berlin, Hamburg, Kiel, Munich, and Essen do much contract research for the federal government. Together they have a combined budget of 60 million deutschmarks and a staff of about four hundred professional economists or about one-tenth of the total number of economists working for West German universities (Müller-Groeling, n.d., p. 6). Their special reports and annual or quarterly forecasts greatly influence West Germany's media and fuel political debates that are not always to the federal government's liking.

The constitutional and political position of the influential Council of Economic Experts, or as many West Germans put it the "Five Wise Men," has been a source of considerable debate. The council was established in 1963 ("Die fünf Weisen," 1977; Dietzel, 1978; Müller-Groeling, n.d.; Roberts, 1979; Spahn, 1979; Welter, 1976; Zinn, 1978). Like the Bundesbank, it is largely independent from the federal government. Indeed some constitutional lawyers grant it a status equal to that of the federal government. In drafting its annual reports, the council has the right of access to all relevant economic information that the government controls. And the federal government has the legal obligation to issue a written discussion of the report's implications for economic policy.

The council's political role was conservative in the 1970s. It was a strong proponent of a neoclassical economic analysis that favored self-regulating markets; distrusted Keynesian aggregate demand management; and attributed unemployment to excessive wage increases. Employers and unions each nominate one member, while the council recruits itself the remaining three. Typically, therefore, only one of the five professors does not subscribe to its neoclassical tenets. Yet unlike the American Council of Economic Advisors, the West German "wise men" are barred from making explicit policy recommendations. Instead their mission is to analyze, on the basis of varied assumptions, the tensions that may arise from the pursuit of price stability, low unemployment, balance-of-payments equilibrium, and steady growth.

Whereas the American Council of Economic Advisors has the explicitly political purpose of serving the president and his administration, the West German council is expected to be independent from all partisan interests. It has a disembodied, abstract, and political scientific expertise. Its role is not to debate the appropriateness of the objective of stability in regard to economic policy but to analyze different ways in which it can be achieved. In filling its role the council has been a persistent critic of both CDU and SPD. Between 1963 and 1968 it saw the major cause of economic instability not in the demands of workers for higher wages, as CDU Chancellor Erhard had hoped, but in the economic policy of the federal government which it deemed inflationary. In the 1970s the council maintained the charge against the SPD-FDP coalition while also pointing in its analysis to the need for restraint in wage increases. In many ways the council could be likened to an auxiliary opposition that impedes, monitors, and criticizes government spending. It is part of the state that checks the executive branch of government and reinforces a predilection for incremental policy.

Industrial Relations. In the area of industrial relations comprehensive legal regulations create a stable and peaceful system of labor-management relations which does not require direct government intervention in collective wage bargaining or in the determination of prices. To date West Germany has had no experience with a statutory incomes policy as occasionally practiced, for example, in Britain or the United States. Instead it features a statutory system of workers' representation in the plant designed to take care of conflicts at the workplace. Factory councils operate under legal rules first established in 1920 and reaffirmed and amended in 1952 and 1972 (see Chapter 3). All the modalities of elections—among others the number of employee representatives, the organization of elections, and the term of office—are precisely specified by law.

The law also stipulates the rights and obligations of the councils. They enjoy far-reaching rights on all decisions affecting personnel management, such as hiring, lay-offs, retirement, overtime, part-time workers, vacation; and the access to detailed information about the company's finances and investment plans to which they are entitled would strike the average American businessmen as ludicrous. At the same time the factory councils also have important obligations designed to ensure a peaceful and stable system of industrial relations. They are not entitled to act as the general collective bargaining agent for the workers. By law they are barred from calling strikes or organizing demonstrations. Indeed, their legal obligation extends to the requirement that they do their utmost to end any wildcat strikes. The councils' mandate is to mediate conflict at the plant level. They are barred from acting politically. Negotiating wage increases and engaging in strikes, under restrictive legal supervision, is the sole responsibility of the unions. But rather than creating tension and conflict, the legislative changes, especially the amendments of the Works Councils Act of 1972, have forged closer links between the councils and the unions. Since the 1950s about 80 percent of the councilors have been union members. The enlargement of the numbers and powers of the factory councils in 1972 has reinforced the position of the unions inside the plant and has made the councils increasingly dependent on the technical expertise that only the unions command. Wolfgang Streeck (1982) has thus rightly pointed to the stabilizing effect that the legal regulation of industrial relations has had for West Germany's unions.

West Germany's system of labor courts illustrates how the state's legal intervention has been adapted institutionally to the presence of the most important economic interest groups. Based on a long German tradition, the courts were legislated in 1953 and charged to maintain or restore peace within the enterprise, dealing specifically with the issues covered in the works councils and codetermination laws (Blankenburg and Rogowski, 1984; Blankenburg and Schönholz, 1979; Blankenburg, Rogowski, and Schönholz, 1978; Körnich, 1978; Ramm, 1971; Wunderlich, 1946). They also have jurisdiction over everything affecting individual labor contracts: they lay down rules for hiring and firing; and more broadly they define the rights of employers and employees. Trade unions and employers' associations participate in recruiting the professional judges. They each nominate the lay judges who also serve on the bench. From the lists of candidates they prepare, the state minister supposedly selects the lay judges. But in the summer of 1985, because of a lack of volunteers, employers and unions in Hesse as elsewhere had recommended only as many candidates as there were vacancies, thus leaving the minister of Hesse no choice. This unconstitutional procedure eventually brought this branch of West Germany's judicial machinery temporarily to a grinding halt (*Der Spiegel,* Aug. 12, 1985, p. 31).

In the federal labor court system two lay judges from each side join three professional judges. The two interest groups give legal counsel to those of their members appealing before court. Because they participate in the court proceedings, business and labor leave individuals little choice but to accept rulings that approximate a form of judicial mediation. The professional judges holds an arbitration hearing alone before regular proceedings commence. And during the entire proceedings she makes explicit attempts, with the consent of both parties, to mediate the dispute. Lawyers are generally not admitted when litigation amounts to less than 300 deutschmarks. Otherwise claimants receive legal assistance from the trade unions and employers' associations. The labor courts emphasize speed in their normal proceedings. For example, no more than three days elapse between an arbitration hearing that seeks a voluntary settlement and the beginning of ordinary hearings. And law suits are extremely cheap since court fees have a maximum limit of 500 deutschmarks. Furthermore, statistics show that labor courts have a much higher rate of settlements than do civil courts. The high number of settlements is a result of the pressure of the judge, "the special necessities of labour law and the especially good conditions for settlement in labour court" (Blankenburg, Rogowski, and Schönholz, 1978, p. 49). Cross-national data illustrate the important role that the labor courts play in West Germany's industrial relations. Table 1-6 points to the importance of West Germany's labor courts. In the mid-1970s the number of cases adjudicated by the labor courts per thousand employees was four times greater than in the United States and six times greater than in Britain; it exceeded the Japanese rate by a factor of twenty.

Social Welfare and Migrant Labor. West Germany's more than 1,500 social insurance funds are another important set of parapublic institutions that in the late 1970s employed a staff of about 175,000 and administered annually transfer payments amounting to about 200 billion deutschmarks, or about one-fifth of the gross national product (Bogs, 1977; Doubrawa, 1969; von Ferber, 1977; Hartwich, 1970; Leopold, 1974; Standfest, 1977; Süllow, 1982; Tennstedt, 1976, 1977; WSI, 1978). Despite these magnitudes, the social funds are, like the Federal Employment Office, not considered credit institutions and thus are not subject to the minimum reserve requirement of the Bundesbank. Three

TABLE 1-6   Use of Labor Courts

	Number of Cases	Civilian Labor Force Employed (1975)	Cases per Thousand in Labor Force
West Germany (Labor Court)	376,186 (1974)	24,828,000	1.515
United States (NLRB)	34,569 (1976)	84,783,000	0.407
Britain	46,996 (1982)	21,314,000	0.220
Japan		52,230,000	
Labor Relations Committees	1,417 (1976)		0.027
Legal Court	2,719 (1976)		0.052

Sources: Tadashi A. Hanami, "The Function of the Law in Japanese Industrial Relations," in Taishiro Shirai, ed., *Contemporary Industrial Relations in Japan* (Madison: University of Wisconsin Press, 1983), p. 177. Erhard Blankenburg and Ralf Rogowski, "West German Labor Courts and the British Tribunal System: A Socio-Legal Comparison," *Disputes Processing Research Program, Working Papers 1984-10* (Madison: University of Wisconsin, Institute for Legal Studies, 1984), p. 15.

major funds administer West Germany's insurance against illness, accident, and old age. With a membership of about 35 million, the health insurance funds cover about 90 percent of the relevant population. The old-age pension insures about 27 million employees. The number of social security recipients was about 12 million in the early 1980s. The obligatory accident insurance funds cover more than 30 million employees. The funds are organized by economic sector, occupational group, and territory. And with the exception of the health insurance funds, which account for about 1,350 of the approximately 1,500 funds employing about 140,000, the system is highly centralized.

As discussed in Chapter 4 the social insurance funds were an integral part of Bismarck's social legislation in the 1880s. Bismarck's intent was to create under a state umbrella cooperative associations that would help administer the new social programs. Because different groups viewed them as powerful bureaucracies linked closely to a vital policy arena, the social funds remained highly politicized institutions until they were absorbed by the Nazi dictatorship. After 1945 political controversies about the purpose and organization of the funds resumed. Social Catholics in the CDU backed by the employers' associations and the FDP disagreed strongly with the SPD and the trade unions on whether the funds should be administered jointly by unions and employers or whether the insured (de facto, the unions) should have two-thirds or even 100 percent control over the funds. As in the case of codetermination (see Chapter 3), a growing political conservatism in the crucial years 1950–52 was reflected in the triumph of the views of the CDU and the FDP. Parity representation of the major economic interest groups, it was argued, was the most likely way of depoliticizing a set of institutions that, since the 1880s, had remained highly charged politically. The traditional dominance of the unions over the health insurance funds and of the employers over the accident funds was thus replaced by a system of parity representation of both. By law up to one-third of the funds' officials can be representatives of the employers' associations and the unions; they are not required to be members of the fund in question. As the frequent amendments to the original legislation of 1951 indicate, political debate has not stopped, because the unions viewed the parity provision as a major setback. And the parity principle is not applied in the governance of all of the social funds. But the only significant exception are the 9.3 million salaried employees who are covered in seven supplementary health insurance funds. These funds are governed only by the insured, with no representation of the employers. Generally speaking though, the joint control of the funds by the two main "social partners" has become a widely accepted fact of West Germany's political life.

The social funds leave it to the major economic interest groups to mediate the state's administration of main social welfare programs. Elections of about 40,000 honorary officials, held every six years, are devoid of democratic meaning for two different reasons. First, the social funds are corporations organized under public law which, under the supervision of the state, administer welfare law. With the exception of the health insurance funds, which retain in some areas the ability to define the level of services and, like the accident insurance funds, have the right to fix the contribution rate, the social funds' main purpose is to administer social services that are determined by law. Thus less than 5 percent of the total transfer payments of 200 billion deutschmarks is determined by the funds. The influence of the honorary functionaries, once elected, is restricted to matters of the funds' internal organization. Second, competitive elections are the exception rather than the rule. If unions and employers present slates of candidates which have no more names than the number of offices being contested, no election will be held. Since 1945 on average this has been the case in 95 percent of all elections. In these cases representatives are simply nominated by the major interest groups. Even in the few instances in which competitive elections take place, the electoral process favors the large economic interest groups through list voting, anonymous candidates, and their privileged position in the nominating process.

In 1953 competitive elections were held in 9 (or 0.42 percent) of the 2,145 social insurance funds. By 1980 the corresponding figure had increased to 49 (or 3.50 percent) of the 1,400 funds then in existence (Süllow, 1982, p. 148). Only twice since 1945 were competitive elections held because employers failed to offer only one slate of candidates. Electoral competition has increased only when the claims of the Union for Employees (Deutsche Angestelltengewerkschaft, or DAG) has clashed with those of the DGB. In 1975 close to two-thirds of the respondents in a public opinion poll did not know that elections had been held the year before. Eighty-five percent did not know either the persons or the organizations representing them in the funds. Only one-fifth had ever voted in one of the elections for the social funds (Infas, 1977, pp. 237, 243, 250). In contrast to the works councils with their electoral participation of 75–85 percent, these data illustrate that politically the social insurance funds are not designed to further democratic participation. Instead they offer a bridge between state and society. Through them the major economic interest groups and the state jointly administer some of West Germany's major social welfare programs.

West Germany's system of unemployment insurance differs in two institutional ways from the other social insurance funds. First, in contrast to management of the social funds, the Labor Ministry supervises the Federal Employment Office (Bundesanstalt für Arbeit), which has 64,000 employees and a budget of about 33 billion deutschmarks in 1985. Second, no provision exists for electing representatives to local, regional, or federal employment offices. The representation of only the main economic interest groups which exists de facto in the case of the social funds exists de jure in the case of unemployment insurance (Bruche and Reissert, 1985; Krautkrämer, 1978).

The structure of the system of labor administration was defined legally in 1952. The Federal Employment Office is a three-tiered system under the supervision of the Ministry of Labor and Social Affairs. The Employment Office works out standardized abstract guidelines that are adapted at the state and local level to the particular conditions of regional labor markets. The Employment Office is located in Nuremberg. It is governed by a president and a tripartite governing board that is assisted by an executive committee. Employers, trade unions, and senior bureaucrats from the federal and state bureaucracy are accorded equal representation on the board. The office in Nuremberg works out the statutes and guidelines for enforcement by subordinate offices. It also allocates financial and personnel resources to state and local offices. However, financial quotas based on employment statistics restrict administrative discretion.

Nine state labor offices and 146 local offices, each of them assisted by tripartite administrative committees, form a centralized chain of command. Below the local offices are 538 branch labor offices. In contrast to other European countries, unemployment benefit offices and placement services are centralized in the same institution. The Employment Office is not under direct governmental authority but is instead a self-governing corporation with standing under public law. It is financed by member contributions. The unemployment insurance tax, 3 percent of an employee's income, is divided equally between employer and employee. But in times of high unemployment, such as the 1980s, the Employment Office also relies on subsidies from the Ministry of Labor and Social Affairs which is responsible for its legal supervision. In contrast to the various social policy funds, the autonomy of the Employment Office is in fact limited by its financial and regulatory dependence on the ministry.

The tripartite form of administration resulted from a process of historical evolution in the twentieth century which saw a deep break between the Weimar Republic, organized around self-governing employment offices, and the institutions that the Nazis imposed soon after 1933 to mobilize the country for war. In the early 1950s the employers' associations and the unions agreed that the system of labor administration should be organized like the social funds, that is, without direct state participation. But the federal government, strongly opposed to any such scheme, convinced a majority of the Bundestag to think otherwise (Dohse, 1981, pp. 143–44). An institution administering questions of employment, including foreign workers, CDU Minister of Labor Anton Storch argued, should not be left only to the social partners but should require also a direct presence of the state. The 1969 revision and amendment of the legislation governing the Federal Employment Office further strengthened the position of the state at the expense of the tripartite governing board: all bylaws and regulations must henceforth be endorsed by the minister of labor and social affairs.

Nevertheless, at the local, regional, and federal levels business and union representatives are intimately involved in the tripartite boards that help run West Germany's system of employment offices. It is the purpose of these boards to guarantee close relations between the Federal Employment Office and the affected interest groups. The tripartite administrative boards have at the federal level 39 members, at the state level between 15 and 27 members, and at the local level between 9 and 21 members. Members and their substitutes are proposed by the trade unions, the employer associations, the federal government, and the peak associations of municipal authorities. Members serve six-year terms.

The "governing board" at the federal level operates like a parliament. It can amend the bylaws; it makes budgetary allocations among different labor market districts; and it is consulted during the nomination process of the president of the Federal Employment Office. For almost two decades Josef Stingl ran the federal office with a keen nose for publicity and a good sense for enhancing the institution's autonomy as well as his own political influence. The "management board" exercises executive powers at the federal level. It is responsible for developing budgetary proposals; it administers all funds; and it controls all personnel matters, including the recruitment of the directors of the offices at the local level. At the state level the tripartite boards are much weaker and are restricted largely to an advisory function. At the local level the boards have at best an indirect effect on policy. Local boards meet on the average two to five times a year. Their primary function is to disseminate to local businesses information about particular employment policies. In the words of one director of a local office: "The board cannot intervene, if I do not want it to. If I do not agree with their 'resolutions', I let them know that I decide what goes on 'in my house' " (Krautkrämer, 1978, p. 46). Board members who were interviewed echoed this sentiment with some resignation. Participation of employers and unions is evidently more important at the federal level than at the local level.

West Germany has a remarkably orderly and centralized system of voluntary welfare organizations which resembles the system of economic peak associations (Bauer, 1978; Heinze and Olk, 1981, 1984; Kirberger, 1978). The rapid evolution of Germany's industrial capitalism since the middle of the nineteenth century, the early development of a conservative welfare state in the 1880s, the effect of military defeats in 1918 and 1945, and the succession of political regimes in the twentieth century have eroded the boundaries between state and society. On the whole state and communes favored the emergence of private welfare associations because they offered welcome institutional resources for achieving their objectives. By 1924 the social legislation of the Weimar Republic had acknowledged this symbiotic relation. On questions of poverty relief, for example, private welfare associations were granted a policymaking role in principle superior to that of the communes. In disbursing its increasing subsidies in the 1920s, the state bureaucracy encouraged the centralization of welfare groups organized in peak associations. The aim of state policy was to create a cartel of peak associations that had a broad institutional presence in society and thus could help implement welfare policy. Independent local and regional associations thus eventually transformed themselves into hierarchically organized, large bureaucracies operating on a national scale.

In the 1950s and 1960s the memories of totalitarian Nazi rule provided a powerful argument for extending legal protection to the privileges and prerogatives of the large welfare associations against potential interventions of the state bureaucracy. As the scope of the federal government's policymaking powers broadened, the welfare state had to rely increasingly on the welfare associations for implementing its programs. More than two-thirds of West Germany's vocational training centers, nurseries, and homes for the elderly are run by the large welfare associations. Together they have 600,000 employees and can count on an army of 1.5 million volunteers. The state finances about 40 percent of the expenditures of these welfare associations. Since 1945 these centralized, professional welfare bureaucracies have been ideologically and financially incorporated into the formulation of policy which, in its implementation, has come to depend crucially on their manpower, institutions, and resources.

In this field the German Association (Deutscher Verein) is one of West Germany's typical parapublic institutions (Hoffmann and Tennstedt, 1980; Orthbandt, 1980; Tennstedt, 1981). Founded in 1880, it was initially no more than an annual convention of welfare workers and specialists in social policy. Between World War I and II it became a small organization with a minimal staff. But since 1945 the German Association has developed a substantial bureaucratic organization that is closely linked to the state. In 1978, for example, the federal government financed two-thirds of the association's budget of 5.6 million deutsch-marks with the state governments contributing another 15 percent. Although the association is de jure a private association, de facto it fills an indispensable public role. For example, twelve of the thirteen members of a working group that the federal government convened in 1955 to consider West Germany's system of public welfare were then or became subsequently members of the German Association. The report that the working group issued in 1958 became the blueprint from which the federal bureaucracy and the Bundestag formulated the Social Welfare Act of 1961. In 1980 its centennial featured President Karl Carstens as a speaker. And quite appropriately the coat of arms of the federal government appeared on the stamp that the Ministry of Postal Affairs issued to honor the occasion.

Although its sphere of activity covers all aspects of social policy, the German Association has a particular impact on all questions of public welfare. For example, since the Ministry for Youth, Family, and Health delegated the task in 1955, the association has authoritatively defined in its commissions and study groups the market basket of goods which it deems essential for a minimum standard of living in West Germany. To discharge its responsibilities the association has a staff of 100, a quarter of whom are professionals producing an unending stream of publications. The association organizes study courses and special seminars for social workers and civil servants. In sum, the German Association has assumed the responsibility for coordinating private and public activities in diverse spheres of social welfare policy. Like the Council of Economic Experts, it aims at playing the role of "honest broker" between the state and its communes, on the one hand, and interest groups, politicians, and social scientists, on the other.

In the welfare field there are several other organizations. The Social Democratic Workers' Welfare Association (Arbeiterwohlfahrt), for example, was created in 1919 to counter the influence of religious and bourgeois welfare associations that had formed in the nineteenth century. Although it formally separated from the SPD in 1945, the association retains a typically Social Democratic outlook on political issues. In addition to the Red Cross, founded in 1864, which has broader international aspects, there is also a peak association for all unaffiliated voluntary welfare associations. Founded in 1920 this association is neutral on matters of religious belief and political ideology. Its express purpose is to make the views of its more than 2,000 member organizations heard at all levels of policymaking; it also assists in the implementation of policy.

The most important welfare associations are arguably religious. In the nineteenth century private, religiously based associations formed which were independent from locally organized efforts to deal with the new poverty of an industrial era (Rinken, 1971, pp. 39–65). In 1957 the Protestant church merged two welfare associations that had been founded, respectively, in 1848 and 1945, into one organization (Diakonisches Hilfswerk). Its Catholic counterpart, Caritas, united in 1897 a broad-based, decentralized effort by the Catholic church and Catholic lay organizations to cope with the social costs of industrial capitalism. During the twentieth century, and especially after 1945, Caritas organized itself systematically along territorial lines to match state authorities from the local to the federal level. Although the Central Welfare Association of Jews, founded in 1917, may have lost its material importance, because of the Holocaust its symbolic significance remains great. It represents the small number (25,000) of Jews now living in the Federal Republic and, more important, provides individual care and counseling.

The existence of these denominational welfare agencies illustrates the primary importance of the Protestant and Catholic churches among West Germany's parapublic institutions. West Germany's Basic Law guarantees freedom of religion and a separation of church and state which has little bearing on the privileged position that the big churches enjoy in public life (Fischer, 1971; Spotts, 1973). As under the Weimar Republic, West Germany's Protestant and Catholic churches are corporations organized under public law. Although this privileged position enjoys little support among constitutional lawyers, it accurately expresses the realities of West German politics. The state is obligated to offer theological instruction for the clergy at the universities. Although the constitutional and political privileges granted once again to the major churches after 1945 disappointed some of their expectations, in the 1960s they enjoyed "a favored position in the state" (Spotts, 1973, p. 190).

One of the most important privileges the churches enjoy dates back to the secularization of 1803, namely, the constitutional guarantee of annual cash payments from the state which amount to slightly less than 10 percent of the total church income. More important is the right, evolved since the middle of the nineteenth century, to levy a church tax. Although actual arrangements are negotiated by the individual states, since 1955 the state has withheld from residents' income a tax, determined by the church, equal to about 9 percent of total income tax receipts; this is then transferred to the churches. The tax is levied on the basis of church membership. Although individuals have the right to leave their church, by the mid-1980s less than 10 percent had in fact done so. Between 1953 and 1968 the income of the Protestant church rose by 500 percent. Although there are no reliable nationwide figures, in 1968 total church income was estimated at 5.6 billion deutschmarks (Spotts, 1973, p. 197). By the mid-1970s the church tax alone had generated more than 5 billion deutschmarks. A decade later the shoe was on the other foot. A tax cut planned for the second half of the 1980s, if implemented, will have a very noticeable effect on church income.

The privileged position that the churches occupy in West Germany's public life is symbolized by the language of the first model treaty signed between the Protestant churches and Lower Saxony in 1955. The treaty speaks of "joint responsibilities" of church and state and makes provisions for active cooperation between these two "partners." As the language indicates, the churches are not merely bodies of public law but share responsibility in the execution of state policy that affects their mission in social, educational, and cultural affairs. This explains why on these issues at state and local levels the churches have an important, though clearly diminished since the 1960s, influence on the appointment of state officials.

In the area of social policy West Germany's churches have far-reaching responsibilities that in other countries are typically left either to voluntary charitable organizations or to state agencies. The churches maintain 9,000 institutions helping, among others, the blind, school drop-outs, and the mentally incapacitated. In addition they operate more than 10,000 nurseries with places for more than 750,000 children; 1,100 hospitals with more than 200,000 beds; 2,500 homes for the elderly; 1,000 rest and vacation homes; and 2,000 student and youth hostels. It is thus not surprising that 80 percent of the churches' formidable income pays the wages and salaries of workers that number in the several hundreds of thousands (Spotts, 1973, pp. 198–201).

Since the churches have the mission and the necessary resources, they are funded by local, state, and federal authorities to carry out various programs. Although the churches bear virtually all of the operating costs of their broad-based network of social institutions, the state pays for the construction and renovation of hospitals (95 percent), nurseries (70–50 percent), and youth hostels, orphanages, and the like (50 percent). At the federal level, the Ministry of Family and Youth relies on private organizations and, most important, on the churches to implement its programs. The Social Welfare Act of 1961 gave ecclesiastical bodies such as the Catholic church's Caritas the right to implement the government's public assistance programs. In the late 1960s church groups received about one-third of the ministry's total budget. The Foreign Office funds churches to do both religious work with West Germany's guest workers and missionary work abroad. And in the 1960s the Ministry for Economic Cooperation gave more than 50 million deutschmarks annually to support the development aid agencies that the churches operated in Third World countries. Although there are no precise figures for total state funds allocated to the churches to aid in policy implementation, one informed participant estimated the total at 800 million deutschmarks in the late 1960s. The important position of the churches in implementing state policy is among several reasons why their role in social policy was so strong in the 1950s and 1960s. "When the two churches worked together on social issues," Frederic Spott concludes (1973, p. 286), "they were able to exert a decisive influence on social policy and social legislation. During this period nothing in this field was—or probably could have been—enacted into law or have even reached the floor of the Bundestag against the clear opposition of the two churches." In the 1970s and 1980s, however, the influence of the churches has declined. Legislation regarding hospital construction, for example, slighted the role of church-affiliated hospitals.

University Reform. Virtually all West German universities are state institutions. Distinguished private universities such as Harvard or Oxford do not exist. Instead universities are public corporate bodies operating under legislation passed by federal and state governments which largely defines the charters of the university. An intricate relation between state and university shapes the structure of the university, its relation to the state administration, its power to grant degrees, administer examinations, develop curriculum, and organize research. Universities are encased by a number of parapublic institutions that embody the merging of public and private power. Since the Basic Law reserved all matters affecting cultural policy, including education, to the states, in the postwar years the increasing influence of the federal government has come about primarily through its appointment of commissions that bring officials of the state and federal governments together with representatives of the academic world and private interest groups.

In contrast to many of the other policy issues covered in this book, university reform has attracted a striking number of organized private groups. (Briese, 1972). The West German Conference of University Presidents, the Association of German Students, and the Association of German Professors, for example, were all founded in 1949 and 1950 as peak associations of constituent groups within the universities. For the promotion of basic research the German Research Association, founded in 1949–50, represents not only all universities but all other major research organizations; it has established itself as the main disburser of research funds. In his detailed description of the institutional network affecting education policy in West Germany, Volker Briese (1972, pp. 32–50) lists another half dozen interest groups. Furthermore, the decentralization of power in the public sector which the Basic Law mandates on issues of cultural policy adds additional complexity. In 1965, for example, the 3 percent that West Germany's federal government was contributing to total educational expenditures was by far the lowest among eighteen industrial nations. The relative contributions of central governments in other federal states, such as the United States, Canada, or Switzerland, tended to be three or four times greater than in the Federal Republic (Cameron and Hofferbert, 1974, p. 231). But the federal role in policymaking increased as early as the 1950s. Coordinating bodies such as the Standing Conference of Cultural Ministers were from the mid-1950s on complemented by a growing number of parliamentary, interministerial, and cabinet committees dealing with science policy. Founded in 1955, the Atomic Energy Ministry was renamed the Science Ministry in 1962 and the Ministry for Education and Science in 1969.

In this complex and dense network three institutions in particular deserve some attention because they illustrate well the West German tendency to create parapublic bodies to solve problems of public policy (Briese, 1972, pp. 25–76; Mushaben, 1981, pp. 65–117). The West German Conference of University Presidents (Westdeutsche Rektorenkonferenz) was founded in 1949. It established its permanent headquarters in Bad Godesberg, close to the federal government in Bonn. The conference is funded in part by the annual dues from its member institutions which are appropriated by the respective state governments. But the federal government subsidizes two-thirds of the budget. It is "as curious an organizational phenomenon as the 'autonomous' university itself: it constitutes a state-financed pressure group, whose independence derives from its ability to play off 'outside' financiers against each other" (Mushaben, 1981, p. 98). The conference includes the small Presidential Committee, which develops general policies, and the State Committee, which includes a university president from each of West Germany's eleven states. Assisted by ad hoc commissions, this second committee negotiates actively with federal and state authorities.

In 1957 the federal government and the states responded positively to the proposal of Gerhard Hess, then president of the German Research Association, creating the new Science Council (Wissenschaftsrat) (Berger, 1974). This organization is governed by a council of forty-four members serving three-years terms. The council is divided into two commissions. The federal president appoints sixteen members of the Science Commission, following among others the recommendations of the German Research Association and the Conference of University Presidents. In addition federal and state governments jointly appoint an additional six members from public life. The Administrative Commission consists of six representatives of the federal government (casting eleven votes) and one delegate from each of the eleven states. Council resolutions require a two-thirds majority; that is, fifteen votes will prevent the Science Council from taking any action.

The initial agenda for the Science Council was to administer federal subsidies for research and to project the future financial and personnel needs for universities and research institutes. Issued annually since 1960, like those of the Council of Economic Experts, its reports were extremely influential in shaping the growing discussion of the future of higher education in West Germany. The Science Council sought to promote research in general, while the states sought to restrict it to the issue of university expansion and reform. State and federal delegates to the Administrative Commission must consider the work of the Science Commission in their budget projections; but under the council's organization, representatives from university and research institutes are not able to influence directly the work of the Administrative Commission. The complex relation between state and university is thus mirrored in the very structure of the Science Commission.

Joyce Mushaben concludes that the Science Council broke new grounds for several reasons. It was created to deal explicitly with the emerging problems of higher education and research. It sought to develop cooperative planning and financial management among academic, bureaucratic, and political elites often pursuing antagonistic interests. By bringing representatives of federal and state governments to the same table on a regular basis, "they enlisted the aid of a 'third party,' whose role they restricted to that of a 'catalyst'. . . . In the final analysis, the Council contributed significantly to the development of cooperative mechanisms for educational reform, but in so doing, rendered itself superfluous as new planning bodies were instituted along similar organizational lines" (Mushaben, 1981, p. 87).

The most notable of these new planning bodies was the German Educational Council (Deutscher Bildungsrat), which was created in 1965 to address what was then perceived to be an imminent shortage of teachers and technically qualified graduates. In contrast to the Science Council, the statutes of the Educational Council did not provide for a common vote of its two commissions. Fourteen of the eighteen members of the Educational Commission were appointed by the states, the other four by the federal government. The eighteen members of the Government Association were chosen similarly. Although the Educational Council was charged specifically to deal with problems of secondary education, issues such as certification or the upgrading of teacher training colleges to university status required a discussion of university curriculum and personnel. Hans Weiler has called (1982, p. 25) the Educational Council a "peculiar semi-corporatist mechanism of policy preparation which, through its ingenious composition of federal, state, and associational representatives and experts had become the dominant force in West German educational policy between the mid-sixties and its dissolution in 1975."

The main agenda item for the Educational Council was the development of a framework for reforming the very structure and governance of West Germany's system of education. Its most important recommendations were published in 1970 after years of contentious bargaining. The council proposed a host of far-reaching proposals to increase participation in West German schools, broaden access to the universities, and eventually lessen social inequality. But as a parapublic institution it was ill-suited to push for major structural change. In this respect the experiences of the Educational Council parallel those of the Science Council whose work became much more difficult once it moved from projections of the future expansion of higher education to the more volatile issue of university governance. In 1975 the joint agreement between the federal and the state governments lapsed for political reasons. Conservative states had objected all along to the work of the Educational Council. They thus made extension of the joint agreement contingent on the council's acceptance of direct control by the states, a demand the federal government adamantly opposed. The substantial amount of educational research which informed the work of the council in the end ran up against the political realities that the institutional restraints of West Germany's parapublic institutions impose on all proponents of large-scale change.

Like West Germany's system of intergovernmental relations, the parapublic institutions I have described here operate largely outside of the limelight of public attention. Yet they are arguably of great importance for any realistic interpretation of the political capacities of the Federal Republic. One might even call them a West German version of the intermediary institutions that Tocqueville 150 years ago saw as so important to American democracy. I have argued that democratic participation by individual citizens is not the primary objective for which these institutions were either originally designed or to which they were subsequently adapted. Parapublic institutions are the trademarks of an oligopolistic style of politics in which the state is neither the central nor a peripheral player. They are both actors who participate and arenas that facilitate a stable accommodation of conflicting objectives. They thus reinforce the tendency toward incremental policy change.

5. Preview

I have argued in this chapter that the domestication of power derives from and is expressed by three nodes of West Germany's policy network which hold together a decentralized state and a centralized society. It is not difficult to illustrate, as I did in section 3, how federalism, judicial review, and other political features decentralize state institutions. Similarly, it is also relatively easy to show the centralized character, for example, of West Germany's producer groups and welfare associations. The difficulty lies in understanding how decentralization and centralization link up in one institutional structure. I argued in section 4 that the composition of West Germany's political parties and the system of coalition governments, cooperative federalism, and parapublic institutions are political, territorial, and functional forms of representation which constrain bold policy initiatives. The restraint that the interaction of these three nodes of the policy network imposes on the exercise of state power explains why policy change in the Federal Republic is incremental even when a new government is voted into office. Analysis of their interaction tells us why West Germany is not the United States, Britain, or France. And they also show why politics and policy in West Germany differ from politics and policy in Social Democratic Sweden and in conservative Japan.

The political structure of West Germany intersects in plausible ways with the political logic of the problems that the country has faced during the last three decades. Five of the six policy areas discussed below (economic management, industrial relations, social welfare, migrant labor, and administrative reform) illustrate that West German politics adjusts incrementally to change. Continuities rather than sharp breaks in policy typify West German policy. In economic and social affairs (Chapters 2–5) the shackling of power results from the interaction of political, territorial, and functional forms of representation. On questions of administrative reform (Chapter 6) continuity results instead from the very structure and strong tradition of the West German state. Major structural changes, however, did occur in West Germany's system of higher education (Chapter 7). Between 1960 and 1980 West German universities were transformed from elite to mass institutions. For reasons that I shall examine in Chapter 7, the institutional constraints impeding structural change were less severe. It is perhaps no accident that in this instance West Germans have not been very happy with the results of government policy. West Germany's way of organizing power creates distinctive capacities and incapacities for public policy. But it is important to recognize that the effectiveness of any political model has its limits. This is the lesson that I draw from West Germany's experience with university reform policies.

The incremental adjustments so typical of West German policy are shaped by three main factors. First, the transformation of West German parties to catch-all parties with mass appeal and the system of coalition governments act as a brake for any major initiatives, such as the attempted reforms of the SPD-FDP coalition in the early 1970s and the efforts of Chancellor Kohl to effect substantial policy changes since 1983. Second, West Germany's "cooperative federalism" has the effect of creating political links among the territorial interests in the Federal Republic which are sufficiently tight to stall all serious attempts at large-scale policy change. Finally, parapublic institutions provide effective mechanisms for representing the functional interests particularly of large producer groups. Because it incorporates many of the institutions that also weaken it, West Germany's state is best described as semiso-vereign.

2 Economic Management

History explains why West Germans and foreigners alike have often associated economic policy in the Federal Republic with its very survival. The political contradictions on which the Weimar Republic was built became fully evident only during the depression of the 1930s. Hyperinflation and mass unemployment encouraged the Germans to support radical parties, both on the Right and on the Left. The lesson of Weimar appeared unambiguous. A stable democracy in Germany required a prosperous economy. There was a second reason for concern. Throughout the twentieth century, Germany had hitched its dynamic economy to an aggressive nationalism that sought to conquer much of Europe and, indeed, the world. Two world wars broke the link between economic success and nationalist expansion. For understandable reasons, then, as in Japan economic policy in West Germany has been viewed as a central policy arena.

The 1950s witnessed West Germany's "economic miracle" without any of the trappings of American laissez-faire policies, British public-sector spending, French indicative planning, Japanese industrial policy, or Swedish labor market policy. Until the early 1980s the Federal Republic was stunningly successful in its economic management. Leaving the political leadership of Europe to France, West Germany became the unquestioned economic leader. As economic performance in Britain began to lag far behind that of West Germany, British policymakers and analysts inquired with increasing urgency into the secret of West Germany's success. Although the answer to that question is far from simple, it appears that the economic and political structures of West Germany were well suited to the purposes of its economic policy: monetary stability at home, international competitiveness abroad, steady growth and full employment.

The configuration of power in this policy sector closely matches the pattern that characterizes the Federal Republic in general. State power is decentralized. The federal government must live side-by-side with state and local governments whose spending decisions it does not determine. Furthermore, West Germany's Federal Reserve (Bundesbank) is virtually autonomous and its influence over economic policy has probably increased over the years. The structure of West German society, on the other hand, and in particular of its major economic interest groups, is very centralized. Government by coalition, a system of cooperative federalism, and parapublic institutions are the three institutional nodes around which the politics of economic policy has unfolded in the Federal Republic. These arrangements have served the Federal Republic well, allowing for incremental adjustments to the tasks of reconstruction in the 1950s, recession in the 1960s, and readjustment in the 1970s. The question that troubles the West Germans is whether the structural shifts underway in the global economy in the 1980s will require a pattern of policy different from what has proven so effective in the past.

Context

Compared to industrial development in Britain, Belgium, Switzerland, and some regions in France and the United States, Germany's industrial development was late and rapid (Gerschenkron, 1962); compared to that in Japan and Sweden, it occurred early and proceeded in an almost leisurely manner. The German path to modernity has avoided both celebrating unrestricted market competition and cherishing what Chalmers Johnson (1982), writing about Japan, has called a developmental state. Instead, from its position of relative economic backwardness, Germany evolved particular institutional and political arrangements that encouraged rapid economic growth at home and soon thereafter expansion abroad.

Germany's investment banks in particular were assigned the role of mobilizing capital on a much bigger scale than had occurred in Britain in the late eighteenth century. For one thing, having entered the process of industrialization later than Britain, Germany did not have the luxury of leisurely developing its textile industry before moving to more capital-intensive industries such as steel. The logic of international military and commercial rivalry demanded otherwise. Indeed, large-scale enterprises such as Germany's railway system required the cooperation of banks and state governments. Large investments and economic recessions spurred the development of trusts and cartels. The government later established scientific research institutes and engineering schools that helped secure Germany's leading role in modern scientific industries—for example, chemicals—as they developed in the late nineteenth century. Germany's stunning achievement in catapulting itself from economic backwardness to economic preeminence within half a century was greeted with applause reminiscent of America's reaction to Japan in recent years. The secret to Germany's success evidently lay in the concentration of economic power in the hands of banks, trusts, and very large firms; the existence of a large number of highly competitive, small and medium-sized firms; and the government's unwillingness to impose the trappings of state power over all of economic life.

Events in the twentieth century reinforced this pattern. World War I was financed largely by domestic loans. After losing the war, Germany could not, as it had in 1871, impose reparation payments on others. Instead, it confronted truly staggering financial demands from the Allied powers. Budget deficits, an unfavorable balance of payments, the wartime erosion in the purchasing power of the deutschmark, and demands for higher wages by a politically assertive trade union movement all turned into hyperinflation. From the beginning of World War I it took more than five years for the deutschmark to fall to about 10 percent of its prewar value. By October 1923 it took only about ten days for a similar drop in value (Hardach, 1980, pp. 19–20). By printing money the government in the end liquidated its debts as well as the assets of a substantial segment of a patriotic German middle class that year after year had purchased government bonds and thus financed the war. The lesson of this episode was not forgotton. West Germany's Constitution gives the Bundesbank far-reaching autonomy as the protector of a stable currency. The management of money, the West Germans have decided, is too important to be left to politicians.

Of similar importance was a second lesson the West Germans learned from the Nazis' eventual control of all important segments of economic life—consumption, investment, and labor—in their mad attempt to impose their "New Order" on Europe. Money income was regulated by very high taxes and wage controls. The price of imports was determined through controls on foreign exchange. Trusts and cartels were favored in controlling domestic prices. Investment controls were imposed to ensure that the armaments industries would expand to support Hitler's foreign policy. The increasing shortage of labor was counteracted through a variety of measures, including a compulsory year of service for women, introduced in 1935, and, eventually, the import of millions of foreign workers to staff the war industries. "The Nazis were slowly but surely creating a governmentally guided economy where state directives instead of the laws of the market determined production and consumption" (Hardach, 1980, pp. 65–66). Although it is true that the Nazis attempted to develop an economy that would differ significantly from both a centrally planned Communist economy as well as from Western liberal market economies, the need to mobilize for war tended to conceal those efforts. In any event, the collapse of Hitler's so-called New Order convinced the West Germans that they wanted the government to play no more than a restricted role in economic life.

After 1945 the time thus seemed ripe for a political reconstruction of economic life which avoided both unregulated market competition and total government planning (Wallich, 1955). The ideological construct that eventually was embraced by all political quarters, the social market economy, offered to the West Germans a third way between liberalism and totalitarianism (Friedrich, 1955; Zweig, 1980). Although this construct built on a venerable tradition in German history, it was debated most actively in the 1930s by a group of economists and lawyers at the University of Freiburg. These men wanted to lay down the principles by which in their opinion German economic life should be reorganized after what they thought would be the inevitable downfall of the Nazi regime. Indeed the very term "social market economy" was coined by Alfred Müller-Armack, under Minister of Economics Erhard later for many years a senior civil servant in the Economics Ministry. The concept expressed the philosophical belief that market competition and social protection were not antagonistic but reinforcing. The growth dividends of a dynamic market economy, it was thought, would be sufficient to alleviate class conflict and to encourage a convergence of interest between business and labor. Furthermore, individual liberty in economic life would be the best guarantor of political liberty. The competing demands of political freedom, social justice, and economic growth could thus be met. This new German ideology spelled consensus (Arndt, 1966; MacLennon, Forsyth, and Denton, 1968, pp. 34–50).

"Godfather" of the economic miracle to some, "the happy piglet" (perpetually puffing a cigar) to others, Ludwig Erhard was an enthusiastic supporter of this new conception. Indeed, during the war Erhard had circulated a secret memorandum to political forces opposing the Hitler regime in which he set forth his view of Germany's future economic and social order. "The paramount objective is a free market economy. . . . To define the role of the state will be one of the most important problems of the post-war economy" (Zweig, 1980, pp. 15–16). In the summer of 1948 Erhard acted on the strength of his convictions. As the ranking German official in charge of economic policy in the British and American occupation zones, Erhard overnight, and on his own initiative, eliminated all wage and price controls and abolished the rationing of food and other essentials. With one stroke he thus legitimated the law of demand and supply and subverted the economic controls that had grown up since the 1930s and, out of sheer necessity, been continued after 1945. General Lucius Clay, outraged by this act of insubordination, pointed out to Erhard that all of the American advisers considered this to be a serious mistake. Erhard is reported to have answered: "Herr General, pay no attention to them! My own advisers tell me the same thing" (Hartrich, 1980, p. 4). Events proved Erhard to be correct. The currency reform of 1948 was a decisive break with the past which set the stage for West Germany's astounding economic reconstruction during the 1950s.

At the same time, Erhard's success was also limited by powerful international and domestic opposition. Because of the Korean War, U.S. High Commissioner John McCloy asked in March 1951 for significant state intervention in the new market economy (Abelshauser, 1983). The Americans were not interested in the ideology of the social market economy and its significance for the political reconstruction of West German politics. They insisted instead that West Germany's industrial production be geared to defense products rather than inessential goods. The American government was in a strong position, for West Germany depended totally on American aid and foreign exchange to finance the imports of raw materials that were controlled by a cartel organized in Washington. "The American High Commission held all the trumps and was prepared to play them" (Abelshauser, 1984, p. 306). Rather than resurrect a state-run economy, the federal government relied on an umbrella association of West Germany's peak associations of business to control the allocation of raw materials and to provide some measure of investment planning. The concept of the "self-administration" of business (see pp. 45–46) was invoked to justify the mobilization of private groups for public ends. Although Konrad Adenauer accepted this arrangement gratefully, this shift of power to large, private groups was clearly a political defeat for Erhard. State reliance on private groups, which this episode illustrates, is an important reason why policy change in the management of West Germany's economy has tended to be incremental.

Domestic opponents also seriously damaged Erhard's concept of a free market economy, as the history of West Germany's anticartel legislation in the 1950s aptly points up (Braunthal, 1965). The Allied powers made the deconcentration of West German industry one of their overriding political aims. Trusts and cartels, they argued, had been active supporters of Hitler's policies. The number of cartels, never considered illegal, increased from 14 in 1871 to about 1,500 at the end of World War I, 2,700 in 1931, and over 6,000 by the end of World War II. American support for Erhard was strong in part because West Germany's first economics minister was also strongly committed to a vigorous anticartel law. The proposed legislation thus challenged a formidable German tradition. The initial bill, drafted in 1950, was submitted to the cabinet in 1951. It became one of the most controversial bills of the 1950s. Industry, otherwise an ally of the CDU, strongly opposed it. In six years of intensive lobbying it forced major modifications of the bill, relying on its supporters in both Bundestag and Bundesrat. With the CDU/CSU deeply split, Erhard was forced to compromise and accepted in the end a bill that had many holes. The law specified eight major exceptions to its application, whereas there were no exceptions in the bill's original version. It was a major political defeat for Erhard. Furthermore, once it was set up, the Cartel Office in Berlin implemented the law very cautiously. Of the literally thousands of mergers and acquisitions which the office has had to approve, it has contested no more than a handful. This difference between the bark and the bite of the Cartel Office illustrates that the ideology of a social market economy has had to accommodate itself to a setting in which economic concentration is not only quietly tolerated but actively embraced. In the 1980s the clarion call for deregulation and more market competition was sounded not only in the United States and Britain but also in the Federal Republic. However, West German conservatives and liberals have responded very cautiously to a political program that appears quite distant from the practical experience of the Federal Republic.

Economic policy has been so important for the Federal Republic because it has served purposes broader than the economic success that the West Germans have enjoyed during the last thirty-five years. In the 1950s, for example, "made in Germany" became a worldwide symbol of West German craftsmanship. The psychology of economic success blended imperceptibly with the politics of success. At home, economic success fortified the political center and made implausible the attacks from the extreme Right and Left. Abroad the West Germans, like the Japanese, began to project power that was not military but economic. The Bonn Republic, as the title of a provocative book called it, appeared to have become "the fourth and richest Reich" (Hartrich, 1980).

Agenda

The agenda of West German economic policy was shaped by the consequences of its own success, by variations in the business cycle, and by changes in the global economy. Yet its objectives have remained remarkably unchanged. Monetary stability, a cautious countercyclical policy, and international competitiveness have been the three dominant objectives to which all of the major players—the federal government, the Bundesbank, political parties, and the major interest groups—have subscribed. Policy change has consisted in slightly altering the relative weights attached to each of these objectives rather than in articulating new ones.

The ideology of the social market economy received its strongest confirmation in the 1950s, a decade of rapid economic growth that an admiring world and the stunned West Germans called the "economic miracle." In hindsight, West Germany's phenomenal economic performance in the 1950s was not miraculous but a result of the convergence of a number of favorable policies and circumstances. Tax policy favored investment over consumption. A pliant labor force was willing to forgo real wage gains commensurate with increases in productivity. Firms invested their large profits in the anticipation of future gain. Furthermore, West Germany's capital stock was young. War production had peaked as late as 1944. In many instances production had been held back by bottlenecks—a broken piece of machinery, a bombed-out road or rail link—which could be fixed relatively quickly. Unlike the Soviet Union in East Germany, the United States did not pursue a policy of dismantling industry located in the Western zones but instead provided generous economic assistance in the form of the Marshall Plan. And the Korean War as well as the increasing liberalization of the international economy under American leadership opened up foreign markets that displayed an insatiable appetite for West German products. The Federal Republic thus embarked in the 1950s on a policy of export-led growth which has been its trademark ever since.

By the early 1960s the immediate task of reconstruction had been completed (MacLennan, Forsyth, and Denton, 1968; Shonfield, 1965). As the Bonn Republic steered an uncertain course into the "era after Adenauer," Erhard assumed the chancellorship. He articulated his and the West Germans' uneasiness with the inadequacies of the social market economy in the face of new challenges, for example, containing inflationary pressures and developing a long overdue program of infrastructure investment. In 1965 Erhard proposed a new corporative society regulated not by authoritarian decrees but by the enlightened self-interest of cooperative groups employing a technocratic politics in the achievement of the common good (see Reading 2-1). Although the second chancellor was not the man to implement his vision of the "formed society," Erhard's diagnosis of the new agenda of West German politics was to the point. Coordination and planning soon became buzz words in Bonn (see Chapter 6). The policy agenda included cautious adaptation of the instruments of fiscal, industrial, and monetary policy rather than debate over new policy objectives.

Although the proximate cause of the arrival of West German–style Keynesianism was the recession of 1966–67 and the fall of Chancellor Erhard, it was preceded by years of debate over the lack of alternatives to the Bundesbank's restrictive monetary policy with which to fight the specter of creeping inflation. While Chancellor Erhard and the CDU/CSU sought to combat the first postwar recession with tax increases, Karl Schiller, speaking for the SPD and the independent Council of Economic Experts (see pp. 63–64), advocated instead that Erhard's "neo-liberalism" be supplemented by his own conception of a "global guidance" (Riemer, 1983). The responsibility of the state would be to maintain aggregate demand specifically by influencing the volume of investment.

Schiller, who in 1967 became the minister of economics, did not press for a sharp break with Erhard's neoliberalism. Instead, he advocated that global guidance, which he distinguished from government planning, be restricted to macro variables (such as investment, prices, and wages) and that at the micro level of individual decisionmaking the market system should prevail as before (see Reading 2-3). He hoped that by modernizing the government's instruments of economic policy, limited growth could be obtained with price stability. Indeed the very title of the most crucial piece of legislation of the 1960s, the Stability and Growth Act of 1967, symbolized the symbiosis between old and new (see Reading 2-2). Introduced by Chancellor Erhard as the "Stability Law" and designed to curb inflation and excess demand, it was broadened significantly to encompass the instruments of policy which the SPD, the Council of Economic Experts, and eventually the Bundesbank regarded as indispensable.

Specifically, the law provided for the presentation of an annual economic report to the Bundestag; the creation of reserve funds and a queue of government investment projects to be undertaken in times of recession; a four-year plan of the anticipated expenditures and receipts of the federal government; a measure of influence over how the social security funds and the Federal Employment Office invest their moneys; a system of consultation between government officials, unions, and employers' associations; and a variety of other measures. The Stability Act introduced three separate steps into the formulation of West Germany's economic policy agenda. First, the annual report of the Council of Economic Experts was to lay out what would happen to the four main policy objectives (price stability, full employment, external balance, and adequate growth) with and without government intervention. Second, the federal government would publish quantified economic targets projected over the coming year. This projection was not binding since the federal government's policy depended on other actors. Finally, in concert with these actors—states, local governments, the Bundesbank, business, and labor—the federal government would arrive at "orientation data" for the economy which did not have to be identical with those of the council but which were to exert the pressure of plain common sense on different groups by making them aware of the ties between their strategies and those of other groups.

Compared to the redirection of economic policy in the United States and in Japan at the beginning of the 1960s, what is noteworthy about West Germany in the late 1960s is its limited departure from its neoliberal orthodoxy. The purposes of policy were not drastically revamped. True, the federal government's scope of action was enlarged but not in a way that diminished its dependence on other actors. On questions of foreign exchange rate policy, for example, the Bundesbank remained a central actor with whom the federal government had to cooperate. Collaboration with other political actors was also imperative, for example, in the system of concerted action described below. The financing of West Germany's first economic recovery program in 1967 illustrates this point (Riemer, 1983, pp. 134–39). A special investment program of 2.5 billion deutschmarks was more than cancelled by equivalent cuts in other expenditures. Fiscal policy and deficit spending were viewed primarily as a problem of debt management and monetary policy. Government borrowing depended on the Bundesbank's pledge to adopt expansionary measures in order to create new liquidity. "The government though thoroughly subservient, was not directly beholden to the central bank. Instead the federal government was dependent on the Bundesbank by way of indirect arrangements that involved the private banks" (Riemer, 1983, p. 136).

West Germany's agenda of domestic economic policy was reshaped a second time in the 1970s. The deep recession of 1974–75 and far-reaching changes in the international economy thereafter—skyrocketing oil prices, wildly fluctuating exchange rates, an international financial crisis of colossal magnitude, and the appearance of new industrial competitors on world markets—created new fears. Policymakers feared that West Germany's global economic policy might no longer be adequate for the task of managing structural changes in the mix of industries in the national economy. This view had been foreshadowed by the growing attention that the West German government had paid to the modernization of industry, especially the support it extended to high-technology industries. Indeed, in 1972 the government renamed one of its ministries the Ministry of Science and Technology. Its mission was to coordinate and reinforce efforts to develop modern industries. SPD reformers in the inner circle demanded more. They wanted an "active structural policy" and more responsibility for the federal government. They saw the new crisis as a political opportunity to press for a more far-reaching regulation of investment. This demand had been suppressed by the party leadership in the heady days of reform in the early 1970s, since it was clearly unacceptable to both the unions and the FDP on whose support the SPD depended.

In any event, because of West Germany's comparatively strong economic performance in the 1970s, Chancellor Schmidt, his cabinet, and the top-level civil servants especially in the Economics Ministry were opposed to any radical, new policies. Confronted with conflicting demands from different quarters, Chancellor Schmidt did what was politically safe. He commissioned from the five leading economics research institutes reports on the structure of the West German economy. These reports, which are periodically updated, reveal that structural policy in West Germany means something different than does industrial policy in Japan or economic planning in France. In West Germany it is not the government's task to cope with structural change. That task is left rather to individual firms, large banks, or industry organizations. Structural policy is clearly less important than either Schiller's global macroeconomic policy or Erhard's market competition policy. In the Federal Republic structural policy aims primarily at affecting the environment in which markets operate (for example, through a stable monetary policy) rather than affecting markets directly (for example, through a policy of corporate mergers). The state does not manage structural change (see Reading 2-7). At best it can remove some of the obstacles impeding structural change. In contrast to the ambitions of French or Japanese policymakers, this conception of the state's role in economic policy is very modest. But it is a conception that with few exceptions is supported by the political and economic leaders of the Federal Republic. On this point as on many others the CDU government elected in 1983 continues to adhere to Chancellor Schmidt's policies.

Macroeconomic policy, competition policy, and structural policy are part of a West German orthodoxy of economic management around which political actors have articulated their different conceptions of how to stimulate growth and reduce the high unemployment rates of the 1980s. On the political Left the unions and factions within the SPD favor an economic policy based on Keynesian demand stimulation: a shorter workweek, higher wage increases, and more consumption will lead to more growth and lower unemployment (see Reading 2-5). On the political Right business, the FDP, and large segments of the CDU/CSU favor the economic prescriptions of the Council of Economic Experts and the Bundesbank: unchanged hours and lower wage increases will increase profits and investment and will thus diminish unemployment. Although the failure of economic policies in other countries has made the advocates of either position aware of the flaws of their preferred policy, remarkably, the politics of West German economic policy has constrained the radical experimentation with either a strong dose of Kexnesianism (as in France between 1981–83) or a strong dose of supply-side economics (as in Britain since 1979). Overall West German economic policymakers have continued to display cautious, step-by-step orthodoxy in their search to defend stability through incremental policy change in a rapidly changing global economy.

West Germany's economic policy was also shaped by its relation to the global economy. Foreign exchange rate policy in particular was the focus of many debates since it had a direct effect on the Bundesbank's monetary policy (Hankel, 1977; Narr-Lindner, 1984; Wadbrook, 1972). Since the late 1950s it has been apparent that West Germany's strategy of export-led growth, based on an undervalued deutschmark, undermined the anti-inflation policy to which the Bundesbank was so strongly committed. An increasing surplus in the balance of payments increased the amount of money circulating in the domestic economy; and attempts to curb domestic inflation by increasing domestic interest rates tended to spur a further influx of foreign capital. Revaluation of the deutschmark appeared to be the only solution to pursuing an anti-inflation policy. The conflict between these two policy objectives reflected a conflict between West Germany's export industries and its banking community. Although the deutschmark was revalued in 1961 and in 1969, the Bundesbank found itself on the horns of a dilemma throughout the decade. Relief came in the 1970s, for, by 1973, international rules had changed and all major countries had opted for a system of floating exchange rates. The deutschmark's subsequent appreciation on international markets (thus increasing the price of West German exports and decreasing the price of imports) assisted the Bundesbank's anti-inflation monetary policy (see Reading 2-4).

Indeed, in the spring of 1973 the Bundesbank decided to impose an extremely restrictive monetary policy in order to squeeze the last drop of inflation out of the West German economy. The strategy was an attempt to compensate for the bank's inability to mount a sustained, coordinated international attack on inflation (Kloten, Ketterer, and Vollmer, 1985; Schlesinger, 1976). The Bundesbank's objective was to lower decisively the inflationary expectations that had become common among workers as well as among businesspeople and bankers during the prolonged boom since 1968. By adopting a highly restrictive monetary policy and not abandoning it throughout the next two years, the Bundesbank served notice that business and labor in particular would have to adjust their bargaining to the targets of money growth which the Bundesbank would from now on announce unilaterally. The fact that business and labor failed to do so in 1974 led to real wage gains much greater than anyone had anticipated. Because of this change the first sharp increase in West Germany's unemployment rate occurred in 1974 (Scharpf, 1984).

The course of unrelenting monetary stability on which the Bundesbank settled in 1973 and which the SPD-FDP coalition accepted throughout the 1970s was central to West Germany's economic relations with other states. Hailed by some as the most important step on the long road to European unification, the creation in 1979 of a European currency bloc, the EMS, centering around the Federal Republic and France, was a West German attempt to create greater monetary stability throughout Europe at the price of marginally higher inflation at home. The establishment of the EMS was feasible in West Germany's domestic politics because it seemed to meet long-standing demands of the dissatisfied unions for monetary expansion, curbed slightly the power of the central bank, and promised to slow down the general upward drift of the deutschmark which had become a major problem for West Germany's export industry. Internationally the EMS was an attempt to insulate the Federal Republic at least in part from the deleterious consequences of a lack of American leadership in the international monetary system by constructing a West European monetary zone.

The stabilization strategy underlying West Germany's export strategy in the 1950s and 1960s was national. The policies of undervaluation of the deutschmark and of fiscal restraint collapsed together with the Bretton Woods system of fixed exchange rates. The stabilization strategy informing West Germany's internationalism in the 1970s was based on the quiet assumption of political responsibilities on a regional scale. However, the Federal Republic was not ready to assume global economic responsibilities. In 1977–78 the United States in particular pressed the Federal Republic to spur domestic growth in order to help alleviate an international recession. But Chancellor Schmidt only grudgingly went along with American policy. He argued instead that the West German locomotive was too small to pull the global economy. The Federal Republic was charged in the late 1970s with being irresponsibly nationalistic and unwilling to help carry the burden of global economic leadership that had become too heavy for the United States; similar changes were levied against Japan in the early 1980s.

West German economic policymaking has permitted numerous conflicts: between banks and export industry over revaluation of the deutschmark, between the Bundesbank and federal government over prudent levels of public indebtedness, and between unions and business over justifiable wage and price levels. But what is remarkable is not the fact that conflicts exist but that they have been so restricted. This is reflected in the nature of political competition over economic issues. Since the mid-1970s that competition has sharpened between the left wing of the SPD and the unions interested in defending the welfare state with Keynesian deficit spending, on the one hand, and the right wing of the CDU/CSU as well as the FDP and business, which have focused on the improvement of the investment climate and deregulation on the other (see Readings 2-5, 2-6). But the centers of the two major parties remain strongly committed to steering a cautious course that veers neither too far right nor too far left and defends economic stability and international competitiveness through incremental policy changes.

Yet an anomalous fact persists which points to a more enduring and important aspect of West German politics (Schmidt, 1982, 1985). In comparison to governments in other countries, CDU/CSU governments in the 1950s and 1960s, both at the state and federal level, were responsible for excessive levels of spending for social and economic purposes given the parties' political orientation and considering the spending averages of other center-right parties in Western Europe. Conversely, the SPD-FDP coalition governments expanded the government's budget at a much slower pace in the 1970s than Social Democratic and many non–Social Democratic governments did elsewhere. Furthermore, a survey of the members of the Bundestag Budget Committee found no support for "Reaganomics" and "Thatcherism" in government spending. Across the political spectrum committee members agreed on the need for the financial consolidation that the SPD began in 1981–82 and the CDU rigorously continued after it assumed power in 1982–83 (Sturm, 1985b). Although the stabilization of the federal budget has significantly slowed the growth of total public debt, debt has continued to increase. A number of reasons exist for these developments. But the "generosity" of the CDU/CSU and the "frugality" of the SPD mirror the pattern of incremental policy change which is so distinctive of West Germany.

Process

In the process of formulating and implementing economic policy, the West German government depends on the cooperation of other political actors. This dependence severely circumscribes all attempts at unilateral, decisive action. I shall illustrate this dependence briefly in the areas of monetary, incomes, fiscal, and industrial policy.

In the area of monetary policy, as I noted earlier, the federal government relies on one of the most independent central banks in any of the industrial nations (Narr-Lindner, 1984; U.S. Congress, Joint Economic Committee, 1981). Government officials can attend the deliberations of the Central Bank Committee, the highest decisionmaking body of the Bundesbank. But they have no vote and their power is limited to the ability to delay decisions by up to two weeks. Its enabling legislation of 1957 specifies that the Bundesbank should support the government's general economic policy but only insofar as it does not undermine the bank's responsibility to maintain price stability. In pursuing its mission the bank is supposed to be " 'independent of government instructions or directives" and if it so chooses can "advise the Federal Government on monetary matters of major importance' " (quoted in Anderson, 1980, pp. 18–19). In fact the Bundesbank's single-minded pursuit of monetary stability has been the most constant element in West Germany's economic policy to the chagrin of the CDU and the SPD alike (see Reading 2-4). The stabilization crisis induced by a highly restrictive monetary policy in 1966 helped push Chancellor Erhard out of office. And in the early 1980s the bank contributed substantially to the problems that tarnished Chancellor Schmidt's reputation as a successful economic crisis manager, thus making him politically vulnerable on other questions.

But perhaps the most dramatic illustration of the power of the Bundesbank occurred in 1972 when its president, Karl Klasen, argued successfully that large inflows of foreign capital required the imposition of capital controls. The cabinet accepted this recommendation against the determined opposition of Karl Schiller who by 1972 had parlayed his successful concept of global steering into control of a "superministry" of economics and finance. It is not implausible to assume that the Bundesbank's tough stand derived not merely from its strong commitment to domestic monetary stability. The Bank was probably also interested in eliminating a personal rival who appeared in the process of building a countervailing institutional power base. The episode did not lack for personal drama for it was Klasen, a prominent SPD banker from Hamburg as well as president of the Bundesbank, who administered what many journalists called a "stab in the back" to SPD Economics Minister Schiller. Schiller had appointed Klasen in 1969.

The economic crisis of 1966–67 focused political attention on incomes policy. The SPD and Schiller insisted on adding to the CDU draft legislation of what eventually became the Stability and Growth Act (see Reading 2-2) a section that required regular meetings to be held among different federal ministries, the leaders of the peak associations of business and labor, the Bundesbank, and the Council of Economic Experts (Hardes, 1974; Molitor, 1973; Seitenzahl, 1974). Schiller thus adopted in modified form a demand that the council had made as early as 1965. Meeting the conflicting objectives of growth, stability, full employment, and external balance, it was thought, required a better coordination of the strategies of different actors. In sharp contrast to some of the smaller European states, West Germany's concerted action among private groups and public-sector officials was voluntary and aimed only at the exchange of information, rather than the establishment of binding wage and price guidelines. Collective bargaining between business and labor remained autonomous from any government interference. But Schiller hoped that the sharing of economic information would alleviate, though not eliminate, the distributional struggle between labor and business (see Reading 2-3).

Between 1967 and 1977 the economics minister convened a meeting about four times a year known as the "concerted action." Thirty-five to fifty members of the German political elite attended. Attendance was voluntary; no votes were taken; and no minutes were kept. Instead, the purpose of the early meetings was to discuss the economic projections of the federal government for the coming year and to confront them with the data of other institutions, specifically those of the Bundesbank, the Council of Economic Experts, the five main economics research institutes that convene twice a year to report jointly on the state of the German economy, and the research departments of the BDI, BDA, and DGB. Subsequently, the concerted action also considered in its deliberations broader questions of foreign exchange rate policy, competition policy, and some areas of social policy. These high-level and secret talks typically concluded with a large press conference held by the economics minister.

The high hopes of the early years were soon disappointed. Concerted action, it turned out, worked only in the trough of the business cycle when labor unions probably would have moderated their wage claims even in the absence of these consultations. But when the government's projections proved faulty, as they did, for example, for 1969 and 1972, wildcat strikes, almost unheard of in West Germany, expressed the frustration of the rank and file with a system of top-level bargaining which had permitted profits to surge while wage increases lagged behind. The more conflictual political climate of the 1970s eventually terminated this concertation of different actors. After the employers filed a lawsuit with the Constitutional Court contesting the extension of codetermination (see Chapter 3), the trade unions declared that henceforth they would not be able to participate in cooperative, secret talks involving government and business.

However, for two reasons the end of the concerted action was not a watershed in West Germany's politics of economic policymaking. First, the objective economic effects of this consultative policy process had always been negligible. Second, Chancellor Schmidt frequently organized small and informal consultations between the government and the major interest groups with aims similar to that of the concerted action. Schmidt reportedly spent 200 of his working hours annually in such meetings (Hofmann, 1980). Ad hoc crisis management and the collaboration of business and labor leaders in national politics was the model that informed this style of government. One of the chancellor's apt aphorisms for his role in economic policymaking was "chairman of the board of directors of Germany Incorporated."

West Germany's fiscal policy also illustrates the dependence of the West German government on others and the great difficulties it has, because of its own internal fragmentation, imposing its objectives for the budget cycle on other actors (Hirsch, 1968; Knott, 1981; Reuss, 1963; U.S. Congress, Joint Economic Committee, 1976). In the 1950s fiscal conservatism reigned supreme. Monetary stability was a prime goal. And the Basic Law stipulated that the federal government balance its books each year. The goal of a balanced budget thus was regarded as a given, irrespective of its effect on national income. Indeed Finance Minister Fritz Schäffer became a legend because by anticipating the future costs of German rearmament he saved hundreds of millions of deutschmarks from soaring tax revenues, unbeknownst perhaps even to Chancellor Adenauer.

With the passing of the Stability and Growth Act of 1967 (see Reading 2-2), West Germany's federal government began to use its budget as a policy instrument for regulating macroeconomic developments. Henceforth, fiscal policy could be discretionary and anticyclical. Together with changes in the Basic Law and the Finance Reform of 1969, the Stability Act effected a number of changes (see also pp. 48–52 and 260–262). It created, for example, an anticyclical reserve fund with the improbable German name of *Konjunkturausgleichsrücklage*. With approval of the Bundesrat, the federal government was permitted to freeze a certain proportion of federal and state tax revenues at the Bundesbank. In addition, the federal government acquired the right to raise or lower income tax rates by up to 10 percent, thus adding to the special reserve fund. These reserves could be spent only in times of recession and only on investment programs developed as special economic stabilizers alongside the normal budget (Knott, 1981, pp. 20–21, 63). Furthermore, in the annual budget cycle the finance minister initially appears to be in a relatively strong position in Bonn. She lays out the general guidelines for the budget, reviews the spending proposals that are developed by low- and middle-level bureaucrats throughout the government, and proposes a draft budget to the cabinet where, together with the chancellor, she carries enormous political weight.

In comparison, the role of the Bundestag is circumscribed. To develop the budget, its Budget Committee works closely with the top-level civil servants of the Finance Ministry. But the partisan debates that the budget receives in the full Bundestag do not recur in the Budget Committee where policymaking is reactive, consensual, and incremental (Sturm, 1985a). By law the Bundestag is not permitted to effect changes that will raise any expenditures in the budget without explicitly proposing the revenue source. Article 113 of the Basic Law permits the government to veto all changes in its budget which result from increased authorizations. To an American president worried about a freely spending Congress, West Germany's tight provisions for fiscal policy must be appealing.

In theory the position of the federal government in fiscal policy appears to be strong. In practice, however, that position has at times been very weak. In the 1970s, for example, the logic of coalition government gave control over the Finance Ministry to the SPD, while the FDP staffed the Economics Ministry. This division of responsibility weakened the federal government's initiatives and created a favorable context for the continuity of policy. For reasons of party politics it proved impossible to cut any items out of the normal budget, given the economic growth at the time. The stabilization budget on the whole raised the expectations of ministries so much that it proved virtually impossible to alter priorities if economic circumstances did not warrant any additional expenditures. The politics of spending, normally decided at the level of the cabinet, has simply proven to be too potent. Only in 1965–66, 1975, and 1981–82 did the pressure of economic crisis spur political parties to some spending cuts.

Furthermore, the federal government controls less than half of West Germany's total public spending and only about 15 percent of public investment. The balance is spent by state and local governments (Johnson and Cochrane, 1981; Knott, 1981). For a variety of reasons their spending patterns are pro- rather than anticyclical. And they are often politically unmoved by the concerns of federal ministries. In the 1970s, for example, the SPD-FDP coalition governed in Bonn while the CDU/CSU controlled a majority of the West German states. Partisan differences thus reinforced normal tensions between federal, state, and local governments. Although constitutional and legislative changes in 1967–69 strengthened the formal role of the federal government, the politics of spending tended to tie the government's hands. Significantly, with rising public expenditures (which increased from 33 percent of gross domestic product in the early 1960s to 46 percent in the late 1970s) and budget deficits (surpluses in the early 1960s had become deficits of around 3 percent of gross domestic product by the late 1970s), the federal government has chosen, since 1975, to follow a restrictive policy, cutting deficits during the most prolonged economic slump since 1945. Between 1981 and 1984, measured as a percentage of gross domestic product, the West German deficit was cut in half while the American deficit quadrupled (Skuca, 1984, Table 11). Yet one knowledgeable student of West Germany's fiscal policy concludes that, because of a one-sided emphasis on stabilization, "less favorable conditions for the exercise of macroeconomic policy would be hard to find" (Knott, 1981, p. 28).

Implementation of policy in the area of industrial adjustment also illustrates the dependence of the federal government on other political actors (Horn, 1982; Küster, 1974). Contrary to the ideology of neoliberalism, the governments of the Federal Republic, both federal and state, are at times intimately involved with different industries. Government involvement is less intimate than in Japan and France, but it deviates substantially from the arm's-length relation that on the whole continues to characterize relations between industry and government in Britain and the United States. Since the 1960s this pattern has been readily apparent in West Germany's treatment of its declining industries (Dyson, 1986; Esser, Fach, and Dyson, 1984; Webber, 1985).

Like that of the rest of the industrialized world, West Germany's ener-

gy policy converted rapidly from coal to oil in the 1960s. The result was
the closing of many mines, a drastic shrinking in the industry's workforce, and the consolidation of the remaining parts of the industry under
the leadership of a holding company, Ruhrkohle A.G., partly owned by
the state. Conversion was accomplished smoothly in comparison to the
bitterly fought, highly politicized miners' strikes that Japan and Britain
experienced in the early 1960s and 1970s, respectively. The West German approach to the coal crisis of the 1960s amounted to concentration
through cooperation. The recession of 1966–67 had revealed that the
defensive, temporizing measures which the government had adopted
between 1957 and 1967 were futile. The formation of the Great Coalition set the stage for a two-pronged policy. First, the federal government
bought out on favorable terms virtually all of the privately owned mines
and consolidated the industry under a holding company in which it
owned substantial equity. At the same time, it upgraded its labor market
and regional policy in order to take better care of displaced
mineworkers. For reasons of energy security the federal government has
continued to subsidize the industry on a massive scale through various
programs adopted in the 1970s. Significantly, both business and unions
were centrally involved in the development of energy policy. The government neither imposed its preferred solution on the industry nor permitted market forces simply to dictate outcomes. Instead, it depended
on other actors to help hammer out a solution to the problem.

Since the late 1970s West Germany has taken a similar approach in
the crisis-ridden steel industry. Outmoded steel plants in the Saar basin
confronted extinction. The kind of trilateral bargaining that took place
in the 1960s has been repeated. This time the federal government has
provided direct support for an uncompetitive segment of an industry
with no demonstrable link to national security. By the standards of most
of its European competitors the government's involvement is not particularly large; but by the standards of West Germany this open-ended
commitment is unusual. Yet the federal government's evident interest in
effecting a reorganization of the West German steel industry in the Ruhr
area has been disappointed. In January 1983 the government appointed
a committee of three advisers (with strong links to the banking community) to recommend the future shape of the steel industry in the Runr
valley. However, some of the firms and unions rejected a final report
that recommended the formation of two groups of firms and a federal
subsidy of 3 billion deutschmarks. By 1985 the reorganization of the

industry was being privately orchestrated. The weaknesses of a "private" approach to industrial policy were revealed by a number of spectacular bankruptcies in the first half of the 1980s (Dyson, 1984). A private approach is likely to continue to rely on grants, loans, and loan guarantees from federal and state governments that have fallen hostage to developments in the international steel market and that apparently have no capacity to impose their solution on this troubled industry.

This self-effacing character of government policy is belied by the wide range of instruments that the government potentially controls. While the SPD was debating, in the mid- and late 1970s, the merits and disadvantages of a more active industrial policy, the federal government was spending large sums of money for industrial subsidies. These figures can be traced more easily in the Federal Republic than in most other countries because neoliberal assumptions have been translated into the requirement that the federal government regularly publish reports on subsidies. Those reports contain, however, only very partial data. The 1980–81 report listed federal subsidies totaling 27.6 billion deutschmarks. This figure excludes about 20 billion deutschmarks for the railways and the EC. Nor does it contain any of the subsidies granted by state and local governments. According to a number of recent estimates, West Germany's total subsidies amount to between 80 and 100 billion deutschmarks in 1980–81. About two-thirds of those subsidies are in the form of grants. One-third is given in the form of tax benefits. The federal government alone directly controls about one-half of the total and directly and indirectly as much as 80 percent of the total (Neumann and Uterwedde, 1986, pp. 145–154). But this notion of control is fictitious. Because of its dependence on other actors the federal government enjoys only a very limited degree of control over the subsidies it grants.

The federal government also does not use public corporations to achieve its objectives. In addition to the publicly owned railways and the Postal Service, some of West Germany's largest corporations are wholly or partially owned by the state: Volkswagen, Veba, Lufthansa, Salzgitter, and Ruhrkohle. In 1984 these five major corporations employed over 500,000 people. And at the end of 1984 the federal government had a stake in 474 corporations. Because of divisions between the CDU and the CSU the privatization of public holdings has proceeded very slowly under the Kohl government. Yet because they are essentially depoliticized, Günther Schäfer concludes (1974, p. 11), "public corporations with few exceptions can not be used as instruments of central public policies." In sum, the policy process illustrates how the dependence of the federal government on other actors makes incremental change rather than large-scale change politically so compelling.

Consequences

By almost any standard West Germany's economic performance since 1945 has been outstanding (Markovits, 1982). World War II stopped, probably once and for all, the military expansion of Germany which had upset the European balance of power ever since the unification of the Second Empire in 1871. But the West Germans were not to be denied stunning commercial and economic victory over their former adversaries. By the late 1950s the Federal Republic had begun to emerge as Western Europe's dominant economy, a position that it has not relinquished in the last thirty years. The unprecedented spread of prosperity among the West Germans in the first postwar decade, chronicled in all its facets in Werner Fassbinder's classic movie *The Marriage of Maria Braun,* contributed mightily to alleviating the understandable fear that the fate of the Bonn Republic might yet again converge with that of the Weimar Republic.

But it would be a mistake to gauge the performance of West Germany by the explosive growth of the first postwar decade. Indeed, as I have argued in this chapter, the Federal Republic's economic policy is distinguished by its preoccupation with achieving both price stability and moderate growth. Table 2-1 compares the economic performance of the Federal Republic with the performances of five other advanced industrial states.

Considering Japan's high rate of inflation in the 1960s, the table shows that between 1961 and 1979 West Germany had experienced by far the lowest inflation rate, one of the lowest unemployment rates, and a respectable growth rate. If we rank West Germany's economic performance against those of the other industrial states along all three dimensions, West Germany emerges as the leader, ahead of Japan in the 1960s and only slightly behind Japan in the 1970s. These numbers reinforce the impression that by economic standards West Germany did extremely well in the 1960s and 1970s. As the world's leading exporter of manufactured goods, with one of the world's hardest currencies and the largest international reserves, the international manifestations of West Germany's domestic economic success were readily apparent to all other countries (Kreile, 1978).

TABLE 2-1 Economic Performance of Industrial States, 1961–79 (percent)

Country	Increase in consumer price indices		Increase in real gross domestic product		Average rate of unemployment		Sum of ranks of three performance indicators	
	1961–70	1970–79	1961–70	1970–79	1961–70	1970–79	1961–70	1970–79
West Germany	28	56	51	30	1.0	3.0	5.0	8.0
Japan	N/A[a]	119	151	61	1.3	1.7	9.0[a]	6.0
Sweden	38	112	48	19	1.7	2.1	11.5	11.0
France	44	121	63	41	1.5	3.7	10.0	11.0
United Kingdom	38	203	28	22	2.0	4.1	14.5	16.0
United States	30	87	43	33	5.3	6.2	13.0	11.0

Sources: Organization for Economic Co-operation and Development (OECD), *Main Economic Indicators: Historical Statistics* (Paris: OECD, 1980); *National Accounts Statistics, 1950–1979*, vol. 1 (Paris: OECD, 1981); *Labour Force Statistics, 1960–1971* (Paris: OECD, 1973); *Labour Force Statistics, 1968–1979* (Paris: OECD, 1981); and International Labour Office (ILO), *Year Book of Labour Statistics 1980* (Geneva: ILO, 1981).

N/A. Not available.

a. Other sources (*OECD Economics Studies*, no. 1 [Autumn 1983], p. 97) suggest that Japan's inflation rate was higher than that of the five states listed above.

However, the doubling of oil prices in 1979 and a severe worldwide recession, brought about and prolonged by extremely high U.S. interest rates, have tarnished West Germany's reputation as an economic leader, causing lagging growth rates and sharply increasing rates of unemployment. In Europe, to be sure, West Germany is holding its own. But it is falling further behind Japan, and in the first half of the 1980s it did not match the growth that the United States financed with its increased military spending and substantial budget deficits. Most worrisome, however, is the fact that additional investments are, at best, having a neutral impact on the total number of jobs. Some political circles are nagged by the fear that past achievements of the welfare state have created political rigidities, especially in labor markets, which will prohibit the attainment of full employment even if the number of new entrants into West Germany's crowded job market declines in the 1990s, as is projected.

What have been the consequences of West Germany's economic policy for other policy sectors? As I shall argue in subsequent chapters, the connections with industrial relations and the question of migrant labor have been very evident. Economic policy was greatly aided by the cooperative relations between business and unions and by the availability of cheap foreign labor imported on a massive scale in the 1960s. Furthermore, the West German approach to social welfare and poverty issues as well as to higher education assumed that economic policy would provide for growth and conditions of full employment. To the extent that this assumption has not been met since the late 1970s, problems in these areas have also increased. Furthermore, West Germany's economic policy, which until the late 1970s was carried by a broad social consensus, has favored not growth, as in Japan, or equality, as in Sweden, but a form of political stability which balances conflicting objectives. The economic orientation of that consensus has now been challenged by the Green party, which wishes government policy to give prominence if not priority to environmental concerns. Furthermore, West German policymakers face the recurrent question of how to maintain economic stability in a rapidly changing global economy to which West Germany is ineluctably tied through its strategy of export-led growth.

Finally, West German economic policy reflects back on the organization of power in West German politics. Here the comparison with Japan is very instructive. With a conservative coalition in power uninterruptedly since 1945, Japan has used major initiatives in economic policy to remake its economic structure twice since 1945 (Pempel, 1982). In the 1950s and 1960s it made the transition from agriculture and textiles to heavy industries and consumer durables such as steel and automobiles. Since the early 1970s it has followed a policy of fostering knowledge-intensive industries such as computers, robotics, and biotechnology. The Federal Republic, conversely, has experienced moderate changes in its dominant political coalition from center-right to center-left and back to center-right which have only marginally affected the evolution of its economic policy. West Germany's economic structure has not been fundamentally reshaped. It continues to be concentrated in the science-based industries (engineering, chemicals, machinery, automobiles) that first propelled Germany into the front ranks of the industrial world around the turn of the century (Deubner, 1984). In the 1980s West German industry adapted to structural change in the global economy without a targeted economic policy but with substantial unemployment.

West Germany's economic policy is simply not well suited to the task of effecting large-scale structural change. This fact should not be credited to a lack of resources or imagination or some other fatal flaw. Rather, we should look to West Germany's distinctive institutional arrangements as the main determinant of incremental policy change. Coalition governments, cooperative federalism, and parapublic institutions create a dense network of multiple dependencies which inhibits all actors, including the federal government, from taking bold steps in new directions. On balance, during the last thirty years West Germany's semisovereign state has been a great asset in the conduct of economic policy. Whether it will continue to be an asset in the next thirty is a question that is beginning to be asked by muffled voices and not only those of the West Germans.

Readings

2-1. THE SOCIAL MARKET ECONOMY AND THE "FORMED SOCIETY"*

In 1948 Ludwig Erhard helped to construct and politically defend the social market economy. By the 1960s in his mind it was undermining

---

*Ludwig Erhard, "Regierungserklärung der Bundesregierung," *Verhandlungen des Deutschen Bundestages,* 5th Wahlperiode, 4th Sitzung, November 10, 1965, pp. 17–20 (selections).

established status and class divisions. In his inaugural speech before the Bundestag Chancellor Erhard articulated his view of the new social order, the "formed society," toward which he saw West Germany evolving. For Erhard the "formed society" was a dynamically evolving process of consensus formation informed by the enlightened self-interest of all citizens and groups. What looked to many like the beginning of a new era of West German politics, hindsight demonstrates was no more than a transition period. Erhard's government fell in 1966, opening the door to a coalition government of the CDU/CSU and the SPD and an entirely different range of public issues.

During the postwar years all political parties have come to embrace a single framework for the reconstruction of German society and economy. Our German model of a modern economic and social order has moved quite naturally from being viewed as a "miracle" to a process that is being tested daily in politics. Today we confront the problem of dissolving the crust that now encases this order; of organically incorporating formerly sheltered economic and social sectors into the process of social progress; and thus of overcoming the continuing tendency to stubbornly defend so-called traditional prerogatives. The real issue that today confronts the German people, this Parliament, and this government is our capacity and will to muster the necessary strength and imagination now that we have passed through the tensions of the immediate postwar period and the phase of economic reconstruction. . . .

Because of the irreducible tension between what can be accomplished easily in the short run and what in the long run is correct and necessary, the Bundestag and the federal government will have to make tough decisions in the next four years. My inaugural speech is marked by both worry and confidence. During the phase of reconstruction important parameters of our economic, social, and foreign policy have changed. The task for the coming years is to acknowledge these new conditions and to draw the appropriate lessons for our policies in subsequent legislative sessions. . . .

What is the fundamental source of Germany's potential strength? Human will and the ability to work toward intellectual and economic advancement. This potential grows in the fertile soil of a liberal order and a modern society. These are the foundation for all forward-looking cultural, scientific, technological, economic, and social endeavors.

The historical memories of our people have rekindled and powerfully reinforced public consciousness of the strong dependence of all citizens on one another. As a result German society is no longer a society divided by social classes. Instead German society has become an achieving society. Nonetheless we should never forget that this achievement society is still frequently threatened by the political efforts to have special interests prevail over the common good.

If we want to continue to travel the road of success, progress as well as political and social peace, German society has no choice but to enter more fully into the modern social order that I shall call here the "formed society."

[*Laughter and cat-calls among SPD members*]

This society cannot be created overnight. It evolves as a social process. The formed society is not organized along the lines of inherited status. Instead it is grounded in the conviction that people are prepared to act on behalf of their own interests not only because of legal compulsion but because of individual reason.

[*Applause among CDU/CSU members*]

The formed society is by no means a philanthropic vision. It does not have unrealistic and other-worldly preconceptions about human nature. This modern achieving society is by no means free from conflicting interests. But these conflicts are no longer elements of its disintegration. They are instead an engine of a continuous process that works toward social compromise informed by the public interest.

This new social order is a result of the social market economy. Indeed the example of the social market economy illustrates that the formed society is no utopian dream. After 1948 concern for the weakest social sectors justified the case against a total deregulation of the post-war economy. Concern centered on the adverse consequences that full deregulation and technological change would have for the overall social fabric and for supply shortages in a period of pent-up demand. Since then all strata and groups of German society have learned that the pursuit of self-interest need not necessarily lead to conflict with others. A reasonable compromise is an excellent instrument of democratic politics. . . .

The formed society is peaceful and rests on the dynamic strength that derives from the achievement of a consensus on all questions of domestic and foreign policy.

2-2. LAW FOR THE PROMOTION OF THE STABILITY AND GROWTH OF THE ECONOMY (1967)*

This act overhauled the economic policy machinery of the Federal Republic. An ambitious piece of legislation, it was adopted with the votes of both the CDU/CSU and the SPD, which had formed a grand coalition government in 1966. It is arguably the most important piece of legislation that the Bundestag has passed on economic policy since 1949.

The Federal Diet in concurrence with the Federal Council has enacted the following Law:

Section 1

The Federation and the laender [states] shall, in formulating economic and fiscal policy measures, consider the requirements of a balanced economy. These policy measures shall to the extent compatible with a market economic system, promote a stable price level, high employment, a balance of foreign payments [consistent with] steady and reasonable growth of the economy. . . .

Section 3

(1) In case of a threat to one of the goals in Section 1, the Federal Government shall make informational data available to the territorial authorities, labor unions, and associations of enterprises for simultaneous and concurrent action (concerted action) for achieving the goals of Section 1. These informational data shall include specially a description of overall economic relationships in reference to the given situation.

(2) The Federal Minister of Economy upon request shall explain the informational data to any of the interested parties.

Section 4

In the case of an external disturbance of the balance of the overall economy, which cannot be avoided by internal economic measures or can be avoided only by jeopardizing the goals mentioned in Section 1,

*U.S. Congress, Joint Economic Committee, "Economic Planning in Five Western European Countries: An Overview," paper no. 1, in *Achieving the Goals of the Employment Act of 1946—Thirtieth Anniversary Review, vol. 4, Economic Planning* (Washington, D.C.: U.S. Government Printing Office, 1976), pp. 48–56 (selections).

the Federal Government shall use all possibilities for international coordination. If this is not sufficient [the Federal Government] shall apply the measures of economic policy at its disposal to protect the balance of foreign payments.

Section 5

(1) The amount and combination of expenditures and the authorization to undertake obligations lasting for future fiscal years, shall be estimated in the Federal budget in such a manner as is necessary to achieve the goals in Section 1.

(2) In case of an expansion of demand exceeding the capacity of the national economy, means for eventual liquidation of debts with the German Federal Bank or for the increase of the fluctuation adjustment reserves [*Konjunkturausgleichsrücklage*] shall be estimated.

(3) In case of a weakening of general economic activity which threatens one of the goals of Section 1, additional necessary funds shall be drawn, first of all, from the fluctuation adjustment reserves. . . .

Section 6

(2) In case of a weakening of general economic activity which may threaten one of the goals of Section 1, the Federal Government may decide that additional expenditures shall be made; paragraph (1), sentence 2, shall be applicable. To prevent a disturbance of the balance of the national economy (Art. 104a[4]1 of the Basic Law), the additional funds shall be used only for purposes provided for in the financial plan (Section 9 in connection with Section 10), or as financial assistance for especially significant investments of the laender and communities (associations of communities). The funds necessary to cover these shall be drawn, first of all, from the fluctuation adjustment reserves. . . .

Section 16

(1) Communities and associations of communities shall take into account the goals of Section 1 in their budgetary policies.

(2) The laender shall strive through proper measures to ensure that the budgetary policies of the communities and associations of communities shall correspond to the policy required by economic fluctuation.

Section 17

The Federation and the laender shall mutually exchange information necessary to carry out a proper budgetary policy on economic fluctuation.

Section 18

(1) A Business Cycle Council [*Konjunkturrat*] for the State shall be created at the Federal Government. The members of the Council shall be: 1. The Federal Ministers of Economy and Finances; 2. One representative from each of the laender; 3. Four representatives for the communities and associations of communities who are appointed by the Federal Council on the recommendation of the head organization of communities. The Federal Minister of Economy shall preside over the Council of Cyclical Economy.

(2) The Business Cycle Council shall deliberate, in accordance with the rules of procedure issued by the Federal Minister of Economy, at regular intervals on: 1. All measures of cyclical economic policy required for the achievement of the goals of the present Law; 2. The possibilities for covering the credit demands of the public establishments. The Business Cycle Council shall be consulted, above all, on measures under Sections 15, 19, and 20.

(3) The Federal Bank has the right to participate in the deliberations of the Business Cycle Council.

2-3. BUSINESS CYCLE POLICY AND THE AFFLUENT SOCIETY*

In 1967 the West German economics minister accepted an invitation from the University of Kiel to give a public lecture; in his speech he set forth the rationale for the new style of macroeconomic policy that he had advocated and implemented after 1966. The expanded lecture was subsequently published. Brief excerpts from this lecture convey Schiller's firm belief in economic rationality.

It took a long time before modern business cycle policy was practiced in Germany. In 1956 the Advisory Council to the Federal Economics Ministery incorporated concepts of the Keynesian model, the Freiburg School, and the neoclassical synthesis for economic policy decisions into its report, "Instruments of Business Cycle Policy and their Legal Institutionalization." From that time dates the "magic triangle."

The Advisory Council suggested that the federal government be re-

---

*Karl Schiller, *Konjunkturpolitik auf dem Wege zu einer Affluent Society*, Kieler Vorträge, N.F. 54 (Kiel: Institut für Weltwirtschaft, 1968), pp. 7–14 (selections).

quired to submit an annual economic program. This program was to be published along with a report on current economic conditions and proposals concerning the future economic policy of the federal government. That is exactly what the federal government's first annual economic report accomplishes in 1968. . . .

Circumstances forced the submission of an economic stability bill in the fall of 1966. However, the scope of this bill remained too narrow. It offered no more than the rudiments of a business cycle policy and failed to exploit the potential for new ideas. In this first draft Parliament was guided solely by the desire to bring government spending under control quickly and thus reduce the pressure on the Bundesbank to maintain stable price levels. The first bill contained primarily restrictive measures. It scarcely considered other possibilities.

The recession of 1965–66 did not have to happen. Monetary and fiscal policy were not coordinated and there existed no common policy between the government on the one hand and powerful autonomous social groups on the other. According to the annual report of the Economic Experts, the result of this uncoordinated approach was in 1966–67 the worst recession in the history of the Federal Republic. . . .

The law promoting economic stability and growth has since been thoroughly revised. It is now the foundation of modern economic policy. It no longer resembles the table with two legs from the 1966 bill but is rather a table that stands on four solid legs. As we know three legs would have sufficed. However, the idea of "concerted action" and provisions for maintaining external economic balance, which were missing altogether in the earlier version, have become integral components of this law. Furthermore, the original law, a purely restrictive measure, was transformed; in its revised version it contained an arsenal of instruments for steering the economy against booms as well as against apparent or real economic recessions. From the point of view of business cycle policy it thus became symmetric or nearly symmetric.

This law has given us a great variety of tools to help control the business cycle. Indeed it is probably the most advanced toolbox of its kind. . . . Even this law did not meet with total approval when it went into effect last summer. "Too many variables" the public was saying. Too many variables! As if the market itself did not include many more variables. Yet the law makes it possible to establish upper and lower limits for these variables. Today after more than six months the toolbox appears to be generally accepted. . . .

This change in social awareness appears to me to be an essential result of "concerted action." As of last summer we have a legal definition for it: according to clause 3 of the Law for the Promotion of the Stability and Growth of the Economy, "the federal government makes orientation data available to state and local governments, unions, and employers' associations for the purpose of coordinating their economic behavior" ("concerted action"). According to that clause, the Federal Minister of Economics is obliged to explain the orientation data if requested to do so by one of the participants. This he does continually.

However, "concerted action" is not just wage negotiations. Although wages as well as profits and investments play a major role in it, "concerted action" is not just an incomes policy or an experiment in incomes policy. "Concerted action" has to do with economic graphs of course, but not just with graphs. It does not have to do merely with marks and pfennigs. Behind all those economic abstractions looms the status of individuals and groups in modern society. . . .

"Concerted action" has changed our sociopolitical landscape and will change it even further. It affirms the existence of organized groups in our free society. Indeed, we have actually found in "concerted action" a flexible method of affording autonomous groups in our society the possibility of participating in the formulation of economic policy.

"Concerted action" does not magically resolve all social conflicts. Social conflicts will surely continue to occur in the future. But the areas of conflict will be more limited because "concerted action" works to inform all parties. There will always be discussions and arguments in a free society about the relationship between wages and profits and about social symmetry.

Yet in this arrangement we actually find a process of social integration. In short, rational communication and information necessarily bring about integration. Therefore, one cannot simply condemn or write off as special interest lobbies those organized groups that have dedicated themselves to this arrangement through, for example, their comments on the report of the Economic Experts. They merely reflect modern society. Experience shows that without good relations with organized groups ultimately we cannot govern this society.

2-4. WEST GERMANY'S PURSUIT OF MONETARY STABILITY*

Originally published in the West German daily Vorwärts, *this article sets forth West Germany's conversion to a policy of monetary stability in the 1970s. Its author was an influential senior civil servant in Minister Schiller's Economics Ministry and a leading banker involved in a massive crisis of a public bank. He is currently a well-known author of books and articles on West Germany's economic policy.*

Now, thirty years after the last war, the US Administration and the Bonn Government consider it an established fact that an economic upswing and full employment will come about of their own accord once economic measures prove successful in stabilising prices and state expenditures and once—and this is a crucial prerequisite—the trade unions realise that restraint in wage demands will enable business to achieve sufficient profits to permit them to invest again.

The most important instrument in bringing this concept of "price stabilisation first and economic recovery later" to fruition on both sides of the Atlantic is the monetary policy. The more rigorously the central banks curtail the still existing scope of prices, state expenditures and wages, the sooner will the rocket of economic upswing ignite itself. . . .

There are two questions that call for a reply. Firstly, what is the explanation for the unholy alliance between US conservatism with its subjugation to the interests of big business—a conservatism which seems to be well on the way to losing the 1976 election—and Bonn's Socialist-Liberal coalition, which dubs itself progressive and is confident of winning the 1976 election? And secondly, what will be the drift of things after 1976 if the forecasts of the recent past suffer the fate of previous prognostications and are proven clearly wrong; if unemployment in the US remains at 8 million and in this country at one million people; and if these people draw considerably worse social security benefits while eagerly waiting for a job—benefits which, even if they do not diminish, are becoming costlier and costlier for the general public to bear?

The first question could be answered off the bat if we were to clarify

*Wilhelm Hankel, "Monetary Stability and the Welfare State," *The German Tribune*, June 6, 1976, pp. 6–7.

how and why a simultaneous change in the economic concept of the US and Bonn came about in the sixties. In the United States a new economic policy came into being in a perfectly democratic way at the end of the Johnson era with its Vietnam involvement. Nixon, who was re-elected in 1972 (although the Watergate affair had already come to light at that time), replaced the welfare state oriented 'fiscalism' by a conservative 'monetarism'. The fight against inflation gained priority over the fight against the depression—a course which gained in emphasis under Nixon's successor.

In this country, the "monetary counter-revolution" took place without an election and a new government, gradually and as an administrative measure. It crept, so to speak, through the back door into the economic policy as a result of a permanent re-interpretation of the Growth and Stability Law which was initiated by the then Chancellor Ludwig Erhard and passed by former Finance Minister Schiller. The equal importance of such aims as economic growth, full employment, equitable distribution of incomes, balanced foreign trade and price stability as envisaged by the Law, was little by little turned into a hierarchy of aims, so to speak, in which monetary stability came first. The idea was that once this was secured it would be easier to realise the other aims.

It is rather interesting to retrace the development which turned the original equality of aims into this new list of priorities. The Law was binding only for the Federal Government but not for the Central Bank, which is autonomous and subject to the older lex specialis (the Central Bank Law of 1957) which clearly stipulates monetary stability as the foremost objective. Although the subsequent general law should have amended the older special law, it was the older law which amended the newer.

But it went even further than that. The thus re-interpreted Law of 1967 became binding for all subsequent Federal governments, regardless of their political hue. They had to pursue the same fixed goals, using the same instruments, as though there had never been a change in the general and world-wide economic situation, no political change, no social progress and, above all, no new findings since 1967.

Since the victory of monetarism over fiscalism in both the United States and the Federal Republic, the economic concepts on both sides of the Atlantic became more similar than ever before in post-war history. The main responsibility for the campaign against inflation lies with the Central Bank. It has the right and the duty to ration the available money and it may permit interest rates to drift, following the dictates of the free markets. As opposed to Keynes' system, the government has neither the right nor the duty to channel state funds for the purpose of securing full employment and utilising available production capacities; if 'deficit spending' at all [*sic*] then this must come about defensively rather than offensively by tax reduction rather than increased expenditure. . . .

The sooner Washington and Bonn realise that monetarism does not pay, the sooner will the conservative counter-revolution be followed by a renaissance of the Keynes thesis—but no longer in the sense of a purely national state-oriented welfare concept along the lines of the thirties and forties, but by an international one.

Schiller's thesis of global control of economic processes and quantities of money would become reality and would no longer be misinterpreted as a national control which, in the final analysis, would do more harm than good to the home country. This would amount to an integration not only of money and commodity markets but also of economic, monetary and political strategies.

2-5. ALTERNATIVE ECONOMIC POLICY*

Dissatisfied by the economic analysis of the official Council of Economic Experts and responding to a deteriorating economic situation, a group of economics professors with leftist beliefs began in the mid-1970s to issue their own assessment of the economic situation. They sharply criticized the analysis of the council as well as the policy of the federal government and proposed an alternative approach.

At the beginning of 1978 the Federal Republic of Germany finds itself in the fourth year of widespread unemployment which continues to remain at record levels even $2\frac{1}{2}$ years after the latest economic crisis's worst point—over 1.2 million unemployed, 250,000 working short hours. This continuing divergence between increasing production and negative employment figures has conclusively proven wrong those forecasters who looked upon the present unemployment as a short-term cyclical phenomenon. They predicted a renewed rise in employment similar to the development in 1967. However, the opposite has hap-

*Arbeitsgruppe "Alternative Wirtschaftspolitik," *Memorandum Alternativen der Wirtschaftspolitik* (Cologne: Bund, 1978), pp. 9–11, 47–48, 59–60, 95 (selections).

pened; 1977 has brought a new turn for the worse. As of October 1977 employment figures have declined again. Isolated improvements have proven to be temporary and unstable. In contrast to mass unemployment after the Second World War (until 1954–55), today's high unemployment figures result from the economic growth process itself and are a long-term phenomenon even though they did not become fully evident until the latest economic crisis. . . .

In 1967 for the first time production levels registered an absolute decline. Since 1971, well before the present crisis, growth rates in major industries have not been sufficiently high to absorb those individuals laid off in other major industries. Since that time the number of industrial workers has been steadily decreasing. The crisis that started in 1974 has only accelerated and intensified this long-term trend. This situation has been made worse by the slackening growth in services and exports. The FRG has entered a phase of structural, long-term unemployment. . . . By 1977 at the latest the FRG had missed the chance to create the conditions for self-generating growth. An important culprit is the policy of "consolidation" of government budgets propagated from many quarters, including the Council of Economic Experts and other leading economic research institutes. . . . Economic projections for the next few years suggest that the FRG will have a large group of constantly unemployed citizens until well into the 1980s. Under present conditions we cannot even be sure that the level of mass unemployment will not increase further.

We observe how unemployment benefits and the national health insurance are being cut; soon social security too will have to be revamped by raising individual contributions and reducing the level of services to the point at which one can "live" with continuing mass unemployment. Adapting to continuing mass unemployment overshadows the effort to tackle the roots of the problem itself. As a result we are sacrificing elements of the welfare state which are especially important for those most in need. . . .

After four years of mass unemployment and general stagnation the Council of Economic Experts alleges to have established, under the phrase "full employment through economic growth," recognized objectives that can be readily agreed upon. The majority of the members of the Council of Economic Experts question neither the extent nor the limits of the economic growth objective. Growth means accumulation through private investment. Growth is said to be a means for solving distributional struggles, for example, the insatiable demands of certain social groups and of the state. This logic amounts to nothing less than forcing the unions to surrender voluntarily in exchange for securing economic growth. . . .

Despite all the other causes of unemployment, the workers are expected to bear the full brunt of the fight against this crisis. Their income is least secure in the distributional struggle. Wages "can be changed at short notice." The relatively weak position of a social group has surely seldom been used so publicly to rationalize an economic policy.

In particular the Council of Economic Experts demands a cost-neutral wage policy "in the strictest sense of the term." This stance abandons cost of living and full productivity adjustments of wages. Employers have no problem granting productivity-based wage increases "only if there is no unemployment."

The basis for the solution suggested by the Council of Economic Experts lies in a chain of events laid out in earlier reports. The chain leads from lower wages or wage costs to greater investments and employment: lower wages—lower costs—higher profits—more investment—more production and employment; at the same time: lower wages—lower costs—smaller rise in prices—greater buying power for average consumer—greater demand—more production and employment.

However, this causal chain is neither empirically nor theoretically as clear as the Council of Economic Experts suggests. Experience over the last few years has demonstrated that unemployment cannot be reduced in this manner. . . .

Confronting high and prolonged unemployment, the federal government has not been sitting on its hands during the last three years. On the contrary, it has gone to a great deal of trouble to pass and to implement a series of special economic programs and stabilization measures whose declared purpose it was to stimulate business investment and to bring about full employment.

These programs and measures have not reached their goal. Mass unemployment has not disappeared; it has not even declined. There are even signs that in the near and not so distant future unemployment figures will increase further. . . .

To be effective, a global and indirect expansionary policy requires that the stipulated close relationships really exist between higher private profits and increasing investments on the one hand and increasing investments and an increasing number of jobs on the other. These relationships are in fact more tenuous than ever.

The indirect and global economic policy practiced until now was condemned to fail because it did not take account of the increasing structural differentiations in the economy and neglected the resulting different and sometimes diametrically opposed ways various branches and business enterprises reacted to economic policy measures. Furthermore it did not consider the increasing structural rigidity of the economy and its resulting inflexibility. Economic policy continues to presume that a given economic impulse will be assimilated and passed on by private industry in the direction in which it was intended.

Sectoral and regional changes in economic structures and the increasing concentration, centralization, and consolidation of markets call for an economic policy that does not merely hope to be effective but instead actively lobbies for its declared policy objectives and sees to it that they are implemented. Otherwise, as is now the case, public funds are squandered in increasing amounts to stabilize the situation. But this leads to reductions in other social services. At the same time the successes in employment policy are harder and harder to see. . . .

If we are to exploit the full potential for the development of productive forces we have to free them from the limitations of the free enterprise system, thus creating the conditions for uninterrupted long-term economic development. This requires drastic measures that work against market forces: a gradual reduction in working hours; substantial political influence on the amount and the structure of social accumulation, and, consequently, on the level of production of investment and consumption goods; and a continuous redistribution of wealth from profits to salary and wages.

These are the directions for the development of a new economic order that would bring about a true socialization of technological progress.

2-6. RECIPE FOR ECONOMIC CURE GETS COLD RECEPTION*

In the summer of 1983 the CDU governor of Lower Saxony drafted a position paper in which he argued that the economic and social policies of the CDU-FDP coalition were destined to fail unless the government adopted a program of truly conservative policies as had been implemented in the United States by President Reagan and in Britain by Prime Minister Thatcher. As the headline for the article indicates, Albrecht's ten theses were very unpopular even in his own party. More clearly than

---

*German Tribune, no. 1099, September 11, 1983, p. 3.

any other episode in the 1980s, this unpopularity illustrates the difference between Anglo-Saxon and West German political conservatism.

There has been opposition on both sides of the political spectrum to economic and social policy proposals by the CDU Prime Minister of Lower Saxony, Ernst Albrecht.

Albrecht wants, among other things, to fight unemployment by giving tax relief for business and increasing [the] value-added tax to make up the financial deficit.

Objectors include Bonn Labour Minister Norbert Blüm, the mayor of Frankfurt, Walter Wallmann (CDU), and the Bavarian Finance Minister, Max Streibl (CSU). According to Associated Press, Blüm said workers should be given the tax relief. It was they who were bearing the brunt of austerity measures. Income tax has risen twice as fast as pay increases. If this continued, the unions would be forced to make unreasonable wage demands. The German news agency dpa reports that Bonn Finance Minister Gerhard Stoltenberg (CDU) will oppose the proposals and work towards lower income tax. Streibl has suggested the introduction of a tax-free portion of salaries as early as 1985–86.

Albrecht's 10 points are:

1. Government measures have not been enough to achieve a sustained upturn and reduce unemployment.

2. The psychological upswing the change of government caused in the business community is waning. Genuine economic measures are needed.

3. The rise in unemployment has many causes, including too small returns on investment and too high wages. The social security costs to be borne by employers have made labour costs even higher and reduced profits still further.

   As a result, liquidity has diminished drastically and the volume of investments is commensurately lower. Business has lost its ability to respond quickly and adequately to changed conditions. Some examples of managerial lack of flexibility: companies find themselves in trouble because the social provisions that have to be made prevent the shut-down of individual production plants.

   Legal provisions to prevent the dismissal of staff lead to overtime rather than new hiring. The co-determination provisions have bureaucratised managerial decisions, favouring the preservation of obsolete structures. Youth protection regulations make it more difficult to place apprentices. Before an industry can be established in a particular site it has to wade through a maze of red tape. Administrative courts contribute their share to the delay of possible investments. Labour has become too expensive, especially due to non-wage costs. The social system is expensive and uneconomical, imposing a heavy burden on employers. The unemployment problem is aggravated further because the yardstick used in financing the social security system is usually based on the labour factor.

4. Tax on business must be reduced noticeably (by about 20 percent). The suggestion that profits ploughed back into business be given more tax relief than those that are withdrawn should be seriously considered.

5. Cuts in income tax would be helpful. If simultaneous tax relief for business and labour puts too much of a strain on the budget, priority must be given to business in the interests of reducing unemployment.

6. Reduced overall tax revenues would be unrealistic in the next four years. The tax relief for business would therefore have to be offset by increased VAT and various sales taxes.

7. Labour costs must come down in real terms. Among the ways of achieving this are: reduced absenteeism, lower health insurance contributions by strengthening the interests of the insured in the thrifty use of funds and the uncoupling of the social net financing from work contracts.

8. The social burdens of economic adaptation processes must be borne primarily by the public. The financial and administrative hurdles for people wanting to go into business—especially the small- and medium-sized variety—must be removed.

9. Everybody has a right to meaningful work: but not everybody can have a highly paid job. The discussion over the benefits and dangers of shorter working lives and working hours should soon lead to specific action. More flexibility is equally important.

10. The distribution mechanisms are in need of a sweeping review. The enormous national product created in factories must be justly distributed. It is doubtful whether wages alone can do this. In any event, capital participation by the staff and later by the nation as a whole must become an important social task.

2-7. ECONOMIC POLICY AND STRUCTURAL CHANGE*

Sharp increases in unemployment and the fear of declining international competitiveness became a prominent subject of political debate in the 1980s. This report of the Advisory Council of the Economics Ministry expresses succinctly the orthodoxy that has informed West German economic policy in the 1970s and 1980s. It shows that the appeal of left-wing and right-wing policy prescription has had little impact on the advice that informs the policy debates within the federal government.

Regaining a dynamic economy requires that we increase substantially the number and quality of the innovations in the German economy; that we manage successfully the structural adjustments in industries under pressure from foreign competitors; and that we simultaneously create more flexible prices in other sectors. In a free enterprise system the solution to these problems requires that, through the specification of general economic targets, business interests work to the benefit of the public as a whole. State intervention in the economy may have merits. Its goal, however, should be the general facilitation of structural change.

In many countries and in Europe as a whole an industrial policy has taken hold recently that has led to a number of interventions in specific industries and that leads to a constantly expanding scope of government action. Such a policy runs the danger of substituting for the advancement of structural change an expanding protectionism of existing structures. Because of the indiscriminate support of some industries the policy has already contributed greatly to distorted competition, outdated structures, rigidity in income levels, and the misallocation of investment capital. Such a gradual increase in government intervention is difficult to avoid. Easily organized special interest groups repeatedly gain the upper hand in political decisionmaking. The costs of granting certain advantages to these groups are usually borne by the population as a whole, rather than by individuals. Public economic policy should work against these weaknesses in the democratic system of government. Regulatory policy must find ways, within the democratic framework, to

*Wissenschaftlicher Beirat beim Bundesministerium für Wirtschaft, *Strukturwandel für Wachstum und mehr Beschäftigung* (Bonn, December 1984), pp. 43–45.

promote structural change without asking the public for unnecessary sacrifices.

The council does not underestimate the problems that the unexpected loss in income has created for social security. However, the solution to these problems lies in the realm of social policy, where institutions and criteria exist specifically for this purpose. Social policy starts with the general income and living standards of the individual and not with the state of affairs in certain branches of industry or individual enterprises. Therefore, it does not require the government to intervene to preserve certain structures. Government measures in favor of certain economic sectors can be justified in the long run only in the interest of national security or because of international effects that are not reflected in product prices but have substantial benefits for the population as a whole. This does not hold true for the preservation of income and employment in certain branches of the economy or in certain regions of the country. Such practices amount to nothing less than discrimination in favor of certain groups of the population. Therefore, we ought to demand that individuals live with the risks of structural change since as employees, capital investors, and entrepreneurs they may also take advantage of the opportunities which these changes bring. If individuals or even whole groups suffer—for example, through structural unemployment in certain occupations—the "social net" can break their fall. A policy that promotes structural change also helps to shorten the period of economic need by creating new job opportunities.

3 Industrial Relations

Mitbestimmung, "codetermination," is an awkward and almost untranslatable word. It refers to the joint participation of owners and workers in the running of West German industry. The term is used sometimes to refer only to the participation of labor on management boards and at other times to include participation in works councils at the factory level. In this chapter codetermination refers to both forms of labor-management collaboration, "bottom up" employee participation in enterprise decisions and "top down" codetermination of labor and business in the boardroom (Thimm, 1981, p. 15). Codetermination is the result of a process of historical evolution which accommodated a socialist labor movement within industrial capitalism. Put starkly, the choice was between revolutionary socialism or evolutionary socialism. Well into the twentieth century, ideology and practice of the German labor movement diverged. Theory was revolutionary, practice evolutionary. The last remnants of Germany's Marxist tradition, which the SPD abandoned with its Bad Godesberg program of 1959, were given up by the DGB in its Düsseldorf program of 1963. That much is well known. But the victory of political and economic reformism at the political summit should not blind us to a long tradition of mutual accommodation of labor and business in Germany's industrial plants. Already in the nineteenth century we find liberal, catholic, and socialist roots of works councils, which institutionalized consultation between management and labor. In the postwar period this consultation has been extended to a system of codetermination which has no analogue in any of the other major industrial states. The contemporary system of West German industrial relations is distinguished by a dual system of worker representation: at the level of the plant, in works councils and the boardroom; in collective bargaining, through unions.

The second distinguishing feature is West Germany's centralized union movement, which is organized along industry lines. British observers in particular have pointed to the difference between Britain's decentralized system of crafts unions and West Germany's centralized system of industry unions as a major reason for the different economic fortunes of the two countries since 1945. The DGB is composed of seventeen industrial unions. In addition, separate union federations exist for white-collar employees and for civil servants. The DGB's power is limited. Unlike Sweden's trade union, for example, it cannot interfere with the collective bargaining of the seventeen member unions. At the same time it is undeniably the group that articulates labor's position in West German politics. That position, especially on questions of collective bargaining, is greatly affected by the labor laws and the labor courts that have ruled out union tactics considered quite normal in other societies. The stability and orderliness of West Germany's industrial relations thus result from several factors: the reformist ideology and practices of unions that are centralized and leave little scope for rank-and-file militants; a well-institutionalized system of works councils which involves workers at the plant level; and laws that constrain what unions and business can do.

Like questions of economic management, West German politics on questions of labor-business relations bears a close resemblance to the pattern of policy and politics that I have sketched in Chapter 1. In the area of collective bargaining, state power is not exercised directly through the legislature or the executive but, rather, through labor courts that have not hesitated to impose substantial limits on union strategies. Centralized interest groups settle among themselves economic issues such as wages, hours of work, and in the 1970s a host of other issues affecting the quality of work life. Together with the political parties, these groups shape the legislation that defines the institutional parameters of West Germany's industrial relations, specifically the system of works councils and of codetermination. Because they elaborate on the argument I developed in Chapter 1, I shall discuss the institutional determinants of industrial relation rather than focus on the collective bargaining process. The core institutions of West Germany's industrial relations system bring together business and labor in a collaborative arrangement that is legally codified. Over the last thirty-five years this system has produced a remarkably stable pattern of politics and incremental policy change which has proven compatible with the requirements of international economic competition. The gradual increase in industrial conflict that has occurred since the mid-1970s illustrates that in times of substantially higher unemployment, unions and business tend to experiment with new strategies. So far these have stopped short of challenging the institutional foundations of West Germany's system of industrial relations. In the 1980s incremental policy in this sector continues to typify West Germany's semisovereign state.

Context

Support for employee representation in the firm predates the rise of German unions. Originally it derived from demands by both employers and employees (Braunthal, 1976, pp. 215–20; Fogarty, 1965, pp. 60– 108; Solyom-Fekete, 1976, pp. 17–34). Employers hoped that improved communication with workers would result in a more committed and stable workforce. Employees, on the other hand, organized friendly societies, modeled after those in mining and the handicraft guilds, that tried to look after the workers' welfare. Workers' committees thus spread, and many of today's leading West German firms, such as Krupp and Gutehoffnungshütte, date their first workers' committees to the early years of industrialization. Indeed, the Revolution of 1848–49 saw not only the discussion of far-reaching proposals of plant and district committees joining workers and owners but also the adoption by the Frankfurt Assembly of a proposal requiring district and regional industry councils with participation of journeymen and workers. These debates and resolutions were prompted by the threat of revolution. When that threat had passed, the pressure for reform declined. The early years of German industrialization thus reveal the seeds of a collaborative system of labor relations which would subsequently grow together, coexist, and eventually supplant labor militancy.

The ideological basis for supporting workers' committees was broad. Liberals in the business community favored them to improve communication on issues such as work rules, discipline, hours, overtime, and wages. Catholics in addition regarded the firm as a family and, focusing on human relations, sought to educate the children of the family—that is, the workers—to become responsible and to practice Christian principles of self-help. Finally, a small number of firms made attempts to set up "constitutional factories" which to a very limited extent curtailed the authority of management. Academic luminaries who had founded the Association for Social Policy (Verein für Sozialpolitik) differed in their assessment of how the workers' committees should evolve. Some, such as Lujo Brentano, were interested primarily in strengthening trade unions. Others, such as Adolph Wagner, favored more forceful state action expecially in wage determination. Still a third group, including Gustav Schmoller, saw the need for state action and stronger unions but insisted on an institutional machinery to represent workers' interests in the firm. Revolution, Schmoller argued, could be avoided only if both workers' committees and trade unions integrated Germany's working class into the emerging capitalist order. But the contribution of the workers' committees evidently went much further. "In 1890 an inquiry on behalf of the *Verein* by the economist Max Sering concluded that the committees strengthened management, improved productivity, increased mutual understanding and co-operation and educated workers. But, he added, it was better for them to grow than to be legislated into existence" (Fogarty, 1965, p. 74).

The crucial push for further growth came not from academics but from German trade unions (Moses, 1982). Legalized in the North German Confederation in 1869, socialist trade unions spread and were united under one organization in 1875. Others including Christian, liberal, and independent trade unions also began to organize. But in 1878 Bismarck exploited the political opportunity created by attempts to assassinate the emperor. Enforcing the Anti-Socialist Bill, the police suppressed not only the Social Democratic party but also the trade union movement, which, technically speaking, was not covered by the law. But after 1890 the trade union movement reemerged, established its formal independence from the Social Democratic party while keeping a de facto close association, and pressed its claim for the establishment of statuory institutions of joint labor-management relations at all levels—industry, region, and national economy. In contrast to the committees that had evolved over decades, labor enjoyed equal participation both under the law and in practice. This demand for equal participation found broad support in a variety of quarters. But the demand for workers' committees in individual plants which were independent of management proved to be much more controversial. Although heavy industry was strongly opposed to workers' committees, legislation instituting them was passed in 1892. But the legislative requirements then imposed on business were not demanding. Every plant was required to issue rules, among others, concerning length of the workweek, breaks, time of payment, and penalties. These rules had to be submitted for comment to the workers before taking effect. For the first time, therefore, the state signaled its direct interest in the structure of individual firms. Workers' committees had been removed from the de facto discretionary powers of business. Instead, in response to the growing power of Germany's political and economic Left, the state for the first time had taken away from business the unmonitored right to manage its own house. By 1905 about 10 percent of all privately owned factories with a workforce of twenty or more had workers' committees.

World War I and the early years of the Weimar Republic provided a decisive push for the workers' committees. These committees were strengthened in 1915–16 and compulsory arbitration was introduced in 1916. The National Auxiliary Service of 1916 permitted the mobilization of all civilian males between seventeen and sixty for the war effort. In return for supporting this bill, the unions got an agreement that workers' committees should be universal and compulsory and should be entitled to take unresolved grievances before arbitration panels staffed jointly by representatives of business and labor and chaired by members of the War Department. At the end of the war the industrialist Hugo Stinnes and the head of the Socialist Free Trade Unions, Carl Legien, signed an agreement that formally recognized the unions, established collective bargaining, affirmed workers' committees, and did much to protect the industrialists from a social revolution. But the powers granted to workers' committees between 1918 and 1922 in fact established a new framework for industrial relations which informed the legislation passed in the early years of the Federal Republic. With the power of socialism at its highest point in the early years of the Weimar Republic, the constitution provided for works councils at the shop-floor, regional, and national levels. However, the national Economic Council was never anything but provisional. Regional councils never were set up. Yet the concept of economic democracy left a legacy. The push for codetermination after 1945 was inspired partly by the plans that the Left had articulated and debated in the 1920s.

Even though in the 1920s management devised strategies to counter some of the advantages it had conferred to workers, the Works Council Law of 1920 extended a measure of economic democracy that went further than any in the past. The democratically elected councils would represent all workers on the shop floor and be charged with overseeing

management's adherence to collective agreements; implementing grievance procedures, safety, and health regulations; participating in the
drafting and application of work rules as well as in regulations for hiring
and dismissal; helping to administer housing and other corporate welfare plans; and joining shareholders in supervising management by
nominating two of its members to serve on the supervisory board. Although the works councils had the right to be informed about the plant's
financial condition and its employment prospects, it could only offer
economic advice to the managers of the company, advice that management was free to reject.

Comparable to the years 1876–90, the Nazi era provided more of an
interlude than a new beginning. The Nazis crushed the labor movement,
the councils, and all of the democratic institutions of the Weimar Republic. They created instead the German Labor Front, which sought to
bridge the conflict between business and labor through compulsory
membership of blue-collar workers, white-collar employees, and employers. The Labor Front assumed all the far-reaching powers that had
formerly been left to the works councils and to free collective bargaining between employers and unions. Although its effect on the dual representation of workers through unions and works councils was nil, the
Labor Front contributed to the centralization of a unified trade union
movement organized along industry lines. West Germany's industrial
unions are represented by the DGB in their external relations but retain
their autonomy on questions of collective bargaining. The old division
between socialist, Christian, and liberal unions no longer exists. Instead
West German workers belong to one of the seventeen unions organized
along industry or multi-industry lines and united under the umbrella of
the DGB. Formally politically neutral since the mid 1950s, the DGB has
organized about 30 percent of the West German employees with the
proportion rising in the 1970s to about 35 percent. If one includes the
white-collar employees and civil servants who belong to two separate
unions, the proportion of the West German workforce that is organized
rose to about 40 percent in the 1970s, about as much as at its high point
in the 1950s (Streeck, 1981, pp. 470–71). Because of their sheer size
and the heterogeneity of interests in each of the seventeen industrial
unions, union leadership cannot easily identify with narrow factions.
Although debate in the union is unrestricted, once a policy has been
adopted, compliance is not only expected but enforced. The result is

that West German unions in general and the DGB specifically have been able to bargain successfully with both business and the state.

The system of industrial relations is an essential component of the economic success and social stability that have marked West Germany's history since 1945. Centralization as one of the two distinctive features of the union movement must be credited to the historical experiences of the 1920s and 1930s. But the principle of dual representation through unions and works councils in the plants goes back to the beginning of Germany's industrialization and has drawn support from variegated social and ideological strata. Only later was it complemented by the workers organized in unions engaged in collective bargaining. Since 1945 a stable system of labor-management relations has helped depoliticize questions of social policy or migrant labor which might have proven more disruptive. But depoliticization and stability were not God-given. They stem instead from deliberate efforts by businessmen, union leaders, and labor judges.

Agenda

In the immediate postwar years the demand for codetermination enjoyed broad political support. Trade unions insisted that labor had to be admitted to the boardrooms of management to prevent big business from supporting extremist, antidemocratic parties as it had done in the 1930s. Business offered labor various plans for participation in management. It thus hoped to win union support against the Allied policy of dismantling West German industry. Indeed, the Allies themselves strongly favored the unions' demand since it fitted well into their plans of decartelizing German industry. Codetermination was legislated in two different forms. The Codetermination Law of 1951 applied only to the iron, coal, and steel industries (Braunthal, 1976, pp. 223–25; Fürstenberg, 1969; Spiro, 1958). The law stipulates that labor be allotted one-half of the seats of the supervisory board (Aufsichtsrat), with representatives of shareholders holding the other half and a "neutral" chair elected by the board to break potential deadlocks. In addition, the board of directors was expanded to include a labor director, to be appointed by the supervisory board from a slate that typically is the result of joint deliberations among the representatives of the employees of a specific company and the representatives of the national trade unions. Although the primary duties of the labor director include supervising personnel matters and social services, she is a full-fledged member of the board with responsibilities extending to general management.

The 1951 legislation fell short of some of the more far-reaching demands the union made in the late 1940s. But it was a political victory. With the political climate changing rapidly, however, the Works Constitution Act of 1952 was a major defeat for the unions. Although it extended the principle of codetermination to the major companies outside of the coal, steel, and iron industries, the bill gave labor only one-third rather than one-half of the seats on the supervisory board. Furthermore, workers' representatives on the board no longer had the power to veto the choice of the labor director. At the same time, however, this law did satisfy some of the unions' demands. It reinstated and extended the works council system along the lines of the Weimar legislation. Works councils were granted a host of functions and rights including monthly meetings with employers to settle grievances; supervision of the enforcement of labor laws; collective bargaining agreements covering wages and hours; agreements covering fringe benefits for individual plants; and limited rights of consultation on questions of hiring, firing, and transfers (Fogarty, 1965, pp. 109–21; Kurth, 1954; Sturmthal, 1964, pp. 63–85). But the important political fact remains that the unions' central political demand, equal representation for labor, had not been adopted. Labor's political agenda for the next three decades was shaped by the attempt to undo its 1952 defeat.

In the 1950s and 1960s the tenacious attempts of the unions were no more than a holding operation. In 1955 the Bundestag passed the Personnel Representation Law, which introduced some employee participation in public administration and established personnel councils. Amended in the 1970s, provisions for codetermination under the Personnel Representation Law are probably stronger than in the works council legislation. In the 1970s it became extremely difficult to run a ministry or, for that matter, any public body, against the wishes of the Personnel Council involved. In 1956 the Bundestag subjected holding companies in the coal and steel industries to codetermination with provisions less advantageous to labor than those in operating companies. In fact, because of mergers and closures the number of firms subject to codetermination was reduced by one-third between 1952 and 1968. But the unions won at least one concession from the respective employers' associations of firms no longer covered by the 1951 law, namely, that supervisory boards and labor directors continue to function, mergers notwithstanding. By 1984, of the 105 companies originally covered less than 20 were still operating (Hartmann, 1970, p. 139; Helm, 1984, p. 2).

While the demand for parity representation remains, over the years the objectives to be served by codetermination have changed. The charge that industry had helped Hitler to seize power had provided a strong rationale for the adoption of codetermination in the early 1950s (Bunn, 1958). As memories of the Third Reich faded, other objectives assumed greater prominence (Hartmann, 1970, pp. 140–42). The unions have argued that because of their social importance large enterprises should be open to some public control short of nationalization. Furthermore, the unions and the political Left have viewed codetermination as a means of extending democracy into the sphere of industry. Finally, they have argued, codetermination would reduce the alienation of workers and increase social stability and economic growth by giving workers a greater stake in the success of the enterprise. Although these arguments are far from precise, they underline the continued urgency that the unions attached to their long-standing demand for parity representation in the boardrooms of the major West German corporations. When the SPD joined the CDU in the Great Coalition in 1966, it pushed for the appointment of a commission to reexamine the system of codetermination (see Reading 3-1). Named after its chair (and later CDU party secretary), Kurt Biedenkopf, the report gave codetermination a clean bill of health. The institutionalization of labor participation had proven compatible with the institution of private property as well as economic efficiency, and it was fundamentally accepted by all major groups. However, in its policy prescriptions for modification and extension, the report fell short of the expectations of the SPD and especially of the unions.

But when in 1969 the SPD assumed power as the senior member of a coalition government with the FDP, the composition of the government changed dramatically in favor of the unions. Since the FDP had opposed the original codetermination bill of 1951 and its extension to holding companies in 1956, it was clear from the outset that a compromise of the coalition government to extend codetermination would be very difficult to achieve. Instead, the coalition prepared a reform of the works council legislation of 1952 (see Reading 3-2). In 1972, after extensive analysis and debate, the new law became effective. It covered 98 percent of all firms in manufacturing and 75 percent of those in wholesale and retail (Wilpert, 1975, p. 53). The law stipulates that works councils shall be elected in all firms with more than five employees and mandates the formation of central works councils in companies with more than one plant. The position of the works councils is strengthened in several areas. Hiring, firing, promotion, transfers, and work allocation all need the advance consent of the works council; management can no longer act unilaterally. The work councils must also approve all plant closings and reductions or alterations in the scale or rate of production. In the eventuality of mass lay-offs, the council and the employer must jointly work out a "social plan" that provides alternative employment in the firm, retraining, or severance pay. The law gives individual workers additional rights, such as access to their files, and grants unions easier access to individual plants. The influence of the works council in the actual management of the firm is less strong. In larger companies with more than 100 employees, works councils appoint economic committees of between four and eight members which are entitled to information on all important issues, including company finances, manufacturing methods, and production programs.

Though gratifying to the unions, the 1972 law was for them no more than a halfway house. After the coalition had won a resounding electoral victory in 1972, the unions pressured the SPD to make revision of codetermination a high priority of the government's legislative program (see Reading 3-3). After years of heated political wrangling between parties and interest groups, the Codetermination Act of 1976 was passed. This act applies to all West German firms with more than 2,000 employees—about 475 firms employing 20 percent of the labor force (Helm, 1984, p. 2). Although the law formally extends to workers the right to equal representation with management on supervisory boards, three qualifications in fact leave workers with less than equal participation (Wilson, 1982). First, labor directors are appointed by a majority of the supervisory board rather than a majority of the labor representatives on the board, as in the coal, iron, and steel industries. Second, the chair of the supervisory board is chosen by a majority of the shareholders' representatives and casts two votes in case of a tie. Finally, the labor members on the supervisory board include white-collar and managerial employees who on account of their position in the corporate hierarchy are more likely to align themselves with the views of shareholders than those of workers.

Neither the unions nor business were satisfied with the results of the prolonged process of political bargaining which accompanies West Germany's pattern of incremental policy change. Unions felt that the bill did not go far enough; business felt that it went too far. In the fall of 1982 the unions started a new campaign for further reform and extension of codetermination. But they conceived of this initiative as an instrument for developing new economic strategies—qualitative growth and the deliberate steering of technological change as well as a shorter workweek—rather than as a political end in and of itself. In the 1970s and 1980s two issues in particular have come to rival the preoccupation of earlier decades with the institutional machinery of labor-management relations: the humanization of work life and the demand for a thirty-five-hour workweek (Markovits, 1986; Markovits and Allen, 1980, 1984).

Because it is vague, the humanization of work life has introduced a broad range of qualitative demands into collective bargaining (Hassencamp and Bieneck, 1983). As in Sweden, demands have focused on diminishing job-related health hazards, reducing repetitive work processes at the assembly line, reorganizing work processes to increase workers' initiative, and enhancing the responsibility of individual workers at the work station, to name a few. Although in principle business favors many of the qualitative demands in the interest of increasing productivity and workers' satisfaction, it is adamantly opposed to having labor dictate the timing and the extent of the changes. For the unions, on the other hand, the issue raises fundamental questions of industrial and economic democracy and, ultimately, of the relative priority of human labor over capital. Reinforced by a special program that the federal government initiated in 1974, the issue became an important feature of collective bargaining in the 1970s.

Sharp increases in West Germany's unemployment rate in the 1980s have, however, moved the demand for a thirty-five-hour workweek to center stage. The metal workers' union (I. G. Metall), with 2.5 million members the largest independent union in any capitalist country, was defeated in 1978 when it made this demand the center of one of West Germany's rare strikes. But in a bitter strike called in 1984, the union succeeded in a shortening of the average workweek from 40.0 to 38.5 hours. The unions want to spread less work among a larger number of workers, thus reducing unemployment rates which reached almost 10 percent in 1984–85. But business is typically opposed to enlarging its permanent workforce in response to temporary upswings in market demand. Increases in production, it holds, will be met by additional overtime or the hiring of part-time labor. Dismissing workers has become increasingly difficult since the extension of the powers granted to the works councils in 1972. But whatever the net effect on employment, in a country that has known few strikes the mere fact that the union struck for a thirty-five-hour workweek symbolizes the DGB's commitment to this demand. In return, however, the unions had to accept greater flexibility in the arrangements for working time negotiated by workers in individual plants. It organized the strike despite the explicit opposition of the CDU/CSU-FDP government and the initial hostility or indifference of much of its own rank and file. The union succeeded in fully mobilizing its membership during a six-week strike and prevailed upon business to accept at least in principle a 38.5-hour workweek. As long as unemployment rates remain high, the demand for a shorter workweek is likely to be an important issue on the agenda of West Germany's industrial relations.

Like Britain's, West Germany's industrial relations during the last thirty-five years have until recently centered on controversies about their institutional structure. But in sharp contrast to Britain, the idea of codetermination has enjoyed broad support from diverse political quarters despite intense conflict over the 1976 reform. Little needs to be said about the commitment of the unions to extending codetermination from the works councils to the boardrooms throughout West German industry. In addition, the SPD could delay but not deny the insistent demand of its strongest political ally. On the other hand, the political initiatives that social Catholics and the left wing of the CDU took in the 1950s and their continued receptivity in the 1970s to a modification and extension of codetermination point to the importance of a corporativist strain in German politics which predates the Bonn Republic. It also helps explain why policy change in the Federal Republic tends toward incrementalism. The federal government has refrained from interfering in any way with the collective bargaining between the social partners, on the one hand; and on the other, it has not objected to the far-reaching rulings passed by West Germany's labor courts especially in the 1960s. Intervention was hardly necessary, for the state's interest in social stability was well served by the institution of codetermination and the involvement of the judiciary.

Process

The political process by which codetermination was instituted in the early 1950s and reformed in the 1970s points to the importance of the centrist tendencies of West Germany's political parties, its system of coalition cabinets, and its parapublic institutions. Only the introduction of codetermination in the iron and steel industries in 1951 was shaped more directly by the personal relations between Chancellor Adenauer and the leader of the DGB, Hans Böckler (Baring, 1969, pp. 196–204; Braunthal, 1976, pp. 223–28). Because in 1950 the DGB's leadership doubted that its demand for full economic codetermination would be supported by a coalition government led by the CDU, it mobilized its rank and file. Böckler offered Adenauer a bargain that was attractive at the time, for the debate about West German rearmament, which followed the outbreak of the Korean War, had agitated the West German public. In return for codetermination in iron and steel, the DGB offered support for Adenauer's foreign policy. Although he resented the extra-parliamentary pressure the DGB applied, it was a bargain the chancellor could not refuse. In January 1951 he personally supervised the dramatic negotiations between the DGB and the BDI which were concluded successfully six days before an unlimited strike was to have begun. The chancellor's bill passed the Bundestag with the strong support of the SPD and the left wing of the CDU, the grudging support of the rest of the CDU and CSU, and against the votes of the CDU's two smaller coalition parties, including the FDP. These smaller parties depended heavily on the financial support of West German business which by then had come to oppose union demands for parity codetermination on the supervisory boards of West German corporations. For a number of reasons—a change in union leadership, the willingness of the FDP in particular to bring down the coalition government, and an increasingly conservative public climate—the unions failed in their political offensive to have parity codetermination extended from coal and steel to the rest of the West German economy. Although it legalized the councils, the Works Council Law of 1952 was for the unions the "greatest disappointment since the rise of Hitler" (Kerr, 1954, p. 552). In large firms it provided only for one-third the number of labor representatives on supervisory boards, rather than equal representation. These representatives were not granted a veto right over the selection of the labor director. Gaining parity remained thereafter one of the principal political objectives of the unions.

The DGB had to wait for almost two decades before political circumstances favored extension of codetermination. In a detailed report named after its chair, a government commission headed by Kurt Biedenkopf provided substantial support for a modification and extension of codetermination (see Reading 3-1). But the narrow Bundestag majority of the SPD-FDP coalition after 1969 and the pressing issue of Chancellor Brandt's policy toward Eastern Europe and the Soviet Union made reform of the Works Council Law of 1952 the only realistic objective of the coalition government. Since the SPD and the FDP were in agreement, after numerous consultations among different ministries, with the trade unions, and with employers' associations, the cabinet approved a draft legislation in December 1970 (Braunthal, 1976, pp. 232–33). Bundestag committees held extensive hearings, a rarity in West German politics, and recommended passage of the government's bill with some modifications. Against the votes of the CDU/CSU, the bill passed the Bundestag and became law in January 1972.

By contrast, even though the SPD and FDP won a solid Bundestag majority in the election of 1972, the haggling among the coalition partners required to reform the Codetermination Law of 1951 was infinitely more arduous (Braunthal, 1976, pp. 234–46). In response to strong pressure from the unions, the SPD convinced its minor coalition partner that reform of codetermination was unavoidable. Yet the FDP remained as opposed to the principle of codetermination as it had been two decades earlier. To maintain its social base of support, it insisted on the representation of white-collar employees in managerial positions on the supervisory board of West Germany's largest corporations. The SPD rejected this proposal, which it regarded as undermining the principle of parity so dear to the unions, arguing with the unions that senior employees were more likely to side with shareholders than with workers. In the end the SPD and the FDP agreed on a compromise that adopted parity representation of workers and shareholders but stipulated that at least one of the workers' representatives had to be a middle-level executive. Both employers and unions voiced their strong opposition to the bill. For the employers the bill went much too far; for the unions it did not go far enough. After protracted hearings and debate in the Bundesrat and the Bundestag in 1974, the SPD and the FDP arrived in 1975 at an impasse that eventually required further concessions from the SPD. After long negotiations in December 1975, a revised bill was agreed upon; in March 1976, despite some misgivings, the CDU/CSU opposition decided to support the bill because it strengthened management's role in the running of the company. The 1976 bill contains the provision that each supervisory board must elect its chair by a two-thirds majority and that the chair is accorded a double vote to break a tie. "Since neither he nor the managing boards themselves can be chosen in opposition to the representatives of capital, the effect is to ensure the continued dominance of private owner-ship in the West German productive process" (Hancock, 1977, p. 10). The opposition of the FDP thus succeeded in blunting the demands of the unions and making possible, after years of political bargaining, only incremental rather than wholesale changes in West Germany's system of industrial relations.

The centrist logic of coalition politics was also evident in the period of policy implementation. The objectives of the 1976 act were threatened by the evasive strategies of firms that, for example, changed their legal status by splitting up into smaller firms or transferred some of their divisions to foreign subsidiaries. Between 1976 and 1978, when the law went into effect, the number of firms covered by the act declined from 600 to 650 to 484 (Streeck, 1984, pp. 402–4). Political controversy over corporate reorganization focused on the attempt of the steel and engineering firm Mannesmann to lease its foundry to a subsidiary, thus anticipating substantial savings, and not incidentally protecting the firm from the 1951 legislation, since without its foundry, sales revenues from iron and steel products would fall below 50 percent (see Reading 3-7) (Spieker and Strohauer, 1982; Thimm, 1981). Strongly opposed to any dismantling of codetermination, the unions demanded that the government pass a "special law." Within a few months of their election victory in 1980, the SPD and the FDP once again confronted the issue of codetermination. After intense bargaining, the November 1980 program of the coalition government headed by Chancellor Schmidt was finalized. It included plans for legislation to provide a six-year transition period during which enterprises would be covered, with only slight modifications, by the 1951 legislation even if their sales of iron and steel products fell below 50 percent of total sales. After that transition period, the weaker provisions of the 1976 act would apply. This compromise satisfied neither unions nor business, and between November 1980 and March 1981 it threatened to unravel almost daily. But after an ideological debate, the bill passed the Bundestag in the spring of 1981.

The policy process was also influenced by West Germany's judicial branch of government. In its prolonged political bargaining with the SPD, for example, the FDP was strengthened by the arguments of most legal experts that a strict system of parity codetermination would probably be held unconstitutional by the Federal Constitutional Court. In the election year of 1976 the SPD obviously wanted to avoid at almost all cost being overruled by the Court. In 1977 twenty-nine employers' associations and nine firms unexpectedly filed a suit questioning the constitutionality of the 1976 bill (Wiedenmann, 1980, pp. 83–85). The political intent of the employers, and in particular of their president, Hanns Martin Schleyer, was barely concealed. If the Court decided to rule in their favor, the 1976 bill would have to be watered down and future attempts by the unions to extend codetermination further would be blocked. If the Court ruled that the 1976 bill was constitutional by making a comparison with the 1951 bill and pointing to the lack of effective parity in the supervisory board as well as to the weaker position of the labor director, the ground would be prepared for a future challenge to the constitutionality of the 1951 law. In March 1979 the Court ruled against the employers (see Reading 3-6). In its ruling the court did not address the question whether parity would be constitutional. Instead, it simply observed that the 1976 legislation did not provide for parity. The Court's decision notwithstanding, the unions viewed the employers' suit as a frontal attack on a political position they had thought secure. In a climate of political confrontation they took the symbolic step, a few days after the suit had been filed, of withdrawing from the concerted action that had been meeting regularly for a decade (see Reading 3-5 and Chapter 2). As is true of all political gestures, this one served a second purpose. Since the concerted action had imposed some strains on their internal organization, the unions were not unhappy to have it end (Alexis, 1983, p. 77).

The court system was also active in the implementation of the 1976 codetermination law. Between 1976 and 1981 the courts ruled in fifty cases, clarifying the provisions of the 1976 act and the executive order regulating the complex procedures for electing employee representatives (Helm, 1984, p. 2). Judicial activism in this particular instance illustrates the far-reaching role that labor law and labor courts play in West Germany's collective bargaining system. West German labor relations are defined by the Collective Bargaining Law of 1949, the Works Council Law of 1952 as amended in 1972, and the decisions of the labor courts. "The entire industrial relations system in the Federal Republic is built on a highly developed series of legal regulations. The aim is to check the conflict of interests and to avoid the resulting political risks" (Bergmann and Müller-Jentsch 1975, p. 248). Legal theory constrains business and labor and seeks to further a climate of "social self-government" rather than unilateral state controls. "The theory goes further (and this now has a more current ring to American ears), 'employees seek a partnership in their places of business' " (Teague, 1971, p. 49). In fact, the theory of partnership severely constrains the options labor has for pressing its demands on business (Riemer, 1975). Court rulings in the 1920s insisted that the Factory Council Law of 1920 had created a "factory community" that imposed risks and responsibilities on workers. It provided the cornerstone of the Nazi legal theory which has shaped legislation and court rulings since 1945. In this community before 1972 the unions were barred from the shop floor. On average 75–85 percent of the eligible workers vote every three years for their councilors. The work councils settle many of the concrete issues of working life in a spirit of social partnership. But they also transform established rights, won by the unions, into bargaining levers for increasing workers' benefits. They do not, however, have the right to call a strike. The Court has also insisted on the equivalency of business and labor, lock-out and strike, in a bargaining relation among the fundamentally equal social partners that confront each other outside the factory. But lock-outs must always be defensive. They can be called only after a strike has started and then only in an "equivalent" proportion to the number of striking workers.

Informed by this legal theory, labor law restrains the representation of workers' interests by factory councils and unions (Bergmann and Müller-Jentsch, 1975, pp. 248–56; Dorscht, 1985, pp. 11–13). Works councils are subject to a general clause of "trustful co-operation" with management. They are bound by a "peace obligation" that makes it illegal to call strikes (including spontaneous strikes) or organize demonstrations. The powers of the councils, though formally quite far-reaching in their scope, thus depend on the power of the unions. Unions bargain with employers on matters such as general wage systems, vacation allowances, schemes for job evaluations, and length of the workweek. Contracts are negotiated at the regional level and often cover more than 100,000 employees in different branches of industry. Wage contracts typically are oriented to average or marginal rather than profitable firms and thus cannot take advantage of the potential for full wage increases. Furthermore, the unions are bound in their wage strategy by the principle of "social appropriateness" in labor disputes. According to this principle, strikes must correspond to the normative order of society as well as to the principles of labor law. The courts have interpreted this vague norm in a conservative fashion. West German labor law makes political strikes illegal; may require a cooling-off period that demobilizes workers; insists on the economic fairness of strikes, thus excluding, as in other countries, the use of force or the economic destruction of the adversary (business or unions); imposes a general obligation to act peacefully for the duration of a contract; and prohibits unions from engaging in any aggressive action, including taking a strike vote, while a contract is in force. Collective agreements, which are legally binding for all members of the employers' associations and the unions, are thus equivalent to legal regulations. In the early 1980s labor relations in the economic sectors, which employed about 90 percent of West German workers and employees, were governed by 43,000 collective bargaining agreements. Such agreements typically apply uniformly to union and nonunion members alike (*Der Spiegel*, April 1, 1985, p. 106). Collective agreements are enforced by the labor courts just as much as labor laws.

Labor courts also mediate the daily conflicts in West Germany's industrial relations at the plant level. As discussed in Chapter 1 (see pp. 65–66), these courts embody the principle of tripartite representation. Business and labor together recruit professional judges who are joined by an equal number, either two or four, of lay judges who are selected in consultation with both unions and employers' associations. In their daily proceedings the courts tend to act as mediators that favor compromise between the parties rather than as judicial bodies that decide a legal case. Often the judges use the procedural tradition of West Germany's civil courts strategically to promote a settlement; about 40 percent of all cases in the lower courts are thus settled. This number is much higher in labor courts than in civil courts. Dismissals contested by works councils or individual employees are typically brought before labor courts. Sixty percent of the employees win their suits in the lower courts; in the three to five years that a normal appeals procedure takes, they cannot be dismissed. In about 95 percent of all the cases brought before West German labor courts, employees are the plaintiffs. An analysis of the system of labor courts in West Berlin found the litigation rate of employees from small firms, which often lack effective works councils, to be five times higher than that of employees from big firms. Claims for payment tend to be more frequent with workers in small firms, while claims against dismissal are brought more often by employees of large firms (Blankenburg, Rogowski, and Schönholz 1978, pp. 5, 16, 21). As is true for West Germany's system of coalition politics, the deep involvement of the judiciary in the policy process encourages incremental policy change.

Consequences

Foreigners and West Germans alike have viewed codetermination as an innovative tool for managing the tensions of a capitalist economy. Abraham Shuchman concluded (1957, p. 244) that codetermination could "mark for the peoples of the world a new course between capitalism and collectivism that leads to a more rational and more just social order." In an early, empirical investigation of the effects of codetermination, William McPherson concluded (1955) that it had created trust and contributed to a consensus style of decisionmaking in West Germany's large corporations. Berthold Beitz, for more than two decades the managing director of Krupp, one of West Germany's largest corporations, was in the 1960s quoted as saying that if codetermination had not been legislated in 1951–52, West German business would have had to invent it. And Philip Rosenthal, a prominent businessman and SPD politician, has described codetermination as " 'a third way', a middle course between unlimited capitalism and bureaucratic communism" (Helm, 1984, p. 1). This middle course has elicited both admiration and criticism from abroad. The EC, for example, present the West German system as a model when suggesting political rearrangements to their member states. On the other hand, during the first Bundestag hearings on the revision of the codetermination bill in 1974, the U.S. Chamber of Commerce charged that the proposed bill infringed on the principle of private property and thus violated the German-American Friendship and Trade Treaty of 1954 (Embassy, 1974; Solyom-Fekete, 1976, pp. 107–31). What these diverging assessments point up is the distinctiveness of the system of industrial relations which has evolved in the Federal Republic.

The political conflicts of the last forty years have left the industrial relations of the Federal Republic with six different forms of workers participation. Table 3-1 shows that in the 1970s only 3.4 million of West Germany's 22.0 million workers had no participation rights whatever, while only 600,000 workers in the coal and steel industries enjoyed the codetermination that West Germany's labor movement regards as satisfactory. Judging by these figures, codetermination has evolved gradually as a series of compromises that, without satisfying fully either business or labor, have left the overwhelming majority of West Germany's

TABLE 3-1   Existing West German Codetermination Legislation

Year	Law	Applies to	Employees covered (in millions)
1951	Montan Codetermination	Montan Industry firms, with more than 1000 employees	0.6
1952	Enterprise Legislation component of Works Legislation Act	Small corporations and small limited liability companies with more than 500 but less than 2,000 employees	0.6
1954	Civil Servants Personnel representation	Federal, state, and municipal employees, including railroad, workers, postal workers, etc.	3.6
1972	Works council component of Works Legislation Act	All German firms with at least 5 employees	9.3
1976	Codetermination Law (*Mitbestimmungsgesetz*)	Corporations and limited liability companies with more than 2,000 employees that are not included in the Montan industry	4.5
	No works council law	Small firms with less than 5 employees	3.4

Source: Alfred L. Thimm, "How Far Should German Codetermination Go?" *Challenge* 11 (July–August 1981), p. 17.

workers with substantial rights to participation. A number of studies have shown that among small firms, in politically conservative states and in the service sector the number of firms with effective works councils that operate independently of management is well below the almost total compliance of the large manufacturing firms with the law. Most observers agree, however, that the high rate of participation among the large manufacturers contributes significantly to the peacefulness of West German industrial relations. Yet unions and employers do occasionally engage in strikes and lock-outs, as they did for example in 1963, 1978, and 1984. Furthermore, strikes and lock-outs increased during the 1970s. But even given the substantial legal barriers that constrain industrial militancy, the West German strike rate has been low throughout the postwar period. Between 1968 and 1978, for example, the number of work days lost due to strikes per 1,000 workers was 545 in the United

States, 446 in Britain, 191 in France, 139 in Japan, and only 49 in West Germany (Wilson, 1982, p. 49).

Specialists evaluating the effects that codetermination has had on West Germany's economic and political life reach more differentiated judgments. In an early assessment Werner Blumenthal concluded (1956) that decisionmaking in practice did not conform to the 1951 legislation. Instead of codetermining issues, labor was dominant on questions of wages and working conditions while management exercised unilateral authority on most other matters. "On balance codetermination in the steel companies proved to be much less radical than expected" (p. 110). Michael Fogarty, underlining the positive aspects of codetermination in iron and steel, emphasized (1965, pp. 133–52) that relatively few firms provided a network of information between employer and employee, created multiple balances of power, and gave the supervisory board an important role. The most comprehensive empirical analysis, the Biedenkopf Report of 1970, arrived at essentially similar conclusions while also noting some partial failures of codetermination (see Reading 3-1) (Hartmann, 1975, pp. 56–58; Mitbestimmungskommission, 1970). The commission concluded in a long and detailed report that codetermination had a greater effect on pacifying labor than in instilling a sense of participation in employees, and that while satisfying the unions it had not interfered with either the economic efficiency or the technical efficiency of firms.

On the other hand, Wilpert in his review (1975) of major studies points to the negative side effects of the double loyalties of employee representatives and the high level of satisfaction among workers with the institution of codetermination in the abstract as opposed to the much lower levels of actual satisfaction with the practice of codetermination. Writing in 1984 Helm reviews (pp. 5–8) more recent studies but agrees with Wilpert that little is known about the broader consequences of codetermination. A research team of the DGB, on the other hand, in a comprehensive empirical analysis of the effects of the 1976 legislation, concluded that the senior white-collar employees elected against the wishes of the unions as representatives of employees had shown themselves "surprisingly cooperative." Furthermore, the appointment of workers' directors on the managing board "surprisingly led relatively infrequently to open conflict" (Bamberg et al., 1984, pp. 238, 245). The union researchers suggest the lack of true parity representation as one possible reason for the unexpected recent consensus in areas so hotly contested before the adoption of the bill in 1976. Yet employee representation on supervisory boards reinforces the position of the works councils and the unions.

In a searching and comprehensive analysis of the effects of thirty years of codetermination, Wolfgang Streeck (1984) has drawn two important conclusions. First, codetermination both on the supervisory board and in the works council is interrelated and has strengthened the position of the unions both in the enterprise and in West Germany's political economy. Legislation has forced a coalition favoring economic productivity. "This constellation has frequently been described as 'integration' or 'co-optation' of labour, or organized labour, in management; with the same justification, it can be seen as 'colonisation' of management, and in particular manpower management, by the representatives of the workforce. The most adequate metaphor would probably be that of a mutual incorporation of capital and labour by which labour internalises the interests of capital just as capital internalizes those of labour" (Streeck, 1984, p. 416).

Second, Streeck concludes (1984, pp. 391, 411–13) that codetermination has changed the way in which employers utilize labor. This change has been accompanied by a partial takeover of managerial responsibilities by representatives of the workforce, which in turn has reinforced the vested interest of workers in a cooperative social partnership with management in the enterprise. In fact, codetermination, especially parity codetermination, has tended to make labor rather similar to capital, a fixed rather than a variable factor of production. Although numerous other factors have also limited the variability of employment, codetermination has offered employers incentives to alter the structure and performance of management in order to deal with the adverse effects of declining flexibility on economic efficiency. Manpower management has become a vital issue, and the board of directors in codetermined enterprises is generally speaking under constant pressure to provide information and to explain its decisions. Furthermore, the works council in particular has assumed de facto comanagement responsibilities that go beyond its preferred area of personnel.

Since they were shaped by incremental changes, the stabilizing effects that the institutions of West German industrial relations have had on other policy sectors cannot be overestimated (see Reading 3-4). For much of the postwar period West Germany's economic policy has focused on containing the conflicts between business and labor which are endemic to a capitalist economy. Between the mid-1950s and mid-1970s social welfare presumed a well-functioning industrial relations system that would facilitate the training and retraining of West German workers. West Germany's policy with respect to migrant labor would have been very different had business and labor not been enmeshed in relatively collaborative arrangements. These arrangements are not due primarily to an enduring German culture favoring consensus. Moreover, as this chapter has amply illustrated, they have not superceded political and economic conflicts that are unavoidable in democratic, capitalist regimes. Instead, collaborative arrangements derive from the specific institutional features of West German industrial relations which shape the diverging strategies of business and labor and thus harness conflict.

One of the great challenges for the future derives from the past success of codetermination. Precisely because it creates a privileged labor force with relatively secure jobs and strong rights, it tends to widen the gap between the core and less privileged workers: the young, the old, female, and part-time workers. Political demands for work-sharing and a shorter workweek derive from the tension between a secure labor force often working overtime, and a shrinking number of jobs and increasing unemployment in the overall economy. Codetermination and especially the system of works councils make the ground in West Germany potentially more fertile for the kind of enterprise unionism that can be found in Japan and in the United States (Jacobi *et al.*, 1986; Shigeyoshi and Bergmann, 1984). The challenge for the West German union movement will be to counteract the growing strength of enterprise egoism with new issues that recreate more solidaristic and collective conceptions of interest. Ironically, it was such collective conceptions that brought about the system of codetermination in the first place (see Reading 3-8).

On this point West Germany's industrial relations both reflect and reinforce the structure of politics at large. Political collaboration results from the intersection of objectives that proved reconcilable, though they were distinctly different, and decisionmaking processes that relied on several institutional mechanisms to diffuse conflict. The incrementalism imposed by West Germany's system of coalition governments, as the political battle of the 1970s showed, is one important mechanism. The tendency to rely on legal settlements of industrial disputes is a second. Finally, codetermination with its different meanings and effects at the shop floor and in the boardroom itself also resembles the parapublic arrangements that are so typical of West German policy and politics.

Readings

3-1. THE COMMISSION ON CODETERMINATION*

The Commission on Codetermination was charged in the late 1960s to take stock of the effects of codetermination and to make recommendations for any future modification or extension of codetermination. As the following selections illustrate, the commission's authoritative report came to positive though cautiously worded conclusions. The report provided the basis for the redrafting of the Works Council Law (1972) and for the revision of the Codetermination Bill (1976).

The Commission bases its recommendations on the co-determination of employees in the undertaking on the assumption that co-determination by employees in the undertaking's governing bodies is not only politically requisite and historically appropriate but is a factual necessity. . . .

The Commission further considers that an important task of co-determination is the institution of compulsory coordination between employer and employee and the introduction of compulsory deliberation and discussion. The creation of compulsory deliberation of this kind and the associated duties of justification to employees is held by the Commission to be necessary. . . . Continued development of social and economic co-determination by employees through institutional co-determination in the undertaking consequently and for these reasons appears to the Commission to be imperative.

The Commission expects that co-determination by employees in the undertaking will have not only these effects but will, in particular, im-

*Anglo German Foundation for the Study of Industrial Society, translation of *Co-Determination in the Enterprise: Report of the Commission of Experts on the Experience Gained so far with Co-Determination (Commission on Co-Determination)*, BT VI/334 (Bochum, January 1970) (selections).

prove information and communication. The hearings before the Commission have shown that an improvement of internal communication systems and the informing of employees on all corporate decisions affecting their work and their economic fate by the earliest possible date is of particular importance. Both the representatives of employees and members of corporate management expressed the unanimous view at the Commission's hearings that an optimization in the flow of information and communication within the undertaking was one of the chief tasks of co-determination. . . .

The compulsion, founded on co-determination, to cooperate and consequently to take attitudes and interests other than the immediately parochial into account alters persons' procedures of thought and behavior and therefore also has both socio-political effects. Entrepreneurs and owners of capital learn to regard the employees' representatives as partners whose concerns are as legitimate as their own. Employees and their trade union representatives experience the economic necessities underlying the undertaking in the market and must now in certain circumstances take joint responsibility for decisions that affect themselves for the worse.

It is obvious that the change in lines of thought and behavior set in motion hereby will effect social and political life throughout. These effects are regarded positively by the Commission. . . .

It is obvious that the inclusion of additional motivators and decision-makers within the undertaking's policy-making process cannot fail to effect the operation of the decision-making process. The dismantling of hierarchical authoritarian relationships in favour of a cooperative corporate management may lead to a temporal lengthening of the policy-making process as will the need for compromise arising from the consideration of additional objectives. Institutional co-determination by employees within the undertaking therefore necessarily means that decision-making processes on important matters will require more time than would be the case without the application of additional, complementary, but also more divergent aspects.

The Commission does not share the view that such an extension of the decision-making process by including additional aspects in the content of discussion and by the need for institutional discussion and justification, will mean necessarily a delay in decision in terms of rational corporate behaviour. At the hearings, the contrary impression was obtained that the inclusion of new aspects through co-determination and, in particular, the need for detailed justification of important decisions, will in many cases contribute to an improvement in the substance of decisions. Co-determination will have the same effect, in the Commission's opinion, if the need for justification and the further aspects as regarding preparation for the decision have already been anticipated, so that delay in the decision-making process may in this way be avoided. The Commission therefore sees no disadvantage in principle in co-determination in the extension of the decision-making process occasioned by it. . . .

The formation of groups by employee representatives—as indeed by shareholder representatives—on the supervisory board of undertakings in the coal and steel industries where co-determination applies shows that the representatives of both sides on the supervisory board see a duality of interests in their functions irrespective of the common orientation towards the interests of the undertaking. The Commission has become aware of only few cases in which individual representatives of the employees (or the shareholders) have declined the "group whip" and have consequently prevented uniform voting by the group. . . .

Even though the Commission takes the view in principle that there is a duality of interests, it does so in the sense that it sees a putting forward of employee interests and aspects as the primary function of employee representatives that justifies co-determination. This must be regarded as the principal motivation of employee representatives. The putting forward of further aspects in discussion and decision and the safeguarding of the undertaking's interests by employee representatives is desirable and lies within the scope of the tasks of employee representatives as members of a governing body of the undertaking. This is not, however, the actual reason for the introduction and development of institutional co-determination. . . .

The Commission's hearings have indicated that employee representatives on the supervisory board predominantly put forward employee interests in such a way that they control the initiatives of the corporate management as to adequate consideration for employee interests. On the other hand, there are relatively few cases where employee representatives have themselves initiated corporate action, i.e., where new kinds of initiative have been introduced into the undertaking's decision-making process through co-determination. . . .

The question of so-called remote control of employee representatives played an important part in the discussions on the extension of co-determination, in connection with the effects of co-determination on the decision-making process in the undertaking. The Commission by remote control means the attempt to influence the autonomous behaviour of the undertaking through external influence on or control of individual members of the corporate governing bodies, particularly the supervisory board. The fears that were voiced in this connection were not confirmed in the course of the Commission's hearings. The Commission therefore considers it necessary to state that the suspicion of remote control expressed against co-determination by employees did not appear to the Commission as founded on fact. . . .

The Commission's hearings, finally, gave no cause for believing that the trade unions wished to develop an independent economic policy with the aid of employee representation on the supervisory boards and to realize this by means of co-determination. There is no evidence that co-determination has so far been regarded by trade unions as a means for the central control of economic processes. The Commission considers it impossible, therefore, that institutional co-determination could be used as an instrument of central control if it is statutorily governed in accordance with the recommendations made by it. . . .

One of the main tasks of the supervisory board is to resolve on the attribution of profits proposed by the board of management. As already stated, it appeared from the Commission's hearings, that the employee representatives on the supervisory board regularly vote along with the corporate management on decisions regarding investment projects and profit distribution. The Commission learned of no case where employee representatives have refused to consent to investment projects or to the distribution of profit, e.g., with the argument that available funds should instead be used for giving benefits to the workforce.

This extensive concordance between corporate management and employee representatives on the supervisory board in dealing with investments corresponds, at least in times of full employment, with the natural interests of employees. Investments serve in the eyes of employees to strengthen the undertaking and therefore to secure jobs. . . .

As experience with co-determination in the coal and steel industries shows, discussion of wage and labour conditions by members of the supervisory board is avoided in the board as these fall within the scope of collective bargaining. On the other hand, works labour [sic] conditions, particularly social facilities, are a matter for discussion on the supervisory board. . . .

The trade unions in the coal and steel industries have so far as a rule, sought only to exercise influence on the appointment of the labour director and not, in fact, upon the composition of the rest of the board of directors. Within the scope of the Works Constitution Act, employee representatives on the supervisory board, as far as the Commission was able to determine, had hardly even come forward with firm proposals. It is, however, quite possible and from the experience of the hearings, only to be expected, that the practical personnel policy of the employee organizations will alter in the future, and much will depend on the extent to which they are in any position to nominate suitable candidates. . . .

Summary of Recommendations

In order to achieve the institutional co-determination of employees in a business, having regard to the conditions imposed by (arising from) the lawful practices special to that business and to the market, the Commission recommends as fundamental the following organizational provisions and statutory regulations:

1.   *Supervisory Board*
1.1 A relative increase in the number of the representatives of the employees on the Supervisory Board of those businesses in which until now the employees' representatives have held one third of the seats, at the same time retaining the preponderance in numbers of the representatives of the shareholders, small though it may be.
1.2 The election by the personnel of the business of all the representatives of the employees, including those employees' representatives from outside the business as will be provided for in the Bill; the right of nominating employees' representatives from outside the business shall however fall to the trade unions represented in that business. . . .

2.   *Management and Workers' Council*
2.1 The representation, laid down by law, in the Management of the personnel side, through a member of the Management appointed for this purpose; his appointment shall be according to the procedure for any other member of the Management (personnel management).
2.2 The formation, laid down by law, of a Joint Workers' Council or

of an employees' representative body with analogous functions in all businesses. . . .

5.   *Application of the recommendation*

5.1   The recommendations should apply to businesses with at least 1,000 to 2,000 employees. Some members of the Commission consider 2,000 to be the significant figure as lower limit. In businesses with fewer employees the industrial law in its present form should continue to operate; in saying this the Commission does not however wish to express any objection to amendments of the industrial law in fields not covered by their recommendations.

3-2. THE WORKS COUNCILS ACT OF 1972*

This selection gives an overview of some of the most important provisions contained in the revised Works Council Law of 1972.

The new Act differs in the following essential points from the Labor Management Relations Act [of] 1952. . . .

The rights of codetermination and cooperation of the works council have been considerably enlarged. This applies specially to social matters, individual personnel measures (Art. 99), measures of vocational training (Art. 98), dismissals (Art. 102), changes of the working place (Art. 91), and the social consequences of changes at the works [plants] (Articles 111 and 112). This extension of the rights of codetermination is strengthened by the possibility of more frequent application to the conciliation board as mandatory arbitration (compare no. 4), and by changes of the burdens of pleading and proof to the detriment of the employer.

The unions represented in the works or, in some cases, in the works council, are the subjects of an expanded catalogue of powers and duties. They may intercede if an election committee is not appointed on time, or if it does not act without delay, or if in a works there is no works council at all. . . . They may also force the works council to convene works assemblies if the works council does not comply with its duty to

---

*Martin Peltzer, *The German Labor Management Relations Act* (London: MacDonald and Evans, 1972), pp. 11–19.

do so (Art. 43[4]). In this respect, the unions have what one can refer to as police functions within this Act.

The position of the unions is further strengthened by the fact that now also a group-majority (the law refers to wage earning and salaried employees as "groups"—see Art. 6) within the works council may demand that a representative of a union represented in the works council be allowed to attend the meetings of the works council. . . . Finally, the law stipulates that nobody who assumes duties within the scope of this act will be restricted in his activities ". . . for their union in the works. . . ." The inclusion of questions of collective labor bargaining, social politics and economics—provided they pertain directly to the works and its employees—among the topics which may be dealt with in the works assemblies, where the representatives of the unions may attend, leads to an indirect strengthening of the unions [sic] position. . . .

The employer (respectively the entrepreneur) has a multitude of new or extended—general or specific—informational duties. . . .

—The employer shall give information at a works assembly concerning the personnel and social matters and the economic situation of the works at least once a year (Art. 43[2]); the same applies to the entrepreneur in the assembly of the works council members (Art. 53[2], no. 2).

—The entrepreneur will inform the economic council in good time and extensively about the economic matters of the enterprise.

—The entrepreneur shall, at least once every calendar quarter, after having consulted the economic committee (in case of smaller enterprises, after having consulted the works council), inform the employees in writing (in case of smaller enterprises, oral information is permissible) about the economic situation and development of the enterprise.

In addition to this, numerous informational duties towards the works council exist in special cases. . . .

The law creates such an abundance of new powers and such possibilities of enforcing them that, in case of extreme and unreasonable use, the freedom of action and disposition so necessary for entrepreneurial success, could be critically restricted. One must therefore trust that the works councils, out of their detailed knowledge of the needs of the works, shall make use of their rights according to the intention expressed in Art. 2 ". . . in the best interest of the employees and the works."

3-3. CODETERMINATION LAW OF 1976*

This brief excerpt contains some of the crucial passages of the most hotly contested domestic legislation of the 1970s.

1. Undertakings Covered
(1) Subject to the provisions of this Act, workers shall have a right of co-determination in undertakings which:
1. are run in the legal form of a joint-stock company, a company with limited partners holding share capital, a limited liability company, an incorporated cost-book company under mining law or a co-operative; and
2. normally employ over 2,000 workers. . . .
7. Membership of Supervisory Boards
(1) The supervisory board of an undertaking:
1. normally employing not more than 10,000 workers shall consist of six shareholders' members and six workers' members;
2. normally employing more than 10,000 but not more than 20,000 workers shall consist of eight shareholders' members and eight workers' members;
3. normally employing more than 20,000 workers shall consist of ten shareholders' members and ten workers' members. . . .
(2) The workers' members of a supervisory board must include:
1. four workers of the undertaking and two trade union representatives, where the board has six workers' members;
2. six workers of the undertaking and two trade union representatives, where the board has eight workers' members;
3. seven workers of the undertaking and three trade union representatives, where the board has ten workers' members. . . .
27. Chairmanship of Supervisory Boards
(1) The supervisory board shall elect a chairman and vice-chairman from among its own number by a majority of two-thirds of the total number of members of which it is required to be composed.
(2) Where the requisite majority under subsection (1) is not attained during the election of the chairman or vice-chairman of the supervisory board, a second vote shall be taken. In this vote the shareholders' mem-

---

*Carl-Christoph Schweitzer et al., eds. *Politics and Government in the Federal Republic of Germany: Basic Documents* (Leamington Spa: Berg, 1984), pp. 275–76.

bers of the supervisory board shall elect the chairman and the workers' members shall elect the vice-chairman, in each case by a majority of the votes cast. . . .

29. Voting

(1) The decisions of the supervisory board shall be taken by a majority of the votes cast. . . .

(2) Where voting in the supervisory board results in a tie and a further vote on the same subject also results in a tie, the chairman of the board shall have a casting vote. . . . The vice-chairman shall not have a casting vote.

3-4. CHANCELLOR SCHMIDT ON THE STABILITY OF WEST GERMANY*

I am often surprised at how many people outside of the Federal Republic of Germany comment on the social and political stability of our country. I believe this social peace is primarily an achievement of our well-developed system of social security, combined with the principle of autonomy under which the labor unions and employers' associations are allowed to pursue their interests and negotiate their differences.

Under our legal system, social policy is accorded the same importance as economic and fiscal policy. . . . Another important element in this system of social peace is the humanization of work conditions. Here, too, new legislative foundations have been laid, covering both job security and more "human-oriented" working conditions.

The entire process of setting wages and salaries is the exclusive responsibility of collective bargaining partners. The Government and Parliament would not even dream of changing this. In our experience, there exists no better solution.

The recurrent rounds of collective bargaining result in continuous cooperation between the unions and the employers' associations. Aside from their encounters at the bargaining table, top-level organizations of both sides meet frequently to discuss related problems of mutual concern, such as arbitration procedures for labor disputes, or other points of contention. Economic and social policy, too, is a topic at these talks which, incidentally, always receive considerable public attention.

*Helmut Schmidt, "The Social and Political Stability of West Germany," *New York Times*, May 22, 1976, p. 23.

One result of this ongoing dialogue has been a low incidence of strikes. In 1973, for example, only 26 work days per 1,000 workers were lost because of strikes or lockouts—and only three in 1972. Statistics show that this is a mere fraction of the work days lost in other industrialized countries. . . .

An important forum for a clearing of interests is the participation of labor and management is the so-called "concerted action conferences." Under the chairmanship of the Federal Minister of Economics, these conferences deal with current economic issues. The "social policy meetings" of the Minister for Labor and Social Affairs fulfill a similar function in that sector.

The Government obtains the opinions of these two groups on all relevant legislation. Representatives of both labor and management are always present at Bundestag committee hearings on such bills.

A particular field of union interest is, as everywhere, always the plant, the office, or the factory itself. Since 1952, the so-called Works Constitution Act gives the union leadership extensive rights to co-determination, participation, consultation and information.

Updated and improved in 1972, the act entitles the elected works councils to a voice in determining work rules, work schedules, overtime, short shifts and vacations. The councils must also be heard on occupational safety programs, measures against job-related illnesses and preventive health care. The same is true for manner of payment, determination of piece-work rates and bonuses.

The council is informed about and heard on plans for new construction, renovation or expansion of production, administrative or technical facilities, introduction of new production technology or working methods, as well as plant closings. Last but not least, the works council must be informed about all plans affecting personnel.

The workers—and in the coal and steel industries the unions as well—elect representatives to the boards of directors of their firms.

In the coal and steel industries, a system of "parity" co-determination and co-responsibility on supervisory boards has been in effect since 1951. In addition, the member of the executive board responsible for labor affairs cannot be appointed against the will of the labor members of the board of directors.

In other industries, workers today elect one-third of the members of the boards of directors, a percentage considered inadequate by the labor unions.

I am profoundly convinced of the fundamental social and political necessity of broad co-determination. Therefore the coalition of Social Democrats and Free Democrats introduced legislation to this effect, which was adopted in the Bundestag on April 9. According to this bill, workers and employees will in the future elect one half of the board members of firms having more than 2,000 employees, with the other members to be chosen as before by the stockholders. In addition, these firms will be obliged to appoint a labor director as a full member of their executive board.

All these rights enjoyed by workers and their representatives give them a greater understanding of the workings of the firm or industry and of the effects of business decisions. This, I believe, creates a climate in which labor refrains from excessive demands and generally asks only for what is reasonable. This belief has been repeatedly confirmed by experience, especially in the difficult year of 1975. And when looking ahead toward labor negotiations of 1976, too, union leaders unequivocally stated that their demands would once again be guided by the productive capacity of our economy.

3-5. INTERVIEW WITH THE LEADER OF THE WEST GERMAN TRADE UNION MOVEMENT, HEINZ VETTER*

In the summer of 1977 a group of employers associations and firms filed a lawsuit challenging the constitutionality of the 1976 Codetermination Law. In response to what they saw as a fundamental break with West Germany's system of social partnership, the unions decided to discontinue their participation in West Germany's incomes policy (see Chapter 2). This selection gives excerpts from an interview with the president of the DGB explaining the stance of the unions.

Spiegel: Mr. Vetter, for the first time since its inception the unions have stayed away from the Concerted Action. Is this a signal to the government and the employers that you are now taking a tougher stance?
Vetter: In the last twelve months we have seen two contradictory developments. On the one hand under the pressure of unemployment we have

---

*"Dann brennt das Feuerchen lichterloh: DGB-Chef Heinz Oskar Vetter über Mitbestimmungsklage, sozialen Frieden und Arbeitslose," *Der Spiegel,* July 11, 1977, pp. 21–23.

tried, at least on this problem, to cooperate closely with the federal government in Bonn and with business. On the other hand, however, the old straw men were once again set up—wage-price spiral, the dictatorship of union functionaries, union state, wage-unemployment spiral. It was like a flight of stairs . . .

Spiegel: . . . whose top step is the lawsuit that business has filed with the Federal Constitutional Court challenging the constitutionality of codetermination?

Vetter: This lawsuit is a climax of the escalation. It is only natural that many of our members are asking themselves: Why should we be the butt of these ceaseless attacks?

Spiegel: What can you do? The employers associations cannot withdraw the suit—simply on account of their own followers.

Vetter: Actually why not? Their rank and file has not yet fully realized the new stakes. The information campaign of the unions for our members has just begun. After all our members should know about the danger zone in which we are now moving. At the same time we shall tell the public about our fears. The employers could then do something they have never done before. They could say, yes, we are living in a time in which we have to prove that our system can solve the serious problems. And that can happen only in cooperation with the unions. The employers could say we shall seek our rights later, if, indeed, they are infringed upon, in normal civil court proceedings.

Spiegel: And if, as appears likely, that doesn't happen, if the employers' constitutional case takes it course?

Vetter: Then we must make it clear that the employers are heading in a direction that opens the gates to tremendous social and political strife. Even if afterward they swear up and down that they hadn't wanted it to happen this way.

Spiegel: How is that?

Vetter: Because this court action endangers the social peace to which we must credit our unparalleled advancement since 1945. Because with this lawsuit codetermination itself may begin to cave in.

Spiegel: You mean the concept as it has been practiced in the coal and steel industries during the last twenty-five years?

Vetter: We wanted the exceedingly successful codetermination in the coal and steel industries extended to all large firms. The reason is simple. We have the best steel industry in Europe. And we have solved successfully the problems of the Ruhr mining industry caused by collapse of the demand for coal. Under our proposal the supervisory board would be composed equally by members representing employers and the employees; and the neutral member, picked jointly by both sides, would have the deciding vote on the second ballot. But the FDP killed our proposal. That is the reason why we got a completely different co-determination bill, a bill that for us doesn't deserve its name. It is not codetermination if in the final decision the other side maintains superiority and can use the additional vote of its chairperson in its favor on the second ballot. In addition we find the voting procedures for the supervisory board objectionable. White-collar personnel in managerial positions are represented independently from the union slate. But all that wasn't enough. Now comes the employers' court case about questions whose answers have all been clearly laid out by the legislation. Why this court case? That's what we keep asking about.

Spiegel: Are you afraid that there is more behind this lawsuit, perhaps an attempt to roll back the gains that the labor movement has made over the years?

Vetter: That danger exists. You can say what you will. By filing this lawsuit the employers have tied their own hands. If the Federal Constitutional Court reaches a decision in two years, the employers may well wring their hands and say that they hadn't wanted things to turn out this way. They may well insist that they favor codetermination in principle.

Spiegel: Do you expect that the judges in Karlsruhe could declare portions of the law unconstitutional?

Vetter: No, but that is not really necessary. It is enough if they write: this law barely conforms with the Basic Law.

3-6. SUMMARY OF THE OPINION OF THE FEDERAL CONSTITUTIONAL COURT OF MARCH 1, 1979*

In 1977 a group of employers' associations and firms filed a suit with the Federal Constitutional Court challenging the constitutionality of the 1976 Codetermination Bill. In late fall 1978 the court heard for four days from more than 130 witnesses, including the leaders of the employers' association, the trade unions, and several members of the cabinet. This excerpt summarizes the court's decision against the employers.

*Herbert Wiedemann, "Codetermination by Workers in German Enterpises," American Journal of Comparative Law (Winter 1980), pp. 88–92 (selections).

The decision of the Federal Constitutional Court is that the expanded codetermination introduced by the Codetermination Act does not encroach upon the basic constitutional rights of the affected corporations, shareholders or employer organizations.

1. The decision concerns itself only with those provisions of the Codetermination Law which are here called into question and scrutinized as to their constitutionality. The question as to whether other rules regulating employee codetermination would be constitutional is specifically left open.

a) The opinion reaches first the basic question of the extent of employee influence established by the law. This is not, in law or in actual operation, a parity situation. Given the second vote of the chairman of the supervisory board, who is normally chosen by the stockholders, as well as the non-homogeneous composition of the employee representatives, chosen separately by the workers, salaried employees and executive employees, we cannot term this parity. This is also true with respect to the codetermination rights of the workers councils. The basic assumption of the complainants is that under cover of an underparity rule, a situation of partial parity and partial overparity is hidden. Furthermore, it is alleged, this is what the legislature actually aimed at, or at least wanted to allow. These assertions have no validity. It does not appear to us that, on the one hand, the objective contents of the statute, which are controlling for purposes of constitutional scrutiny and, on the other, the actual effect of the rules, are incompatible. . . .

c) The Federal Constitutional Court has confirmed its previous position on the question [of] whether the provisions of the Codetermination Law being examined here, when regarded as the reasonable prognosis of the legislature, are compatible with the constitution. . . . The Basic Law does not prescribe or guarantee a particular economic order or a concrete constitutional basis for the fashioning of economic life. Rather, it leaves ordering the economy to the legislature, which is free to choose such an order [from] within the parameters set by the Basic Law. Such actions require no further legitimation. This legislative discretion may not be limited in the name of an interpretation of basic principles any more than is demanded by individual basic constitutional rights. . . .

2. This opinion concludes that sections 7, 27, 29 and 31 of the Codetermination Law are compatible with the Basic Law.

a) The statute's provisions do not infringe upon the property of the shareholders, or upon that of the enterprise. . . . It is true that the legal rights of the shareholders are reduced by the law though not "halved," since the shareholders retain a determining influence in the enterprise. However, these limitations must be considered within the context of the social nature of property, which varies according to the degree to which the particular property has a social impact and a social function. The personal aspect of the rights of the shareholders are not generally affected by the Codetermination Law. On the other hand, these rights do possess a far-reaching social aspect and an important social function, especially since collaboration of the employees is always required in utilizing the property of the shareholders. The basic rights of the employees are thus affected. To the extent that any questions arise concerning the property of the corporations which own enterprises affected by the law, we may not go beyond the prognosis of the legislature and assume that broadened codetermination would prevent the enterprises from functioning, or will result in a situation approximating functional incapacity. If changing the organization and the process of decision-making on the supervisory board of the corporation in fact causes any difficulties, these must be considered within the context of the more social nature of the property of large corporations.

b) The basic right of freedom of association is likewise not infringed. It already appears doubtful whether the focus and content of Art. 9(1) of the Basic Law allow the application of this guarantee to large corporations. In these corporations, in contrast to those falling within the primary intended protective sphere of this basic freedom, the personal element is negligible. We leave open the question as to whether the regulations here attacked infringe upon Art. 9(1) of the Basic Law, should it be applicable to this situation. The regulations do not come into conflict with the principle of free association nor do they unconstitutionally infringe upon the functional capability of corporations. Likewise, they do not interfere to an impermissible degree with the right of corporations to control their internal organization and decision-making. Nothing is changed by the fact that there must be two or three union representatives among the supervisory board members chosen by the employees. This rule does not contradict corporate law in principle; nor is it inappropriate in this case, since this makes it easier for the employees to enjoy highly qualified representation. This will help to prevent or at least dilute the "enterprise egoism" expected in the wake of expanded codetermination.

3-7. CODETERMINATION AND MANNESMANN*

The conflict between SPD and FDP over codetermination exploded once again shortly before the federal election of 1980. Legal maneuvering by West Germany's largest pipe manufacturer, Mannesmann, was aimed at exempting the company from coverage by the stringent 1951 Codetermination Act and moving it under the less far-reaching 1976 Act. Pressure in the SPD for passage of a special law was very strong. Chancellor Schmidt, who wrote the following memorandum, succeeded eventually in convincing his party of the futility of a strategy of conflict escalation. Instead the dynamics between his coalition government and the FDP required a strategy favoring delay and eventual compromise. The memorandum was leaked and published in a West German weekly which sets the context in the first paragraph below before excerpting Schmidt's memo.

With a thirteen-page memorandum Chancellor Helmut Schmidt has succeeded, as of Monday last week, in persuading the SPD parliamentary leadership to follow a course concerning codetermination different from that laid out by the SPD's Bundestag Whip Herbert Wehner. Before the Bundestag elections Wehner had convinced almost the entire party to sponsor a bill by means of which the concept of codetermination in the coal and steel industries in the Mannesmann Corporation could be preserved. Schmidt had first sent his position paper to Wehner and then circulated the document among a few parliamentary party leaders. The paper describes private conversations the chancellor had with Mannesmann executives and with the president of the metal workers union, Loderer. In the document Schmidt tears apart Wehner's conflict strategy and threatens to resign ("grave consequences will result for the federal chancellor"). Excerpts:

8 a) From the point of view of the FDP the so-called group-sponsored SPD bill was submitted without prior consultation within the coalition about either substance or procedure. From the perspective of the FDP this constitutes a serious violation of the tradition of cooperation between coalition partners. . . . The FDP's public rejection of this group-spon-

---

* "Knüppel hinter der Tür: Ein internes Papier von Helmut Schmidt zur Mitbestimmung bei Mannesmann," *Der Spiegel,* August 25, 1980, p. 26.

sored bill was preprogramed (and was indeed anticipated). Earlier this week FDP Minister Genscher expressed to the chancellor his serious concerns not only with regard to the effect this initiative might have on the election campaign in which the coalition partners will confront each other, but also on the prospects for a renewal of the coalition government. Moreover, Genscher mentioned the difficulties he anticipated in preventing group-sponsored bills by his own party should the coalition government be resumed. Minister Genscher's personal opinion was that we are moving to a growing test of strength between the two coalition partners, a test the severity of which probably no one imagined.

8 b) Dr. Kohl would have no difficulty achieving full agreement among members of his party for a special session of the Bundestag. After all the compromise suggestion made by Overbeck [the chief executive of Mannesmann] preserves, in the eyes of the employees' wing of the CDU, Adenauer's legacy.

8 c) As a result the SPD would find itself isolated in a special session of the Eighth Bundestag.

9) The coalition and particularly the federal cabinet will have to coordinate policy at the very latest when the expected contested Bundestag voting draws near. Until then members of the government will remain uncommitted. However, almost all SPD members of the cabinet signed the group-sponsored bill. With regard to the coming difficult domestic and foreign policy issues expected in the next legislative period I shall simply not put up with the fact that members of the government will vote against one another in open disagreement in the Bundestag. I do not want to leave the impression that the federal chancellor is unable to bring his cabinet into line. The federal chancellor might be compelled to prevent members of his government from participating in the Bundestag debate by means of his constitutionally guaranteed prerogative to determine the guidelines of policy. It is doubtful whether such a measure would succeed. If it failed, grave consequences will result for the federal chancellor.

10) The mood of the metal workers' union is not uniform. The two presidents Loderer and Maier are clearly more cautious than is Judith who is in charge of the steel industry. In the meantime the union has probably sensed that it could use more public support from other unions and the German Federation of Trade Unions. On the other hand, for the first time in ages this development could open up a field of operation for the executive board of the German Federation of Trade Unions and its

president. However, this development would not have only positive consequences for the leadership of the metal workers' union. . . .

12) Conclusions. (a) We have to create public pressure for possible solutions by means of carefully worked out objective arguments [*Sach-argumentation*]. Similarly we must create party and union pressure for possible solutions along the lines which the chancellor suggested originally in his conversations with Overbeck and Christians. (b) At the same time the door needs to stay open for the possibility of adopting Overbeck's proposal in modified form after negotiations between Mannesmann and the union on the one hand and between these two partners and the three Bundestag parties on the other. (c) In a small discussion group we need to decide whether and when in the course of future negotiations a private meeting with the relevant leaders might be advisable. The chancellor would participate if need be. However, some political demands notwithstanding, at the moment it appears to be premature for the chancellor to play the role of mediator.

3-8. WEST GERMAN UNIONS: AN ATYPICAL SUCCESS STORY*

Despite a bitter and prolonged strike in 1984, according to this article, West Germany's system of codetermination has protected the unions from the erosion of their political influence typical in other West European countries. Legal barriers that constrained union militancy in the 1960s and 1970s helped protect their influential position in hard times.

Karlheinz Weihs is a manual worker at the big Thyssen steel combine at Duisburg, just north of Düsseldorf in the Ruhr. But he is also the most important union member there, and under the West German system of co-determination, he sits on the company's supervisory board. His principle, he said as he sat in Thyssen's crisply modern office tower just across the street from the blast furnaces and rolling mills, is that "if you want to take part in decisions, then you also have to accept some of the responsibility." "Labor and management have different tasks," said Mr. Weihs, a stocky, hearty man in his 50's, "and so they have different

*R. W. Apple, Jr., "West German Unions: An Atypical Success Story," *New York Times*, January 21, 1985, p. A4.

opinions. Our negotiations are sometimes tough, but without work stoppages." ·

"I don't need to carry around a mental picture of management as the enemy," he said. "And we don't see our strategy as blocking roads and having street fights with the police in order to keep individual plants open. "Nor," he added, "do we see our role as getting every pfennig we can in wages in difficult times like the last couple of years. There is a German saying, 'Don't slaughter the cow you expect to milk the next morning.' Our members understand why they have had to take token pay increases, less than the rate of inflation, to help the company recover." Mr. Weihs's union is IG Metall, which represents not only the workers in the Ruhr steel factories but also those in the auto industry and in countless small machine shops and garages across West Germany. With 2.5 million members, it calls itself the largest single free labor union in the world, and unlike other unions in Western Europe it has lost relatively few of its members—about 200,000—and little of its economic and political clout. The West German labor-union movement is, in fact, probably the outstanding single exception to the systematic decline of such movements in Europe in the last decade. . . .

Hans Gert Wöllke, the Thyssen director responsible for industrial relations, says he worries about whether the country's industries can afford "quite so dense a social safety net" and six weeks' paid vacation for most workers. That it has managed it up until now, he said, is a tribute to "the fact that the German worker doesn't work very often, but when he does work, he works very, very hard"—and to the attitude of the unions, which he calls "most sensible, even if we do grumble."

To a visitor from Britain, where the wildcat strike and the slowdown are a key part of union tactics, the absence of such activity in West Germany is startling. By law, the West German unions are bound to insure that their members fulfill their contractual obligations. A complex system of worker councils, which exist at every level from the individual plant to huge conglomerates, is used to iron out disputes before they burst into flame. "It costs money, of course," Mr. Wöllke said. "Somebody from my staff meets with representatives of one of our councils almost every day. But the system is so successful that if it didn't exist, I would be out campaigning for the establishment of something like it. . . ."

Erwin Kristoffersen, head of the international department of the DGB, or Deutscher Gewerkschaftsbund, says he thinks the IG Metall strike has left a residue of bitterness that could poison the previously healthy relationships between labor and management in West Germany. "We have had very little class warfare here," he said, "but perhaps the idea of class struggle was always in the back of the employers' minds, and now they think they can assert it. It was visible in the initial unwillingness of the employers even to negotiate on a 35-hour week, and it shows up in some key people in Government. You can see it in all the Western countries to one extent or another, an unwillingness to take joint responsibility for unemployment, an eagerness to cut the net of social support just when we need it. We are not looking for, and certainly not hoping for, a new kind of class conflict here. We don't need it. But that sort of thing can be imposed from above, if people start behaving like robber barons." Still, that kind of development seems a long way off at Thyssen headquarters in Duisburg. Mr. Weihs says the time will soon come when workers will want to recoup some of the sacrifices they have made, now that the company has returned to profitability. Asked how he will react, Mr. Wöllke answers, "Our attitude will be positive, because we have to take into account the way in which the work force has helped."

4 Social Welfare

The concept of the welfare state is inextricably linked with German history. In a variety of ways social welfare had been provided before the Industrial Revolution, and compulsory unemployment insurance was legislated as late as 1927. But it was Bismarck's Germany that, first among all of the industrial states, passed national legislation in the 1880s insuring a small proportion of its population against sickness, accident, and old age. Bismarck's social policy was a highly charged political affair. Social welfare legislation was the carrot that accompanied the stick of antisocialist legislation. State officials hoped thus to blunt political agitation on behalf of the Social Democratic party and to win the support of a sizable segment of the working class. Subsequent, unintended developments similarly underline the political aspects of social policy: the successful move of leaders of the union movement into a decentralized system of health insurance funds in the early 1890s, the countermobilization of doctors and employers in the first decade of the twentieth century, stalemate and conflict in the Weimar Republic, and the Nazis' radical elimination of left-wing forces and centralization of power after 1933.

Since 1945 West Germany's social policy has been based on the premise that "both market economy and social policy are necessary if the overall aims of society are to be achieved" (Zacher, 1982, p. 367). Step-by-step reforms of West Germany's pension system in 1957, its system of social welfare in 1961, and its system of labor market administration in 1969 made it possible, at least for some time, to view West Germany's social policy as shaped by the logic of modernization rather than by policy and politics. But this view has lost some of its plausibility as a result of the economic crises of 1970s and the 1980s. Its plausibility is also undermined if we compare West Germany's experience with that of other countries. In contrast to liberal America and statist Japan, the two other leading powers among the industrialized countries, West Germany is distinguished by the generosity and comprehensiveness of its social welfare spending.

In 1979, for example, West Germans derived one-quarter of their disposable income from the institutions of the welfare state. Different, often overlapping groups of recipients of social benefits included 14.2 million parents receiving child support payments, 12.9 million elderly people receiving social security, 6.1 million living in subsidized housing, 2.3 million receiving veterans' benefits, 2.1 million living on welfare, and 1.5 receiving rent subsidies (Alber, 1984, p. 235; Schmidt, 1982). West Germany's social welfare system stresses preventive health care, accident prevention, training, retraining, and rehabilitation. Benefits are financed through earnings-related cash benefits once a contingency occurs. They equal about 60 to 100 percent of previous income, and most are adjusted regularly to take economic changes into account. Contributions are also related to income. They are assessed up to a certain ceiling of "insurable" income that falls short of total income. In 1984 the deductions amounted to about 35 percent of insurable earnings: 19 percent for old-age, survivor, and disability pensions; 12 percent for health insurance; and 5 percent for unemployment insurance and labor market assistance. The industrial accident insurance is financed through a levy imposed on employers alone. All other contributions are shared equally by employers and employees. West Germany's economic prowess is compatible with—indeed, it requires—a broad array of social policies.

Political patterns concerning social policy in West Germany resemble those concerning other issues. Decentralization characterizes the state's provision of many of its welfare payments and services. At the same time, the legal norms that regulate, for example, the disbursement of old-age pensions, are a unifying force. The centralization of West Germany's system of economic interest groups is reinforced by the presence of a number of groups not active on the broader stage of West German politics: for example, peak associations of physicians and municipalities. Coalition governments, cooperative federalism, and parapublic institutions are the three important nodes of an institutional network that has shaped the policies through which West Germany reformed its system of social security, welfare, and labor market administration between

1949 and 1969. And as I have shown in Chapter 1, in the 1970s this network also encouraged the adoption of a "concerted action" to contain spiraling health care costs. West Germany's response to sharply rising unemployment in the 1980s has not been to dismantle the welfare state but, rather, to calibrate its requirements with the economic climate of modest growth.

Context

Social policy in the industrial states can be viewed from two perspectives. As a response to the ravages of industrial capitalism, it seeks to protect individuals from some of the vicissitudes of unregulated market competition. And it is also a response to international competition, war, and revolution (Alber, 1982; Flora and Heidenheimer, 1981; Machtan, 1985; Mommsen, 1981; Rimlinger, 1971; Tennstedt, 1983; Zöllner, 1982). In Bismarck's Germany both perspectives on social policy appear to have converged. The social and political consolidation of the Second Empire at home went hand in hand with national self-assertion and imperialist expansion abroad. Of course, Germany's preindustrial legacy also had a substantial impact on the kind of social welfare state that an autocratic government conferred upon its subjects in the 1880s.

As had been true of Britain in earlier decades, liberalism in the 1840s and 1850s sought to distinguish the poor who could not provide for themselves from an emerging working class that could as long as it secured paying jobs (Tennstedt, 1981). Insurance against factory accidents and the uncertainties of old age thus became the hallmark not of a radical attack on the eradication of poverty but of a conservative policy of demarcating workers from "lower" social strata. These lower strata were left to the care of local governments, which administered welfare in a decentralized manner. In the 1870s only a few large municipalities organized a local welfare policy that aimed at providing benefits not only for the poor but for workers, and indeed all citizens. In addition to providing water, gas, electricity, and transportation, they set up communal dining halls, municipal nurseries, hospitals, clinics, and public housing programs. Compared to both the national, earnings-related insurance system for workers and local welfare for the poor, these initiatives are noteworthy precisely because they highlight a path that the German welfare state did not choose. With the exception of health insurance, German welfare policy has aimed at granting transfer payments to individuals rather than providing collective goods for social consumption.

Bismarck's legislation centralized prior social policies. It built on a series of laws such as the 1839 restrictions imposed on child labor, the 1845 reorganization of the Prussian guilds which contained some elements of social policy, and legislation passed in 1849 and 1854 that provided, respectively, for the establishment of company and local insurance funds (Tampke, 1981). In the 1850s and 1860s slightly less than half of Prussia's blue-collar workers enjoyed some minimum of protection. The Great Depression that started in 1873 reinforced Bismarck's conviction that liberal capitalism was causing a social disintegration that required positive state action (Tennstedt, 1981). His aim was no less than to reintegrate through a program of social legislation the mass of German workers whom Germany's rapid industrialization had uprooted.

To this end Bismarck sought to impose on workers a unified national system of insurance funds that would tie them to the state. In his approach, Bismarck agreed with academic socialists such as Gustav Schmoller rather than with the economic liberals who dominated the top echelons of the Prussian bureaucracy or the conservative aristocrats whose interests he sought to defend. Yet, politically the enactment of his program on the support of liberals and conservatives who thus were able to effect significant modifications in Bismarck's proposals. To prevent strengthening an already powerful executive, the liberal parties successfully slowed down Bismarck's program in favor of a decentralized system of insurance funds. Conservatives, on the other hand, restricted the scope of coverage by excluding poor agricultural workers and cottage industries and by restricting the new programs to Germany's politically volatile blue-collar workforce, which needed to be appeased.

Health insurance, introduced in 1884, was the first of Bismarck's social legislations (Tennstedt, 1976). Compared to Britain, which developed its comprehensive unemployment insurance system two years before its health insurance system, the forty years' lead time of Germany's health insurance over its unemployment insurance deserves special notice. That unions had made the greatest inroads in institutionalizing social services for the working class in the health sector illustrates the politically conservative impetus behind Bismarck's reform. Health insurance embodied the guiding principles that, with the exception of health care, have informed Germany's social welfare state ever since:

earnings-related compulsory contributions based on gross wages, entitlement to payments without means-testing, administration by parapublic insurance funds, and recourse to specialized administrative courts. The proportion of the workforce covered by health insurance doubled from 5 to 10 percent between 1880 and 1885 and increased to about 25 percent by the eve of World War I.

Because the new national system built on existing institutional foundations, the administrative organization of the parapublic insurance funds was complex. There were roughly twenty thousand insurance funds. Each municipality had a large number of occupationally specific insurance funds that gradually consolidated into the *Ortskrankenkassen*, insurance funds operating in each locality. Employers and workers often preferred the "supplementary funds" (*Hilfskassen*), which had existed on a voluntary basis for some time. The employers' preference was understandable since they did not have to contribute one-third of the costs of this private system of health insurance. Workers liked the superior benefits (a result of screening the health of prospective members) and the full political autonomy that the funds enjoyed. However, in the early 1880s German workers switched in large numbers to the *Ortskrankenkassen*. To attract workers away from the voluntary, union-dominated funds, Bismarck's legislation granted workers a two-thirds voting majority in the new health insurance funds. That the German labor movement would transform the funds so soon into a stronghold that provided it with political leverage over and access to the state bureaucracy was certainly unintended and unforeseen. The funds also were channels of upward mobility for the leaders of the trade union movement (Heidenheimer, 1980; Tennstedt, 1976).

The increasing centralization of health insurance into regional funds and the founding of a national peak association of local health insurance funds, dominated by the trade unions, prompted German doctors to organize in 1900. By 1913 about three-quarters of all licensed physicians were organized and expressed, at times with militant strikes, their preference for private market solutions in health care. The Imperial Insurance Code of 1911 also hoped to undermine the power of the compulsory health insurance funds. The code stipulated, for example, that the supplementary funds be used to organize the health insurance of white-collar employees, thus contributing to the stratification of Germany's blue- and white-collar workforce. The 1920s and 1930s witnessed a continuation of this political struggle, which increasingly favored the doctors. New government regulations adopted in 1931 amounted to a de facto abolishment of the principle of autonomous self-government by the funds and made the peak associations of physicians the central actor in the formulation of German health care policy. The Nazis' seizure of power in 1933 ratified this development. The Nazis fired the left-wing leadership and staff of the *Ortskrankenkassen* and replaced them with politically reliable party members. Furthermore, the Nazi regime finished centralizing the organizations of health insurance funds and physicians, established both as bodies of public law in 1937, and eliminated the funds once and for all from the provision of any medical services.

Only after three draft bills had been discussed did the Reichstag in 1885 pass workmen's compensation legislation. The final bill dropped the substantial government subsidies that Bismarck had proposed, and made employers' contributions responsible for underwriting the cost of this accident insurance scheme. The Imperial Insurance Office in Berlin and a large and growing number of occupational associations, united in 1885 as a national peak association, worked together quite effectively to develop plans for and enforce safer regulations for the workplace. Starting with accident-prone industries, such as coal mining, these regulations spread gradually throughout manufacturing and agriculture. Implementation was largely a matter of self-policing by the associations. During the 1920s and 1930s the system was further centralized and improved. Since workers' participation in the system of occupational associations had been outlawed as early as 1911, the effect of Nazi Germany on this insurance system was less noticeable than its effect on the health insurance funds.

Because his policy of wooing the German working class had evidently failed, by the time the legislation concerning invalidism and old-age pensions passed the Reichstag in 1889, Bismarck had lost interest in his social programs. Although old-age pensions were minimal, 15 million Germans were covered in 1908, compared to 13 and 24 million covered respectively by health insurance and workmen's compensation. For the benefit of white-collar employees, the Imperial Insurance Code of 1911 set up a system of invalidism and pension funds in order to create a distinct "private sector bureaucracy" to complement Germany's conservative civil service.

The millions of casualties that resulted from World War I greatly affected invalidism insurance. Between 1913 and 1924 the number of pensions for widows increased from 12,000 to 200,000; those for orphans increased from 40,000 to 1,300,000 (Tennstedt, 1976, p. 460). Urgent negotiations with the central government and its subordinate agencies led the regional insurance funds to create a peak association as early as 1919. Although payments improved quite substantially, by the end of the 1920s about 70 percent of the recipients of invalidism pensions were also on public welfare. This statistic illustrates the dramatic difference that existed between the "social security state" before 1945 and the institutionalization of a comprehensive "welfare state" after 1945. The old-age pension was affected by the postwar inflation more than by World War I itself. Its assets drastically diminished, the pension's financing depended largely on current contributions. As unemployment rose sharply in the Great Depression from 1929 on, the pension fund found itself confronting a growing deficit as revenues declined sharply. Selective cuts imposed by emergency decree in 1931 and a substantial consolidation of the fund's financial basis in 1932, which included the payment of government subsidies, preceded the Nazi seizure of power by only a few months. The Nazis used a large amount of the capital of the pension funds to pay for their rearmament program. They also sought to centralize and simplify the insurance system, with no more than mixed success.

The history of these three major programs illustrates the increasing role that the central government played in implementing policy (Heidenheimer, 1981a, pp. 286–87). By the time the 1927 unemployment insurance law had been adopted, self-administration had been largely robbed of its social content. As early as 1911 the Imperial Insurance Law in fact had created a uniform judicial structure for the entire insurance system, significantly constraining the administrative discretion of the health insurance funds, the most decentralized of the system's three pillars. Because it was administered by the municipalities, Germany's welfare system retained its decentralized structure (Leibfried and Tennstedt, 1985a, pp. 64–93). For a long time the level of poverty relief granted depended on local circumstances. Here too, though, central control began to be exerted albeit less strongly than in the insurance systems established in the 1880s. Voluntary agencies began to receive government subsidies for providing welfare services in 1924. The same year dates the first attempt of the central bureaucracy to establish a more uniform level of welfare. The state issued a set of guidelines, made compulsory for the first time by the Nazis in 1941, for the amount of welfare granted by different localities. But despite these incursions, the role of municipalities has remained central in the provision of welfare services.

Local governments were in fact the first to recognize that an efficient system of employment offices and, eventually, a system of unemployment insurance was the only way of containing the escalating costs of welfare which they had to shoulder alone (Faust, 1981, pp. 150–63; National Industrial Conference Board, 1932; Weisbrod, 1981, pp. 188–204). In the late nineteenth century more and more people began to recognize the intimate link between poverty and unemployment which the doctrines of economic liberalism had always denied. Local employment offices, both public and private, appeared with increasing frequency in the 1890s, although their presence was often bitterly contested. The fact that the unions demanded unemployment insurance simply reinforced the strong opposition of industry and agriculture and prompted the state to avoid so controversial an issue.

The Weimar Republic confronted the question of how to create an unemployment insurance fund only after the postwar inflation had been stabilized in 1923–24. But the unified, national insurance provided for by the Unemployment Act of 1927 was based on the faulty assumption that unemployment was cyclical rather than structural. The growing employment crisis demanded increasing government subsidies for unemployment. Such demands split the democratic Left from the democratic Right, then united in a coalition government. The proximate cause of the fall of the last parliamentary government before Hitler was a battle over whether or not to raise unemployment insurance contributions by half a percent. The Left argued for increased contributions, the Right for fewer benefits. Fundamentally, however, this split indicated the lack of a social consensus on whether unemployment was a social risk rooted in the structure of capitalism and thus to be covered by insurance, or an individual risk demanding a means-tested provision of welfare payments. From the passage of Bismarck's health insurance to this bitter struggle over the nature of unemployment in the waning years of the Weimar Republic, German social policy had thus always been an explosive political issue that both reflected and shaped the balance of power among the state, business, and labor.

Agenda

The institutions that characterize West Germany's semisovereign state have transformed this struggle and created instead an inclination for incremental policy change. The system of social partnership was institutionalized when the various insurance funds were reorganized along the lines of parity representation. Despite their strong opposition, the trade unions sacrificed the two-thirds majority that they had enjoyed in the self-administered health insurance funds before 1933; and the employers were willing to concede their monopoly over the accident insurance funds (von Ferber 1967; von Ferber and Kaufmann, 1977; Hockerts, 1980, pp. 131–46, 1981; Kaim-Caudle, 1973; Michalsky, 1985; Rimlinger, 1967; Tennstedt, 1976; Zacher, 1980). The political conflict over the distribution of power in the insurance funds was fought with intensity. After all, the funds were administering sums that in 1950 amounted to two-thirds of the total federal budget. Despite the Bundestag's far-reaching determination of contributions and services, the self-governing funds retained important areas of discretion, for example, in the investment of the capital of the pension funds, in the negotiations over the fee structure of the health insurance funds, and in the decisionmaking regarding the construction and management of hospitals and convalescent homes of all three insurance funds. Furthermore, at a time of high unemployment the funds controlled a combined total of almost 100,000 jobs. In the end the left wing of the CDU, which represented the Catholic trade unions, proved decisive for the adoption of the parity solution. Anton Storch, their leader and the first minister of labor, saw the principle of equal institutional representation of business and labor, and the subsequent political tranquillity of the funds, as the most likely way to transform the confrontation of class enemies into the cooperation of social partners. The connection to the political debate about codetermination (see Chapter 3) was very evident for Storch.

The West German government was pressed in the early years of the Bonn Republic to deal with the immediate emergencies that World War II had created for different groups—refugees, invalids, widows, orphans, and Jews. World War II had left West Germany with 9 million refugees; 4 million invalids, widows, and orphans; between 3 and 4 million displaced people who had lost all of their property; and between 1 and 2 million prisoners of war who returned from the war as late as 1955. Hindsight shows that the agenda for reform between the mid-1950s and the late 1960s was a step-by-step reduction and eventual elimination of want through the indexation of pension entitlements in 1957; the redefinition of public welfare to focus on the provision of temporary help in special situations rather than on the permanent provision of means-tested help in 1961; and the development of an active labor market policy with the aim of achieving full employment by continuously retraining the West German labor force in 1969. The corners of this "magic triangle" of social policy were interdependent. The indexation of pensions broke an important link between old age and poverty and thus permitted welfare policy to focus increasingly on providing help in special situations. In addition, an active labor market policy was needed to maintain a full-employment economy able to finance generous welfare state programs.

The pension reform of 1957, the first important major social policy reform, was a response to a number of pressures, foremost among them the legislative improvisations of the early postwar years, the growing legal confusions and contradictions that impaired policy implementation, the rapid escalation of government subsidies to the pension fund, and finally the competition between the CDU/CSU and the SPD in the federal election of 1957. In the inaugural address of his second four-year term, Chancellor Adenauer promised a comprehensive and all-embracing transformation of West Germany's system of social policy. For Adenauer the future of the Federal Republic rested on the twin pillars of a foreign policy of Western integration and a domestic policy of social consolidation.

When the first comprehensive statistical inquiry commissioned by the federal government in 1953 revealed that the existing pension system failed to protect a substantial number of old people from poverty, Adenauer decided to focus the political energies of his cabinet on a comprehensive reform of the pension system. The central idea that eventually prevailed did not emerge from within the government but was formulated by experts outside the government (see Reading 4-1). It departed from past government policy (individualistic, based on the principle of self-help) and from the orthodoxy of past demands by the opposition (a collective insurance scheme based on the principle of government assistance). The new pension system was based on a "solidarity pact" between generations in which the present working-age population supported the aged in return for being supported by the contributions of successive cohorts of younger workers. Because the system linked benefits to past earnings, it retained its insurance character and did not tamper with the pay inequalities of labor markets. But by tying pensions to increases in wage levels, and thus productivity gains as well as inflation, the new system allowed the elderly to participate directly in the material gains of West German society. The powerful opponents to the pension reform of 1957 included the Ministries of Finance and Economics, the Bundesbank, and the business community. Despite numerous political battles, the essential features of proposals by the CDU and of the SPD were remarkably similar. Under Adenauer's leadership the CDU accepted the principle of inflation indexation, while the SPD was willing to let go of its preference for a uniform, egalitarian pension scheme.

The 1957 pension reform was followed in 1961 by the new Social Welfare Act (Leibfried and Tennstedt 1985b; Walker, Lawson, Townsend, 1984). It shifted emphasis from a system of means-tested welfare payments covering ordinary living expenses to the provision of special assistance to individuals who could provide for their normal living costs but temporarily needed special help, catalogued in the bill under eleven headings. The courts had sanctioned entitlement to a life-style in agreement with "human dignity" as early as 1954. All parties supported the new legislation and with it a further depoliticization of West Germany's social policy. Public welfare came to be defined as a safety net that was tailored to individual needs and covered whatever holes were left by the earnings-related pension system as well as by the administration of West Germany's labor markets. That principle was reinforced again in 1974 when the system's coverage and the level of benefits were substantially improved.

The third corner of the magic triangle has been West Germany's labor market policy (Blankenburg, Schmidt, and Treiber, 1975; Krautkrämer, 1978; Scharpf et al., 1982; Schmid, 1985). Until the mid-1960s employment policy was not a matter of great political concern. By the late 1950s unemployment had disappeared. The task of the Federal Employment Office in Nuremberg was to administer West Germany's unemployment insurance system, to supervise the regional and local employment offices, and to organize West Germany's system of vocational guidance. But with the number of open jobs substantially exceeding the number of job applicants in the 1960s, the Employment Office also had to help ensure an adequate supply of labor. It did so in two different ways. Beginning in the late 1950s it organized the import of foreign labor on a massive scale (see Chapter 5). In addition, it devoted a small amount of its resources to retraining programs. The recession of 1966–67 increased the salience of employment issues. To be sure, the recession was brief and unemployment never topped 3 percent. Indeed by the time the Employment Promotion Act was passed in 1969, unemployment had again fallen below 1 percent. But unemployment was concentrated both regionally (in North Rhine-Westphalia, which lost 360,000 jobs in 1966–67) and sectorally (in the coal and steel industries). Both the CDU/CSU and the SPD agreed that unemployment had to be combatted by an active policy that aimed at retraining workers before they became unproductive.

Modeled after Sweden's active labor market policy, West German policy was redesigned in 1969 to enhance workers' mobility via retraining and vocational training courses. In fact the law gives individual workers a legal claim to financial assistance of up to 90 percent of their wage during the retraining program. Furthermore, the law provides for an impressive array of policy instruments: among others, subsidies for workers put on short hours, for construction workers in winter, for people employed in public works, and for unemployed who have difficulty in finding jobs. But in contrast to Sweden, these measures are financed not from tax revenues and the government's budget but from the revenues of the unemployment insurance. Finally, the law designates specific groups of workers—women, the elderly, the handicapped, those living in disadvantaged regions—as deserving special attention.

In this respect employment policy reinforced a development foreshadowed in the evolution of West Germany's workmen's compensation policy (Tennstedt, 1976). Extended and improved through successive reforms in 1952, 1956, 1961, 1971, and 1974, the law was rewritten in 1963 to redirect policy more explicitly to the prevention of accidents rather than the provision of accident insurance. Conceived of as part of an ensemble of economic policies such as the Stability and Growth Act of 1967 (see pp. 90–91, 98) and the Joint Task for the Improvement of the Regional Employment Structure of 1969 (see pp. 55–56), the Employment Promotion Act was an important bridge to West Germany's welfare system. By stipulating that some portions of the insurance funds should be used before the onset of unemployment, the act sought to secure the economic foundations for the indexation of pensions; moreover, it expressed the expectation that unemployment, like poverty, could be avoided through an anticipatory, targeted policy.

We know by now that these optimistic expectations have been disappointed by the developments since the mid-1970s. The number of officially registered unemployed hovered around 5 percent (1 million) in the second half of the 1970s and increased to about 9 percent (2 million) in the prolonged depression of 1981–83. West Germany's employment and social policy thus began to focus solely on cutting expenditures to meet reduced revenues. As early as 1975, employment policy shifted from the retraining objective to the provision of public works. Unemployment insurance contributions were raised several times and benefits were cut substantially in the early 1980s. In 1975 and 1978 the federal government made it increasingly difficult for recipients of unemployment compensation to turn down opportunities for employment even if the new job required lower qualifications, offered less pay, and was further away from home. In the late 1970s and early 1980s increases in social security were temporarily and partially uncoupled from changes in wage levels. Among thirteen OECD (Organization for Economic Cooperation and Development) member states studied, only in West Germany and the Netherlands did real social expenditures rise more slowly than the gross domestic product (Alber, 1985; Markham, 1984). These cutbacks in turn have increased the financial pressure on West Germany's welfare system. The proportion of recipients of long-term welfare payments has increased sharply since 1982. Growing unemployment and fiscal frugality have severely strained the carefully knit social policy net.

Process

Policy formulation shows the importance of heterogeneous social alliances within parties, especially the CDU, as well as of coalitions between parties. And policy implementation has been shaped by West Germany's parapublic institutions and its system of cooperative federalism. I shall illustrate these political tendencies briefly by discussing the passage of the Pension Reform Act of 1957 and the Employment Promotion Act of 1969 as well as the way in which pensions and welfare payments are adjusted.

The pension reform bill was the most important piece of social policy legislation of the 1950s. It illustrates three different aspects of West Germany's policy process: the importance of the convergence of CDU and SPD objectives, the fragmentation of the federal bureaucracy, and the ambiguous role of the chancellor (Heidenheimer, 1981b; Hockerts, 1980 and 1981). The convergence in policy objectives resulted from developments within and between the two major parties. The CDU was moved initially (1953–56) by the commitment of its chancellor to consolidating both the young Bonn Republic and the rule of the CDU, in domestic politics; later (1956–57) it was the electoral competition with the SPD that pushed the party to action. The SPD had moved toward favoring the indexation of pensions ever since it had outlined its ideas in a very general program drafted before the 1953 elections. The party subsequently refined its proposals and introduced a bill in the Bundestag before the CDU-led coalition government had finalized its own plan. This broad convergence facilitated informal contacts with and consultation between the labor wing of the CDU, which enjoyed full access to the Labor Ministry, and SPD opposition as well as the trade union movement. This "informal" great coalition was in fact strong enough to eventually overcome the united opposition of the business community, the precursor to the Bundesbank, and the Ministries of Finance and Economics. At stake in this conflict was the choice between indexing pensions to wage increases (as the "progressives" preferred) or to productivity gains, which do not reflect changes in inflation rates (as the "traditionalists" demanded).

A second distinguishing feature of policy formulation was the fragmentation of the federal bureaucracy as well as its lack of conceptual innovation. The contrast to the visionary Swedish and British civil servants in charge of social policy, as Hugh Heclo describes (1974), is very striking. In fact, for the idea of indexation Chancellor Adenauer went outside of the federal bureaucracy, to an academic expert, Wilfried Schreiber. Schreiber's central ideas were summarized in a position paper drafted in the chancellory and forwarded to the CDU leadership and the Labor Ministry. Furthermore, Hans Günter Hockerts's detailed account shows that the Labor Ministry and the Finance Ministry in particular were preoccupied, respectively, with obstructing both Chancellor Adenauer's demand for a comprehensive social reform and the development of legislation embodying fully the chancellor's political demand for wage-based indexation. In this instance, the informal coordination of the federal bureaucracy in the 1950s (see Chapter 6) simply did not work. Finally, supporting the analysis of Chapter 2, neither macroeconomic policy nor Keynesian considerations were articulated at any point by the Economics Ministry, then under the leadership of Ludwig Erhard. The decentralization of policymaking—the focus of unsuccessful reforms in the early 1970s (see Chapter 6)—is readily apparent in this case of policy formulation in the 1950s.

Last but not least, Chancellor Adenauer was a key player. In this episode at least he was not aloof from or uninterested in domestic policy formation. Instead Adenauer pushed energetically for an innovative reform which he regarded as essential to the consolidation of the Federal

Republic. Although the chancellor's role was very important, the politics of social policy does not fit the description of West Germany as a "Chancellor democracy." For example, Adenauer had enormous problems convincing the Labor Ministry to cooperate with him. The ministry torpedoed his public commitment to develop one all-encompassing reform for all of the major social insurance systems. Such large-scale change was simply unacceptable. Instead, the ministry prevailed with the view that the different sectors of policy should be reformed one by one. Later in the policy deliberations Adenauer repeatedly encountered resistance from his finance minister, who often was in alliance with Minister of Economics Erhard. The intense political and bureaucratic infighting was understandable considering the importance of the task. But the chancellor's constitutionally guaranteed right to determine the guidelines of policy was in many instances much less important than a stylized description of West Germany's "Chancellor democracy" might suggest. Adenauer frequently found himself in the midst of political battle without control over his own troops.

In the mid-1960s the West German government charged an expert committee to evaluate West Germany's social security system. The government intended to act on whatever changes were considered necessary in the 1957 reform. However, the experts reaffirmed the basic model informing West Germany's social policy and recommended only incremental changes (see Reading 4-2).

The formulation of the Employment Promotion Act of 1969 also points to the importance of coalitions across party lines for effecting policy reform (Blankenburg, Schmid, and Treiber, 1975). Although the Labor Ministry had begun to prepare for a far-reaching reform, efforts by CDU/CSU–SPD coalition (1966–69) made passage of the law relatively smooth and uneventful. Whatever disagreements existed did not focus on the objectives of the new law but on the details of implementation. The left wing of the CDU cooperated closely with the SPD and the unions. Furthermore, smooth passage was helped by the fact that the CDU minister of labor and the CDU head of the committee for labor in the Bundestag were close personal friends and played important roles in the CDU and in the Catholic labor movement. As had been true of the pension reform, the Bundestag committee played a nonpartisan role and saw its role as providing additional information and reinforcing the consensus that already existed. When the bill was submitted to the Bundestag for a first reading, there was no debate.

Conflict did however exist between the top echelons of the Labor Ministry, which pressed for adoption of a new "active" labor market policy, and the bureaus inside the ministry as well as the Federal Employment Office, which were organizationally strongly committed to the traditional task of administering a "reactive" unemployment insurance fund. As discussed further in Chapter 6, the minister as well as the senior civil servants made up for the lack of bureaucratic support by enlarging the planning and coordination staff at the top of the ministry. Moreover, they recruited some economists rather than the customary lawyers or former employees of the Employment Office. In fact, the center of opposition was the Employment Office, which was charged with implementing the new law. The office objected to three aspects in particular: it was reluctant to grant an individual entitlement to retraining; it wanted to finance the new program from the federal budget or a new payroll tax rather than from workers' unemployment contributions; and it was wary of potential infringements on its autonomy. In the end, however, the opposition of the Employment Office proved fruitless.

The Employment Promotion Act of 1969 also points to the constraints that West German politics imposes on large-scale policy change. In the late 1960s the political leadership and the senior civil servants in the Labor Ministry pushed for a comprehensive reform of West Germany's vocational training as part of the new legislation. The original legislation had in fact envisaged the creation of a more centralized policy network. However, it soon became apparent that a comprehensive reform was impossible because of the competition for turf with other ministries, the absence of a centralized network for implementing policy, and the lack of a system of financing (Blankenburg, Schmid, and Treiber, 1975). Important in the deliberations were the Chambers for Industry, Commerce, and the Crafts which are independent of the federal government. In the early phases of policy formulation, economic interests closely tied to the chambers enjoyed much greater access to and influence over both the executive and legislative branch, and succeeded in preventing any far-reaching measures. The eventual reform of the vocational training system passed in 1975 was thus only further piecemeal reform of West Germany's system of labor market administration (Offe, 1975).

The dependence on cooperative arrangements between the federal government and other political actors is also very evident, for example, in the process of policy implementation in the areas of health, pensions, and welfare. The reorganization of the health insurance funds with parity representation of both employers and unions set the stage for a far-reaching depoliticization of policy implementation. Furthermore, in 1955 the state organizations of the local funds together with the associations of doctors were given standing under public law, and their relations were reorganized (Tennstedt, 1976, pp. 415–17). Rewarded as it turned out by subsequent developments, the general hope was to diffuse conflict in an area that had been explosive politically before 1945. A general contract covering all health insurance practices was negotiated in 1959 and has been amended periodically. National negotiations set the guidelines for these general practices. Negotiations over money occur not between local funds and individual doctors but between the provincial associations representing funds and doctors, respectively. In these negotiations the doctors typically try to get the best results by negotiating separately with the different types of health insurance funds in each state and then using the best offer as a target figure which they ask all funds to match. In practice the difference between states is small. Negotiations are rarely so conflictual or prolonged that they require the intervention of an arbitration panel that has the final word. The organizations of physicians process claims, receive payments from the health insurance funds, pay the doctors, and try to review the utilization of services (Glaser, 1978). In sum, "the German experience is a good example of how government can enact the rules and then leave the doctors and sick [*sic*] funds to carry out the program with little government intervention. . . . The result is national uniformity with provincial flexibility" (Glaser, 1978, pp. 109–10).

A similar process occurs in the area of pensions. The 1957 reform tied an earnings-related entitlement to pensions to the wage level prevailing at the first time the pension was paid. Subsequent changes in the wage level are reflected with a slight lag in the level of pensions. As a result of the complex political bargaining in the 1950s, the link between wages and pensions is semi-automatic. Chancellor Adenauer's attempt to remove party politics from this important arena of the welfare state was successful. The Social Advisory Council, after considering all relevant economic data, recommends to the federal government an annual adjustment in pensions on which it must act. In extraordinarily tight fiscal times, the government must ask for approval from the Bundestag to partially decouple the link between wages and pensions. Normally, though the actual provision of pensions is devoid of overt politics. It is a purely administrative act that links the individual and the vast bureaucracy of the pension fund.

Although until the late 1970s West Germany's means-tested public welfare system compensated for changes in price levels rather than wages, it reflects a tendency to minimize conflicts in policy implementation. In 1955 the German Association, representing the major public and private welfare organizations, calculated an average consumer goods basket that would meet the legal entitlement of Germany's poor to a dignified standard of living. That basket was recalculated and substantially improved in 1961 and again in 1970. In money terms it defines a practically uniform national standard of welfare payments of about 350 deutschmarks in 1983 (Adamy and Naegele, 1985, pp. 114–29; Galperin, 1985, pp. 161–62). Indexation left the real purchasing power of public welfare unchanged between 1974 and 1982 but permitted the gap between real wages and welfare payments—and thus the gap between average consumption patterns and those permitted by welfare payments—to widen. Although invisible in normal, daily politics, the reaction of the West German poor was poignant (see Reading 4-4). Since welfare is provided by municipalities that increasingly lack the funds needed to upgrade payment levels, the plight of the poor has increased in the 1980s. Attempts to recalculate an average basket were obstructed in the mid-1970s and again in the early 1980s by the peak association of communes.

Although national standards are uniform, the bureaucracy's administration of benefits appears to be restrictive. In time for the federal election of 1976, the CDU made the "New Social Question" an important issue (Geissler, 1976) (see Reading 4-3). According to the CDU's calculations, more than 2 million households with almost 6 million persons received a net income below the poverty line of 1974, as compared to the half a million households with 0.9 million persons which were listed in government statistics. Although the experts disagree on the magnitude of the gap between the official statistics and social reality, there is widespread agreement that the gap is substantial. Stephan Leibfried has argued plausibly that its root lies in the nature of West Germany's welfare bureaucracy which creates a number of screens to filter out the claims of individuals legally entitled to receive welfare payments. Leibfried summarizes (1976) one layer of these screens under the label of "passive institutionalization." Passive institutionalization is the major reason why the programmatic and political differences that separate West German welfare policy from American welfare policy are in fact sharply diminished in the process of policy implementation (Leibfried, 1978). Passive institutionalization, especially in times of increasing need and decreasing resources, is apparently greater in the countryside, in the south, and in states and localities dominated by the CDU/CSU than in urban areas, in the north, and in states and localities dominated by the SPD. Estimates are that only half of the West Germans with legal entitlements actually received welfare payments in the mid-1980s (Hartmann, 1985). Bureaucratic shackles, analyzed in Chapter 6, thus reinforce the distinctive institutions in West German politics which make incremental policy change so pervasive.

Consequences

By most standards West Germany is one of the leading welfare states in the contemporary world. Table 4-1 summarizes data on the broad array of social benefits that cover most of the population. Furthermore, the balance between transfer payments and taxes has some redistributive consequences. A government committee calculated, for example, that a married West German employee with two children earning 2,500 deutschmarks in 1976 would receive back in the form of transfer payments (allowances for children, housing, educational expenses, and a bonus for a savings account) her 30 percent income tax. Within the broad middle stratum of West German society, the balance between transfer payments and taxes favors the bottom over the top. Those earning 1,000 deutschmarks end up with 1,800; those earning 5,000 deutschmarks with 3,750 (*Der Spiegel*, Jan. 30, 1978, p. 38).

A detailed comparison with the United States in the mid-1970s shows that programs outside the area of public welfare absorb one quarter of West Germany's gross national product as compared to a much smaller figure in the United States. By contrast, West Germany's welfare payments absorb only 1 percent of GNP compared to almost 3 percent in the United States. The number of welfare recipients per 1,000 inhabitants is four times greater in the United States than in West Germany (Leibfried, 1978, pp. 65–67). At the same time, it is also clear that the rate at which social expenditures have increased has been slower in Germany than elsewhere. History offers one plausible reason. Germany was the first country to introduce various benefits in the nineteenth century; and it was the first country with a fully developed pensions system to index social security payments in the 1950s. West Germany's budget for public expenditures was the highest among the welfare states in the mid-1950s; two decades later it ranked only in the middle (Alber, 1980; OECD, 1978, p. 13). West Germany's economic stabilization strategy evidently constrained the growth in welfare spending especially in comparison to several of the smaller European democracies.

Aggregate financial statistics, however, do not accurately gauge the extent to which policy objectives were actually achieved. On questions of social policy, West Germany's agenda was both surprisingly ambitious and limited. In its reform of pensions, public welfare, and employment, West Germany aimed at nothing less than the preventive treatment of the risks of old age, poverty, and unemployment. The moves toward the indexation of pensions, the provisions of special public welfare for individual need, and the development of an active labor market policy were carried by a broad political consensus. Throughout the 1960s the pressures generating action were primarily bureaucratic, professional, and, though only intermittently, electoral. This particular way of addressing policy choices was rooted in a strong consensus on the desirability of—indeed, the constitutional mandate for—keeping the Federal Republic a well-functioning social welfare state (Hartwich, 1970).

Both the SPD's preference for basing pensions on a flat rate, thirty years later advocated by the Greens (see Reading 4-5), and the CDU's predilection for relating pensions to earnings were compromised by the 1957 reform. Pensions were in fact linked to average national income while continuing to reflect the length of work life and the level of earnings before retirement. As a result of this compromise, absolute differences between pre- and postretirement incomes have diminished, whereas the relative differentials in postretirement income have in fact widened in the 1960s and 1970s. Although the attitude of the CDU and the SPD governments differed in the 1960s—with the CDU favoring a reactive social welfare policy while the SPD championed an active social planning approach—the evolution of policy was in fact marked by a bipartisan consensus on the gradual expansion of benefits. When the SPD was voted into office in 1969, it instituted a number of innovations, including some to make relevant information available to high-level policymakers. For example, a new social budget was constructed for the purpose of projecting costs and revenues of the major programs. And the government has, since 1970, regularly issued a social report. But these innovations were largely procedural rather than substantive. They did not seriously affect the contours of West Germany's welfare state.

When consensus could not be found, however, little progress was

TABLE 4-1   The Provisions of Social Insurance Laws in the Federal Republic of Germany, 1949, 1969, 1978

Scope of insurance	Pension Insurance			Health Insurance			Unemployment Insurance			Accident Insurance		
	1949	1969	1978	1949	1969	1978	1949	1969	1978	1949	1969	1978
No. insured (millions)	15	19	21	13	17	20	9	19	20	21	24	23
% of work force	66	70	84	57	63	79	38	60	80	90	90	92
Monthly income limit for compulsory coverage (deutschmarks)	600[a]	all workers and employees		375[b]	990[c]	2,775[d]	600[a]	coverage includes all workers and employees		coverage includes all employed persons and, for 1978, students, and school children		
Benefits	27 (% average net wage, maximum)	66	72	50% of gross earnings	full salary for 6 wks, then 75%	full salary for 6 wks, then 80%	20.40 ([deutschmarks] weekly, for earners of average wage)	114.60	247.80	first 6 weeks under health insurance; nursing benefits if helpless		
	60 ([deutschmarks] average pension)	353	641				45.0 (% of average wage)	62.5	68.0			
Maximum duration of benefits (in weeks)	N/A	N/A	N/A	26	78	78	26	52	52	N/A	N/A	N/A
Contributions as % of gross wages	10.0	17.0	18.0	6.0[e]	10.5[e]	11.4[e]	4.0	1.3	3.0	employers contribute about 1.5% of payroll		
Sources of funds	equal contributions from insured persons and employers[f]			equal contributions from insured persons and employers			equal contributions from insured persons and employers[g]			contributions from employers only		

Income limit for contribution purposes (deutschmarks)	600^a	1,700^h	3,700^i	375^b	990^c	2,775^d	375^b	1,300^h	3,700^i	
Controls: Length of waiting period (days)	N/A	N/A	N/A	3	0	0	7	0	3	0	0	N/A	N/A	N/A	0

Source: Adapted from Jens Alber, "Der Wohlfahrtsstaat in der Krise? Eine Bilanz nach drei Jahrzehnten Sozialpolitik in der Bundesrepublik," *Zeitschrift für Soziologie* 9 (October 1980):318.

Notes.

1949: Provisions of *Sozialversicherungsanpassungsgesetz* (for accident insurance, law dated August 10, 1949).

1969: Provisions of the laws in effect before the social-liberal coalition of 1969.

1978: Provisions then in effect.

All given income limits are statutory. Percentages of wages are statutory earnings replacement ratios in health and unemployment insurance since 1969. All other percentages calculated by author, based on wage statistics in *Sozialbericht* (1978), p. 316 (net) and p. 319 (gross). Wage figures from 1949 are interpolated from data from 1948 and 1949 given in Bundesministerium für Arbeit und Sozialordnung, *Übersicht über die soziale Sicherung 1970* (Bonn, 1970), p. 67 (tax rate assumed to equal 1950). Figures for pension insurance refer to workers' scheme.

N/A = not applicable.

a. 3.2 times average wage.

b. 2.0 times average wage.

c. 1.0 times average wage.

d. 1.2 times average wage.

e. Averages for all funds.

f. Federal government's contribution to pension insurance fund varies from 15 to 19%.

g. Following the maximum duration of unemployment benefits, the federal government continues to pay welfare; the rate is lower than the rate for unemployment insurance.

h. 1.7 times average wage.

i. 1.6 times average wage.

made. In the late 1950s, for example, shortly after the passage of the pension law, the Labor Ministry attempted to introduce a far-reaching reform of the health care system which was predicated on the notion of cost containment and cost sharing of patients (Heidenheimer, 1981b; Safran, 1967). The cost-sharing formula that Minister Theodor Blank tried to introduce was daringly novel. As developments in the 1970s later proved, Blank was remarkably prescient of inflationary pressures. But for a variety of reasons, both physicians and trade unions, the providers and the consumers of health care, were strongly opposed to the adoption of this new policy. What came to be known as the Great Coalition favoring the status quo mobilized inside the major parties. The Labor Ministry's draft bill was fair game when it reached the Bundestag committee. Chancellor Adenauer, sensing the strength of the opposition and the absence of an electoral bonus, failed to back his minister. After years of debate, Blank's bold initiative was eventually dropped in the mid-1960s. A decade later the explosion of health care forced the "concerted action" in health care described briefly in Chapter 1 (pp. 33–34).

West Germany's active labor market policy also points to the limits of policy change possible in West Germany's institutions. Informed by Swedish policy in the 1950s and 1960s, the move toward an active labor market policy, as measured by financial allocations, remained incomplete. Measured in terms of the share of GNP between 1973 and 1978, Sweden spent twice as much as the Federal Republic, and the effect on employment of Swedish measures was almost three times larger (Bruche and Reissert, 1985; Johannesson and Schmid, 1980; Scharpf et al., 1982, p. 17; Webber, 1983). That Sweden's unemployment rate remained very low throughout the 1970s was the result of an ambitious labor market policy never applied with similar determination in West Germany. The Labor Promotion Act of 1985 was an attempt by the CDU coalition government to infuse West German labor markets with more flexibility. Because of Sweden's prior record with labor market policy, such legislation would be unthinkable there. But West Germany's cautious steps would not be acceptable either to a conservative government in the United States seeking to push more fundamental changes. In this policy sector as in many others in West Germany, change is incremental.

Like other industrial states, West Germany since 1973 has had to cope with the social consequences of a restructured global economy. Lower economic growth and sharp increases in unemployment have stopped the further growth of the welfare state and prompted successive governments, led first by the SPD and later by the CDU, to implement substantial savings programs. These programs have affected virtually all aspects of welfare spending just as the need for such spending increased greatly. They have hit the poorest sectors of society hardest. Rising unemployment causes both an explosion in social spending and revenue losses in taxes and social insurance contributions; as a result, it puts great financial pressure on the state. But these pressures were reinforced also by some serious mistakes in policymaking (see Reading 4-5). For example, based on sharp increases in wages between 1968 and 1972 and a growing number of foreign workers, projections for West German pension funds suggested a surplus of 200 billion deutschmarks over the next fifteen years. The pension reform legislation of 1972, supported by both the SPD-FDP government and the CDU/CSU opposition, generously dictated the appropriation of funds that existed only as statistical projections. Only five years later Chancellor Schmidt had to deal with the direct consequences of the previous government's policy in a different economic climate. Yet even then, economic pressures were mild compared to those of the early 1980s (Groth, 1977). Between 1980 and 1983 total expenditures for unemployment compensation doubled to 17 billion deutschmarks, while the average unemployment ·compensation per recipient declined by 11 percent. Benefits were cut even further in 1984 (Alber, 1985; Bosch and Sengenberger, 1984, p. 9). The cumulative impact of a restrictive fiscal policy between 1982 and 1985 cut an annual average of 54 billion deutschmarks from the federal budget (Adamy and Steffen, 1984, p. 7). It is too early to evaluate the social consequences of fiscal frugality. But it is spawning an important debate on the premises underlying West Germany's social welfare state (see Readings 4-6, 4-7, 4-8).

That debate is spurred not only by high unemployment but also by the demographic changes that are transforming West German society (*Der Spiegel,* Dec. 23, 1985, pp. 68–75; Dec. 30, 1985, pp. 56–63; Jan. 6, 1986, pp. 62–74; Jan. 13, 1986, pp. 70–79). Since the late 1960s the West German birth rate has dropped dramatically. Between the 1980s and the year 2030 the proportion of people over sixty will double. To maintain the current living standard of social security recipients, contributions would have to double: 60 to 70 percent of gross wages and salaries would go toward financing the welfare state. Alternatively, if the present rate structure were to remain unchanged, living standards for the elderly would be cut in half. These are two improbable political scenarios. In the debate about future policy choices, CDU Minister of Labor Norbert Blüm speaks for the center and left wing of his own party as well as for the SPD opposition in support of incremental changes in the insurance principle of the present system. This informal coalition between the two main political parties must, however, contend with criticisms from some segments of the CDU and FDP on the Right and the Greens on the Left. For different reasons, both groups advocate an entirely new insurance system for the elderly (see Readings 4-6 and 4-8). For the present, however, this debate is occurring in a period of consolidation rather than dismantling of the welfare state. A broad political consensus supports consolidation. The cuts in welfare spending that the SPD coalition government initiated unwillingly in the mid-1970s have been continued rigorously by the CDU coalition government since 1983 (Alber, 1985).

West Germany's social policy is linked intimately to the other policy sectors that reflect similar political links between the three nodes of the policy network. In West Germany coalition governments, cooperative, federalism, and parapublic institutions constrained the explosive growth of social expenditures that has made the need to tighten belts in neighboring Denmark and the Netherlands much more urgent. Questions of employment policy are addressed not only by the Federal Employment Office in Nuremberg, which straddles one national system of employment offices, but also by the welfare payments that West Germany's municipalities distribute in a decentralized manner. The joint participation of employers and unions in a variety of insurance funds mirrors, without any of the acrimonious conflicts, the principle of codetermination that is a key feature of West Germany's system of industrial relations. West Germany's social policy thus both reflects and reinforces political arrangements that typify its politics more generally. A closely knit institutional web limits the exercise of unilateral political initiatives by any one actor and encourages incremental policy change. In a word, it makes the West German state semisovereign.

Readings

4-1. A DYNAMIC SOCIAL SECURITY SYSTEM*

This excerpt is from a report that helped prepare the ground for a fundamental restructuring of West Germany's system of social security in 1957. It proposed the adoption of a social security system that deviated radically from the old insurance-based system.

The dynamic character of a modern economy depends on the following factors: the natural increase of the population; technological progress; entrepreneurial leadership; market competition, which increases production and productivity; the spread of markets; governmental intervention especially through policies regarding business cycles; the power of public opinion, which demands progress and an increase in the standard of living. The dynamic character of a modern economy shapes the GNP and the standard of living. The size and composition of the GNP will change but the buying power of money—inflation notwithstanding—will always diminish (as it did, for example, between 1870 and 1914). Personal savings, accumulated for retirement, will have less buying power in forty years than they have today.

A pension system financed on the basis of accumulated savings is open to a number of serious criticisms. Capital accumulated on such a vast scale constitutes a formidable, anonymous source of power. It risks losing some of its purchasing power over time. It is easy prey for the ravages of inflation. And in times of economic crisis it can be liquidated only with great difficulty if at all.

Contributions to the pension fund should not go into a savings fund. Rather they should finance the pensions of the elderly; or help create a reserve for hard times which could be used to strengthen the principle of

*Hans Achinger, Joseph Höffner, Hans Muthesius, and Ludwig Neundörfer, *Neuordnung der Sozialen Leistungen: Denkschrift auf Anregung des Herrn Bundeskanzlers erstattet von den Professoren Hans Achinger, Joseph Höffner, Hans Muthesius, Ludwig Neundörfer* (Cologne: Greven, 1955), pp. 107–9.

self-help, for example, by making construction loans available to the younger insured population.

Since the dynamism of a modern economy leads to perpetual changes in the GNP, social security recipients will enjoy a living standard that corresponds to the general standard of living only if the pension system provides for a contractual bargain between the generations. Solidarity between the active and the retired segments of the population must be complemented by solidarity between the generations. According to this logic, the working population could be mandated to make a given percent of its income available to the social security fund benefiting today's pensioners; future generations will in turn provide for today's workers. In this manner pensions could be adjusted to the prevailing standard of living. For it to work, the system would have to anticipate future increases in the number of old people.

4-2. A REAFFIRMATION OF THE DYNAMIC PENSION*

In the mid-1960s an extensive government report investigated many aspects of West Germany's social welfare policy and reconfirmed the system's basic premise, relating pensions to earnings.

There are four models of social security. The first model maximizes private initiative in the provision for as well as consumption of social security and minimizes the influence of public and institutions. Since only the state has the power to redistribute income and wealth, social security automatically depends solely on private savings. . . . this model falls short of total success. . . .

The second model also seeks to maximize private initiative. However, in this model it is not necessary to reduce the influence of publicly provided pensions on private initiative. . . . The attempt to create a maximum of individual responsibility requires that, as in the first model, the compulsory old-age insurance be restricted to the provision of a minimum standard of living. Tax revenues should finance this basic pension for everyone.

The third model adheres to the principle of an earnings-related pension system. Like the first two, this model does not rely excessively on the state. In contrast, however, it requires not a minimization but only a

Soziale Sicherung: Sozialenquête in der Bundesrepublik Deutschland (Stuttgart: Kohlhammer, 1965), pp. 122–24 (selections).

restriction of state influence. . . . The fourth model, frequently debated under the misguided slogan of the "welfare state," values redistribution more highly than private savings. According to this model, in cases of need each individual should be insured on an equal basis regardless of his or her prior income and contribution to the pension fund. The amount of social security should depend not on any conventional definition of a minimum level for existence but on the productive capacity of the national economy. . . .

Despite occasional differences . . . this commission bases its discussion of social policy on the third model, for three main reasons. (a) The third model corresponds in principle, even though by no means completely, to the social security system that currently exists in the Federal Republic. Adhering to a different model would require a transformation of the existing system. . . . (b) The third model fits well with the general system of the Federal Republic. This is particularly evident in the case of the economic order. In contrast to the system of laissez-faire, West Germany's social market economy stresses the imperative of market competition rather than that of the passive state. Competition should occur preferably with a noninterventionist state. But the social market economy permits state intervention should the principle of competition be at risk. (c) Finally, the third model enjoys strong popular support.

4-3. THE NEW SOCIAL QUESTION*

In 1976 a prominent social policy expert of the CDU, and subsequently secretary of the West German CDU and cabinet member, Heiner Geissler, wrote a report in which he charged that the social policy of the SPD and FDP had overlooked a new hidden poverty. Although the book was frequently dismissed at the time as a crude attempt "to pass the SPD on the left" it rekindled a debate about West Germany's system of welfare which intensified in the 1980s when the SPD opposition made the same charge to criticize Geissler and the CDU/CSU-FDP coalition government.

The struggle between labor unions and employers which intensifies inflation shows that neither side can gain a lasting advantage over the other. But from those who are not organized—large families, single mothers with children, old people, the disabled, and the handicapped—

*Heiner Geissler, *Die Neue Soziale Frage: Analysen und Dokumente* (Freiburg: Herder, 1976), pp, 15, 26–29, 38, 42 (selections).

organized groups may obtain some advantage. Normally the unorganized lose when they confront well-organized, large interest groups. The conflict between labor and capital has been augmented by conflicts between organized and unorganized interests, minorities and majorities, city and country, between those groups that exercise power and those that do not. Here lies the "new social question." . . .

Because of the passive attitude of the federal government in the past years, especially since 1969, the political responsibility for income and income distribution in West Germany has become a chief responsibility of the collective bargaining between employers and unions. Meanwhile, the government has largely forgotten that a married worker with children cannot make a living from the wage he earns. He remains dependent on social welfare benefits, for example, child allowance, rent subsidy, or vocational training subsidy. These services are among the social welfare benefits that the state in redistributing income finances through tax revenues. . . .

The Federal Republic of Germany again lives with bitter private poverty. There are 5.8 million people in 2.2 million households whose incomes are below the poverty level. We are not talking about lazy bums but rather about 1.1 million households with 2.3 million persons living on social security, 600,000 blue-collar families with 2.2 million people, and 300,000 white-collar families with 1.2 million people. The silence of the poor should not deprive them of public attention without which little happens in a mass democracy. Though often bashful and hidden, poverty does exist in this country. The number of people whose income lies below the level for social assistance is about seven times as large as the actual number of recipients. . . .

Female gender, old age, and large families are today's signs of poverty. This is true regardless of one's position in the production process. . . . Sociologists agree that it is almost always the elderly, women, and large families who are underprivileged. Incidentally, this is true for poverty analyses in other countries such as England and the United States. . . .

We propose five strategies to repair the inequities of the current benefits system: (1) social benefits must be targeted towards the truly needy; (2) social benefits must be restructured to attain more distributive justice without raising overall expenditures; (3) social benefits must be administered to encourage personal social engagement; (4) social services must be organized more humanely and economically; (5) particular situations and individual wishes must be accommodated. A decisive prerequisite for making these strategies acceptable is to release the thinking behind social policies from the traditional polarity between rich and poor and thus from traditional ways of thinking. Only then will citizens begin to understand the tasks that lie ahead. . . .

For the problems of the late 20th century, socialism offers no perspective. Indeed in the past socialism has never been able to give the right answers. But in the 19th century, socialism did pose the right questions. It appears that socialism is no longer capable of doing even that. We need to reorient ourselves. In this process the Christian-Democratic Union of Germany may succeed if it draws from the existence of the new social question the correct political lessons.

4-4. THE IDEAL WELFARE RECIPIENT*

This drawing was created by a group of single parents in Lübeck, all of them welfare recipients. The original is drawn on wrapping paper, roughly 3 meters by 1, and dates back to 1979. Although the drawing makes fun of West Germany's welfare program, it has an undeniably bitter undertone.

Key

1. An empty brain—a ticking bomb
2. A sensitive antenna to register the prevailing climate in the welfare department
3. Safety helmet to protect against administrative hammers
4. Cross-eyed, to look at everyone in the welfare office in the right way at the same time
5. A good nose for trouble is a precondition for survival
6. Ears need to be adjusted to continuous draft (in one ear, out the other)
7. Especially big mouth to be assertive
8. . . . sharper than a serpent's fangs . . .
9. It is often useful not to reveal everything
10. Special protective device for the neck against attack from behind

*Arbeitsgruppe Begleitforschung, *Entwicklung humaner Arbeitsstrukturen* 2, interim report (Bremen: 1980), pp. 90–91.

11. Broad shoulders to carry all the dead weight without breaking down
12. Cool collar for temperature control
13. A heart that has grown quills
14. It is necessary to appear in rags to have a chance of obtaining new clothing
15. Especially thick skin helps endure all sorts of situations
16. Especially sensitive skin is also necessary to open oneself to the problematic existence of administrative personnel
17. The bile is always flowing
18. Catheterization of the gall bladder to drain the bile
19. Babies unwanted due to cost increases
20. . . . off limits for single mothers
21. A good stomach to digest leather
22. . . . strong bladder control to avoid being pissed off
23. A microscope to detect payments, if any . . .
24. Wanted: a wedding ring and a bounty hunter for recoupment of spouse support
25a. An Irish folk saying, sanctioned by old German sources ("Götz"): "Kiss me arse"
25b. Callus on your "arse" for the waiting room
26. Beggar's staff (the equivalent of a badge of poverty)
27. Beggar's knee pads
28. Ibid. (see note 27 above)
29. This boot is made for walking—back and forth between the welfare offices
30. Broad sole for (under-)standing
31. Preventive medicine against "abuse"
32. This boot is custom-made for "economy and efficiency"

4-5. THE CRISIS WAS PREDICTABLE*

In this article a former senior civil servant in Bonn argues why the crisis of West Germany's social and economic policy, though predictable, was inevitable for reasons that inhere in the policy process and in competitive party politics.

*Thilo Sarrazin, "Die Krise war vorhersehbar." *Der Spiegel*, March 28, 1983, pp. 102–12 (selections).

Analysis of the worsening crisis of the global economy reveals remarkable things. Almost all of the negative trends had emerged by the mid-1960s or even earlier: declining growth, higher inflation and unemployment, higher taxes, and larger budget deficits. And in all states public policies have fallen far short of addressing the growing list of structural problems. . . .

To credit this mismatch simply to the "stupidity" or "opportunism" of the politicians would be shortsighted. Even the electoral cycle does not explain everything. Electoral competition increases the pressure on the public purse. The tendency to suppress problems altogether or to push them aside is strong. However, because of a systematic bias, the policy process favors short-term considerations at the expense of long-term perspectives. This can be fatal in times of far-reaching structural changes which require long-term perspectives.

One example is the pension reform of 1972. The high growth of wages and salaries after 1968 and a simultaneous increase in total employment had created a substantial surplus in the pension fund. Projections for West Germany's system of social security estimated that the surplus would grow over the next 15 years to over 200 billion deutschmarks. These projections assumed uninterrupted, high economic growth, a continuous high level of employment, and substantial increases in wages, in nominal terms 7 to 8 percent annually. Simple alternative projections showed that the billions would shrink to zero if the optimistic assumptions were changed only slightly. This fact was, however, disregarded. Government and opposition treated the 200 billion deutschmarks as if they had already been earned. So they were distributed. . . . That is how a pension reform was adopted which spent all of a surplus in the social security fund that existed only hypothetically on the basis of unrealistic projections. The cost of social security thus accelerated rapidly, setting the stage for the subsequent financial crisis of the social security system.

The story concerning the projection of labor-market policies is similar. . . . The projections of the Economics Ministry were not altogether mistaken. But they presented a narrow spectrum of unfailingly optimistic if highly improbable future trends in labor markets.

One of the main causes for the shortsightedness of policy and politics is *static thinking*. By this I mean the tendency to mistake the present and apparently prevailing trends for the design of the future and thus to eliminate from political consideration possible changes in underlying conditions. . . .

This has also something to do with the second factor, *the dynamics of habitual styles of thought.* For example, since the 1950s social policy was based on the assumption that "more" meant "better." The change in office from Hans Katzer (CDU) to Walter Arendt (SPD) was much less of a break than either party was later willing to acknowledge. Since the 1950s the two major parties have jointly supported all of the major social reforms that are creating headaches today. This was true also of the pension reform of 1972. To measure social progress solely according to increases in social services and to view a year without the introduction of new social services as a step backward—these are patterns of thought whose dominance over all social policymakers must simply be incomprehensible to those a step removed. Those who matured politically in this environment could hardly escape from such patterns. . . .

Disregard for the overall context is an additional culprit. The concept of the division of labor prevails in politics. Over time most politicians become advocates of a relatively small selection of ideas and interests which largely dominate their behavior. One pleads for the civil servants, the next fights for women's equal rights, a third against increases in defense spending, and a fourth for the German coal industry. Only a small minority ever show any interest in seeing the whole picture and focusing on the common good. And this minority typically is in a very weak position when it confronts the representatives of well-organized groups. For example, if in either party the steel lobby forms an alliance with the welfare lobby, the financial specialist simply does not stand a chance. . . .

Many politicians have internalized the interests of the groups they represent to such a degree that they have become the objects rather than the subjects of current events. They have given up truly independent thought. Only a few muster the courage (or cynicism) to admit to themselves as well as to others that the pressure of interest groups narrows the range of choice in some cases and precludes some choices altogether in others. The greater the disjunction between the objective pressures for action and the interests of groups supporting a government, the more hectic and shortsighted becomes the public policy process.

4-6. THE NEED FOR A NEW DEBATE*

Meinhard Miegel is the author of a controversial study, issued by a CDU think-tank, which advocates increasing reliance on private initiative and savings in the provision of social welfare services. In these selections Meinhard Miegel answers the charges that critics on the Left leveled against him in a spirited debate in the West German weekly Die Zeit.

For its defenders the welfare state is an institution that always gives and always does well. They do not consider the fact that the state must take in at least as much as it gives out. This becomes particularly clear when Jens Alber [one of the participants in this debate] offers the following revealing computation. The average household income amounts to 3,400 deutschmarks. Of these 900 deutschmarks are government transfer payments. Without this sum the net income of private households would amount only to 2,500 deutschmarks. He concludes that "Miegel's studies leave open how with such an income, covering an average household of 2.4 persons, one can cover not only current expenses but also save for unexpected expenses in the future."

Those calculating in such terms have not grasped the mechanisms of the welfare state. Alber does not recognize that household income on average must have been reduced by at least the 900 deutschmarks by which they are subsequently increased through transfer payments. To put it differently, for the household with statistically average net income, whether a state-run system of transfer payments does or does not exist is inconsequential; average income in any case is 3,400 deutschmarks.

Though banal, this statement is nonetheless quite important. The welfare state does not enrich us. At best it influences the distribution of welfare. Whoever in his life earns an average income, is rarely ill, and dies around 70 years of age is only disadvantaged by the welfare state. Whoever corresponds to the statistical norm neither wins nor loses anything. Only the frequently unemployed or ill and possibly also those who grow to a very old age enjoy a higher standard of living thanks to the institution of the welfare state.

*Meinhard Miegel, "Angst von einer Debatte: Die Verteidiger der traditionellen Sozialpolitik wollen eine Anpassung an die Realität verhindern," *Die Zeit*, September 23, 1983, pp. 36–37 (selections).

This is not an objection to the legitimacy and the benefits of the social welfare state. But as the example makes clear, today's welfare state has increasingly assumed the character of a large insurance company. Only in some marginal areas such as welfare policies are services and benefits directed from the productive segments of society toward the needy. By far the greatest part of public transfer payments is awarded without a means test. The magnitude of prior contributions to the welfare system decides who will receive what. Whoever has contributed little, will receive little.

Old age insurance and unemployment insurance by and large reflect this principle. Both insurance systems are earnings-related. Lacking in redistributive intent, they attempt to maintain social differences between rich and poor even when gainful employment has been either interrupted or terminated. Health insurance, on the other hand, is organized on the basis of each according to his capacity and each according to his need. But characteristically, in the case of health insurance, the economically strong has the option to leave the public insurance system and thus to protect himself against a redistributive policy that he would have to help subsidize.

Many valid arguments support an insurance system that emphasizes earnings capacity rather than need. Yet whoever embraces this type of welfare state as social progress cannot at the same time wrap himself in the mantle of social equality, greater justice, and a new morality. The welfare state evidently has gradually become a service-oriented institution that could be organized in different ways. Reasons for maintaining its present organization grow increasingly less persuasive. To accomplish its social tasks—the necessity of which no one questions—the state can rely on other institutions.

The central weakness of the traditional welfare state is its neglect of these changes. The traditional defenders of the welfare state are at best willing to acknowledge the demographic transformation in the state. But they do not comprehend far-reaching changes in economic and social life, in public consciousness, and in long-term political developments. They simply project past trends into the future, thus committing the same mistake as those economists who naively projected, and at times continue to predict, unchanging relative growth rates. Traditionalists of all stripes simply cannot sense basic discontinuities. Like all other institutions, the welfare state is not immune to real-life changes. It would indeed be very peculiar if this institution, which has been shaped in its present form by the social conditions of the first part of the twentieth century, continued to expand quantitatively without changing qualitatively into the next century. . . .

Like all other social institutions, the welfare state should continually and radically be reevaluated and debated. Otherwise the foundations of the welfare state risk quiet erosion and eventual collapse. One has to be blind not to see that this process of erosion is now well under way, not, as the traditionalists maintain, because of the policies of the federal government, but as a result of the attempts of millions of citizens to circumvent the welfare state. . . . These citizens are slowly learning how to live with their new-found wealth. A forward-looking social policy must be intent on supporting this development by, for example, cautiously loosening some of the strictures of the welfare state which, as the unofficial economy of cash-for-labor illustrates, will ultimately be circumvented. In the past the enforced social solidarity of the welfare state was a historical necessity. Today it is the task of a forward-looking social policy to reinterpret the meaning of solidarity to a wealthy industrial society and its autonomous citizens. Because of the way in which the institutions of the social welfare state are now operating, many citizens are now violating traditional concepts of solidarity.

4-7. THE FUTURE OF THE SOCIAL WELFARE STATE*

In this discussion paper a commission of the SPD recognizes the new challenges that derive from a different economic context, demographic changes, and the erosion of social solidarity. It also outlines the SPD's reasons for a policy of incremental change.

The working group holds the view that the economic conditions of previous, successful social policies in the future will either not recur or will not have the same impact. It is thus necessary to get ready and face new changes. Future economic growth will not match the rates of the 1950s and 1960s. The rationalization of industrial production progresses faster than economic expansion. This process replaces human labor progressively and thus diminishes the demand for labor.

The social policies of the next decades must adjust to the fact that full

*Arbeitsgruppe Sozialpolitisches Programm der SPD, "Die Zukunft des Sozialstaats," interim report (Bonn, March 19, 1984), pp. 6, 8, 14 (selections).

employment will no longer be attainable solely through economic growth. A policy aiming at economic growth at all cost is open to criticism for reasons of ecology as well as social policy, as is illustrated by the need for a humanization of work life.

In contrast to the past economic growth and full employment can no longer be taken as the unquestioned foundations of social policy. Instead for the foreseeable future any social policy must consider unemployment as a problem that can no longer be solved only with traditional policy instruments. . . .

New lifestyles have spawned criticisms of the welfare state which question any social consensus that is reached by those whose positions are other than conservatism and liberalism. This criticism, partly embraced even by Social Democrats, is not directed against the very concept of social welfare. Instead it aims at some instruments and institutions of the welfare state which in West Germany as elsewhere have a specific historical origin and social profile. Criticism is directed in particular against the preference for a remedial rather than a preventive social policy, against the "professionalization" and "bureaucratization" in the implementation of social policy, and against the atrophy of the principle of self-help so typical today among the insured. . . .

A comprehensive reform of the social welfare system which extends beyond isolated changes in specific policy arenas is necessary. Since 1973 social policymakers have learned the hard way that a comprehensive reform is the only alternative to a succession of illiberal and fiscally motivated cuts that typically hit the underprivileged hardest. Social Democrats will defend the welfare state successfully against its conservative and liberal critics only if they call publicly for its comprehensive reform.

In the foreseeable future the economy simply will not support a social policy that aims solely at increasing the relative share of the social budget in national income. As the financial capacity declines, rising unemployment, an aging population, and an explosion in the cost of health care are some of the growing social burdens. In the future it will therefore not be possible to finance existing social services without substantial increase in taxes and withholdings. Although limited increases may be inevitable, it is doubtful whether substantial increases will be either possible or desirable.

Instead, financial resources available for social objectives must be targeted more specifically and utilized in a more just manner to preserve the existing quality of welfare services. Future social policy shall thus not only distribute increases in services but also redistribute different entitlements to social welfare. This requires that we set clear priorities. We need to decide under which conditions one is to receive welfare benefits and which conditions in life will have to be met by private means or with the help of family. Clear rules should stipulate who is to contribute financially and who is not. Social policymakers can no longer afford to have existing structures dictate the priorities of social policy.

A comprehensive reform of the social welfare system is needed for reasons other than financial. The injustices that derive from a system organized along the lines of occupational status are numerous, as are the situations where equal social conditions are treated differently both in the claims that are permitted and in the financial assistance that can be granted. Social legislation and its interpretation by the courts have become so complicated that to the average citizen the social welfare system is virtually impenetrable. We lack a minimum level of insurance for everyone. Various social insurance funds are so fragmented that it is very difficult for them to organize effective preventive measures, rehabilitation, and well-planned, necessary, and cost-effective social services.

A reorganization of the social welfare system can be undertaken only in small steps over a long period of time. The social welfare state requires that we honor well-established entitlements and avoid massive interventions into the plans of individuals. The working group knows that the achievement of comprehensive reform is a long-term task. The group is, however, convinced that it should be possible to approach this target in the foreseeable future. . . .

4-8. BASIC ELEMENTS OF A "GREEN" PENSION REFORM*

This pamphlet represents an early attempt of the Green party to move from ecological to other social issues. Seeking to forge an alliance with West Germany's elderly population, the party advocates a comprehensive flat-rate pension system. This would break drastically with the earnings-related social security system that has evolved in the Federal Republic and would in particular benefit women.

*Jürgen Borchert et al., *Grundrente statt Altersarmut: Die ''Grünen'' und die ''Grauen Panther'' fordern Rentenreform* (Berlin: Verlagsgesellschaft Gesundheit, 1985), pp. 77–79, 97.

A basic reform of social security must contain the following elements: 1. A basic pension of at least 1,000 D.M. for everyone. 2. A system of pensions that assures women independence in old age. 3. A uniform social security system for all people.

A basic pension of at least 1,000 D.M. for all. The centerpiece of the alternative pension system which the Greens propose is the demand for a basic monthly pension of at least 1,000 deutschmarks to be paid to all German citizens and foreign residents of 60 years of age. This basic pension is an individual entitlement that is unrelated to prior earnings and independent of the recipient's way of life (single or married). This basic pension should secure a lifestyle that does not offend the dignity of old age. Today's welfare payment is so low that it offends old people (and the young!). A basic pension of 1,000 deutschmarks is possible now. For starters we propose that the basic pension be financed by general tax revenues, a solidarity fund into which the whole society pays. Pensions should be fully indexed, that is, linked to the general development in wages and prices. The additional revenues needed should be raised through a tax on the gross production value added. This tax would replace the wage-related fringe costs that employers must pay. In any case the basic pension that the Greens and the "Gray Panthers" [the lobby for the elderly] demand favors the poorer segments of the population. The basic pension will prevent poverty among the old. A basic pension of 1,000 deutschmarks would guarantee an elderly couple 2,000 deutschmarks each month (without any additional private old age insurance). This is far more than the average payment in today's public insurance system.

A pension assuring women some independence in old age. Independence for women in old age could be reached by combining a basic pension financed through tax revenues with a supplementary insurance-based pension that divides contributions equally between spouses and a child-rearing "pension credit system" (at a minimum three years a child credited at 100 percent of average income). The existing structure of social security makes it much more difficult, if not impossible, to reach the same objective. To assure older women some independence, we must have a basic pension that is not tied to prior earnings since, compared to men, women on average earn only a little more than one half. . . .

A uniform social security system for all. We must eliminate today's social security system, which is organized in a feudal manner along the lines of occupational status. Only powerful and privileged interest groups defend the "organically grown," "differentiated" system. That the very people who without any scruples ravage our forests and pollute our rivers suddenly become quite conservative when they defend a system that is "organically grown" is not surprising. Today's chaotic system of social security is not designed to increase freedom of choice for the individual citizen. Instead, employees are pushed into one system or another virtually at birth. This fragmented social security system is expensive and inefficient. It spawns an enormous administrative apparatus, wastes scarce financial resources, and in the end prevents a socially equitable pension system for all. That is why the Greens propose including the whole population in a social security system composed of a basic pension and a supplementary insurance.

Who pays? A comprehensive reform of social security organized along the lines of this "alternative pension model for all" can be financed. Poverty among the old cannot be justified with economic reasoning as our calculations make abundantly clear. A basic pension of at least 1,000 deutschmarks, a social security system that guarantees old women their independence, and a uniform system of social security are not mere illusions but the demands of a forward-looking reform policy. Whether these demands will be translated into reality depends largely on whether we can successfully apply political pressure to the defenders of the status quo. This reform of social security, it is patently clear, would have to be paid for by corporations; public employees, especially civil servants; and men with high earnings. Women would be the main beneficiaries.

5   Migrant Workers

The politics of recruiting and then adapting to the presence of migrant labor opens an uncomfortable chapter in German history. This is reflected in the very concept of "guest workers" which the West Germans have coined to describe the millions of Southern Europeans who have moved to the Federal Republic since the early 1960s. One of the possible German translations of "foreign workers" (*Fremdarbeiter*) was stigmatized by the Nazis' deportation of more than 6 million people, especially from Eastern Europe, under this name to staff their war machine. The concept of guest worker retains the illusion of temporary migration despite the reality of permanent immigration. It also offers a jarring juxtaposition of social courtesy and menial labor. Furthermore, because of its past, observers of West Germany are nervously watching the crescendo of xenophobia in the economic crisis of the 1980s for signs of a displaced form of antisemitism (Hoskin, 1985).

The West Germans are largely ignorant of the living conditions of workers. In 1985 a free-lance journalist, Günter Wallraff, published his book *At the Very Bottom,* the West German analogue to John Howard Griffin's *Black Like Me*. The book records Wallraff's dismal experience, disguised as a Turk, living in West Germany. Selling 650,000 copies in the first two weeks, the book became an all-time best-seller. As Walraff shows West German society is deeply split. Compared to the United States, German culture has traditionally been inward rather than outward looking. Turkish-Americans proudly parading down New York City's Fifth Avenue are one example of "social integration by hyphenation." This is a heretical concept in West Germany. You can be Turkish or you can be West German, but you can't be both. The absorption of millions of foreigners, especially Turks, in times of high unemployment is evidently testing the insecure politeness with which the West Germans refer to their foreign workers.

By the end of World War I Germany had lost all of its overseas colonies. It thus has not had to address the vexing question of race and citizenship which has been so important in Britain and France (Freemann, 1979). Instead, at the end of World War II millions of Germans left Eastern Europe where they had settled centuries ago. But as in all other advanced industrial countries, since 1945 a growing international migration has affected West Germany (Böhning, 1970; Lohrmann and Manfrass, 1974). The liberal international economy that the West Germans embraced and labor mobility in the EC put West Germany's export industries in an enviable position. Among the advanced industrial countries only Japan resisted the attractions of importing a foreign workforce. Instead, the Japanese exported their plants to neighboring countries. But in Northern and Western Europe, West Germany's reliance on foreign labor is hardly unique. Since the late 1950s, Britain, France, Scandinavia, the Low Countries, Austria, and Switzerland have also imported a substantial foreign workforce. Like the Federal Republic, these countries are now struggling with the social consequences of cultural heterogeneity in a period of high unemployment.

As has been true of the economic and social issues discussed in Chapters 2–4, policymaking on questions of migrant labor has been incremental. Between the late 1950s and 1973, the key actors and their relationship resembled the political arrangements typical of the Federal Republic more generally. On questions of recruitment, centralized interest groups for business and unions interacted with the Federal Employment Office in Nuremberg which in turn operates under the jurisdiction of the Labor Ministry. Social issues deriving from the growing cultural heterogeneity of German society were administered by private welfare associations, especially the churches, as well as state and local governments. In this institutional network, the consequences of importing a large number of foreign workers were never seriously discussed. Policymakers assumed that increasingly labor mobility in the EC should be encouraged and that foreign "guests" from other countries would return home should West Germany's economic fortunes decline.

The ban on any further recruitment of foreign workers announced by the federal government during the first oil shock in November 1973 prepared the ground for proving both of these assumptions wrong. Although the number of foreign workers temporarily declined, the number of foreign residents increased. Foreign workers evidently were not returning home. Yet until the late 1970s West German policymakers kept insisting that the Federal Republic was not a land of immigration. Furthermore, because it anticipated a further large-scale influx of Turkish workers, West Germany opposed granting Turkey an associate membership in the EC. Yet policy change continued to be incremental and vaccillating as the issue became increasingly politicized. Growing social problems and public resentment of foreign workers have to date not altered the customary incremental approach of West German policymaking elites.

Context

Germany's delayed but rapid industrialization in the nineteenth century proved an irresistible magnet, attracting Poles from Russia and Austria-Hungary to Eastern Prussia (Bade 1984a, 1984b; Dohse, 1981a; Spaich, 1981). What came to be known as the "Polish Question" was shaped by an increasingly aggressive German policy of acculturating its Polish population, which in turn spread Polish nationalism. With this policy the Prussian government hoped to permanently annex formerly Polish territories. To defend this policy against the "subversive" influence of a growing number of Poles, the Prussian government deported 30,000–40,000 Poles in 1885–86 and closed its eastern border.

However, this policy conflicted sharply with the economic interests of the landed aristocracy in Eastern Prussia as well as the mining industry in Upper Silesia. Eastern Prussian agriculture increasingly lost its rural labor force to other parts of Germany where wages were higher. The political tensions over this issue in the Prussian elite grew, and in 1890 the Prussian government cautiously opened its borders to unmarried, seasonal workers who were restricted to employment largely in Eastern Prussia. In addition to their demand for higher agricultural tarriffs, Prussian landowners in 1900 tied their support of Germany's naval armaments program to a further liberalization of migration policy. Although they were partly successful, Polish labor continued to be admitted only on a seasonal basis.

The government imposed less onerous political restrictions on industry, and the import of foreign workers made it possible for business to contain wage increases. Even the Prussian state benefited from the effect that foreign labor had on the cost of public works. Its power to deport foreign workers was unrestricted and useful for deterring these workers from organizing in unions or participating in collective bargaining. Labor shortages in World War I were met by recruiting—increasingly through the use of force—Poles living in Russian territory that the Germans had seized and by further restricting the movement of Poles already working in Germany. By the end of the war there were 700,000 Poles in Germany.

The conflict between the political and the economic interests of the Nazi regime were even more striking than they had been in Imperial Germany (Homze, 1967). The German war industry could not function without forced foreign labor, which numbered more than 6 million by the end of the war. These foreign workers were joined by 2 million prisoners of war and the inmates of the hundreds of concentration camps dotting the German countryside. This labor pool helped arm the 13 million German soldiers whom the Nazis had drafted. Yet by the standards of the Nazis' racist ideology and practice, to the extent that they came from Eastern Europe, foreign workers, prisoners of war, and the inmates of concentration camps were all inferior and potentially all subject to extermination. The deportation of workers was organized by the German Employment Office and often assisted by the army, the Gestapo, or the Nazi storm troopers. German industry cooperated closely with the Nazi regime. More than 40 percent of the workforce in some of Germany's key industrial firms—Krupp, Flick, I. G. Farben—was foreign. In the aircraft industry the proportion was as high as 90 percent. German industrialists refused to admit to any wrongdoing after the war, notwithstanding voluminous evidence to the contrary (Ferencz, 1979). In any case, German industry had had substantial experience employing foreign labor before the influx of workers from Southern Europe began in the late 1950s.

This migration from the South was in fact the third wave reaching the Federal Republic. First, at the end of World War II all of the Eastern European countries expelled more than 7 million Germans who had settled there, some centuries ago (International Labour Office, 1959). Second, 2.6 million refugees from East Germany crossed the West German border before the Berlin Wall was erected in 1961. Adding the children of refugees subsequently born in the Federal Republic brings the total to more than 12 million. The overabundance of labor in the 1950s was one of the important ingredients of the "economic miracle" of the 1950s (Kindleberger, 1967) (see Chapter 2). In contrast to the subsequent migration from Southern Europe, these 12 million Germans were fully absorbed into German society within a generation. Special government programs such as the "Equalization of Burdens Act" sought to distribute more fairly the social consequences of the war among those who had lost little and those who had lost everything. Special housing programs for refugees were generously subsidized by the government. The strategy of export-led growth created jobs for a swollen labor force. By the early 1970s the two waves of German refugees had become fully assimilated into West German society. When in the late 1970s a much smaller number of Germans arrived from the Soviet Union, Poland, and Romania, it was absorbed with little controversy even though the issue of foreign workers was by then highly charged.

But a third wave of migrants began arriving in the late 1950s. The Iron Curtain had cut West Germany off from its traditional supply of labor in the east; hence, these migrants came from the south (Berger, 1975). Two world wars had left the Federal Republic with a lopsided demographic structure. Between 1962 and 1972 its working population decreased by 6.6 percent, a loss of more than 3 billion working hours (Rist, 1978, p. 110). Guest workers were recruited to fill the gap. The number of migrant workers, most of them Italian, increased from 100,000 in 1955 to half a million in 1961 and reached 1 million by 1964. Like workers from all other EC member states, Italians enjoyed legal rights comparable to those of West German workers. Political restrictions on the status of migrant labor could only be applied to citizens from countries that did not belong to the EC, such as Turkey or Yugoslavia. But in the 1960s labor mobility was very much in agreement with the economic doctrine of neoliberalism and its insistence on the central role of markets. No group or party thought about the problems that substantial immigration would eventually create for West Germany's social policy in such areas as housing or education. Indeed, until the late 1970s West Germany's migrant labor policy was remarkable for the lack of public debate it provoked, on the one hand, and the far-reaching effects that the migrants had on questions of economic, social, educational, and foreign policy, on the other.

Agenda

The agenda for policy affecting guest workers was shaped not by the political plans of the government or important interest groups but by developments in the global economy and the international state system. West Germany's spectacular economic growth in the 1950s rested on an export strategy geared to increasingly liberalized international markets. The building of the Berlin Wall in August 1961 shut the West German economy off from a stream of East German refugees, many of whom were skilled and needed no special assistance to integrate fully into West German society. Hiring foreign workers, rather than shifting production abroad or accepting lower rates of economic growth, was then viewed in all political quarters as the only sensible response. The oil shock of 1973 and the stabilization crisis induced by the Bundesbank (see Chapter 2) led the federal government to ban any further recruitment of foreign workers, whose numbers had increased from 1.5 million in 1969 to 2.6 million in 1973. By 1980 increasing political repression in Third World countries together with the continued strength of the West German economy throughout the 1970s had created a new wave of more than 100,000 political refugees, many of whom came to the Federal Republic intent on finding a job and staying. Since Article 16 of the Basic Law of the Bonn Republic grants all political refugees an unconditional right to stay, the West Germans suddenly confronted a new type of migrant workers.

But the policy agenda was structured also by the gradual pressures that the increasing number of migrant workers put on different policy sectors. The increase in numbers was very rapid in the 1960s. One million guest workers had come by 1964, 2.0 million by 1970, and 2.6 million by 1972. Although the number of guest workers decreased between 1973 and the early 1980s by about half a million, the total number of foreigners did not; for the number of dependents grew sharply, reaching 2.5 million in the early 1980s. Because they were staying increasingly longer, guest workers either married and had children or, more typically, brought their families with them. This influx created problems in the fields of education and housing; social integration began to trouble West German policymakers under the rubric of "the second generation." The "Polish Question" of the 1890s has been transformed to the "Turkish Question" in the 1980s.

The objectives of the major groups of producers derived from their position in the German economy (Dohse, 1981a, pp. 145–65). By the mid-1950s labor shortage had become a serious constraint for West German agriculture, which demanded that the government recruit foreign workers. Industry soon followed suit. Business was interested in recruiting more workers and in containing the demands for higher wages which West German workers could make in increasingly tight labor markets. Full employment appeared a threat rather than a blessing. At times firms collaborated regionally by refusing to hire workers who had left their former employers to obtain higher wages and better fringe benefits. Importing migrant labor in the face of buoyant demand came naturally, especially to large corporations that had operated throughout World War II with large numbers of forcibly imported foreign workers (Castles and Kosack, 1985; Markovits and Kazarinov, 1978).

Because the import of foreign workers slowed the changing balance of power between employers and workers, the unions for agricultural and construction workers who first confronted the new labor pool were opposed. But the trade union federation agreed with a policy that integrated West Germany's national labor market into the wider European market (Barkin, 1966; Castles and Kosack, 1974). It insisted, however, on two conditions: foreign workers should be paid the same wages as West German workers; and at all times local employment offices should give preference to West German workers and workers from EC countries. Business accepted the first condition. The second found expression in ministerial decrees and administrative regulations. Although its basic demands were met, in the mid-1950s the trade union federation was reluctant to agree to active recruitment of foreign labor as long as the West German economy had not reached full employment. The year in which the West German government negotiated its first agreement with Italy was in the union's view not yet a year of full employment. The union evidently preferred to fully exploit West Germany's labor reserves, both the unemployed concentrated in particular regions and women. But in principle unions supported the policy of recruiting foreign labor.

In the late 1950s the conflict of interest between business and unions was muted. With perfect hindsight, we can say that the 1950s were remarkable for the lack of an open political debate of the issue. The unions, in particular, were preoccupied with other questions—codetermination and rearmament, for example—and did not make foreign workers one of their prime concerns. The admission of foreign workers in increasing numbers was viewed simply as an unavoidable part of an encompassing dual strategy—neoliberalism at home and European integration abroad—that promised a decisive break with the German past.

The economic crisis of the 1970s and 1980s revealed once more that business and unions did not differ fundamentally on how to deal with migrant workers (Dohse, 1981a, pp. 307–58). When in 1973 the federal government imposed a ban on the influx of additional foreign workers from countries that were not members of the EC, the Federation of Employers lobbied to be allowed to recruit seasonal workers, albeit under strict government supervision. It quickly accepted the fact that the recruitment of foreign workers for the long term was no longer acceptable in an era of growing unemployment. Although business was unsuccessful, as demanded by business, the Federal Employment Office was instructed by the Budget Consolidation Act of 1975 to tighten the eligibility requirements for those West German workers who received unemployment compensation while refusing to accept low-paying or low-skill jobs. Sharp increases in unemployment rates prompted the unions to support the restrictive policies that the federal government adopted after 1973. Without any public debate, the labor movement simply adhered to the principle that it had articulated two decades earlier and that had informed government policy ever since: in times of unemployment West Germans and workers from EC member states were to be granted preference over all other foreign workers, such as Turks or Yugoslavs.

Between 1960 and 1980 the agenda of the federal government was largely economic. In the 1950s a coalition government led by the CDU favored the demands of the business community. Its policy aimed at price stability in times of high economic growth; and labor immigration was conducive to a low-inflation policy. After 1973 a coalition government led by the SPD banned any further immigration, thus honoring the unions' expectation that West German workers would be preferred in hard times. But throughout the 1970s, in the absence of sustained public debate government policy rested on a basic contradiction, as indeed it had ever since the late 1950s. Time and again the politicians repeated that West Germany was not a "country of immigration." Instead, the government's migration policy was predicated on the assumption that the guest workers would eventually return home. Yet with every passing year it became more evident that in fact this was not happening. The expectation that foreign workers would be the shock absorbers of the West German economy in times of economic adversity had been plausible in the 1960s. In the short recession of 1966–67 at least 300,000 and perhaps as many as 500,000 foreign workers left. This return migration seemed to suggest that West Germany might not have to incur the substantial costs of investing in the housing and education of the migrant workers and their families. But the 1970s proved otherwise. By 1980 two-thirds of the foreign workers and one-half of the foreign population had lived in the Federal Republic for more than ten years (Bade, 1984a, p. 40).

In the summer of 1973 a series of wildcat strikes among the foreign workers spread from the sprawling Ford plants in Cologne to numerous other places throughout the Federal Republic. "These strikes preoccupied German officials and seemed to endanger not only the government's stabilization policy and its wage strategy, but the entire social partnership system designed to maintain labor peace" (Miller, 1981, p. 110). The restrictive course of policy adopted in November 1973 was undoubtedly influenced by the previous hot summer. Furthermore, in June 1973 the federal government issued the first of several reports which for the first time took account of the growing social problems that accompanied a policy of favoring the importation of foreign workers (Mehrländer, 1978, pp. 120–27; Schiller, 1975). Specifically, the report recommended that prior to granting a work permit the government insisted that adequate housing should be secured, that the regional concentration of foreign workers should be taken into account, and that the processing fees for employers should be increased from 300 to 1,000 deutschmarks. In addition, the illegal import of foreign workers should be punished more severely, and the legal position of long-term foreign residents should be improved. This tentative move toward a more restrictive admissions procedure and a greater concern for the social integration of foreign workers was short-circuited by the total ban on recruiting foreign workers imposed in November 1973. The swiftness with which the government imposed its ban in November 1973 resulted largely from the realization that the international economic context had greatly changed (Huber and Unger, 1982, pp. 124–94). Yet this drastic change in policy did not eliminate numerous problems.

The government's new approach was reflected in a series of policy decisions made after 1973 (see Reading 5-2). All of these measures followed from the view that the problem of migrant labor was a strictly economic affair and that all measures should reflect the legal requirement expressing the unions' demand that available employment opportunities be reserved for West Germans. Work permits were to be issued for no more than one year, thus making it possible for local employment offices to continually reassess regional labor market conditions. Foreign workers were also discriminated against in the payment of unemployment compensation (Dohse, 1981b, pp. 20–24). Work permits were refused to family members who came to West Germany after November

1974. This policy affected thirty to forty thousand foreign teenagers entering West Germany's labor force annually in the mid-1970s. Cities were required to ban further immigration once the number of foreigners had reached more than 12 percent. The short-term effects of these measures produced the desired results. In the first two years after these actions were taken, the number of foreign workers with legal jobs declined by 450,000 (Rist, 1978, p. 113).

In 1977 a commission of the federal and state governments charged to produce a new plan for the government's policy dealing with migrant workers issued its report (see Reading 5-3). This report revealed the contradictory premises of government policy. It reiterated the traditional position that West Germany is not a country of immigration, while insisting that the foreign workers then living in the Federal Republic would be needed for an indefinite future. The report also stressed that policy should make it more attractive for migrant workers to return home, short of expulsion or deportation, while recommending that the legal status of foreign workers should be made more secure.

The status of foreign workers was improved in 1978 with passage of a reform that made it possible for foreign workers to attain the status of long-term residents after only five years; however, they still lacked sufficient legal protection against expulsion. The general shift in policy toward a consideration of social issues was symbolized in 1978 by the creation of a new position, the "commissioner of the federal government for the integration of foreign workers and their families." In 1979 a report by the first commissioner (the Kühn Report) addressed the vexing questions of how to deal with the integration of the "second generation," that is, the children of foreign workers (see Reading 5-4). In particular it advocated a sharp improvement in the legal, economic, and social position of children based on the assumption that the Federal Republic had become de facto a country of immigrants. It urged, among other recommendations, an extension of suffrage in local elections to all foreign workers.

The increasing concern over the growth of West Germany's foreign population has been evident in the growing number of reports and policy initiatives since 1979. In 1979 a commission convened by the minister for work and social welfare assembled representatives of political parties, parapublic institutions, and the bureaucracy from different levels of government. Its detailed recommendations aimed at facilitating the social integration of the children of guest workers. For the first time, a commission's report took account of West Germany's complex policy network. In March 1980 the federal government announced new guidelines for a policy of social integration which were based in part on the recommendations of the two reports issued in the previous year. Characteristically, these guidelines could inform but not determine the policies adopted by states and local governments. In December 1981 the federal government issued guidelines harmonizing the regulations of the different states governing the immigration of the dependents of foreign workers. In March 1983 a blue-ribbon commission developed detailed recommendations for the new government of Chancellor Kohl (see Reading 5-7). On many substantive points the commission remained divided. Finally, in November 1983 the Bundestag passed a law providing financial incentives to encourage foreign workers to leave the Federal Republic.

In sum, during the 1970s and the 1980s the federal government's policy continued to vaccillate. In the words of Ray Rist (1978, p. 113), policy was characterized by a "structural ambivalence" that permitted only incremental change. It was based on contradictory premises and advocated inconsistent objectives. In contrast to Britain and France, the issue was not seriously debated by political parties in national politics until the late 1970s. The inconsistencies of federal policy in the 1970s were in fact manifestations of a broad agreement that any major departure in policy would be too costly, economically, socially, and politically. Excluding expulsion and assimilation as unacceptably extreme solutions, West German policymakers advocated a vaguely defined policy of social integration that permitted a broad spectrum of interpretations by all of the relevant political actors (see Reading 5-8). Consensus is mirrored in the fact that policymakers significantly altered only two policy measures. The restrictions imposed on internal migration in 1975 were rescinded two years later, evidently because they were not effective. The regulations imposing initially severe restrictions on the movement of the dependents of foreign workers to West Germany were also subsequently modified.

Process

Policy formulation occurs in a network in which state institutions are tied closely to the major interest groups. The position of the Federal Employment Office and the role of the federal government are strong (Dohse, 1981a). The principle of parity representation of business and unions in the recruitment of foreign workers had been accepted during the early years of the Weimar Republic but was eliminated in 1933 by the Nazis' successful efforts to centralize power in the hands of state officials. Almost unnoticed by the unions then preoccupied with the issue of codetermination, the minister of labor reactivated that statist framework by administrative decree in February 1952. Inside the government, coordinating committees between different federal ministries affected by foreign workers were set up in 1962; similar coordinating committees linking the federal and state governments were established in 1965. Since 1971 the Labor Ministry has had four sections that deal with questions of foreign workers. They formulate strategy, deal with questions of work permits, maintain contact with the private welfare agencies that typically serve foreign workers, and supervise policy measures designed to further the integration of foreign workers in German society, such as language training and special education for the young.

The Labor Ministry has also become the center for organizing corporatist-style consultations involving the major interest groups. Representatives of the major economic interest groups are, as discussed in Chapter 1, represented on the board of directors of the Federal Employment Office. Such actions illustrate the indirect support of business and unions for state policy in the 1960s and 1970s. To the extent that government policy was criticized by the rank and file, union leadership could be counted on as a strong defender. In addition, since 1965 the ministry itself has convened a "coordination circle" that helps formulate policy. Other groups particularly involved in the implementation of policy are also included in the circle, specifically, the welfare organizations of the unions, the Catholic and the Protestant churches, and the peak association of municipalities. For example, the employers' request for the admission of seasonal migrant workers following the imposition of the ban of November 1973 was referred to this circle since it convenes regularly to discuss social policy issues. In this instance the circle formed a subcommittee for further study and consultation.

The important role of the bureaucracy is also reflected in West Germany's method of recruiting foreign workers in the 1960s. In contrast to Britain, France, and Sweden, West Germans did not view recruitment as a political issue to be organized by an office in charge of immigration. Instead, the issue was defined exclusively in terms of labor market management and was thus given to the Federal Employment Office. According to the Labor Promotion Act of 1969, the Employment Office was charged with preventing conditions of labor shortage. Between 1955 and 1968 the Federal Republic and the major Mediterranean states signed seven bilateral treaties that regulated recruitment. Recruitment centers of the Employment Office were opened in Athens, Verona, Madrid, Istanbul, Belgrade, Lisbon, Casablanca, and Tunis; staff numbered in the hundreds. These offices acted as conduits that relayed the requests of German firms for workers to the relevant government organizations in the host country. The employment office of the host country proposed suitable applicants. The West German recruitment center examined the occupational qualifications and the health of these applicants, issued labor permits, arranged for residence permits and a contract with the prospective employer, and provided transportation to West Germany. The whole process was organized with a precision chillingly reminiscent of the 1930s and 1940s (see Reading 5-1). Until June 1973, the prospective employer was charged a fee of 300 deutschmarks for each foreign worker hired. The proportion of foreign workers recruited through these official channels increased from 40 percent in the early 1960s to over 70 percent in the early 1970s.

In the 1970s and 1980s the different actors diverged somewhat in their policy preferences. Generally speaking, the private welfare agencies and the municipalities favor liberal solutions to specific questions involving foreign workers. The Labor Ministry, the Federal Employment Office, and business typically follow a more restrictive line. The unions and the major parties fall somewhere in the middle (Huber and Unger, 1982, pp. 169–82; Reimann and Reimann, 1979, p. 85). The issues that divide a liberal from a restrictive policy stance focus on the conditions under which a permanent residence permit should be granted (supported by the churches and the municipalities), the principle of giving employment preferences to German citizens (favored by the welfare agencies and the churches), suffrage for foreign workers in local elections (opposed by the CDU/CSU), and the status of the Federal Republic as a de facto country of immigration (denied by the SPD, the DGB, and segments of the CDU/CSU). The government has continued to view policy problems primarily from the perspective of labor markets. Accordingly, it has tended to seek agreements with the major economic interest groups and the Employment Office first and only subsequently and less intensively with other institutions. These consultations are often carried out in a group that the employers and unions set up in December 1973 to discuss questions of foreign labor. Since its inception, the Labor Ministry and the Federal Employment Office have been invited to such consultations as permanent "guests." Despite some differences of opinion over details, this process has helped maintain consensus among the most important actors (Reimann and Reimann, 1979, p. 75).

The greatest political threat to the established structure of policy making came from the troubled relations between unions and workers (Castles and Kosack, 1974, 1985, pp. 116–79; Miller, 1981, pp. 155–59, 166–70; Rist, 1978, pp. 120–32). For many reasons class solidarity between West German and foreign workers remained weak. In the hierarchy of skill and pay foreign workers were at the bottom. Differences in language and culture rekindled traditional ethnic prejudices. Finally, differences in legal position and political rights were a constant reminder of the potential threat of competition between West Germans and foreigners over scarce jobs.

Until the late 1960s the attitude of the unions toward foreign workers was to accept them as a necessary but hardly welcome factor in the continued economic expansion of the Federal Republic. In the late 1950s the unions fought successfully for two demands: that the principle of equal pay for equal work should govern all recruitment of foreign workers, and that recruitment should be done only by the Federal Employment Office. Under the assumption that foreign workers would stay only for a year or two before returning home, the DGB accommodated itself to their rapidly growing numbers. "When the 1967 recession sent 300,000 foreign workers back home, the DGB closed its newly opened foreign worker section as if to mark symbolically the closing of this temporary worker chapter in German labor history" (Miller, 1981, p. 157).

However, the subsequent doubling in the number of foreign workers between 1967 and 1971 greatly changed the attitude of the DGB's leadership. It issued its first public position paper calling for the social integration of foreign workers in 1971. But the crux of the matter was not the inadequate access of foreign workers to housing or education, issues on which the unions, like the large welfare associations, had already worked in the 1960s. Instead, wildcat strikes among foreign workers threatened the unity of the labor movement in 1969 and 1973. Foreign workers objected strongly to their marginal position in the organization of the unions and on the works councils (see Chapter 3). In the early 1970s the number of union members among foreign workers was much lower than among West German workers. Only 2.4 percent of all shop stewards and 2.2 percent of all members of works councils were foreigners. Responding to the threat by foreign workers to form a splinter union, the DGB pressed the federal government to include in the 1975 revision of the Aliens Act important demands of foreign workers. They included stronger protection of free speech and free association, reforms in the rules governing residency permits, representation of foreign workers on government advisory boards, and improved access to language and vocational training.

At the same time the DGB also devoted more of its own resources to recruiting foreign workers to union ranks. It increased the number of shop stewards and gave them the right to call meetings, parallel to regular union meetings, in which foreign languages were used. In part because of these changes, between 1974 and 1982 the proportion of foreign workers who were union members jumped by ten points to 35 percent. Foreign workers accounted in the mid-1980s for almost 10 percent of the DGB's membership. But foreign workers remain seriously underrepresented on the works councils (Andersen, 1984, p. 20). Although the attitude of foreign workers toward the DGB remained ambivalent, the greater efforts of the unions to integrate foreign workers and the employment crisis of the 1980s were sufficient to defend the established, centralized structure of policymaking.

That the foreign workers themselves are in no way involved in the policy process merits attention. Since West Germany is not a country of immigration, policymakers have consistently denied the extension of political citizenship, despite beginning to address the issue of social integration. Specifically, in contrast to Britain, foreign workers do not have the right to vote. The number of naturalized foreign workers is infinitesimal, in part because West German administrative practice is highly restrictive on this score, in part because the foreigners themselves are reluctant to become naturalized. In 1982 in West Berlin, for example, a citizenship campaign was aimed at 30,000 of the city's 100,000 plus Turkish inhabitants who were eligible; 50 applied (Viviano and Browning, 1983, p. 6). One reason for the low response is the strong distaste foreign workers feel for the idea of becoming West German citizens. In a 1981 survey 94 percent indicated that they had no intention of relinquishing their old citizenship in favor of a new West German one (Andersen, 1984, Table 11).

As awareness spread that West Germany's foreign workers were likely to stay, the question debated actively in the late 1970s and early 1980s was the extension of suffrage in local elections. Whereas the SPD, the FDP, and the Greens favored such a move, the CDU and the CSU were opposed. There is as yet no substantial majority in favor of what is basically a constitutional issue. Although community- and state-level boards and foreign councils exist to advise the municipalities about the concerns of foreign workers, politically they have been largely ineffective and count for little at least in the eyes of most foreign workers (Miller, 1981, pp. 124–36). This is not surprising. Although the different ethnic groups in the Federal Republic have developed an extensive net of political organizations (Thränhardt, 1984), these local advisory councils must by law have West German representatives, typically chosen from city offices or welfare associations that deal with the social problems of foreign workers (Andersen, 1984, pp. 18–19; Rist, 1978, p. 143). That proponents who seek to solve the problem of citizenship through an extension of naturalization are often accused by West German liberals as "blackmailing" the foreign workers (to choose between their "old" and their "new home" country) may seem odd at first (Sievering, 1981). But it makes sense if viewed against the background of Germany's long tradition of a racist ideology of pan-Germanism and Nazism. West Germans shrink from any measure that smacks of assimilation, be it cultural or political.

For a variety of reasons, the Labor Ministry and the Federal Employment Office play strong roles in policy implementation. These institutions enjoy a large amount of bureaucratic discretion, for example, in the granting of long-term residence permits that free foreign workers from having to apply annually to renew their permit, as was necessary before the adoption of new administrative guidelines in 1978. By administrative fiat, the minimum length of stay before a worker became eligible to apply for a long-term permit was increased from five to eight years. In Hesse, a liberal state traditionally governed by the SPD, 876 of the 434,257 foreign workers, or 0.2 percent, held a long-term residence permit in 1977 (Huber and Unger, 1981, p. 141). For the years 1972–81, the annual average number of foreign workers who were granted West German citizenship was 12,585 or about 3 per 1,000 (Andersen, 1984, Table 10). By 1983 only 95,000 foreign workers from countries that are not EC member states, or 5 percent of those eligible, had a long-term resident permit that offered reasonable legal protection against expulsion. The legal foundation of the bureaucracy's discretionary power is the German Aliens Act, which is based on a bill that the Nazis adopted in 1938 and in its new version puts "the interests of the Federal Republic" ahead of the well-being of the foreign workers. Although considerable public debate led in 1975 to an alteration of the Aliens Act, the bureaucracy's power was left largely intact.

At the same time, generally speaking, the legal cast of West German policymaking has left the figure of illegal migrants working in the Federal Republic, after the ban on further recruitment was imposed in 1973, at about 10 percent. In comparison to the United States this figure is low. Part of the reason probably lies in the very stiff penalties—up to 100,000 deutschmarks and prison terms of up to three years—for employers caught illegally recruiting foreign workers (Reimann and Reimann, 1979, pp. 67–68; Rist, 1978, p. 78). But unfortunately we lack good data on the extent of enforcement of these regulations. Compared to those in other European countries, such as Britain, West Germany's foreign workers appear to have experienced less discrimination at the workplace in the 1960s. W. R. Böhning attributes (1970, p. 22) this to "the tight network of regional employer-trade union agreements (rather than [to] the almost non-existent anti-discrimination legislation), which the trade unions cannot, for ideological as much as practical reasons allow to be broken."

The provision of social services for foreign workers once they were in the Federal Republic was delegated largely to private welfare agencies, mainly religious ones, or left to the municipalities. The government viewed the recruitment of foreign labor for so long as an economic issue in part because on questions of social policy it lacked an institution analogous in its mission to the Employment Office. In the 1970s all private welfare agencies combined employed about six or seven hundred case workers to deal with foreign workers. The agencies divided the six main ethnic groups along religious lines. The Catholic organization (Caritas) takes care of the Catholic groups: Spaniards, Italians, Portugese, and some Yugoslavs. The Protestant organization (Diakonisches Werk) is in charge of the Greeks. And the union organization (Arbeiterwohlfahrt) is responsible for working with the Turks and some Yugoslavs. In the formulation of policy these three act, as noted above, as advocates for foreign workers. They monopolize the welfare field. Although they all receive substantial subsidies from state and local authorities as well as from the Federal Employment Office, only the Arbeiterwohlfahrt is almost wholly dependent on government subsidies. They are truly parapublic institutions (see Chapter 1). The discretion that the public bureaucracy enjoys in dealing with foreign labor also characterizes these private bureaucracies. Case workers, often of foreign descent, have a free hand as long as through their conduct they do not imperil the interests of the agency (Thränhardt, 1984, p. 6; Weber, 1965, p. 41). These interests are shaped by the welfare agency's integration into a broader policy network that involves all levels of government as well as the major economic interest groups (Weber, 1965, p. 41).

Uniform implementation of policy has been constrained by West Germany's international treaty obligations. Since West Germany and Italy were both members of the EC, Italian workers were exempted from a number of administrative restrictions in the 1960s and were guaranteed unrestricted access to the West German labor market in 1968. The restrictions that the federal government placed in 1975 on the movement of foreign workers into highly congested urban areas were removed in 1977 because the pending EC membership of Greece, Spain, and Portugal, and the eventual membership of Turkey, exempted an overwhelming proportion of the foreign workforce from the government's regulation. In the 1980s the effect of international obligations has remained noticeable. Turkey applied for associate membership in the EC in 1964. A protocol about the eventual implementation of labor mobility was signed in 1972. By the mid-1970s it was estimated that more than 1 million Turks were ready to move to the Federal Republic. Political elites in the Federal Republic were in broad agreement that this would strain the social and political capacities of the Federal Republic beyond endurance. Turks and Yugoslavs thus remain the only sizable ethnic groups without EC status. Their legal position in West Germany is precarious. But even after a ten-year transition period lapsed in 1986, the West German government remained adamantly opposed to honoring the treaty obligation of granting free labor mobility to EC members should Turkey be formally admitted as a full member. Instead, in bilateral negotiations with the Turkish government West Germany offered increased military assistance.

Equally noteworthy are the contrasting approaches that different states, governed either by the CDU or the SPD, have taken on the question of socially integrating foreign workers (see Reading 5-7). Regulations pertaining to foreign spouses and children who intended to join their families already living in the Federal Republic were applied much more restrictively in the CDU/CSU strongholds of Bavaria and Baden-Württemberg than in Hesse or Hamburg, which are governed by the SPD. Similar differences are also evident in the administration of social welfare policies. But by the late 1970s the attention of West German policymakers was increasingly focused on the problem of how to integrate the "second generation" of guest workers, specifically through the school system. Education is a matter that does not fall under the jurisdiction of the federal government (see Chapter 7). Policy has thus failed to converge despite the guidelines that the cultural ministers issued in 1964 and subsequently revised in 1971 and 1976. Education policy is informed by two different models. "Liberal" states ruled by the SPD, such as Bremen or Hesse, tend to pursue a policy of social "integration"; "conservative" states governed by the CDU or CSU, such as Baden-Württemberg or Bavaria, typically pursue a policy of "rotation." The first model exemplifies educational policies that aim at the assimilation and eventual absorption of foreign communities into West German society; the second model is based on the assumption that foreign communities are transient (Rist, 1978, pp. 204–44). An important government commission that issued its report in March 1983 documents in great detail that the restrictive approach favored, for example, by Bavaria, Baden-Württemberg, and the BDI differs markedly from the more liberal approach of Bremen, Hesse, and the federal commissioner for foreign workers (see Reading 5-7).

These striking differences in party philosophy are reflected on other questions. For example, CDU Governor Hans Filbinger of Baden-Württemberg advocated in the mid-1970s a policy of the "golden handshake" whereby he sought to encourage foreign workers to leave by offering them a cash bonus. The proposal follows logically from the "rotation" model and has been criticized strongly by the unions and the SPD. It was adopted by the federal government in November 1983. In 1984 an estimated 545,000 foreign workers and their families left the Federal Republic each with a government payment equivalent to $3,600 (and $500 dollars for each child) (Gupte, 1984, p. 86). On average every second foreign worker who left also received a substantial cash bonus from her former employer. These payments were in lieu of social services to which returning workers would have been entitled had they stayed in the Federal Republic. Since during 1975–82 annual return migration swung from a high of 600,000 in 1975 to a low of 366,000 in

1979, it is not yet clear whether this policy initiative achieved its intended purpose. Informed analysts estimate the numerical effect at less than 50,000 (Dohse, 1985, p. 15). This figure appears plausible in view of the fact that in subsequent years the government has substantially cut the cash incentives.

But at the federal level the ambiguous yet enduring consensus that has supported a policy based on contradictory assumptions does not permit these partisan differences to dominate the relations between parties, producers, local governments, and private welfare agencies. In his inaugural address Chancellor Kohl identified foreign workers as one of four high-priority areas, equal in standing to unemployment, social welfare, and national security, that his government would seek to reform fundamentally. But as is true of other sectors, incremental policymaking has dulled the edge of a conservative reorientation. The policy of the CDU government is distinguishable from that of its SPD predecessor only in matters of detail. The basic policy line, anchored in a set of parapublic institutions and collaborative political arrangements, has remained remarkably unchanged.

Consequences

The most obvious consequence of three decades of incremental policymaking on the issue of foreign workers is the fact that West Germany has become a culturally and ethnically pluralistic country of immigration. In the early decades of this century Poles who had migrated to the Ruhr faced considerable hardships before integrating with German society. Like American blacks, they used sports as a vehicle for social mobility. For example, one of the most respected soccer clubs of the interwar period was Schalke 04 which had many players with Polish backgrounds and called Gelsenkirchen, a center of the Ruhr area, its home. As late as the 1950s West Germany's national team had players with names such as Tilkowski, Szymaniak, or Kwiatkowski. Today's Turks play in separate soccer clubs. Although it is too early to tell whether or not they will eventually be assimilated into West German society, we know that state and society in West Germany were more receptive, both in the policies adopted and in the values espoused, toward integration of the 12.0 million Germans from Eastern Europe and East Germany than toward the 4.5 million Southern Europeans who are presently living in the Federal Republic. A major difference is political. Article 113 of the Basic Law granted automatic citizenship to German refugees from Eastern Europe. Political pressure from the Allies and fear of political radicalization among the refugees made a policy of social integration plausible. Moreover, since the refugees had the right to vote, what was plausible became compelling in the electoral strategies of the political parties. In contrast, international pressures for the social integration of the migrant workers from Southern Europe are weak, and they are denied the right to vote. Nothing symbolizes this difference better than the willingness of conservative politicians to attempt to solve the problem in times of great fiscal restraint by bribing foreign workers with a cash stipend.

Advocated several times since the mid-1970s, this "golden glove" policy illustrates the shifting balance between the economic benefits so evident to West German business in the 1960s and the social costs so evident to West German politicians in the 1980s. Rough economic calculations that take account of the prior investments of the home country in education and subsistence of foreign workers and the cumulative annual investment of these savings in West Germany arrive at a figure well above 100 billion deutschmarks (Rist, 1978, p. 37). But the political impact of such a figure is close to zero today. Since the late 1970s West Germans have worried not about the reasons for past economic successes but about the factors contributing to present social burdens. Competition for jobs is increasing. In decaying inner city districts West German schools must make substantial investments to accommodate foreign children whose proportion often exceeds one-half or even three-quarters of the total student body. Foreigners have access to a broad range of social welfare services that even in hard times for most of them make life in the Federal Republic economically more attractive than moving back to another country that many of them, especially the younger ones, have no reason to call home.

But facts that to the West Germans signify economic cost to the foreigners often symbolize political marginalization and social segmentation. Unemployment among guest workers was 14.9 percent in 1983 as compared to 9.5 percent for the total population, reversing the temporary convergence in unemployment rates of foreigners and West Germans that occurred in the mid-1970s (Zuleeg, 1985, p. 298). And in the 1980s specialists estimate the actual unemployment rate among foreign workers to be ten percent higher than the official figure (Dohse, 1985, p. 14a). About half of the foreigners do not have the unlimited working permit that assures them of unemployment compensation. These workers depend on finding employment during the one-year grace period that the local employment offices customarily grant. Many other social services are extended by discretion of the welfare bureaucracy. Deportation becomes more probable if the foreigner cannot earn a living (Zuleeg, 1985, pp. 300–302). In general social policy grants support to individuals in times of need such as illness, unemployment, and old age. This logic is reversed in the case of migrant labor. Potentially repressive state action, such as expulsion, comes into play only when migrant workers lose their jobs. Economic risks are not counteracted but reinforced by politics.

Whereas the number of foreign workers declined sharply from 2.6 million in 1973 to 1.9 million in 1976, it decreased by only another 200,000 in the next seven years (see Table 5-1). The growth in the number of dependents explains why the total foreign population has increased from 4.0 million in 1979 to 4.6 million in 1983. West Germany's population increased from 40 million in 1870 to 56 million in 1976. But a current long-term projection by the Office of Statistics based on the decline of the birth rate in the 1960s and 1970s, predicts a German population of 52 million in the year 2000 and of 39 million in the year 2030 (Bade, 1984b, p. 622; Klauder, 1984, pp. 696–730). Whatever the merits of any particular set of projections, the conclusion is inescapable: the relative number of foreigners will increase. This is a source of great worry for the political Right (see Reading 5-5). All official pronouncements to the contrary, West Germany has become a country of immigration. In 1980 the average length of stay for foreigners was more than nine years. In addition, more than half of the foreigners had spent more than eight years in the Federal Republic (Dohse, 1981b, p. 6).

Tendencies toward social segmentation are well documented in numerous studies especially in the areas of education, vocational training, youth unemployment, workplace relations, and housing. Compounded by the continuing uncertainties about their residence permits, this interlocking syndrome of social disadvantages relegates the second generation of foreign workers especially to a position of permanent economic and social marginality. The number of foreign children under 16 increased from 364,000 in 1969 to 768,000 in 1974 and 1.2 million in 1981. More than half of these children were born in the Federal Republic. They face severe educational handicaps (Baker, Lenhardt, and Meyer, 1985). Between 10 and 25 percent do not attend school. Those who do are seriously underrepresented in secondary schools leading to higher education. Half in fact leave school without the required certifi-

TABLE 5-1 Foreign Workers in West Germany, 1960–83

Year	(1) Total Number of Employees (in millions)	(2) Employed Foreign Workers (in millions)	(3) Foreign Workers as % of Total Employees	(4) Total Number of Foreigners (in millions)	(5) Total Number of Foreigners % of Resident Population
1960	21.96	0.33	1.5	0.69	1.2
1965	21.35	1.22	5.7	1.22[a]	2.1[a]
1967	21.09	0.99	4.7	1.81	2.8
1969	21.45	1.50	7.0	2.38	3.9
1971	21.76	2.24	10.3	3.44	5.6
1973	21.81	2.60	11.9	3.97	6.4
1975	20.68	2.17	10.5	4.09	6.6
1977	20.10	1.87	9.3	3.95	6.4
1979	20.83	1.94	9.3	4.15	6.7
1981	20.88	1.90	9.1	4.63	7.5
1983	20.16	1.71	8.5	4.53	7.4

Sources: Cols. (1) and (2): For 1960–75, Ray C. Rist, *Guestworkers in Germany: The Prospects for Pluralism* (New York: Praeger, 1978), p. 62. For 1977–83, Uwe Andersen, "Political Participation of Immigrants in Germany" (paper prepared for the European Consortium for Political Research, 12th ECPR Joint Sessions of Workshops, Workshop on Political Participation of Immigrants in Western Europe, Salzburg, April 13–18, 1984), Table 1. Cols. (4) and (5): Der Beauftragte der Bundesregierung für Ausländerfragen, *Bericht zur Ausländerpolitik* (Bonn, March 19, 1984), p. 72. Martin Frey, "Ausländer in der Bundesrepublik Deutschland: Ein statistischer Überblick," *Aus Politik und Zeitgeschichte* B 25/82 (June 26, 1982), p. 3. Hermann Korte, "Labor Migration and the Employment of Foreigners in the Federal Republic of Germany since 1950," in Rosemarie Rogers, ed. *Guests Come to Stay: The Effects of European Labor Migration on Sending and Receiving Countries* (Boulder: Westview, 1985), p. 32.

a. Employed migrants.

cate to obtain vocational training. Although foreigners make up 9 percent of the labor force, they fill only 3 percent of the apprenticeships. Thus almost half of the fifteen-to-seventeen-year-old foreigners were either unemployed or working illegally in the shadow economy (Castles and Kosack, 1985, pp. 500–502).

The "social time bomb" that a growing number of West Germans are perceiving has prompted some changes in policy since the late 1970s. By and large, though, the process of social segmentation appears to be proceeding stronger and faster than the halting, slow, and contradictory steps of a policy that wavers between "integration" and "rotation." West German policy has brought short-term economic benefits to West Germany in the 1960s. But it has also had a profound effect on the structure of West German society. In creating a new "underclass" it severely damages the chances of a substantial minority. And it strains the political capacities of West German institutions to deal with the social consequences of a policy for too long narrowly defined as economic.

The political consequences of West Germany's way of dealing with foreign labor became evident when, largely in response to the ban of 1973 and West Germany's generous welfare policies, the number of applicants for political asylum increased dramatically in the late 1970s and early 1980s. Although the annual figure had fluctuated in the mid-1970s between 4,000 and 9,000, it grew in 1980 to a high of 108,000. After a sharp decline in 1981–83, it doubled from 35,000 in 1984 to 73,000 in 1985. Two-thirds were from Third World countries. Furthermore, the type of refugee changed. Since the mid-1970s most of the traditional "political refugees" from Eastern Europe had been replaced by "economic refugees" from Turkey and from Third World countries. Many of these "economic refugees" booked charter flights to East Berlin and continued from there to West Berlin and West Germany. In 1985 the two German states agreed to try to plug this hole. The East Germans are no longer permitting the deplaning of some passengers who lack the proper papers to enter the Federal Republic. In return the West German government increased its allocation of interest-free credit to East Germany from 600 to 850 million deutschmarks. Ironically, twenty-five years after it was built, the West Germans have come to see some usefulness in the Berlin Wall.

Because 800,000 Germans found political asylum abroad in the 1930s and 1940s, the Federal Republic has, by international standards, an exceptionally liberal law governing the granting of asylum. Article

16 of the Basic Law guarantees to all political refugees an unconditional and absolute right to asylum. But political practice differs from constitutional guarantees. According to one newspaper article in the mid-1970s, West Germany let in only 40 percent of the political refugees applying for asylum, more than Britain, Italy, and Austria but less than France, Switzerland, Denmark, Norway, Belgium, and the Netherlands. Constitutional guarantees have increasingly been subordinated to a bureaucratic filter that checks whether reasonable grounds exist for inferring that the refugee turning up at West German borders is misusing the right to asylum for economic and social gain. The exercise of this discretionary bureaucratic power is controlled by administrative courts (see Reading 5-6) (Zuleeg, 1985, pp. 302–3). In 1984 8,067 foreigners were deported. This figure, however, is much smaller than the about 200,000 refugees who did not apply for asylum or whose application was turned down (*Der Spiegel,* Sept. 2, 1985, pp. 40–43; March 17, 1986, pp. 101–7).

Since work permits are not granted before an application has been ruled on (which can take up to seven years) and may not be granted thereafter, applicants have little choice but to accept living in state-run camps. Living conditions in these camps are often appalling. An amendment to the Social Welfare Act of 1961 which passed the Bundestag in 1982 specifies that until the legal status of an applicant for asylum has been determined, that applicant is entitled to no more than the bare necessities of life normally provided for by in-kind services rather than cash payments. The political commitment to a social minimum standard of living is thus undercut for a substantial number of people who have little recourse against the discretionary power of a welfare bureaucracy that runs their lives. The bureaucracy is interested primarily in the economic and social deterrence of foreigners whom it suspects to be "economic tourists" rather than "political refugees." One of the consequences of West Germany's migration policy in the 1980s was to make the administration of poverty a weapon by which the state defends itself.

As this chapter has shown, the links between migrant labor and other economic and social issues are numerous. The preference for incremental policymaking resembles the political logic that we have discovered in other policy problems. In the 1960s government policy was little but a handmaiden of a West German labor market that increasingly extended into Southern Europe. The economic and social changes of the

1970s have undoubtedly increased the role of the federal government. In collaboration with the major economic interest groups and relying on the services of West Germany's private welfare agencies, the federal government has adhered to a policy carried by an ambiguous consensus based on contradictory assumptions. But the lack of significant change in policy before 1983 has been repeated since, despite the programmatic commitment of CDU Chancellor Kohl and his new cabinet. West Germany's system of coalition governments, cooperative federalism, and parapublic institutions constrained policy divergences especially at the federal level. Policy is thus shaped by collaborative, centralized institutional and political arrangements that, in turn, it sustains.

Migrant labor has, however, some peculiarities as a result of which the pattern of policymaking resembles economic management more than industrial relations or social welfare. Until the mid-1970s policymakers viewed the problem almost exclusively in economic terms. The ban on recruitment of November 1973 during the first oil shock was part of a quick adjustment to a radically altered international economy. By contrast, recognition of the fact that West Germany was becoming a multiethnic society did not lead to any break with policy incrementalism. Furthermore, I noted in Chapter 1 that labor market policy is one of the few sectors in which the federal government relies on its own bureaucracy. For this reason the federal government and bureaucracy was a more active player in this sector than in economic management. Finally, in this case incremental policy led to large-scale social transformation. In economic management, industrial relations, and social welfare, policy incrementalism paralleled a gradual evolution of economic and social life. But in the case of migrant labor policy, incrementalism has effected a structural change in the character of society. West Germany has become a multiethnic society and as a consequence is now confronting a broad range of new policy problems.

West Germany's policy on migrant workers has consisted of a multitude of incremental adjustments. The Aliens Act of 1965 and the Labor Promotion Act of 1969 left undefined the legal status of West Germany's migrant workers. This is only one reason why, as in other policy sectors, the courts have played a central role in developing and implementing policy on a day-to-day basis (see Reading 5-6). On questions of political asylum, for example, the position of the courts was particularly strong. Since the early 1970s, as this chapter has shown, there has been a variable cascade of policy measures including, among others: the ban on further recruitment (1973), a change in the Aliens Act (1975), an administrative clarification of the residency status of foreigners (1978), changes in regulations governing the admission of dependents (1979), federal guidelines for the development of a more coordinated policy (1980), and legislation against the abuse of asylum rights (1980).

The political initiatives of the Kohl government fit this general pattern. Heralded as a major departure in policy, a new government commission was charged in 1983 to define alternative policies for a revision of the Aliens Act and policy more generally (see Reading 5-7). But the FDP quickly blocked the CDU's preference for a more restrictive policy. And the options of the CDU are also constrained from abroad. The new minister of the interior wanted to lower the maximum age at which children of foreign workers can join their families in West Germany, from eighteen to six years. But Turkish opposition was so strong that he had to settle for sixteen years instead. Should Turkey become an associate member of the EC, the degree of restriction on labor mobility which the CDU/CSU government will be able to impose may quite possibly become a matter for the European Court of Justice. It seems highly unlikely that the government will succeed in reducing through strict controls and a policy of repatriation the total number of foreigners in the Federal Republic by 1 million. As in economic management, industrial relations, and social welfare, incremental policy change is the politically most plausible option in West Germany's semisovereign state.

Readings

5-1. TRANSPORTING FOREIGN WORKERS TO WEST GERMANY*

This excerpt from an article describing the immigration of foreign workers conveys the logistical problems of organizing the transportation of foreign workers. The bureaucratic rationality of the process

*H. M. Dreyer, "Immigration of Foreign Workers into the Federal Republic of Germany," *International Labor Review* 84 (July–August 1961):15–16.

evokes chilling parallels with the policy of Nazi Germany, which was of course carried out under political circumstances and with political aims totally different from those of the Federal Republic.

On the basis of the prepared transport lists, all local labour offices in Germany which will be concerned with conveying workers to their destinations are provided from the start with relevant details such as final destination, contract numbers and total number of workers to be expected. The local labour offices nearest to the German border responsible for routing workers advise the receiving offices. Travel escorts are provided principally by the individual receiving labour offices. Before setting out, workers leaving for Germany receive sufficient food supplies to last until they reach the distribution centre in Germany. The travel escorts are supplied with drinking water containers.

Travel arrangements vary according to the point of departure. A special train, or a group of special carriages, leaves Verona for Munich five times a week. It takes workers from northern and central Italy who have come to the German Commission's Verona centre during the day, been medically examined and found jobs. There is also a special train, or a group of special carriages, leaving Naples five times a week, four times a week via Switzerland to Singen and once a week via Verona to Munich. After registration, medical examination and placement, workers coming from southern Italy are housed for one night at the Naples centre. . . .

The chief transit station for distribution and routing is Munich, where the Federal Institute has built an underground hall next to the central station, with room for 700 workers to be temporarily accommodated. Provisions for the next stage of travel and hot meals are also distributed here. A large number of workers can be housed for the night if it is too late for them to leave the same day.

From Munich to the areas covered by the various local labour offices, regular trains are used, the necessary number of places being reserved. Large groups may be accompanied by an escort at this stage too.

The other transit stations, Singen, Karlsruhe and Cologne, also have the appropriate machinery to distribute and route the groups arriving. The receiving labour offices are responsible for smooth distribution of groups arriving at their final destination. In cases where groups arrive too late at a rail centre to be sent on to their final destination the same night, appropriate accommodation is provided.

5-2. DRAFT GUIDELINES FOR A FEDERAL POLICY FOR MIGRANT WORKERS*

In October 1975 a committee of the federal government issued a draft of seventeen theses for a new migration policy. Because of its narrow economic focus and highly restrictive character, this draft elicited strong critical reactions from the churches and the broader public.

In an analysis of its policies regarding foreign minorities, the federal government put forward the following theses. . . . It is necessary to limit the employment of foreigners not only because of the long-term policy of "modernizing our economy" but also to accelerate rationalization and structural change. Such a limitation coincides with the interests of foreign workers whose social integration still remains problematic. On the other hand, the German economy cannot function without foreign workers, at least in the foreseeable future. The federal government does not contemplate taking any drastic measures in order to reduce the number of foreign workers. Also, for humanitarian reasons the federal government rejects a compulsory rotation of foreign workers. . . .

More and more children of foreign workers employed in the FRG will soon be old enough to be able to work themselves and will therefore want to work here as well. If they have immigrated before December 1, 1974, children of foreign workers can be given a working permit even under present labor market conditions. This regulation will not be rescinded in the future. Children of foreign workers who immigrated after December 1, 1974, are now refused a working permit. . . .

The federal government considers it neither necessary nor justifiable to budget for financial incentives to support the return of foreign workers to their home countries. And it does not plan to change the legislation governing the return of prior contributions to social security. Measures supporting and facilitating the return and professional reintegration of foreign workers into their home countries—especially from the perspective of development aid—are not affected by this regulation.

The federal government takes it for granted that the regulation limiting foreigners' movement into regions already overpopulated will remain unchanged. The regulation was passed on April 1, 1975, based on an arrangement between the federal government and the states, to bal-

*Frankfurter Rundschau, February 23, 1976, p. 14 (selections).

ance the great interest these regions have in the future employment of foreigners with the need to provide for their adequate social integration. This regional policy inhibits the formation of foreign ghettos. And it counteracts the development of regional and infrastructural supply deficiencies. Generally, the social integration of foreigners is thus encouraged. . . .

In principle the federal government maintains the equality of foreign and German workers under labor and social legislation. However, labor market and fiscal policies justify the government's limiting of unemployment compensation to foreigners without working permits to the period during which they have paid into the system. In order to ensure that German workers take precedence over foreign workers, foreigners will not automatically be entitled to a working permit after five years of continuous employment. . . .

The federal government continually attempts to facilitate the social integration of foreigners working and living in the FRG. The government aims, therefore, at an adequate consolidation of the legal status, especially on questions of residence, of those foreign workers who have been working in the FRG continuously for a longer time. . . .

The federal government holds that it is not necessary to add special regulations for foreign workers to the legislation governing naturalization. Naturalization presupposes a process of assimilation and therefore demands a substantial period of residence.

The federal government does not intend to make it more difficult for foreign workers' families to move to the FRG. The government continues to consider a waiting period of one year as well as proof of adequate living quarters as both necessary and sufficient. . . .

One of the main objectives of the government's migrant labor policies is to make clear to foreign workers the benefits of returning to their home countries, both for themselves as well as for the economic and social development of their native countries, based on the careful utilization of the knowledge and skills that they have acquired in the FRG. The federal government considers the professional and social reintegration of workers who want to return to their native countries to be very important. For years, the government has emphasized the possibilities inherent in return migration for development policy. As in the past, the government will support contacts with the foreigners' home countries, will give incentives for return migration, and develop new models. The federal government holds to the opinion that a permanent solution for the employment problems of migrant workers can be achieved only in the framework of the European Economic Community.

5-3. RECOMMENDATIONS OF THE JOINT COMMISSION OF THE FEDERAL GOVERNMENT AND STATES*

In the political debate surrounding migrant labor, this comprehensive report reflects the contradictory policy of the 1970s. Its main recommendations are excerpted here.

Future policies governing the employment of foreigners should reflect the following basic postulates.

1. *The Federal Republic of Germany is not a country of immigration.* West Germany is a country in which foreigners reside for varying lengths of time before they decide on their own accord to return to their home country. Over the long-term this basic orientation serves the economic and social interests of the Federal Republic of Germany as well as those of the home countries.

2. *A permanent freeze of foreign workers must be maintained over the long run.* In view of a sharply growing domestic labor force during the next ten years, the recruitment of additional foreign labor would infringe upon the interests of German as well as foreign workers already living here.

3. *Foreign workers will be needed in the Federal Republic of Germany on a long-term basis.* However, the capacity of the labor market to absorb foreign labor is declining. This means that the level of foreign labor will continue to decrease in the years ahead.

4. *We need to reinforce the readiness and the ability of foreign workers and their families now residing in West Germany to return. The countries of origin have to share in this responsibility.* Each foreign worker should decide on his own when he wants to return home. In this context forceful repatriation is unacceptable.

5. *Foreign workers and their families living in the Federal Republic of Germany should enjoy a secure social and legal status, and they should live fully integrated into West German society.* Efforts to achieve

*Der Bundesminister für Arbeit und Sozialordnung, *Vorschläge der Bund-Länder-Kommission zur Fortentwicklung einer umfassenden Konzeption der Ausländerbeschäftigungspolitik* (Bonn, February 28, 1977), pp. 3–4 (selections).

a full social integration of foreign workers and their families should be strengthened in the future aided by the personal initiatives and active cooperation of foreign workers and their families.

6. *In the future employment policies dealing with foreign workers should pay special attention to the problems of the second generation of the children of foreign workers growing up in the Federal Republic of Germany.* Neglecting this task would not only amount to a serious handicap for individuals but would also place a heavy burden on the social stability of the Federal Republic. Social integration of foreign workers and their families, on the one hand, and consolidation of the employment level of foreigners, on the other, should in the future constitute essential and complementary components of a well-developed, comprehensive concept for the employment of foreign workers. Thus a socially acceptable compromise can be fashioned by calibrating the fundamental interests of the German population, especially of the employees, with the legitimate social and economic demands of foreign workers and their families now residing in the FRG.

5-4. NEW DEPARTURES*

In 1978 Chancellor Schmidt appointed a former governor, Heinz Kühn, as advisor to the federal government on questions of migrant labor. Released a year later, this report by Kühn marked a watershed in the evolution of policy. Its premise was that West Germany had become a country of immigration and that public policy would have to develop strategies for integrating foreign workers, especially their children. Kühn advocated a number of measures, including the right to vote in local election, easy naturalization, and integrated school classes. His report was heavily criticized by West German conservatives because of its new premise and the total cost of policy measures, estimated at 600 million deutschmarks. Similarly a substantial segment of the foreign population vociferously opposed the proposal of full educational integration. The report spurred the federal bureaucracy and government to develop new programs for the 1980s.

*Heinz Kühn, *Stand und Weiterentwicklung der Integration der ausländischen Arbeitnehmer und ihrer Familien in der Bundesrepublik Deutschland: Memorandum des Beauftragten der Bundesregierung* (Bonn, September 1979), pp. 2–4, 10–11, 59 (selections).

Because the prospect of one million foreign children and teenagers living in the Federal Republic is alarming, comprehensive efforts are necessary in order to prevent great damage to individuals and society. Current problems are small compared to those we shall confront in the future if no dramatic action is forthcoming. If we fail to act now these problems may well become unmanageable. This would have disastrous consequences.

Up to now labor market policies have had an excessive influence on social developments and public policies. Broader social perspectives on the other hand have been unduly neglected.

Against the background of the intensifying crisis of foreign workers and their families, the new policy approach will have to more fully incorporate broader social perspectives. We are confronting an irreversible social process. Our responsibility toward foreigners and their children, many of whom were once actively recruited and have lived in West Germany for a long time, goes well beyond any measures we might take in response to the fluctuating conditions on labor markets. For the (presumably large number) of migrant workers wishing to stay, especially those of the second and third generations, we must commit ourselves to unconditional and permanent integration.

Ill-considered proposals offering integration for a limited period are contradictory and unrealistic and simply fail to measure up to the realities of daily life. Even attempts to encourage return migration, limited as they are in their effectiveness, make sense only if they are carefully targeted on those foreigners for whom such a prospect might be at all relevant. In any case, even such a policy presupposes that the reasons speaking for and against returning be fully spelled out.

Accordingly, this report proposes an uncompromising policy of integration focused specifically on: (1) recognizing that West Germany has de facto become a country of immigration (which continues to prohibit further recruitment); (2) increasing considerably our efforts to achieve the social integration especially of children and teenagers in nurseries, schools, and vocational training courses; (3) terminating all policies of segregation such as separate classrooms in school; (4) honoring the claims of foreign youths to unrestricted access to apprenticeships and jobs; (5) granting all foreign youths born in the Federal Republic the right of naturalization; (6) revising all laws covering foreigners and the process of naturalization so as to secure the legal status of foreigners and their families and to take account of their specific, legitimate interests;

(7) extending the suffrage in local elections to foreigners who have resided in West Germany for some time; and (8) reinforcing social services for foreign workers which help to address specific problems. . . .

Past evaluations of foreign workers have emphasized considerations of employment policy and labor markets. This perspective was reinforced by the disturbances that since the early 1970s have characterized developments in labor markets. The assumption that the immigration of foreign workers was temporary and largely influenced by variable conditions on labor markets remained unchallenged.

This basic orientation in the past has shaped the policies affecting foreign labor. The legal status of foreigners was left largely to the discretionary powers of the bureaucracy. The granting of a residence permit was linked directly to a work permit, which in turn depended in principle only on labor market conditions. Policies of social integration for a long time merely aimed at providing a minimum of service and concentrated largely on facilitating the transition to a new working environment. However, the legal position of German and foreign workers is more equal on narrower aspects of employment and social policy. With this exception, however, any special measure affecting foreign workers has been a heavy-handed intervention dictated by conditions on labor markets, for example, the ban on any further recruitment of foreign workers and the regulation governing the granting of work permits for the children of foreign workers.

However, it is quite evident that officials in all walks of life (federal, state and local government, the main economic interest groups, churches, welfare organizations, and private sector initiatives) have tried to respond to pressures which go well beyond those normally occurring in traditional labor markets. Halting steps toward more coordinated steps in this direction can, however, be found only in the proposals that the "Federal-State-Commission for the Development of a Comprehensive Conception of the Foreigner's Employment Policies" issued in the spring of 1977. . . .

The successful implementation of this proposal for a reoriented policy will depend decisively on the ability of numerous organizations and officials, especially among different levels of government in our federal system, to reach a consensus. Since agreement on the alarming conditions today is astonishingly widespread, it may not be far-fetched to hope for coordinated efforts to address the pressing tasks that lie ahead.

5-5. THE HEIDELBERG MANIFESTO*

The sharply declining birth rate of West Germans and the continued increase in the foreign population (because of the reunification of guest-worker families and the high birth rate among an exceptionally young foreign population) has raised the specter of a gradual erosion of German culture and society. This possibility has made West German conservatives very nervous. Fifteen prominent scholars signed the following memorandum for what they called the "Heidelberg Circle." It was published in the February 5, 1982, issue of the liberal weekly Die Zeit. The call for public action with which the memorandum ends received scant public notice.

It is with grave concern that we observe the infiltration of the German nation by millionfold waves of foreigners and their families, the infiltration of our language, our culture, and our national characteristics by foreign influences. In 1980 alone, despite the freeze on hiring, the number of registered foreigners increased by 309,000, including 194,000 Turks. Our birth rate is now barely one-half the rate needed to ensure the continued existence of our nation. Many Germans are already strangers in the places where they live and work.

The immigration of foreigners was encouraged by the federal government for reasons connected with uncontrolled economic growth, which is now seen as a dubious phenomenon. The German people were given no explanations regarding the significance and the consequences of this policy, and they were also not consulted on it. For this reason we call for the establishment of an association that, independent of parties and ideologies, will work for the preservation of the German people and its spiritual identity on the basis of our Western, Christian heritage. On the basis of the Constitution we reject ideological nationalism, racism, and the extremism of the Right and the Left.

Biologically and cybernetically, nations are living systems of a higher order, with different system qualities that are transmitted genetically and by tradition. The integration of large masses of non-German foreigners and the preservation of our nation thus cannot be achieved simultaneously; it will lead to the well-known ethnic catastrophes of multicultural societies.

*Population and Development Review 8 (September 1982):636–37.

Every people, including the German people, has a natural right to preserve its identity and its individuality in its habitat. Respect for other peoples requires their preservation but not their fusion ("Germanization"). We regard Europe as an organism of peoples and nations that are worthy of preservation on the basis of their common history. "Every nation is a unique facet of a Divine Plan" (Solzhenitsyn).

The Constitution of the Federal Republic of Germany does not posit the concept of "the nation" as the sum total of all the peoples within a state. It is based on the concept of "a people," specifically the German people. The President of the Republic and the Members of Parliament take an oath of office to dedicate their strength "to the well-being of the German people, to promote its advantage, and to defend it from harm." The Constitution thus makes the preservation of the German people an obligation.

In the Preamble to the Constitution, the goal of reunification is established as an obligation. How is this obligation to be met if a portion of the nation's territory becomes ethnically foreign? The current policy toward foreigners promotes the development of a multi-racial society. This is in violation of the Constitution, which obligates all Germans of the Federal Republic to protect and defend our people's right to exist.

Hundreds of thousands of children are now illiterate in their native languages and in German. What hope for the future can they have? And our own children, who are being educated in classrooms where the majority of students are foreigners: what hope for the future can they have? Will the billions being spent for the defense of our country ultimately be worth such a price?

Only vigorous and intact German families can preserve our people for the future. Our own children are the only foundation for the future of Germany and Europe.

Technological development offers, and will increasingly offer, opportunities to make all employment of foreigners unnecessary. Bringing the machine to the human being, rather than the human being to the machine, must therefore be the highest guiding principle for the economy.

The problem must be attacked at its roots, and this means concerted development assistance to improve the living conditions of the foreign workers in their native countries—not here in our country. For the Federal Republic of Germany, which is one of the most heavily populated countries of the world, the return of the foreigners to their native lands will provide ecological as well as social relief.

To achieve continued public response, we call upon all organizations, associations, citizens' groups, and other groups to dedicate themselves to the preservation of our people, our language, our culture, and our way of life, and to form an umbrella organization that will permit both group and individual membership, with each association retaining complete independence and freedom. A supervisory board should be appointed to oversee the work of this organization and to protect its ideological and political independence.

5-6. INTERVIEW WITH HORST SENDLER, PRESIDENT OF THE FEDERAL ADMINISTRATIVE COURT*

Because of the ban on foreign immigration, in the late 1970s and early 1980s "economic refugees" from Third World countries came to the Federal Republic in growing numbers asking for political asylum. The severe strains that this new wave of immigrants put on West Germany's judicial system is evident in this interview with the president of the Federal Administrative Court.

Spiegel: Mister President, your court is continually setting new records and is thus becoming a subject of gossip. What were the latest figures? Do the March figures for the court's handling of applications for political asylum again top the figures of previous months?

Sendler: In fact, last month was a record. We completed rulings on 1,550 files, which exceeds even the record number of new applications of 1,230.

Spiegel: Let's translate these numbers. This exceptional performance must be credited to the ninth Senate of your court which deals with applications for political asylum. With its five judges this court normally deals each month with about 1,500 appeals or about 75 each day. Including breaks it adds up to about eleven cases per hour or about one case every five minutes. This is a world record for a higher court. But does it still resemble in any way the adjudication of justice?

Sendler: Undoubtedly yes . . . in most of the cases lawyers make their requests on standardized forms. The immigration Senate faces a very large number of similar cases and a significant number which lack any substantive form of legal justification. The law prescribes, however,

Der Spiegel, April 26, 1982, pp. 46–60 (selections).

such a justification as well as a written presentation of the case. The files where these legal requirements are not met take only a few seconds since the appeal has to be rejected on formal grounds.

Spiegel: Last year alone the immigration Senate has thus shoveled aside about 8,700 such cases.

Sendler: "Shoveled aside," as you put it, sounds as if we just got rid of these cases. You can't describe our work in these terms.

Spiegel: This reminds us of Tucholsky: judgement is being passed without looking.

Sendler: Yes, without looking at the person but not without looking at the case. Each file is examined as much as the legal brief warrants. We don't do more—that is the rationalization of work.

Spiegel: All that, including the decision, in five minutes? In how many of these 8,700 cases has the court approved the appeals of the plaintiffs?

Sendler: Not in a single case.

Spiegel: You could have thrown these files into the waste basket—the end result would have been the same. . .

Sendler: No, neither you nor I should advocate this as a prescription. It goes without saying that each individual case is analyzed. There are important things to be uncovered. But it takes special skills for recognizing them. This requires that you study a file closely. As it happens, in 91 cases we have ruled on various grounds that the lower courts reopen the case. . . .

Sendler: The distribution of work within the immigration Senate is organized by the names of the lawyers filing the appeal. The lawyers are for the most part specialists. Their number is much smaller than one might imagine considering the 10,000 odd cases each year. The same names recur time and again. Many use standard forms for establishing a case; they only add the name of applicant for asylum. Occasionally they use a false name and quite often a false country of origin. These lawyers keep coming back with the same legal reasoning.

Spiegel: And thus they end up getting the same answers?

Sendler: That's how it really is. It is not surprising that the same legal reasoning always gets the same answers. Rather, what is astonishing is that despite these answers, the same stereotypical legal reasoning is offered. After a consideration of the legal reasoning informing its decisions, the Senate has organized them in "text modules." These modules are stored in a wordprocessor and, depending on any given brief, can be combined in different ways. There exist, for example, different procedures for rejecting a case and different reasoning for recognizing the legal importance of a case. We simply put together a written decision from these text modules. And you should not forget that the judges are assisted in their work by five legal experts.

Spiegel: . . . Who for constitutional reasons do not have the right to decide a single case.

Sendler: That is correct. But they help prepare the decisions of the court. This facilitates the work of the judge and must be deducted from the time which you calculated. You came up with 5 minutes per case because you start with a weekly work load of 40 hours per judge. In fact judges work much longer hours. In any case decisions are made only by judges or groups of judges. They read the drafts which the experts have prepared and edit them, at times heavily.

Spiegel: Assuming 60 working hours each week the court reaches on average a decision every nine minutes. That is not much of an improvement. How many text modules do you have in stock?

Sendler: I asked for a collection of modules which contains about one hundred units. For a variety of criticisms they offer canned answers. These answers are altered depending on the specifics of a case. Occasionally I stop by the typing pool and listen to the grievances of my colleagues. Occasionally the typists complain about the additional work they have because the judges, for any given case, quite often insist on rewriting the text modules. These complaints illustrate graphically that each case is being examined individually.

Spiegel: After looking at a file, does the judge write on a cover note 13, then 26 and eventually 37 and does the typist then proceed to compose a text from modules 13, 26 and 37?

Sendler: That is how we work. But in practice it looks like this: module 26, unchanged; module 37 with deletions of the following words and addition of this paragraph. Although this creates additional difficulties in the office, it is inevitable. We cannot afford to be too fully automated lest one could charge us with "shoveling away" cases or sweeping unpleasant ones under the rug.

Spiegel: Many foreigners view the Federal Administrative Court as an institution which in judicial robes decrees eviction.

Sendler: I have never before heard this accusation. It would of course be totally unjustified.

Spiegel: When the foreigners learn that 99.9 percent of the appeals have been rejected.

Sendler: . . . Only 98.9, but this is really not a substantial difference.

Spiegel: Then one should not be surprised about the impression this creates with the plaintiffs.

Sendler: I can only concur. We must alter the court's procedure so that this high percentage figure does not have such a frightening effect. To an outsider it makes the court's work look like pure nonsense.

Spiegel: We know about the flood of applications for asylum. Today more than 200,000 applicants live in the Federal Republic. Only 5,000 came in 1972, 51,000 in 1979, and 108,000 in 1980. One should not belittle the consequences of this flood. Don't the "records" in the number of appeals denied by your court create the suspicion that here a federal court has degraded itself to become the whore—or to put it less offensively the safety net—of the executive branch of government which is intent on getting rid of as many foreigners as possible?

Sendler: No, that's not the case. Last year the Federal Bureau in Zirndorf granted political asylum to 7,800 applicants. The lower courts recognized 700 or 750 more and the appeals court an additional 3. Last year the Federal Administrative Court had to decide more than 10,000 cases out of which only 91 were successful—they were referred back to the lower court.

Spiegel: By and large, how long does it take to decide on an application for political asylum, from the first filing of papers until the final negative decision of your court?

Sendler: Negative decision—well yes generally speaking you are right. It takes on the average three and a half years. Some cases move faster but others last much longer, some as much as up to eight years. We have applicants for asylum, whose case has been referred back to the Federal Administrative Court up to four times. But we decide 50 percent of the cases within 3 months; an additional 30 percent are decided within 6 months; and another 15 percent within one year. The remaining 5 percent take a variable amount of time.

5-7. COMMISSION REPORT ON FOREIGN WORKERS*

In his first speech before the Bundestag as the head of the CDU/CSU-FDP government, Chancellor Kohl made reconsideration of migrant labor policy one of his four political priorities. A commission of repre-

---

*Kommission "Ausländerpolitik" aus Vertretern von Bund, Ländern und Gemeinden, *Bericht* (Bonn, February 24, 1983), pp. 18–21.

sentatives of federal, state, and local governments delivered its report in March 1983. Based on the three principles informing government policy—limitation of further immigration, support of integration, and encouragement of return migration—the commission prepared an extensive set of recommendations that neglected, surprisingly, the objective of further integration. This excerpt is a summary of the commission's recommendations.

The commission agreed upon a set of principles and recommendations (numbers 1 to 15); on other points, agreement proved to be impossible (numbers 16 to 24).

Fundamental agreement was reached on the following essential points:

1. The goals of policies toward foreign workers are to integrate socially foreigners who are long-term residents; to limit further immigration particularly through an unconditional stop of any further recruitment of foreign workers irrespective of future economic developments; to promote the willingness of foreign workers to return home; to help maintain the potential for their return, but not to force return migration.

2. The immigration of the spouses of foreign workers shall no longer be restricted. Legislation should be passed governing the immigration of the families of Germans and foreign workers now living in Germany. (The legislation should define those eligible and the requirements for receiving a residence permit).

3. Legislation should be passed governing the immigration of the families of Germans and of foreign workers now living in Germany. (The legislation should define those eligible and the requirements for receiving a residence permit).

4. Foreign spouses and minors of German citizens shall be granted a legal entitlement to a residence permit.

5. The immigration of foreign adults who have been adopted by Germans shall not be permissible in principle. Exceptions can be made in special cases.

6. Additional control measures shall be taken to stop the illegal residence and illegal employment of foreigners. Illegal immigration should be stopped through taking a variety of measures at the border and the government should seriously consider extending the number of countries whose citizens will be admitted only if they are in possession of a valid visum.

7. In the future the granting and extension of residence permits shall be governed by legal decree as well as dictated by the objectives of our policy towards foreigners.

8. The Law for Foreigners shall specify concrete legal grounds for the denial of residence permits (such as illegal immigration).

9. With the exception of the controversial issue of the subsequent immigration of children of foreigners now living in the FRG (see number 16), the entitlement for a residence permit shall be extended to minors of less than 16 years of age. Minors residing illegally in the FRG shall, by force of law, be accompanied back to their home countries.

10. A residence permit shall be extended only if the applicant has adequate financial means, rents an adequate apartment, and has avoided serious infractions of German law.

11. Foreigners, whose residence is granted for a specific, temporary reason (i.e. studies, medical treatment, tourism) shall be granted a special residence permit which shall automatically preclude subsequent application for a permanent residence permit. The German government shall consider the creation of a special residence permit for family members of foreigners residing in the FRG.

12. The time of residence of foreign applicants for study shall be limited according to their plan of study.

13. Additional measures should be taken, on an individual basis, against political extremists from abroad such as a ban on travel and the withdrawing of a residence permit.

14. Amendments of the law concerning political asylum which was passed on August 1, 1982, shall be considered only after a report about a one-year trial period with that legislation has been completed by August 1, 1983.

15. The Standing Conference of the Ministers of Interior of the states is being asked to reconsider its decision of August 26th 1966 concerning special regulations for the expulsion of citizens from Eastern Europe.

No consensus has been reached in the following essential areas:

16. Regulations governing the move of children (from states which are not members of the European Communities) joining foreigners residing in West Germany (reduction of the age limit, entitlement to a residence permit).

17. The move of spouses (from states which are not members of the European Communities) joining foreigners of the second or subsequent generation in the FRG.

18. Proposals for making the legal status of foreigners dependent on the extent to which they have become socially integrated, and to make the extension of a residence permit and the permission for the subsequent immigration of family members dependent on the proof of adequate housing.

19. Facilitating the naturalization process and the imposition of sanctions if foreigners refuse to avail themselves of this process.

20. Dismantling barriers impeding unrestricted access to jobs.

21. The length of time during which applicants for political asylum are ineligible for work permits.

22. List of reasons for expulsion.

23. The reinforcement of protection from expulsion for specific groups.

24. Concessions of a return option for foreigners who do not take advantage of the resettlement allowance.

5-8. DISAGREEMENTS AMONG DIFFERENT STATES*

Heinrich Lummer is a CDU politician who in 1981 became mayor and senator for the Department of Home Affairs of West Berlin. His restrictive policies diverge from the liberal approach taken by Minister of Interior of the state of Hesse Horst Winterstein, representative of a coalition between the SPD and the Greens. Their discussion illustrates the different policies that are pursued in West Germany's federal system of government.

Lummer: The problem would be easier to solve if the foreigners were not so concentrated in certain regions but, rather, distributed more evenly throughout the Federal Republic. At the present time 12.5 percent of West Berlin's population is foreign and that inevitably creates some difficulties.

Spiegel: The city of Frankfurt has to cope with 23 percent foreigners.

Lummer: That is the reason why the Mayor of Frankfurt, my party colleague Walter Wallmann, fights the policies of the land government of Hesse. . . .

Spiegel: . . . Mister Winterstein, you are responsible for easing restrictions on the immigration of family members of foreigners and for

Der Spiegel, October 15, 1984, pp. 85–94 (selections).

making expulsions more difficult. Are you now going to have to welcome the Turks whom Mister Lummer no longer likes to live in Berlin-Kreuzberg?

Winterstein: That is possible. But it would only be a small number. The decisive political question for us was how to give some measure of security to foreigners who live here, whom we recruited in the first place, and who want to stay here. That is the context for our policies.

Lummer: It is certain that we should not expect a large number of people to move from Kreuzberg to Hesse, at least not in the near future. But the difficulty is in the reverse flow of migrants. If Hesse adopts a more liberal policy, many Turks will first move to Hesse before settling in other states.

Spiegel: Mister Winterstein, with your liberal policies towards foreign migrants, the government of Hesse has made a virtual turnabout. Only two years ago Minister-President Börner wanted "to close the borders tightly against any further influx of additional foreign workers."

Lummer: I also wonder about this turnabout.

Winterstein: Mister Lummer, times have changed . . .

Lummer: Yes, the Greens are now backing you.

Winterstein: Frankly, if the Social Democrats in Hesse had the absolute majority, we would certainly not have made these changes so quickly. But we now have an agreement with the Greens which I personally back since I was part of the negotiation commission. We are giving the Law for Foreigners a more humane touch than you or Dr. Zimmermann [Minister of the Interior of the Federal Government] would like. This does not hurt a Social Democrat. . . .

Lummer: I think that your policies are viable only if the other states cooperate. But at this time I don't see any other state ready to follow suit. Not even North Rhine-Westphalia.

Winterstein: Mister Lummer, if uniformity means that in Hesse I should implement a policy towards foreigners that is to the liking of the majority of states dominated by the CDU, then I favor a more humane approach over a more uniform one.

Lummer: The majority of the states agreed that the policies towards foreigners had to be changed, in a more restrictive direction. You are doing exactly the opposite. Now we are confronting the prospect of different states pushing in different directions.

Winterstein: But you can't simply assume that as a Social Democratic Minister of the Interior I would simply accept a majority agreement of the Standing Conference of Interior Ministers which is to your liking. You have stated that you intended to cut in half the number of foreigners living here, in West Berlin . . .

Lummer: No, I have never said that.

Winterstein: But you have said something like it. Like you we don't want to open the border, but we think it is simply inhumane when, for instance, Turkish workers are allowed to have their children under six years of age join them while the older ones must stay in Turkey. . . .

Spiegel: What you call a flood of foreigners is only the smaller part of the problem. The return migration of the Turks began long ago, in any case, several years ago. More Turks are returning home than are newly arriving in the FRG.

Lummer: In the second and third generation, there are undoubtedly young people who grew up here and who are possibly already socially integrated. And why should not they make the decision to apply for German citizenship?

Winterstein: But what are you expecting of these people? A few decades ago the Polish coal miners moved into the Ruhr area. These were people from a roughly similar cultural background. Yet it took three generations until they were genuinely accepted. And the Turkish workers come from a completely different cultural background.

Lummer: In as far as you are discussing migrant workers, I certainly feel that I can hold my own. My ancestors on my mother's side were immigrant coal miners who looked for work in the Ruhr area. I am, in a manner of speaking, second generation. My mother came from Yugoslavia. I would like to claim that my social integration was a complete success.

Winterstein: I was born in Yugoslavia. On this score we have something in common.

Spiegel: Mister Winterstein, Mister Lummer, thank you for this interview.

6 Administrative Reform

For many foreigners the essence of German history is the ascendance, triumph, and ultimate destruction of the German state. The rulers of a sandy patch of land in northern Germany in the seventeenth century began to enlarge their territory. By the end of the Seven Years' War, Prussia had become a major player in European diplomacy. During important periods of German history the processes of statebuilding and warmaking were coterminous. In the next century the Prussian monarchy developed a meritocratic civil service that soon became a model of administrative rationality for other states. Ito Hirobumi, an advisor to the Japanese emperor, traveled in Europe in 1882 after the Meiji Restoration. Upon his arrival in Berlin he is reported to have sent only one brief cable back to Tokyo: "I found it." In rebuilding their state Japanese officials modeled many of their institutions after the Prussian bureaucracy.

Theory followed practice. Hegel and German idealism enshrined the Prussian state as the high point in the evolution of modern history. The security of the state was the justification for foreign expansion. The machinery and the ideology of the state were thus in place. The Industrial Revolution after 1850 provided the power and German nationalism the emotion that, molded by the German state tradition, led to two catastrophic world wars and a profoundly authoritarian domestic politics.

West Germany's administrative reform policies have been virtually unnoticed by the general public. Social groups have neither strong interest in the arcane aspects of the politics of the state bureaucracy nor, typically, standing in policy deliberations. Yet precisely because administrative reform is carried out in relative isolation from society, it is informative for an analysis of the organization and political capacities of the West German state. In the last twenty-five years there have been numerous political attempts to address what West German political elites viewed as adverse consequences of the decentralized structure of the state. Policy coordination needed improvement if the various initiatives of the 1960s and 1970s were to succeed. The goal of administrative reform was to enhance efficiency, openness, and rationality by institutionalizing more planning within ministries, between ministries, and between different levels of government. The "reactive" state of the 1950s, it was widely thought, should be transformed to an "active" state in the 1970s. The political model was France, the U.S. Defense Department, and later Japan. Policy planners of all stripes, however, were to be disappointed. The West German state, and for that matter the state in general, is not a surface easily imprinted by the fleeting steps of reform-minded enthusiasts. Instead, state institutions have their own durable structure shaped by history, reflected in deeply held legal norms, and sustained by a large and powerful bureaucracy.

The West German bureaucracy presents structural obstacles to large-scale changes no less formidable than the interaction of coalition governments, cooperative federalism, and parapublic institutions. Failed structural reforms have, however, not prevented incremental changes that, far from diluting state power, have maintained the structural decentralization that elicited the demand for reform in the first place. Yet the state bureaucracy mobilized all resources when it saw social change seriously challenging its integrity. This happened in the 1970s when it sought to bar from public service people whom it classified as "political radicals." Although it has been tamed by political parties, social groups, and parapublic institutions, the West German state retains its basic structure. Its decentralization gives the state a presence in all sectors of society. Civil servants feel a deep attachment to legal rules that they execute rather than question. The West German state thus remains central to the setting of the norms informing policy and politics.

Context

The historical evolution of German bureaucracy is characterized by an absolutist coalition for bureaucratic autonomy (Armstrong, 1973; Gillis, 1971; Hanf, 1968; Mayntz, 1984; Rosenberg, 1958; Shefter, 1977). The origin of the Prussian civil service dates back to the concerted effort of the crown to create a standing army under direct command of the king. To finance such an army the king needed to create an administrative apparatus to raise the necessary revenues, thus bypassing the estates on whose support he had previously depended. The corps of civil servants which the crown gradually recruited became both a group of professional public administrators and a political status group. Civil servants were recruited from both the aristocracy and the middle class. Over time the emphasis shifted from noble birth to talent and education, especially in classics and jurisprudence. The autonomy and power of the bureaucracy grew over time. Prussia's political absolutism and late industrialization retarded the emergence of political counterelites. In the first half of the nineteenth century Prussia's senior civil service thus became de facto a ruling elite that assumed the most important functions of government. Although it remained nonpartisan, the bureaucracy played a crucial political role.

The second half of the nineteenth century saw the emergence of new elites in business, finance, arts and sciences, and politics. The gains of middle- and working-class politicians gradually put the senior civil service on the political defensive and narrowed the scope of its power. At the same time, however, the bureaucracy, like the army, remained fully autonomous. The new political groups had limited access to the top level and virtually no access to the lower levels of bureaucracy. In a time of rapid economic and social change, liberal elements in the bureaucracy were gradually purged. In the late nineteenth century state bureaucrats increasingly identified with the conservative and monarchist cause. In the Weimar Republic many civil servants viewed the new democratic order with reservation or hostility. But the norm of enhancing the state's interest and the nation's welfare through expert, nonpartisan service outweighed their deep dislike of the new regime. In addition, the democratic parties relied on the bureaucracy so heavily that they did not challenge the principle of bureaucratic autonomy. After 1933 the Nazis were more effective in weakening the bureaucracy. Democrats, socialists, and Jews were quickly dismissed. Political partisanship in support of the Nazi cause became an explicit precondition for state employment. The norm of serving the state remained strong. Until the bitter end the civil service served the cause of the Nazi state obediently.

Despite Allied Occupation and the program of de-Nazification, after 1945 continuity in civil service personnel was as great as it had been in the transition from the Second Empire to the Weimar Republic in 1919 and from the Weimar Republic to the Third Reich in 1933. A decade after the collapse of Nazi Germany, about two-thirds of the senior civil servants held positions in the Federal Republic comparable to those in the administrative structure of Hitler's Germany (Edinger, 1960, p. 66). A critical piece of federal legislation, passed in 1951, gave all regular civil servants the right to be reinstated, including those who had been dismissed after 1945 because they had been members of the Nazi party. Only 1,000 of the 53,000 civil servants initially removed from office after 1945 were permanently barred from the bureaucracy. This was a preferential policy, adopted not to favor ethnic minorities or women, as in the United States in the 1970s, but to favor state bureaucrats. If we view the de-Nazification program as an attempt at administrative reform, then we must judge it an abysmal failure (Cole, 1952; Herz, 1957; Hochschwender, 1962; Montgomery, 1957). At the same time, the Basic Law charged civil servants to be active supporters of the new democratic order rather than neutral bystanders. This constitutional mandate, as I shall describe below, became the center of a highly charged political controversy in the 1970s.

As in all other industrial states, the number of public-sector employees has increased sharply in West Germany. In the 1970s West Germany recorded a much greater increase in the number of public-sector employees than did the United States, Japan, Britain, and France. Only Sweden surpassed by a significant margin the West German figure (*Süddeutsche Zeitung,* April 6, 1982; Sept. 6, 1985). Between 1960 and 1982 the number of full-time civil servants almost doubled from 1.6 to 2.8 million. The Postal Service, the federal railways, and public corporations accounted for another 850,000 employees in 1982. Seven hundred thousand part-time employees brought the grand total to about 4.5 million. The growth in public-sector employment has been a strain on the public purse. In the mid-1970s, in a rich city state such as Hamburg, 46 percent of the state budget went to salaries and wages, compared to 80 percent in the Saar, one of the poorest states. On average personnel costs accounted for 15 percent of the total expenses of the federal government, 30 percent of local government, 42 percent of state government, 55 percent of the postal system, and 67 percent of the federal railways. As I noted in Chapter 1, because West Germany has a field system of administration, the number of federal bureaucrats (317,000) is dwarfed by those at state (1,589,000) and local levels (933,000). Public-sector personnel are concentrated at the federal level in defense, at the state level in education, and in local government in social welfare and health.

The West German bureaucracy consists of three types of public servants: 1.2 million civil servants (*Beamte*), 1.1 million employees (*Angestellte*), and 0.5 million workers (*Arbeiter*) (Keller, 1984; Miko, 1976). The expansion of the public sector has occurred mostly in the category of "employees." The category of "workers" primarily comprises blue-collar workers who are excluded from many of the benefits, privileges, and obligations of civil servants. The qualification of civil servants and public-sector employees has increased sharply. Between 1960 and 1982 the relative share of the top ranks in the public service increased from 12 to 18 percent, while the proportion in the bottom ranks declined from 7 to 3 percent (*Süddeutsche Zeitung,* Sept. 6, 1985).

In addition to unions that represent workers for the postal service, the railways, the police, and the teaching professions, public-sector employees are organized for the purpose of collective bargaining by one of West Germany's seventeen industrial unions representing both workers and salaried employees. This union has successfully leveled some of the differences that separate employees from civil servants. Chancellor Brandt, for example, resigned in 1974 not only because of the embarrassment that a spy had been discovered in his inner circle of advisors but also because he had become politically vulnerable after giving in to stiff union opposition to his publicly announced plan for a noninflationary salary increase in the public sector.

Although civil servants do not have the right to strike, they are permitted to organize. Their union is independent of the DGB and a powerful defender of extensive benefits (see Reading 6-6). Civil servants enjoy life-time job security, pensions up to 75 percent of their salary, protection against arbitrary political decisions, and the right to sue the government in regular courts in case of financial disputes. Civil servants receive salary supplements that are determined by their marital status and by the number of children they have. They do not contribute toward their pensions as do all other employees in the Federal Republic. And they have to pay for only one-half of their medical costs. Because it defends these and other benefits despite the sharp increases in salaries in the 1960s and 1970s, the civil servants' union has been a major barrier to a reform of the civil service. Backed by the constitutional guarantee of Article 33 of the Basic Law and a powerful lobby of Bundestag members from all major parties drawn from the ranks of the civil service, the union has so far successfully defeated all efforts to level the differences that still exist between the three types of public-sector employees (see Reading 6-6).

Civil servants are divided into four categories that are legally codified and used to be very rigid. In the past it was virtually impossible to pass from one category into another. More recently opportunities for moving from one category to the next have greatly improved. Members of the "basic" and "middle" service perform manual or low-level clerical work. The "executive" service includes administrative positions without policymaking responsibilities. Entrance requirements are a high school or technical school diploma, a probationary period lasting three years, and a passing score on an examination. The "higher" service encompasses about 10 percent of the civil servants. At the federal level, for about 2,800 civil servants it is the avenue to the top policy positions. A university degree and an extended probationary period are necessary for admission. In the federal bureaucracy careers are made within particular ministries rather than by moving among ministries. Furthermore, the strong position that civil servants have in the personnel councils, the analogue to the works councils described in Chapter 3, typically prevents outsiders from entering the middle or top levels of the bureaucracy. Newcomers start at the bottom. A legal education is still the normal channel for recruiting members of the higher service who work for federal and state governments. That the judiciary trains West Germany's administrative elite accounts largely for the strength of legalism in many of West Germany's policy debates. It is also a strong support for the norm of a nonpartisan civil service operating "above politics" so central to the West German concept of state service.

Agenda

The political restoration masterminded and presided over by Chancellor Adenauer in the 1950s required a skillful handling of the federal bureaucracy in Bonn. Adenauer's administrative chief of staff in the 1950s, Hans Globke, exemplified the continuity of Germany's administrative elite across the growth and collapse of different political regimes in the twentieth century. Before 1945 Globke had been a high official in the Ministry of Interior where he had played a controversial role in the drafting of the official commentary on the 1936 Nuremberg Race Act, an important link in the chain of events leading to the Holocaust. Because of these circumstances Globke advised Adenauer not to make him head of the chancellory. Yet Globke was probably Adenauer's most important political associate. For a time he succeeded in making the chancellory the hub of the Bonn government, overcoming the decentralization that has confronted all West German governments since

1949. More than any of Adenauer's other advisers, Globke had the greatest part in organizing and running the chancellory from the day he was hired. In the fall of 1953 he became head of the chancellory.

Yet by the early 1960s West German policymakers sensed that the policy formulas that had worked so well during the era of economic reconstruction under Adenauer's chancellorship were failing. Political debates about planning inside the EC were forced by the French and stoutly resisted by the Federal Republic. Planning became a widely accepted symbol of administrative and political reform only during the Great Coalition (1966–69). In fact, for a brief time the topic of administrative reform became politically contested ground for both the CDU/CSU and the SPD. After some haggling over jurisdictions, a cabinet committee drawn from five ministries constituted a "reform cabinet" chaired by Chancellor Kiesinger. Under its direction a group of civil servants began to work on developing a strategy for administrative reform. The first of three reports was delivered shortly before the 1969 federal election that ushered in the SPD-FDP coalition. The new government decided to move ahead with administrative reform and began to develop a comprehensive reform concept (see Reading 6-2) (Faude, 1974; Mayntz and Scharpf, 1973, 1975; Scharpf, 1973, 1974; Schmid and Treiber, 1975; Seiler, 1984; Waterkamp, 1974). By the time it had finished that initial stage of its work, precious months had passed and the reform impetus of the new government had begun to dissipate. From then on the work of the group became increasingly restricted in its scope and soon politically irrelevant. Even though the procedural changes the group suggested in its third report in 1972 had little resemblance to the substantive reform proposals of 1969–70, most of them were not implemented (see Reading 6-3).

In the political environment of the 1960s and early 1970s the chancellory defined as its task the imposition of central coordination on the ministries (see Reading 6-2). Unlike his predecessor Ludwig Erhard, Chancellor Kiesinger had shown some interest in instituting policy planning while he was governor of Baden-Württemberg. But once in office in Bonn he was preoccupied with the political management of the Great Coalition. The small planning staff formed in the chancellory in 1967 was inconsequential. But with the election of Chancellor Brandt in 1969, the formulation and implementation of a broad range of reform policies under the SPD suddenly became a high priority. The SPD's political objective was to ensure that the top civil service was responsive to the new government's reform initiative; it had no intention of allowing its initiatives to be torpedoed by a bureaucracy whose outlook had been shaped by the personnel policies of two decades of CDU rule. For the SPD reformers the political agenda after 1969 was clear. The success of the government depended heavily on the creation of an administrative machinery that would be responsive to the programmatic concerns of the new government.

But the chancellory's desire to acquire greater capacities was shared by individual ministries (Murswieck, 1975). Forced by the medium-term financial plan (see Chapter 2) to rationalize its acquisition purchases, the Ministry of Defense, for example, adapted the planning procedures of the U.S. Department of Defense. The Transportation Ministry unveiled a long-term transportation plan named after its minister, Georg Leber. In the early 1970s individual ministries developed plans in the areas of urban development, health services, environmental regulation, regional structure, and social policy, among others. In most instances long-term plans merely indicated that general lines of policy, were nonbinding, and self-consciously eschewed the setting of concrete targets. These plans illustrated that the ministries had moved rapidly to develop their own in-house planning capacities. The same was true of some of the eleven states, namely Hesse, Hamburg, West Berlin, North Rhine-Westphalia, Rhineland-Palatine, and Lower Saxony.

The agenda of administrative reform affected not only the "horizontal" coordination of the work of the federal bureaucracy in Bonn but also the "vertical" coordination between federal, state, and local bureaucracies. The impact of the economic crisis and the fall of Chancellor Erhard in 1966, for example, gave a big push to reforms in the administrative machinery of policymaking. In the area of economic policy, financial planning was rapidly implemented. The coalition government introduced a number of innovations under the heading of "general economic framework planning" and "medium-term finance planning." The Stability and Growth Act of 1967 (see Chapter 2) provided for interdepartmental working committees dealing with general economic forecasts, tax estimates, and long- as well as medium-term economic projections. In addition, the economic policies pursued at federal and state levels were coordinated by the Economic Council, the Finance Planning Council, and a number of working committees that were charged to coordinate policy but lacked the power to adopt binding resolutions. Finally, the concerted action acted as an umbrella linking different levels of government, the major interest groups, and parapublic institutions. The reform agenda was clearly set. But, as discussed in Chapter 2, the hope for rational, planned, and consensual decisionmaking based on the sharing of information and a clear articulation of policy objectives was a dream that contrasted starkly with the reality of the federal government's multiple dependencies on important actors whose behavior it did not control.

Vertical coordination also was an important aspect of a reform commission charged to consider a reorganization of West German federalism (Lehmbruch, 1977). But the reform objectives of the major political actors were quite varied. Some, especially in relatively wealthy states, wished to strengthen the traditional separation of powers between federal and state governments. Others, especially in relatively poor states, insisted that the financial equalization between different states be improved further. Finally, a third group, including a large number of politicians and civil servants at the federal level, were eager to develop a more coordinated and uniform set of planning policies that would be shaped by the federal government. Since the states could not in fact agree on one basic position, they opted for the line of least resistance: adherence to the system of intergovernmental relations which had been modified when West Germany's system of public finance was overhauled in the late 1960s (see Chapter 1).

In the mid- and late 1960s the reform of West Germany's system of local government also got off the ground (Albertin, 1980; Gunlicks, 1977a, 1977b, 1981, 1984, 1986; McDermott, 1981). For about a decade the debate had focused on the need for modernizing and increasing the efficiency of the system of local government. In the early 1960s, for example, the largest locality in North Rhine-Westphalia had 750,000 inhabitants while the smallest had only 13. With such disparities it was difficult for the government to fulfill the constitutional mandate of achieving a uniform standard of living throughout the Federal Republic. Revenue sharing might provide the funds, but many of West Germany's 24,500 communes simply lacked the administrative infrastructure necessary for the delivery of adequate social services. More efficiency in this instance meant greater administrative centralization. By 1978, however, each state had adopted its own distinctive version of municipal territorial reforms.

The policy agenda of political elites aimed to effect changes in the structure of the state. But in one instance that cut to the core, the agenda was just the opposite, to preserve rather than alter the character of the state bureaucracy (see Reading 6-9). Under West German law civil servants are permitted to be politically active as long as their politics do not undermine the democratic institutions set up by the Basic Law. In response to the perceived threat of Marxist student organizations intent on moving from the universities to the secondary schools (see Chapter 7), Chancellor Brandt and the Conference of State Governors adopted in January 1972 what came to be known as the "Radicals' Decree" (*Radikalenerlass*) (see Reading 6-4) which barred from employment in the public sector those whose political affiliations state or local government officials deemed to be opposed to "the free democratic basic order" (Dyson, 1974, 1975b; Frisch, 1977; Hirsch, 1980; Kvistad, 1986).

Debates surrounding the adoption of the decree emphasized that it was largely aimed at the teaching professions. Segments of the radical students who had opposed the Great Coalition (1966–69) as part of an "extraparliamentary" opposition and who were disappointed by the timid or failed reforms of the SPD-FDP coalition had joined Communist groups or the Communist party. They were the targets of a policy designed to defend the Basic Law and state institutions against subversive political influences (Kvistad, 1984, 1986). To many West Germans the fears of the bureaucracy were exaggerated. But the Radicals' Decree had deep roots in traditional concepts of the rights and obligations of the civil service dating back to the nineteenth century. Shared for a while by the politicians in all of the major parties, the issue was framed as a defense of state institutions against the enemies of democracy.

Process

I shall illustrate the implementation process of administrative reform policies by analyzing the planning mechanisms in the chancellory and, more briefly, the efforts at territorial reform and the politics of the Radicals' Decree. These examples illustrate that West German state institutions strongly resist political attempts to impose major structural reforms, such as the planning policies designed to improve policy coordination in the late 1960s. On the other hand, using different methods for orchestrating the work of the federal governments, in the 1950s and 1970s the chiefs of staff of Chancellors Adenauer and Schmidt achieved creditable results. The federal bureaucracy thus has resisted the attempt to impose large-scale changes on its structure and operation.

Furthermore, the state bureaucracy cooperated in reform ventures, such as local government reform, that enhanced its control. And it invoked norms and practices that defended the bureaucracy from the insurgence of social forces, which bureaucrats deemed a threat to the state.

One of the clearer illustrations of these norms came after the SPD's victory in the fall of 1969. Chancellor Brandt subsequently appointed Horst Ehmke as head of the chancellory, a man strongly committed to a rational and planned approach to the new government's program (Dyson, 1973, 1975a; Faude, 1974; Hanf, 1973; Lompe, 1970; Schatz, 1976). Ehmke reorganized the chancellory by adding two new divisions: domestic reform and planning. The planning division was given 38 positions out of a total of 351 in the chancellory. The intention was to strengthen long-term "goal" planning by integrating sectoral plans—for example, in transportation, finance, or the environment—into a comprehensive system of broad government objectives.

To this end the new planning division set up a new computer-based information system designed to provide for an early coordination of the government's general policy objectives, on the one hand, and medium- or long-term planning for particular tasks or sectors, on the other (see Reading 6-2). The coordination required individual ministries to inform the chancellory about any policy initiatives they were planning over the next six months. In return for sharing this information, the chancellory made available to each ministry a weekly print-out summarizing the plans of all federal ministries. By 1970 information on nearly 500 projects was stored in this data bank. The intent was to give the chancellor and the cabinet earlier and fuller information about the internal workings of the bureaucracy, thus reducing their need to accept the preliminary decisions of the ministerial bureaucracy without considering other political alternatives. Task planning, the planners hoped, would precede financial planning.

The planners had in fact an extremely critical view of the predominance of financial over substantive planning (see Reading 6-5). The lack of reform initiatives, they argued, resulted from an orientation that viewed political problems in terms of ceilings and constraints rather than objectives. Financial planning tended to encourage ministries to defend their pet projects. It reflected rather than reshaped budgetary practice. Task planning had to go beyond a five-year time horizon to coordinate policies before interest groups inside or outside the government assumed rigid postures. Thus in 1970 the planning division in the chancellory started long-term functional planning for the years 1976–85, an exercise that even the planners themselves did not really take seriously.

Because Ehmke and the head of the planning division, Reimut Jochimsen, were aware of the danger of working in a political vaccum, each ministry was given a planning delegate charged with the task of providing for a two-way flow of information. Unfortunately for the planners, several of the key ministries, such as Finance and the Interior, chose marginal people for this position who were isolated from main departmental activities. New interministerial committees were set up to improve horizontal coordination between ministries. Continuing an old tradition, the state secretaries met weekly in a committee chaired by Ehmke to share information and prepare cabinet meetings. The planning delegates also attended regular meetings in a committee chaired by planning head Jochimsen.

The obstacles that the planners confronted were numerous, and for a variety of reasons they proved insurmountable. One reason was the inevitable clash between the short-term electoral considerations of party politicians and the long-time horizons of the planners. Planning for the decade 1976–85 appeared preposterous to a government whose slim parliamentary majority was dwindling by the month. From the preliminary inventory that seven interministerial working groups and seven federal-state committees on functional planning completed, the federal cabinet picked only a handful of proposals that appeared to be particularly promising for winning the next election.

The prime issue for the first Brandt government was in the area of foreign rather than domestic affairs. Brandt's main interest was to build on his substantial expertise and accomplishment in foreign policy. As mayor of West Berlin, Brandt had lived at the center of the Cold War, and in 1961 he had seen Berlin divided by the Wall. For a variety of reasons the international system favored a major change in West German foreign policy. Brandt's political energies after 1969 were thus channeled primarily toward implementing his detente policy with the East. The foreign and East German affairs division in the chancellory thus became politically more important than the planning division. Because these divisions had mistrusted from the beginning the coordinating role assigned to the new planning division in 1969, they did their best to perpetuate the relatively unimportant role of the planners.

Finally the reformers faced serious opposition from within their own party as well as from within the FDP. Although run by SPD ministers, the Finance Ministry, which in 1971 was amalgamated with the Economics Ministry into a "superministry" (see Chapter 2), was a particularly adamant and powerful opponent. Since that ministry's development of a system of medium-term financial planning was well advanced, it was opposed to a different planning system. It viewed such a system as a clear rival for bureaucratic turf. The chasm between goal and financial planning was not narrowed when the Finance Ministry developed its own rudimentary version of functional planning. Finance Ministers Karl Schiller and later Helmut Schmidt were unwilling to share their powers with Ehmke and Jochimsen in the chancellory. Schmidt disparagingly referred to his rivals in the chancellory as "Ehmke's toy steam engine" (Dyson, 1973, p. 357).

But the planners also contributed to their failure through their own action. In the summer of 1970 the planning division in the chancellory made its first recommendation about the political priorities of different projects. Data that the ministries had shared for the inventory of the early coordination system were unexpectedly used to rank the political priorities for the federal government. Politicians and senior civil servants in the ministries were incensed at what they saw as a ruthless attempt of the government's political center to curtail the constitutionally guaranteed principle of ministerial autonomy. The reaction was an instantaneous politicization of the data that the ministries were willing to feed into the early coordination system. Projects were no longer reported routinely by low-echelon officials. Instead, senior civil servants relied on tactical political considerations to screen the projects that should be reported. The information flow between the ministries and the chancellory thus soon reassumed its traditional pattern. As a result of these obstacles, planning efforts in the chancellory were curtailed sharply after the SPD election victory of 1972.

It is instructive to compare the sobering results of the implementation of policy planning with the less confrontational approach used by the chancellory to coordinate the work of the federal government in the 1950s and 1970s. Like the reformers in the chancellory after 1969, Globke confronted in the 1950s a decentralized federal bureaucracy to which he wanted to impart some central direction (Katzenstein, 1969). Globke devised an ingenious system of informal penetration of ministries through a clever rotation of personnel, an active social calendar, and his appointment powers. In working around the bureaucracy rather than trying to confront it, the "system Globke," as it came to be called, was quite successful in enhancing policy coordination.

Globke was convinced that an unrestricted and ample flow of information was a necessary prerequisite if Chancellor Adenauer was to control effectively the formulation and implementation of the policies of his government. This need for information required the construction of a system that would give Globke and the chancellor full knowledge of and effective influence over important legislation that the ministries prepared.

Globke divided the chancellory into different sections that were assigned to keep in close contact with a number of ministries and thus to keep Globke and Adenauer fully informed. At times the sections were told to intervene in debates going on within a ministry. The chancellory's highly qualified staff evaluated the legislative proposals submitted by the ministries to the chancellory and recommended alterations or adoption to high officials in the ministry or to the chancellor and his top aides. The staff kept in informal but close contact with key assistants in the ministries that it was assigned to cover, thus maximizing the chancellory's influence at the early but critical stages in the preparation of important legislation. This system amounted to an informal penetration of all important ministries by the chancellory and the establishment of good channels of communication between the chancellory and the ministries far below the level of the undersecretary of state. In some situations, especially when time was pressing, the chancellory's aides prepared decisions that the chancellor had to take on substantive issues without consulting the ministry most directly concerned. Globke's system of control was not based on abstract and diffuse political objectives. Attention to detail, personal acquaintance with key officials, and the discrimination between important and unimportant policy issues were more important. It was a system of informal influence which helped to ensure that the chancellor's views, when he had some, were followed in the formulation of legislation and subsequent amendments.

This system was supplemented by Globke's genius in establishing good working relations with the top senior civil servants in the different ministries. He created a "rotating system." Young, first-class civil servants were hired away from their ministries and given assignments in the chancellory where their specialized knowledge would be of greatest use. These elite civil servants came to appreciate the importance of the chancellory's coordinating and supervising function. They were rotated back into higher positions within their old ministries after they had ceased to be useful. Many of Bonn's highest civil servants followed this career pattern. Detlev Rust, for example, had covered economic affairs in the chancellory before being promoted to the position of division head in the Economics Ministry and assuming the position of under-secretary of state in the Ministry of Defense. Karl Gumbel had worked for the chancellory in the area of domestic policy before starting to climb the administrative ladder of the Defense Ministry up to the position of undersecretary of state. Heinrich Barth was Adenauer's personal assistant and became undersecretary of state in the Ministry for Family Services. Herbert Blankenhorn was head of the division for foreign affairs in the chancellory before he became division head in the Foreign Office and later ambassador. The system thus ensured that there were a number of high officials in most ministries who had worked in the chancellory and were probably more receptive to suggestions and more open to direct influence than could otherwise have been expected.

Globke had a third technique by which he increased informal contacts between the chancellory and other ministries. He organized informal dinner parties, frequently in his own home, for all undersecretaries of states and their spouses. This practice soon became an institution that survived even Globke's retirement in 1963. Globke's organization of the chancellory and the net of informal associations and friendships which he was able to cast over all departments increased the influence of the chancellory in policymaking. He created an efficient institution, an un-ending stream of information, and potential for effective coordination and supervision, while maintaining a firm grip on the ever expanding administrative machine. The "system Globke" was an essential reason for Chancellor Adenauer's dominance over the cabinet and foreign policy.

In the 1970s the "system Schüler," adapted to the needs of the SPD government, was similarly successful in coordinating the work of the federal bureaucracy (*Der Spiegel,* Aug. 9, 1976, pp. 21–24; *Frankfurter Allgemeine,* Dec. 2, 1978). At the age of only forty-two Manfred Schüler, a trained economist, became Chancellor Schmidt's senior administrator. In his view, which was similar to Globke's, the task of the chancellory was to coordinate the work of the federal bureaucracy quietly and efficiently and to keep the chancellor and her cabinet on top of the policy process. As it had been for Globke, the control of information was for Schüler the key. To this end Schüler worked hard to revive a practice his predecessors had neglected: the rotation of bureaucrats between ministries and the chancellory. The different divisions of the chancellory were well staffed and sections knew what was happening in "their" ministries.

The West German state bureaucracy resisted the heavy-handed efforts of the planners in the chancellory to effect far-reaching changes in its structure. It did, however, prove responsive to the less ambitious objectives that Globke and Schüler pursued in the 1950s and 1970s with a lighter political touch. Resistance to large-scale change and accommodation to smaller changes appear to be part of a broader pattern. In 1970 the Bundestag, for example, instituted the Commission of Inquiry for Constitutional Reform. It was charged to deliberate on an imposing catalogue of issues including, among others, the governability of West Germany, the openness of decisionmaking, the prospects for enhanced citizen participation in politics, and the constitutional and legal limits to government planning. A preliminary report issued in 1972 received harsh criticism. Reconvened in the spring of 1973, this commission proposed in its final report of December 1976 that the financial reforms of the late 1960s needed to be corrected; it claimed that West Germany's cooperative federalism had encouraged a decline in accountability and participation. Although there was much agreement about the commission's assessment of the situation, the constitutional amendments that it proposed were never taken up. Moreover, in none of the other areas did six years of work on the big topics of state organization and West German politics lead to any tangible results.

On the other hand, the more limited question of the reform of local government was resolved by focusing on the issue of procedural efficiency. In the 1970s the number of West German municipalities had declined by two-thirds, from 24,500 to about 8,500. The number of counties was almost halved (Gunlicks 1977a, 1977b, 1986). To be sure, in states that were dominated by the CDU or CSU, such as Baden-Württemberg or Bavaria, the average municipality or county was smaller than in states dominated by the SPD. The CDU and the CSU were less ambitious in their reforms and tended to criticize the centralizing instincts of the SPD. In addition, West Germany's states also differed in their administrative organization and traditions. What opposition existed against the reform of local government was typically defeated in the courts. Outside of local politics the process of territorial consolidation generated remarkably little political or bureaucratic opposition. It was widely viewed as another move toward centralization.

Relevant for democratic practice was the fact that the number of offices to be filled by local elections were halved to about 140,000 elected local councilors. To counteract the growing psychological and physical distance separating citizens from city halls, the states amended their local government charters to provide for a variety of institutional forms of devolution (Albertin, 1982). But the state bureaucracy was much more reluctant to implement administrative devolution than territorial consolidation. Administrative preponderance in local affairs thus increased. "To the extent that administrative reform in this sense of administrative decentralization has remained incomplete, the original reform goals have not been met" (Gunlicks, 1977a, p. 26).

The implementation of the decree that sought to protect the West German civil service from infiltration by political radicals shares one important feature with the case of territorial reform; in the process of implementation the bureaucracy determined its own course and was largely unaffected by party control. The Radicals' Decree, adopted jointly by the Conference of State Governors in 1972, did not create new law; it merely reaffirmed some provisions of existing civil service law (see Reading 6-4). But it did create new administrative practices. The background of applicants for civil service employment (including school teachers, university professors, and employees of the Postal Service or railways) henceforth had to be investigated (see Reading 6-8). A ruling of the Constitutional Court in 1975 left the executive branch with a substantial amount of latitude (see Reading 6-7). Bureaucracies in states dominated either by the CDU/CSU or the SPD interpreted the decree in remarkably similar ways (Kommitee, 1982; Kvistad, 1984; Schmidt, 1980, pp. 112–24). They constructed an exhaustive screening procedure that, generally speaking, left no part of an individual's past unexamined and that applied stringent but often differing criteria for judging which memberships in political parties or which activities were judged to be "undemocratic" (see Reading 6-8). State intrusion into the private life of its citizen was extensive. In Cologne, for example, an employee of the municipal utility company was dismissed as a "security risk" because he lived together with Christel Ensslin, sister of Gudrun, a prominent member of the accused Baader-Meinhof terrorist group. In a notorious case, Communist party member Volker Goetz was denied a position in the judiciary not because of his membership in the Communist party but because of his opinion, stated in a private conversation, that Yugoslav-style socialism was to be faulted for its imitation of capitalism (Kvistad, 1984, p. 483). The statistics of policy implementation illustrated the extensiveness of the investigations. Between 1973 and 1980 the Office for the Defense of the Constitution together with state and local governments had screened about 1.3 million applicants. Of these about twenty-seven thousand admitted to have had extremist connections and about thirteen hundred, or less than 0.001 percent, were finally barred from public-sector employment (Landfried, 1985, p. 214). In the mid-1970s more than 80 percent of all denials were based on nonpolitical criteria. Put differently, a search of 1.3 million applicants netted only about three hundred politically justified denials (Kvistad, 1984, p. 491).

Policy implementation was eventually affected by party differences. By 1976, an intensive political debate especially in the SPD-FDP coalition, a decision of the Constitutional Court in 1975 (see Reading 6-4), and a policy declaration by the Bundestag dating from the same year had led to an official break between government and the opposition. The SPD-FDP and the CDU/CSU disagreed about how restrictively the 1972 guidelines should be interpreted in the process of policy implementation. The states governed by the SPD-FDP coalition subsequently adopted practices more respectful of individual rights than did states governed by the CDU/CSU.

Consequences

The record of West Germany's administrative reform policies is unambiguous. Major structural reforms of the federal bureaucracy, West German federalism, and the Constitution have failed. The reason is simple. The state bureaucracy, as Max Weber argued, is at its core an institution that has absorbed and merged external and internal interests that are very difficult to dislodge. Frederick the Great called himself "the first servant of the state" in part out of modesty, in part because in the eighteenth century the bureaucracy began to impose its own structure on absolutist, royal power. In the nineteenth century, the German state in many ways shaped an emerging industrial society. The political pocketknives of the planners of the 1960s proved somewhat too small to carve this hard trunk.

But it would be too simple to conclude that in the absence of major structural reforms, nothing has changed (Ellwein and Hesse, 1985; Hesse, 1982). Administrative reform has meant many different things over the last twenty-five years, and small changes have indeed occurred in many areas. Some of these took place almost unnoticed in the aftermath of failed major reforms. A permanent legacy of the planning work in the chancellory, for example, was an expanded and refined method of data collection which describes each project under forty different categories (Schatz, 1976, pp. 55–56). In the mid-1970s about eight hundred projects were on file, and their number increased by about twenty each month. Given the role of a clearing house and facilitator, the planning division developed also a calendar for the work of the cabinet, an indispensable aid in the decisionmaking procedures of the federal government. Similarly, the planning methods adopted by individual ministries strengthened the administrative capacities of the federal bureaucracy while making coordinative planning by the chancellory less necessary.

West German scholars have debated at great length whether administrative reform is shaped by the internal restrictions of a decentralized, large-scale bureaucracy or by the external restraints of a capitalist society. In the end, most knowledgeable analysts have concluded that the truth is somewhere in the middle. Important for our line of argument is the fact that the various planning exercises initiated by individual ministries never coalesced; the traditionally decentralized system of policy making in the federal government was never visibly altered. Similarly, failed efforts to reform West German federalism did not stop the reform of the system of local government. Indeed, a variety of regional and subregional planning bodies have emerged, especially for large metropolitan areas, which are coordinating the work of different levels of government. Although the territorial reform of the local government system was successfully completed by the late 1970s, "the allocation of authority between the two basic levels of local government . . . is still a matter of dispute even though territorial reform has meanwhile been completed" (McDermott, 1981, p. 199). In fact, West Germany's administrative system, epitomized by its "cooperative federalism," has opened the door to multiple administrative tiers that link the three basic levels of government and maintain the ambiguity between different units of local government. West Germany's administrative structure has defied all attempts to impose major structural change. But because it is a loosely coupled system of agencies rather than some massive Behemoth, it has accommodated incremental change.

Compared to the issues of economic management, industrial relations, social welfare, and migrant labor which I discussed in Chapters 2–5, the case of administrative reform is largely about a depoliticized game of politics within West Germany's decentralized state. West Germany's major interest groups and parapublic institutions remained total-ly uninvolved. The impossibility of effecting major changes in policy is the same in all five policy case studies. But the factors that determine similar outcomes differ. The shackling of power through the system of coalition politics, cooperative federalism, and parapublic institutions has prevented large-scale change in economic and social policy. In the case of administrative reform, the resistance of state institutions to ex-ternally defined or imposed changes has led to the same result. It is thus only fair to assume that more recent proposals for simplification of the structure of the state bureaucracy will not lead to administrative changes of the magnitude that has characterized, for example, the United States in the 1980s (Ellwein and Hesse, 1985).

The internal resistance to large changes in administrative structures and procedures and the accommodation of incremental changes are re-flected in the ambiguous relation between the state bureaucracy and West German politics more generally. The norm of a nonpartisan senior civil service that serves the state and operates "above party politics" has been deeply ingrained since the nineteenth century. But during the last two decades that norm gradually has changed. A number of empirical studies have concluded that West Germany's senior civil servants are now defining their role in the policy process as more political (Grottian, 1974; Herz, 1957; Putnam, 1975, 1973; Steinkemper, 1974, 1980). The contrast with traditional German perceptions of nonpartisanship is as striking as the similarity with the perceptions of bureaucrats in other countries. The reasons for this change are numerous and complex and include political changes in West Germany, the promotion of a new generation of civil servants trained after 1945, and the recruitment of a larger proportion of senior civil servants not trained in law. In fact, many of the planners brought into government in the late 1960s were viewed with suspicion by senior civil servants because of their training in the social sciences.

Middle- and top-level recruits for West Germany's civil service are trained in what the Germans call "state science" (*Staatswissenschaft*), which focuses largely on public law. All eleven states as well as the federal government, the Postal Service, and the armed forces operate at least one university-style academy in which the future cadres of state administrators are trained. However, not all training for the civil service is as tightly controlled by the state. West German universities train a large number of applicants who pass state-administered examinations and seek entrance to the civil service. With the Radicals' Decree of 1972 the state bureaucracy mobilized fully to keep applicants judged as politically unreliable out of state employment. "Planners" could be defeated or at times be accommodated in a political game that took place within state institutions. "Radicals" were to be kept out of state service despite troublesome constitutional issues and very substantial political costs for the government. The inevitable tensions between accommodating flexibly to some social and policy changes and resisting fiercely others that touch the very core of the bureaucracy aptly characterize West Germany's state as semisovereign.

Readings

6-1. LAW ON THE STATUS OF CIVIL SERVANTS ELECTED TO THE BUNDESTAG (1953)*

The intensifying controversy in the 1970s over the privileges of civil servants and the growing number of Bundestag members with civil service status dates back to legislation passed in 1953.

Art. 1 - A civil servant or judge on salary who is elected to the German Bundestag shall be put on the retired list beginning on the day of his acceptance of the election.

Art. 2 - (1) A civil servant or judge (Art. 1) shall receive the salary for his previously held office during the month in which he accepts his election as a Member of the German Bundestag. (2) After the expiration of the period for which salaries are allowed the civil servant or judge shall receive a pension.

Art. 3 - (1) After the termination of his membership in the Bundestag a civil servant or judge (Art. 1) shall, upon his request, be accepted into his former condition of service, provided that he can still meet the general civil service requirements. The position to which he is appointed must be a line identical with or equivalent to the position he last held

---

*John C. Lane and James K. Pollock, eds., *Source Materials on the Government and Politics of Germany* (Ann Arbor: Wahrs, 1964), p. 121 (selections).

and must provide a basic salary at least equal to it. . . . (3) If a civil servant or judge does not present a request, pursuant to paragraph (1) above, he shall remain on the retired list. His superior service authority may, however, recall him into his previous condition of service by an appointment to a position meeting the requirements of paragraph (1), above; provided that at the termination of his membership in the Bundestag he has not yet reached the age of fifty-five. Should he refuse the appointment he shall be deemed discharged from service. The two preceding sentences shall not apply to a civil servant or judge who was a member of the Federal Cabinet during his service as a Member of the Bundestag.

Art. 4 - The period of service in the Bundestag until the age of sixty-five shall, in case of re-entry into the previous condition of service (paragraph (3), above) or after the end of the term of the Bundestag, be counted as term of service for purposes of the salary and compensation laws.

Art. 5 - (1) The provisions of Arts. 1 through 4 shall apply accordingly to salaried employees in the public service. . . .

Art. 6 - The discharge of a civil servant or judge or the giving notice of dismissal to a salaried employee after the completion of their service in the Bundestag because of their activity as a Member shall not be permissible.

Art. 7 - This Act shall not apply to teachers with civil service status at technical institutes, to persons holding honorary offices or not receiving fixed remuneration, nor to civil servants chosen for limited terms (*Wahlbeamte*). The legal status of civil servants chosen for limited terms and elected to the Bundestag shall be regulated by Land [state] legislation.

6-2. DEVELOPING PLANNING MECHANISMS IN THE FEDERAL GOVERNMENT*

In the following Reimut Jochimsen, head of the planning division in the chancellory after 1969, describes the political efforts to improve the capacity of the chancellory to coordinate the work of the federal government.

*Reimut Jochimsen, "Establishing and Developing an Integrated Project Planning and Coordinating System for the West German Federal Government," *International Journal of Politics* 2 (Summer–Fall 1972):51–77 (selections).

An evaluation of the present situation reveals the following pattern: on the one hand, there are varying degrees of planning being carried out independently within different specialized areas, including budgetary and finance planning; on the other hand, there is still a clearly recognizable tendency to adhere to the old, hierarchic, regimented system of sovereignly defined authority in selecting and performing governmental tasks . . . .

We could spend a great deal of time demonstrating how the principle of maximum output works at the section level (the principle does, after all, have certain positive features and effects). The section head contacts the various social groups, business associations, and others—for example, professional groups—within his area of responsibility. Through this contact he arrives at the tasks to be undertaken. Most of these tasks are, indeed, extremely important. But the point is that as long as the section heads themselves have reached an agreement, there will generally be no check or control over whether it lies in the common interest to attack these problems at precisely this moment or in just this manner. And since the section heads follow the maxim "if you strike, I'll strike back," if I may express it so crudely (everyone wants to pilot his own ship once in a while!), the final result is an amalgam of reports, legislative bills, and other proposals that differ quite widely from one another depending on where they originated. Negative coordination alone is not enough. . . .

Any look at the situation in the United States should lead us rather to deplore the fact that duplication of planning—in the Departments, on the one hand, and in the Executive Office of the President and in the Presidential commissions, on the other—can cause even greater waste due to friction among government bodies. Thus, it is not a question of whether to centralize or not to centralize. It is not a matter of amending the Constitution; rather, it is a question of allowing free play to all the various balances and counterbalances already provided for in the Constitution, and here I would place the main emphasis on restoring the cabinet principle. Cabinet sessions in which each minister participates exclusively as a departmental head speaking only on matters relating to his own department continue the practice of purely negative coordination. It is like limiting concern to the children who have fallen into the well while, to extend the metaphor, the surroundings and safety of the well—and its purpose as a playground—are not planned. . . .

What are the alternative theoretical approaches to the problem of establishing and developing a project planning and coordinating system, capable of reducing difficulties for the Federal Government? Here we might distinguish two competing and diametrically opposed principles: total, centralized coordination, and comprehensive decentralized coordination. . . .

Since it is not possible to simply take over a planning system—even the best of planning systems—from somewhere else, we are faced with the problem of how to plan a planning system for the Federal Government.

The key to the first phase was the realization that there was one completely new and absolutely essential task to be performed: we had to create a base of information. Without this base, planning and coordination in the government were impossible. Let me give just one example. Shortly after the present government was formed, preparations were being made for the Hague Conference between the heads of government of the six EEC countries. In those preparations the question arose of what sort of offer we should make in the negotiations. This was in effect also asking the question of what promises and commitments we had actually made already—in the Council of Ministers or in the other EEC organs. Naturally, it was assumed that this could all be cleared up in a matter of minutes with a telephone call. That was not the case. After fourteen days of searching, the only thing we were certain of was that we had still not discovered all our promises.

Creating this information base is the first, absolutely essential, step toward developing a task planning and coordinating system. The Federal Government has begun by appointing to each ministry a planning representative charged with the integration of planning efforts within and among the various departments. Together, these planning representatives form a permanent body which meets every two weeks in the Federal Chancellor's Office to discuss procedural coordination of governmental projects with respect to priorities of content, finance, and timing. . . .

The second step in developing the system is presently being taken. A survey on reform plans, programs for carrying them out, and planned measures to put these reform proposals into practice during this legislative period, as well as preparatory work for plans reaching into the future are all now under way. This work will be the basis for implementing and extrapolating the government program and for actually making possible its coordination with regard to content, finances, and time.

One of the central problems in this connection can be described by the term "early-stage coordination." Our information system has actually been constructed from the wrong end: it has been built up on the basis of projects to be started in the next six months. Yet these are generally those projects that have reached such an advanced stage of preparation, that have already been operationally so well delineated, as it were, within the departments, that apart from the matter of timing little actually remains to be done—at the most, a sort of negative compatibility check. This is an extremely hazardous affair because it means that the effort to improve coordination is begun at a most difficult—i.e., a very late—stage instead of in an earlier stage when intentions, qualms, and first efforts at a solution had indeed emerged, but when the final solution, the model, the proposal, as it were, had not yet been put forward. The principle of maximum output that I postulated earlier has a corollary, namely, maximum efficiency in handling this maximum output within departments. This of course creates sources of conflict at a time, moreover, when at the government level the projects have obviously long since been made public and have been discussed with the various interest groups and parties, and have generally reached such an advanced stage that the only way left to coordinate the project will be either by cutting the necessary financial appropriation by half or by postponing the project for a year. This is indeed what happens today. . . .

In other words, we must be able to solve problems within a given frame of reference; it is this frame of reference that we need. But it must be a frame of reference that is not already conclusively defined by the technical limits of our present organizational structure, which simply fails to provide for certain complex tasks. Let me illustrate this with an example.

In August 1969, the Bundestag passed the Vocational Training Law. It passed this law despite the fact that three months earlier it had amended the Basic Law so that the new Article 91b gave the Federal Government the right to enter into an administrative agreement with the states enabling it to initiate comprehensive planning in all areas of education, including vocational training, with no restrictions. The law was adopted by the Bundestag with a view toward making optimal use of the Federal Government's existing powers in this area. This meant that general education was excluded. The law dealt only with vocational training, and the objectives of the latter were brought in line with the educational tasks and goals over which the Federal Government had jurisdiction—namely, the providing of competently trained manpower for the labor market. That meant that many aspects of educational policy that today appear almost as parts of a whole were approached in quite a different manner last year. The organs to have responsibility in this area included the Federal Ministers for Economic Affairs, for Social Affairs, and for Youth, but none of the states' ministers of culture. Because of the vertical distribution of powers there is a temptation to say, in effect: "General education—that is the states' affair. They each have their minister of culture; he is completely apart from the system of federal departments and the Federal Government. But vocational training—that is a matter of producing skilled labor for the market. That is the affair of the Federal Government."

If this problem had been tackled in good time outside the organizational structure and the distribution of responsibilities between the federal and state governments and among the various government departments, then we would certainly have anticipated, even as early as 1969, the widespread public debate on education as it has now developed, and as it is expressed in the amendment to Article 91a, where the word "higher" is eliminated before the word "education."

Similarly, we could have foreseen the planning and budgetary difficulties we now face in trying to carry out the federal-state administrative agreement on education. In other words, it is always easier to predict planning conflicts between specialized sectors and spheres of responsibility if one listens—as we could easily have done in this case—to opinions from experts, the public, and interest groups, and if one seeks organizational forms for problem-solving that I would describe as "broadly conceived project planning": problem-oriented, not department-oriented. Our solutions must go beyond the view that the present organizational structure of the departments, the organization determined by the Chancellor for a given legislative period, is something absolute and valid for all time. . . .

I think, that planning in a democracy expands and does not constrict the limits of our freedom. This is aimed at recreating the freedom of action, which by common avowal we all lost in the Bundestag in 1966, and which we have won back only to a small degree through our present medium-term financial planning. I mean specifically a freedom of action such that the Parliament and the government (with members elected on the basis of their commitment to specific concrete alternatives of action) can decide what will happen in the future; a freedom of action such that these two bodies become more than simply the ratifiers of decisions handed down from another level and for which they can hardly assume political responsibility.

6-3. PROPOSALS FOR A REFORM OF THE STRUCTURE OF THE FEDERAL GOVERNMENT AND BUREAUCRACY*

In this third and final report a reform commission develops its conclusions about how the work of the federal government might be improved. This reform commission generated much of the work that led to a revival in state theory and public policy among West German scholars. The commission's political impact on the other hand was fairly small. The selections that follow develop ideas about how policy planning and budget planning could be more closely linked.

The commission's proposal aims at strengthening existing efforts towards program-oriented task planning in the federal ministries and by the federal government in concert with the financial planning process. A planning procedure is needed which makes it possible to combine program and budget planning within the framework of a "program budget." This proposal can be implemented only gradually.

The proposed new procedure would first affect program planning in the ministry. The openness of administrative processes would be improved and policy objectives clarified if each federal ministry were to organize the activities of sections into programs at the level of division which in turn could be brought together in the form of a ministry's program. The divisional programs should conform with the goals of the ministry's program. To achieve this purpose the ministries must develop a goal-oriented program structure.

Analogously, a goal-oriented program structure must be developed for merging the ministerial programs into a comprehensive program of the federal government. The planning activities should be initiated by a central office in each ministry and for the government as a whole.

*Projektgruppe Regierungs- und Verwaltungsreform beim Bundesminister des Innern, *Dritter Bericht zur Reform der Struktur von Bundesregierung und Bundesverwaltung* (Bonn, November 1972), pp. I/65–I/78 (selections).

Therefore, a "planning division" is to be set up in each ministry which above all will depend on a successful cooperation among the divisions for budgeting, organization, and personnel. We recommend therefore that these sections be grouped together. Because this "coordinating group" will need support at the top of the ministerial hierarchy, it should be attached to the office of state secretary.

For the development of planning of the federal government, we recommend the formation of a working group of representatives of the chancellory and of the Ministry of Finance. This group would assist individual ministries in the development of their planning structures; it would define the objectives of the comprehensive plan of the federal government; and it would organize the reporting system. This working group should from the beginning have full access to the ministries' expertise and it should also have the option of drawing upon the assistance of experts outside of government. . . .

The proposals of the commission take into account the considerable time pressure under which the budgets for 1973 and 1974 will be drawn up. We thus envision a development, a trial, and an implementation phase.

Beginning in 1973 we propose to develop planning structures in the ministries and to define the objectives of the federal government's comprehensive program by listing the activities of sections on activity data sheets and of divisions on program data sheets; by relying on the planning section in each ministry to develop a financially realistic ministerial plan based on program data sheets; by articulating the objectives of the federal government in a working group of the chancellory and the Ministry of Finance; by drafting in the planning division of the chancellory the federal government's comprehensive plan based on the ministerial programs and program data sheets; by forwarding to the Ministry of Finance drafts of the planned ministerial budgets (along with data sheets) to ensure the financial feasibility of all proposed activity; and by having the cabinet debate the comprehensive program.

In the trial phase, the draft budget for 1975 will be prepared using rough estimates, as has been customary, and filling out additional program budget data sheets that in the meantime have been developed by the working group of the chancellory and the Ministry of Finance. The planning process, running parallel to the budget cycle, should include the following steps. Within the ministries financial requests together with program budget data sheets will be filed with the planning division.

The planning division in each ministry will prepare not only an estimate for each budget item but also a draft plan for the ministry. As has been customary, these estimates as well as the program budget data sheet will be forwarded to the Ministry of Finance to assist in preparation of a draft budget and a financial plan. The draft plan of each ministry and the program budget data sheet will be forwarded to the chancellory to aid in preparation of the federal government's comprehensive program. After negotiations with the individual ministries, the chancellory and the Finance Ministry cooperate in preparing a proposal for the cabinet. . . . The cabinet's decision will be prepared by a coordinating committee comprised of the state secretaries who supervise the coordinating groups in each ministry.

With the budget cycle for 1976 we shall be able to implement the budget procedures that have already been described. . . .

The commission proposes altering the federal government's planning system in order to improve the process of program planning and to link more closely task and financial planning. The new procedure permits a systematic assessment of programs beginning at the very sections and divisions within the ministries which develop program activities. At the same time this system promises to incorporate individual plans into a consistent federal comprehensive program that links program planning with financial planning. Further interministerial perspectives could be incorporated into the plans as soon as the necessary sources of information have been created. This process would qualitatively improve the cabinet's work. These continuous planning activities will allow the government to concentrate on the important issues and to present policy more effectively to the public. Furthermore, the proposed planning system offers new possibilities for enhancing the control of the Bundestag and for beginning a permanent dialogue with the general public about the character and extent of state activities.

6-4. EMPLOYMENT OF ENEMIES OF THE CONSTITUTION IN THE CIVIL SERVICE (RADICALS' DECREE)*

The Radicals' Decree of January 28, 1972, became the subject of an intense political debate in the 1970s. Its defenders viewed it as simply

---

*Erhard Denninger, ed., *Freiheitliche Demokratische Grundordnung* (Frankfurt: Suhrkamp, 1977), 2:518–19.

an agreement to coordinate administrative procedures at the federal and state levels—a reaffirmation of existing law. Critics interpreted the decree as a contradiction of basic human rights and the substance of democracy, and an expression of an illiberal spirit sanctifying authoritarian practices that are to be deplored and resisted. The debate illuminates contrasting perceptions about democratic rights and state interest.

On January 28, 1972, the minister-presidents of the states of the Federal Republic, in consultation with the chancellor and on the advice of the standing conference of the interior ministers, have agreed to the following principles:

1. In accordance with the civil service law of the federal and state governments only an individual can be appointed to the civil service who can guarantee that he will intervene on behalf of the free democratic basic order as defined in the Basic Law. A civil servant is duty-bound, during service and nonservice hours, actively to stand up for the maintenance of this basic order. These provisions are binding.

2. Every individual case must be tested and decided on its own merits. The following principles are to be used for that purpose:

2.1 APPLICANTS

2.1.1 An applicant who has been engaged in activities that are hostile to the constitution will not be appointed to the civil service.

2.1.2 If an applicant belongs to an organization that pursues goals hostile to the Constitution, that membership establishes reasonable doubt whether he would intervene on behalf of the free democratic basic order at all times. This doubt normally justifies a denial of appointment.

2.2 CIVIL SERVANTS. If, on account of activities or membership in an organization that has aims hostile to the Constitution, a civil servant does not meet the requirements of section 35 of the Civil Service Law—whereby he is duty-bound to acknowledge the free democratic basic order as defined by the Basic Law in his entire conduct and intervene to uphold that order—his supervisor has, from circumstances to be ascertained case by case, grounds for the requisite conclusions. Such supervisor should especially consider whether dismissal of the civil servant is advisable.

3. The same principles are valid for public-sector workers and employees—in accordance with their employment contracts.

6-5. THE FEDERAL GOVERNMENT'S VIEW OF ADMINISTRATIVE REFORM*

In this report the federal government responds to three separate written questions submitted by different members of the Bundestag concerning the reform commission's work. In the following selections the government highlights some of the conceptual innovations and successes of the reform commission.

In its first report, the commission pointed out that the creation of larger ministries would require placing a larger number of policy sectors under the jurisdiction of subordinate offices. . . . Such a move, the commission believed, would make it easier to implement future structural adjustment processes [in the federal bureaucracy].

The numerous initiatives of the German Bundestag and its committees and the equally numerous suggestions of the Federal Delegates for Administrative Efficiency aimed to strengthen and encourage the ministries to delegate some of their powers. The commission thus sought to define anew the difference between ministerial and nonministerial activities. In so doing it hoped to establish precedents for transferring responsibility for policymaking to subordinate agencies. Until then . . . nonministerial tasks had primarily included those that dealt with individual decisions, were restricted to the implementation of political decisions, or involved solely administrative activities. After critical examination of foreign models—especially the organizational separation of political administration and functional administration in Sweden—and after in-depth study of the solutions tried out by individual states, the commission proposed to rely on the political content of the administrative steering process. The commission proposed considering as ministerial only those duties that continually require political direction. With this new measuring rod the commission hoped to transfer integrated sets of public tasks rather than only fragmented duties to subordinated agencies, thus strengthening the involvement of public-sector employees in these agencies. . . .

Further proposals aimed at rationalizing the relationship between ministry and subordinate agency, based on the premise that such agencies should be supervised by general guidelines and that direct interventions by the ministries should be resisted. In the event that delegated tasks became politically explosive, ad hoc working groups (minis-

*"Antwort der Bundesregierung," *Deutscher Bundestag Drucksache* 7/2887 (Bonn, December 4, 1974), pp. 21–26, 80–88 (selections).

try/subordinated agencies) were instructed to exercise authority jointly for a limited time. . . .

Informal activity by the commission has already had practical results. By cooperating with the commission, individual ministries have increased their awareness of the necessity of structural changes and gained support for many independent initiatives. Following the commission's lead, some ministries took practical steps for implementing their own planning procedures.

Disseminating the results of the commission's work to the interested lay public also strengthened the ministries' initiative to implement planning procedures even before binding decrees to that effect were issued. Reports and special studies delegated or written by the commission have been circulated among the committees and members of the Bundestag, and offices outside government. These reports have sparked new discussions—especially in the field of public administration—that have clarified further the commission's findings.

Foreign governments have been very interested in the work of the commission. A substantial portion of the commission's proposals have been put into practice. Rudimentary experiments with planning have been developed further to include proposals for introducing planning delegates in the ministries; developing a comprehensive planning procedure and planning organization in the Ministry of Agriculture; developing goal and program structures for some divisions in the Ministry of Economics; introducing a planning group in the Ministry of Family and Youth Affairs; combining functional with financial planning; improving the presentation of goals for the purpose of policy evaluation; establishing a work group—"program planning"—for planning coordination and policy evaluation in the Ministry for Science and Technology; organizing an early coordination system in the Ministry of Postal Services and Telecommunications; and establishing an information system in the Ministry of Economic Cooperation.

6-6. INTERVIEW WITH FORMER PRESIDENT GUSTAV HEINEMANN ABOUT THE PRIVILEGES OF CIVIL SERVANTS*

In this conversation with journalists of the West German weekly Der Spiegel, Gustav Heinemann publicly elaborates his criticisms of the

*"Selbstbedienungsladen derer, die drin sind?" Der Spiegel, December 16, 1974, pp. 41–46 (selections).

privileges enjoyed by the bureaucracy. Published a year after the re-
lease of a report recommending many changes in the civil service, this
interview expresses the intensity of criticism by the advocates of a re-
form that never materialized.

Spiegel: Dr. Heinemann, in your last speeches and interviews as federal
president you warned of developments in the civil service. You ex-
plained among other things that there was an imbalance between what
the civil service accomplished and what the public could rightfully expect of it. Are you afraid that Germany is on the way to becoming a
republic of civil servants?

Heinemann: One should never give pat answers. There are people in
public service who perform superbly, more than can be expected of
them. And then there are others. My worry about developments in the
civil service lies in large part in the fact that interests have coalesced in
such a manner as to make any reform or improvement extremely
difficult.

Spiegel: You mean the role that the civil service plays in wage negotiations and in reforms of its own affairs. In these instances it not only
articulates the demands but at the same time also tries to maintain the
status quo on the side of the employer or in legislation.

Heinemann: Yes, my greatest concerns are in this direction. Increasingly parliaments are composed of men and women who are civil
servants. Almost half of the members of the federal and state parliaments belong to the civil service. If the interest group for public servants makes demands for higher wages or other improvements, you
cannot expect any great opposition from those who are part of that
group. The reason is simple. All members gain from the success of
those who are putting on the pressure. That is true to the extent that the
salaries of legislators depend upon the pay civil servants receive. Or that
a lord mayor in Lower Saxony, the political representative of the community, functions at the same time as an official of the union representing public servants. Any way you look at it collusion is inevitable.

Spiegel: Linking the salary levels of the legislators with the pay scales
of the civil servants was done by the Bundestag. Do you attribute this
action to the fact that civil servants make up 40 percent of the Bundestag?

Heinemann: Yes, I do. If you look carefully at specific committees in
the Bundestag, for instance the Committee for Domestic Affairs or the

Budget Committee, you will find there too many people from the civil service, at least to my way of thinking. Can you recall the Budget Committee ever taking a hard look at a governmental agency and asking the question: "Does this one have to exist?" Take for instance the coal agency. It has, as far as I am concerned, no longer any reason to exist. When will it finally be abolished?

Spiegel: Agencies that exist are taboo.

Heinemann: Almost every time a new government forms in Bonn we find that responsibilities are taken from one ministry and slipped over to another. This raises the natural question, "Do the people responsible for these issues in the old ministry move over to the new ministry?" I doubt greatly that this happens. But where is the opposition in the Bundestag that checks up on such things? The CDU/CSU is just as saturated with civil servants as are the governing parties. On this specific point I have yet to be successful in getting the opposition to check the influence of the civil service through the Bundestag.

Spiegel: Have you asked the opposition to do so?

Heinemann: I have spoken to legislators right up to the party leaders and have said, "This is actually your responsibility" . . .

Spiegel: What do you think about reductions in the length of the work week in the public service? Do you think that too many concessions have been made over the years?

Heinemann: Yes, I am convinced of it. I have to confess that this rapid reduction in the number of working hours really has concerned and annoyed me. As it is now we cannot finance our educational plans; we cannot finance our penal institutions as the Justice Department has planned it. There are a lot of things we cannot finance. At the same time we are reducing the work week to forty hours. There is a tremendous contradiction in this state of affairs. If we want all sorts of things, we have to be able to afford and pay for them. . . .

Spiegel: We certainly will not be able to touch such sacred cows without attacking other vested rights—foundations on which the state rests.

Heinemann: Oh yes, those vested rights. I once said jokingly that all public servants, from doormen and couriers on up, ought to be promoted to state secretary. Then we would not be bothered for at least half a year. Afterwards, however, the state secretaries would start to subdivide into senior state secretary, head state secretary, executive state secretary, and so forth. . .

Spiegel: . . . and so on. Would it not be a good idea, if there is to be a reform, first to do away with the constitutionally mandated system of life-time tenure for professional civil servants? After all, the other privileges can be traced back to this one.

Heinemann: In view of the excesses that have taken over in the public service we will most likely have to consider even this question carefully. Unfortunately the guarantee stipulated in Article 33 of the Constitution impedes any sweeping standardization of the rights of the civil service. . . .

Spiegel: Until now all attempts have failed, particularly those aimed at standardizing the rights of the civil service in addition to creating a fairer and more efficient career course and wage system. As things stand now, the top layers of the federal bureaucracy would have to formulate such a reform. But how are you supposed to reform a government bureaucracy which is unwilling to entertain such a course of action?

Heinemann: If I really knew a way to help you, I would tell you. I am afraid, however, considering the unreasonableness of the people involved, that this episode will not end happily.

6-7. GUIDELINES OF THE CONSTITUTIONAL COURT CONCERNING THE OBLIGATIONS OF CIVIL SERVANTS*

On May 22, 1975, the Federal Constitutional Court in Karlsruhe ruled on the Radicals' Decree. The ruling is based on guidelines that are excerpted here. They reiterate the substance of the West German civil service law and its requirement for a special obligation of West German civil servants to be ready always to serve the state.

1. It is a traditional, distinctive and fundamental principle of professional civil servants (Article 33, paragraph 5 of the Basic Law) that the duty of a civil servant includes a particularly high degree of political loyalty to the state and its constitution.

2. The loyalty requirement demands an affirmation of the state and its accepted constitution even if that constitution can be changed by process of amendedment. This affirmation should not be merely verbal. It should also be evident in a civil servant's professional actions. He

*Presse- und Informationsamt der Bundesregierung, *Bulletin* 60, (May 25, 1976), p. 562.

should follow and fulfill those constitutional and statutory laws and administer the duties of his office in the spirit of these laws. Political loyalty requires more than a formally correct but otherwise indifferent, cool, inwardly distant attitude toward the state and its constitution. It requires in particular that civil servants clearly distance themselves from groups and movements which attack, oppose, and defame the state, its constitutional authorities, and the current constitutional order. Civil servants are expected to recognize and honor the state and its constitution as a supreme positive value worth standing up for. Political loyalty continues in times of conflict and in serious conflict situations in which the state has to depend on its civil servants to side with it.

3. Violation of this sense of loyalty by public servants during their probationary period of work should result in dismissal. Violation of this official duty by civil servants with tenure can result in their removal from the service after formal disciplinary action.

4. One of the constitutional prerequisites for entrance into the civil service (Article 33, paragraph 5 of the Basic Law) and recognized in normal law requires the applicant to guarantee that he will support the liberal, democratic basic order at all times. . . .

8. A portion of the conduct which can be of considerable importance in judging the personality of an applicant for the civil service is entrance into or membership in a political party whose goals are hostile to the constitution. It is not relevant whether the unconstitutional nature of the party has been ascertained in a decision by the Federal Constitutional Court.

6-8. TRANSCRIPT OF AN INTERVIEW OF AN EMPLOYEE OF THE POSTAL SERVICE ABOUT HIS MEMBERSHIP IN THE GERMAN COMMUNIST PARTY*

Hired for a probationary period by the Postal Service, a twenty-seven-year-old engineer and member of the Communist party was interrogated by a panel of state officials over a period of three days about his political views and the possible activities of the German Communist party. These are excerpts of a transcript published in a liberal daily paper.

*Frankfurter Rundschau, September 27, 1976.

Q: Were you aware at the time when you joined the German Communist Party that government agencies had repeatedly expressed that the German Communist Party has goals contrary to the Constitution?

A: A government cannot ascertain whether a party or its goals are contrary to the Constitution. This is the duty of the Federal Constitutional Court alone.

Q: Were you aware that by joining the party you were obliged to contribute actively to the party, to engage yourself everywhere in society on the party's behalf, and to work within the rules of party discipline?

A: I joined one of the authorized political parties in the Federal Republic of Germany in order to help take part in the democratic political process. In the course of this political activity I shall always stand up for liberal democracy as it is spelled out in the Basic Law. It belongs to my official duties as a civil servant, something I swore to uphold and still stand by today. Loyalty to the Constitution comes before party discipline. . . .

Q: Do you stand by the goals of the German Communist Party without reservation—socialist revolution and the dictatorship of the proletariat (or as the German Communist Party calls it these days: the supremacy of the working class or "antimonopolistic democracy") in which the principle of the separation of power does not exist (as Lenin indicates in "Theses on Bourgeois Democracy and the Dictatorship of the Proletariat")?

A: At the moment I am not able to see the significance of the question in detail. Socialist revolution and the dictatorship of the proletariat are academic concepts which I cannot explain completely because of their complexity. The path to a socialist society should not be chosen against the will of the people. In this society the basic rights set forth in the Basic Law of the Federal Republic of Germany and the freedom of the individual must be guaranteed. I affirm the separation of powers set forth in Article 20 of the Basic Law.

Q: To what extent have you studied the concept of "academic socialism [*wissenschaftlicher Sozialismus*]"?

A: I have read some articles about this question. I cannot recall any of the titles of these articles. I did read Marx's *Communist Manifesto* some time ago. I refer here to the basic right to academic freedom. . . .

Q: Do you feel bound to carry out the aims of the German Communist Party?

A: Yes, in as much as they agree with the Basic Law and the oath I took. . . .

Q: Why did you not actively contribute toward the realization of the objectives of the German Communist Party at your place of employment?
A: I need refer only to my oath of office. The law prohibits political activity of a civil servant during working hours. . . .
Q: How much have you worked actively—verbally or otherwise in some externally recognizable fashion—for the basic liberal democratic system?
A: I have always worked for the basic liberal democratic system in everything I do—both professionally and otherwise—as prescribed by the oath of office I took. If you want me to give examples, you will have to formulate the question more precisely.
Q: Could your attitude toward the basic liberal democratic system be described as neutral?
A: No, on the basis of my acknowledgment of the basic liberal democratic system I do work actively for this system; that includes my oath of office.
Q: Do you think that the "Radicals' Decree" of January 28, 1972, is contrary to the Constitution?
A: I am not familiar with all the details of the decree. Like some legal scholars, I do consider it at least questionable in its constitutionality. To give a definitive answer I would have to read the decree and think this through. Only the Federal Constitutional Court can determine whether such a decree is contrary to the Constitution. . . .
Q: What is more important in your opinion: the loyalty of a civil servant and the right of the state to refuse to appoint someone to become a civil servant who is against the basic liberal democratic system or the interest of political parties in protecting themselves against measures taken by the state that affect the parties?
A: Every civil servant has the right to make use of the party privilege set forth in the Basic Law. If the employer has reason to doubt the loyalty of the civil servant to the Constitution, there are legal provisions by which a court can ascertain any constitutional impropriety. I see no contradiction in these two equal, basic freedoms. . . .
Q: Do you believe that supporters of the NPD [Nationaldemokratische Partei Deutschlands; another politically extreme party that has not, however, been prohibited] should be allowed to take part in state service when you claim this right for members of a communist and, therefore, politically extreme party?
A: It is not for me to decide whether members of the NPD, a party

which is not outlawed, should be allowed employment in public service. As far as I know, the courts have classified the NPD as the successor of the Nazi party. According to my knowledge and interpretation of the Basic Law of the Federal Republic of Germany, which says that members of successor organizations of the NSDAP shall not be granted access to public office, I would argue that no NPD member should have access to public office. I am in agreement with the Incompatibility Decree of the German Trade Union Association which refuses NPD members membership. . . .

Q: Do you agree with the revolutionary means that Marx, Engels, and Lenin suggest to reach your political goals?

A: The concept of "revolutionary means" is in my opinion not clearly delineated in this question. I point to the concept of academic freedom as defined in the Basic Law. There are different paths to socialism. Furthermore, I would like to emphasize that I am first and foremost a communications technician and not a sociologist or political scientist. . . .

When asked in closing whether conditions indicated that the applicant had at any time failed to carry out his official duties, his supervisor replied that he had proven himself to be an interested, competent trainee. As far as his personal attitude was concerned nothing negative had yet come to light.

6-9. A DISCUSSION OF THE RADICALS' DECREE BY THE SPD MINISTER OF SCIENCE (WEST BERLIN) AND THE CSU MINISTER OF CULTURE (BAVARIA)*

The sharply different political interpretations of the Radicals' Decree in the public debates among the SPD-FDP and the CDU/CSU is mirrored in the following debate between two of the most articulate spokespeople of government and opposition in the 1970s. It deserves to be reiterated here that in the process of policy implementation the difference between government and opposition tended to be quite small.

Spiegel: Should teachers be allowed to be Communists; should Communists be allowed to be teachers?

---

* "Die Angstfigur des deutschen Bürgers," *Der Spiegel,* October 9, 1978, pp. 29–34 (selections).

Maier: No, clearly no. The margin of tolerance in every democracy is substantial, but there are limits. The history of the Weimar Republic has taught us that these limits cannot be stretched too far. Otherwise the political center ultimately becomes too weak. Whatever is true for the Communists is, of course, true also for extremists on the Right. . . . I believe that the Bonn Republic has to defend itself more against the Left than against the Right. After all the taboo against violence was not violated after 1945 by the Right but rather by the Left. We have to keep these things in mind. . . .

Glotz: Party membership alone should not decide whether a Communist is allowed to be a teacher or not. The Federal Constitutional Court has indicated this very clearly. We have to examine every Communist very carefully in order to ascertain what kind of person he is. I know how very difficult this is. Yet that is what our laws tell us to do. We have to stick with the examination of individual cases.

Spiegel: One Communist should be allowed to become a teacher while the other one should not?

Glotz: Yes, and that is what the courts have stipulated. . . . I do not mean to advocate putting all Communists in the school systems; but I do feel that the world will not come to an end if once in a while a member of the Communist Party teaches somewhere. And I also do not believe, "Aha, membership in the party? Now we know everything. Get lost."

Maier: But if you do allow a Communist into the school system and he behaves himself for a couple of years, then you cannot get rid of him. Look at the decisions our labor courts have reached. They illustrate the pressure these precedents create for the state. . . .

Spiegel: It appears to us that the means used to keep so-called enemies of the Constitution out of the civil service are even more threatening to the democracy than would be a handful of radical leftists. Since the Radicals' Decree in 1972 More than 1.5 million citizens who wanted to join the civil service have been investigated. The Office for the Protection of the Constitution recorded "findings" in the cases of 15,000 applicants, and approximately 1,000 of these were rejected. This practice of sniffing around is surely much more detrimental to a democracy than the damage that Communist teachers can inflict—those few that we have and the few more we would have without a Radicals' Decree.

Maier: I take exception to your reference to "the practice of sniffing around." A civil servant in a liberal democracy must guarantee his loyalty to the Constitution and allow himself to be examined. That has nothing to do with infringing on the free choice of occupation [*Berufs-verbot*] as the measure has been foolishly labeled. Whoever cannot prove his loyalty to the Constitution simply does not possess the proper qualifications. Whoever wants to join the civil service has to undergo the investigation. No one else has to be investigated, but everyone applying does. This has been our practice since 1946. In this regard the Radicals' Decree did not change anything. People are acting as if this practice of investigating applicants were brand new.

Spiegel: True. But in the past nobody necessarily checked with the Office for the Protection of the Constitution.

Maier: Only the computer files are checked. If the applicant has never been involved in activities contrary to the Constitution, then the answer is negative, i.e. there is no evidence against him. Besides, the Radicals' Decree created no new law.

Glotz: No new law but an entirely new state of affairs. . . . My point is that what is happening creates fear among our young people, even among those who are not affected by this legislation. . . . I would say that half of our 900,000 students are really afraid. Out there in the real world I have seen two classical reactions to petitions. One side says, "I'll sign. It really doesn't make any difference as far as I'm concerned. I won't get a civil service job anyhow." The other side says, "No way I'll sign. Who knows what effect that might have on my chances if I want to become a teacher." That just goes to show how we are surgically removing the backbone from a substantial part of an entire generation. . . .

Maier: The tremendous expansion of the "test of conscience" came about because the simple, old catalog of organizations hostile to the Constitution has gradually disappeared. The CDU/CSU still recognizes them, but the SPD no longer does. Therefore, especially those states governed by the SPD have gone over to a "test of conscience," something which some people claim is nothing more than snooping around in someone's private affairs. When the objective criteria are gone, you have to investigate people's private thoughts. I reject this idea. . . .

Glotz: We have to put this idea of objective criteria to rest once and for all. After all a decision of the Federal Constitutional Court in 1975 states that no applicant can be denied employment in the civil service merely because of his membership in a party such as the German Communist Party. We cannot just act as if all we have to do is return to the golden years of Konrad Adenauer.

Maier: However, I have to note that the Federal Consitutional Court clearly stated that a civil servant has to recognize and honor the highly positive value of this state and its constitution. Political loyalty maintains itself in times of crisis and in conflict situations when the state has to depend upon each civil servant to side with it.

Glotz: That is quite true. The only problem is to find out how someone really feels or thinks.

7 University Reform

West Germany's university reform policies are noteworthy because they have defied the pattern of incremental policy change which distinguishes the other social and economic issues examined in earlier chapters. Instead, since 1960 higher education has been transformed dramatically from an elite system to a mass system. The last major change in the German universities occurred at the beginning of the nineteenth century after Prussia's defeat in the Napoleonic Wars. Reorganization provided universities with considerable autonomy from state intervention. German idealism throve in an institution that was dedicated to the task of facilitating scientific advances and of providing cultivation. The pursuit of knowledge required personal independence and institutional detachment. Yet intellectual advances in the universities also benefited the state by elevating and rationalizing the purposes informing state policies. The university did so directly by providing the best possible training for the future servants of the state and indirectly by strengthening the private professions and thus the whole nation.

The elitism of this particular conception of the German university grew in the nineteenth and twentieth centuries. Even the destruction of the universities' autonomy by the Nazis did not shatter it. It took instead sharp demographic shifts and the concerted political reforms of the 1960s to transform an elite system into a mass system. In the process virtually all institutional norms and rules were challenged. Different types of universities emerged. The internal structure of the university was reorganized. The content of education was debated. Relations between the universities and the state bureaucracy were redefined. On questions of education the relation between state and federal governments changed. By opening universities to all applicants and preventing

296

governments from regulating access to the university, the courts actively shaped the opportunities and career options of the younger generation.

Until the constitutional amendments of 1969 and 1971, the Basic Law had given the states rather than the federal government sole jurisdiction over cultural affairs, including the universities. Coalition politics at the federal level thus proved to be relatively unimportant. The pattern of decentralization was reinforced by the presence of a relatively large number of groups representing different constituencies in the university. Since university reform was an emotional issue in party politics, decentralized policymaking became fully politicized, especially in the 1970s. Parapublic institutions lacked the backing of the major economic interest groups. Uncharacteristically for West German politics, these groups operated largely on the sidelines of the reform. Without their support, parapublic institutions became arenas for rather than actors in the policymaking process. Since they enjoyed substantial autonomy from state interference, the universities proved more open to the currents of social change that were affecting West Germany in the 1960s and early 1970s. The result has been a structural reform of West Germany's university system and a largely unsuccessful search for consensus through continuous policy experimentation.

Context

The history of the modern German university dates back to Prussia's defeat in the Napoleonic Wars. Universities had lost much of their standing in the eighteenth century. In the face of the intellectual reforms of the Enlightenment and the political upheavals that followed the French Revolution, more than one-half of all the universities in the German-speaking countries permanently closed their doors (Schelsky, 1963). Prussia was home to a few outstanding universities, for example, the university of Halle. At the beginning of the nineteenth century Prussia's intellectual life was exuberant. But existing institutions of higher learning did not serve it well. The reputation of the university had by then sunk so low that Prussia's minister of justice, who was responsible for higher education, seriously proposed that all universities should be closed and replaced by professional academies (Fallon, 1980, p. 8). Napoleon's humiliating defeat of the Prussian army at Jena in October 1806 was the cataclysmic event that legitimated far-reaching institutional reforms in Prussia.

One of these reforms focused on the universities. Between 1808 and

1810 the groundwork was laid for a new university in Berlin. Wilhelm von Humboldt's name became indelibly associated with this new university. He personified the concept that inspired the founding of this university and became a symbol of the rescue and re-creation of the university in hard times. During his sixteen months in 1809–10 as the king's privy councilor and section director, he thoroughly revamped Prussia's system of secondary education and established the University of Berlin. A clear-thinking and broad-minded intellectual with practical experience in government, Humboldt held a unique position of authority during his brief tenure. Because he was active in both politics and scholarship, Humboldt, rather than scores of other intellectuals who committed both more time and effort, developed and implemented the concept of the new university. In the discussions of the 1960s and 1970s the "Humboldtian" university was constantly invoked by both the proponents and the opponents of reform.

Three main principles informed Humboldt's organization of Prussian universities in the nineteenth century. First, the university should guarantee academic freedom, an unrestricted "freedom of teaching and research." As a liberal, Humboldt was a firm believer in appointing the best brains and giving them maximum freedom. This was particularly significant since nineteenth-century Prussia had no tradition of free speech (Ben-David, 1971). Second, the university should reflect the "unity of research and teaching." The frontiers of knowledge were extended within the same institution by the very people who were also charged with educating the next generation of civil servants, professionals, and scholars. The university was both elitist and professional. Finally, power within the university should be held by the full professors, the German mandarins (Ringer, 1969). In Humboldt's conception the enlightened king furthered the development of his state by creating the best education system. "The state provided higher education in the finest traditions of independent inquiry, and the students educated in this manner provided the state with enlightened ministers" (Fallon, 1980, p. 24). Since before 1945 two-thirds of all universities were located in Prussia, with the exception of a few universities in southern Germany, this Prussian university system served as a model for the rest of Germany.

The relations between the university and the state were in fact more complex than Humboldt conceded. Universities had a dual legal nature. They were state institutions as well as independent corporate bodies.

"In this double life . . . lay the productive tension of the German university system" (Hennis, 1982, p. 2). On questions of finance and personnel state bureaucrats exercised control. On academic questions—curriculum, research, promotions, and recommendations for new appointments—academic bodies were in charge. The system of university-administered state examinations illustrates the symbiotic relations between the administrative and the academic sectors. Chronologically, the development of the bureaucracy, the university, an academically tracked secondary school, and the state examination system all coincided in the early years of the nineteenth century. Through a system of state examinations administered by the universities, state authorities were able to maintain standards in most professions. "As a result, there was hardly an area or discipline for which some sort of state examination was not eventually devised. . . . The free and learned professions absorbed much of the available middle-class talent, and a species of private officials grew up side by side with the regular civil service. One is tempted to speak of a 'social fusion' in which the administrative and higher professional classes were drawn together. The officials contributed aristocratic and bureaucratic values, but it was the academic ideology of "cultivation" which provided the most important bond between the various elements of the alliance" (Ringer, 1967, p. 132).

The administrative and the academic realm clashed unavoidably, especially on questions of new appointments. Between 1817 and 1900, for example, the ministries of various German states disregarded the carefully prepared recommendations of academic bodies for new appointments one-third of the time in theology and one-fifth of the time in law and medicine (Fallon, 1980, p. 49). Universities after all were state institutions financed fully from state budgets. Professors were civil servants. The most important examinations were entrance examinations for civil service positions. University administrators such as Friedrich Althoff, for many years division head for higher education in the Prussian Ministry of Culture, or Carl Heinrich Becker, head of the same ministry in the 1920s, were in fact instrumental in engineering the rise of the German universities to world fame. One could well argue that the separation of and tension between state and academic administration is one important reason why "the German universities were among the few German institutions before 1933 to find praise and imitation in the entire world" (Hennis, 1982, p. 3).

Not so after 1933. Despite the many apologies that have been written,

German academics, since 1945, have had to live with the charge of having failed as the intellectual leaders of the nation. Historians can document tales of individual courage, commitment, and opposition to the Nazi regime. Moral cowardice, ideological indifference, and political opportunism thus did not reign supreme. On balance though, the corporate structure of a self-governing university offered little protection against the political design of the Nazi state. "The weakness of the university lay in confrontation with the law of the land, its strength in the interpretation of decrees . . . and the judicial power the rector possessed as leader (*Führer*) of the university to interpret them" (Giles, 1976, p. 3). Individual resistance was the exception, institutional collaboration the rule.

For a variety of reasons the collapse of Nazi Germany in 1945 left the principle of university self-government intact and circumscribed state intervention. After 1949 cultural policy, including the regulation of higher education, became once again the prerogative of the individual states rather than the federal government. Senior civil servants were suspect, and the entire concept of the state's cultural policy was totally discredited. After the Nazis' excesses, the state was seen only as a threat to intellectual freedom and university autonomy. The universities aimed—on the whole, successfully—to enhance their rights of corporate self-governance to include many administrative matters previously left to state supervision. An incipient debate in the American and British zones of occupation about other changes in university structure and governance was cut short by the Berlin blockade of 1948 and the Cold War. "What the universities saw as a restoration of their long-abused autonomy, then, was in reality a more extreme version of it than they had ever experienced" (van de Graaff, 1975, p. 3). Subsequently, efforts focused on the physical reconstruction, modernization, and expansion of the universities, almost half of which had been destroyed during the war (Kloss, 1968, p. 323). University reform does not appear as an important item on the political agenda until the 1960s (Hahn, 1963).

West German universities form the apex of a vertically structured system of education (see Figure 7-1). After four years of primary education, at the age of ten, students choose one of three types of schools (Teichler and Sanyal, 1984, pp. 95–102). The main school is traditionally integrated with the primary school. After nine years of full-time school most students attend part-time vocational schools, while also

FIGURE 7-1   The West German Educational System

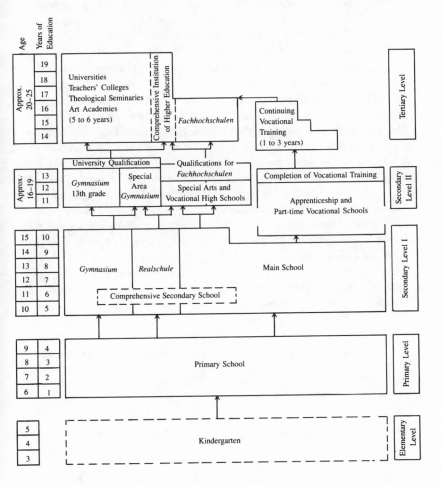

Source: H. Peisert and G. Framhein, *Systems of Higher Education: Federal Republic of Germany* (New York: International Council for Educational Development, 1978), p. 9

Note: The chart does not indicate quantitative proportions of the individual institutions. The arrows indicate the most common transitions.

learning a trade as an apprentice, until they reach the age of eighteen. The *Realschule* is a particular type of secondary school which leads to a variety of technical schools granting qualifications for middle-level occupations. The *Gymnasium* tracks students academically for university studies. The final examination after thirteen years of schooling traditionally serves both as the certificate for successful completion of the *Gymnasium* and admission to the university. Figure 7-1 illustrates that this system has been softened by a variety of reforms that have slightly enhanced opportunities to transfer between different types of schools. Such transfers make it possible to reach the tertiary level of education without passing through the *Gymnasium* on the traditional academic track. Although the number of students in main schools and part-time vocational schools has remained remarkably constant between 1960 and 1980, the number of students in intermediate and academic tracks of secondary education has expanded greatly. Students who leave secondary school, having completed the academic and higher vocational tracks, have increased from 5.5 percent of their age cohort in 1960 to 20.0 percent in 1980.

An equivalent increase has also occurred in the number of university students, which topped 1 million in 1980. Higher education in West Germany has thus lost the elite status it had less than a generation ago. About 70 percent of the students attend universities and engineering schools. Another 20 percent attend vocational training colleges (*Fachhochschulen*) to which they are admitted without studying on the academic track of secondary schools. The rest attend a variety of other institutions (comprehensive universities that cover both university and nonuniversity education, teachers' colleges, theological seminaries, and art academies). About two-fifths of all university students are female. That proportion has increased over the last twenty-five years, although at an uneven pace. For a variety of reasons West German students are significantly older than their American counterparts. In 1980 only 13 percent were 20 years or younger; 56 percent were between 21 and 25 years, and 20 percent between 26 and 29 years old; 11 percent were over 30 years of age. As we shall see, the agenda for the reform discussion of the 1960s was set in part by the emergence of mass institutions of higher learning. However, in the end policy was more important than demography in shaping this significant era of German politics.

Agenda

West Germany's university reform occurred in different phases. The early 1960s were dominated by what critics would subsequently refer to as "the technocratic phase." The primary concern focused on the quality of research, particularly in the natural sciences and in medicine. Discussion centered on the consequences of international competition, the inability of West German scientists to keep pace with the United States, and worries over the "brain drain" of thousands of younger researchers to the United States for which the traditional structure of the German university was seen responsible. American universities and to some extent Britain's experience with new universities in the 1950s were widely regarded as viable models. The archaic structure of German universities was too hierarchical and sluggish. It did not facilitate an interdisciplinary organization of research. Since it appeared questionable whether the old universities could be refashioned, conservative reformers such as the well-known sociologist Helmut Schelsky pushed for the founding of small, interdisciplinary, new universities such as in Constance, Bielefeld, and Ulm.

The second phase of the reform movement was marked by concerns over quantitative expansion rather than qualitative improvement. The publication in 1962 of the British Robbins Report on the reform of British universities indirectly opened up this debate. The appendix of this report contained statistical data that showed how far the Federal Republic, despite its notable economic strength, lagged behind most Western European countries in its expenditures for higher education as well as the number of students admitted to institutions of higher learning. In 1965 Torsten Husén, a noted specialist in the field of comparative education research, singled out West Germany as " 'a present day European example of a failure to plan' " (quoted in Mushaben, 1984, p. 425). Gradually increasing demographic pressures began to put the established institutional arrangements of West German universities under stress (Fuhrig, 1966; van de Graaf, 1978). Two popular books in particular marked the beginning of an intense and sustained public discussion. Georg Picht, a philosopher and historian, warned (1964) that the "catastrophe of German education" might soon bring economic growth to an end because of the lack of qualified manpower (see Reading 7-1). For Picht a dramatic increase in the size of higher education was the only possible solution. Ralf Dahrendorf, one of West Germany's leading sociologists, argued (1965) that if West Germany was to become a liberal, modern society, its educational system needed to be opened up to working-class youths and members of the lower social strata. The agenda of university reform was shaped by the intersection of greater economic efficiency and social equality—concerns, that is, which also characterized the issues of economic management and social welfare (see Chapters 2 and 4).

A doubling in the number of university students between 1955 and 1965 to more than 300,000 and forecasts of a deficit of 100,000 schoolteachers by the end of the 1960s gave this discussion unusual urgency and made dramatic changes in policy acceptable to all political quarters (see Reading 7-2) (Kloss, 1963). For reasons linked to long-term economic growth, political conservatives in the CDU/CSU supported much greater investments in education. They were also open to a reform of and experimentation with West Germany's universities. Maintaining an internationally competitive West German economy in an era of high technology would require more scientists, engineers, skilled workers, and in general a better educated society. It turned out later that this economic argument for university reform was not the only one that defined the political agenda. To be sure, SPD proponents on the left of the political spectrum did not disagree with the economic arguments. In addition, though, SPD and FDP proponents also emphasized the themes of social equality and political democracy. The rigid pattern of stratification of West German society rested largely on the highly restrictive access that the secondary school system granted to a university education. Broadening access to university study offered a promising avenue for ameliorating these social inequalities.

Government officials adopted a variety of measures to sharply increase student enrollments. Most important, the proportion of students leaving secondary school was increased. Existing university facilities were reorganized and expanded. Specialized institutions were given regular university status. Engineering schools revamped and broadened their curriculum and were accredited as universities. A new stratum of junior faculty was hired to restore student-teacher ratios to the levels of the 1950s. The number of university "assistants" increased from 9,000 in 1960 to 28,000 in 1971. State governments founded eighteen new universities, among them Bochum and Regensburg (Mushaben, 1984, p. 426).

But in the third phase of reform the political agenda went beyond qualitative improvement and quantitative expansion. Proponents on the Left argued as early as 1964 for a reform in the very structure of university administration. The power and prestige concentrated in the hands of the German professoriat were to be dispersed among all members of the university: senior faculty, junior faculty, students, and staff. Academic autocracy was to be replaced by participatory democracy in a university enshrining the principle of codetermination. By 1970 many of these demands had, in modified form, been accepted by the federal government, together with the concerns over scientific progress, economic growth, and social equality (see Reading 7-3). All political parties supported initiatives to regulate the relationship between state and university as well as the university's administration of nonacademic matters, especially general administration and finance (van de Graaff, 1975, pp. 6–7).

The broad political consensus of both parties for university reform was consolidated very briefly by the political demands of the student movement that swept university campuses throughout the Federal Republic in the 1960s. That movement was directed against the Great Coalition of the CDU/CSU and the SPD, which governed in Bonn between 1966 and 1969, and against American involvement in Vietnam. All political parties were challenged by student activism on behalf of both a democratically organized university and a socially more relevant and self-aware pursuit of science. After 1967 campus disruptions and student unrest galvanized the programmatic commitment for change into action. Before 1967 only the state of Hesse had introduced modest structural changes in its universities. After the onset of massive student unrest in 1967, all of the states initiated a period of intensive legislative activity which by 1973 resulted in drastically new university structures throughout West Germany (van de Graaff, 1975, p. 7). As a byproduct of these legislative initiatives, the relations between state and university, as defined in the early nineteenth century, also experienced drastic change.

Illustrative of the commitment to greater social equality and increased access to the university was the decision to respond to the drastically growing number of students leaving secondary, academically tracked schools. In 1971 the federal government adopted a means-tested system of grants for both university students and students in secondary schools. Financed by the federal government, these grants were administered by a student self-help organization (*Studentenwerke*). This system of grants was considerably more generous than the frugal financial assistance that had been available for students since the late 1950s. Between 1971 and 1977 student financial assistance tripled, reaching 150 million deutschmarks (Bork and Klee, 1979–80, p. 28).

The federal government's plan to change the character of German university life by creating a new type of university also illustrated its commitment to greater social equality. Federal legislation proposed in 1971 aimed at uniting the different kinds of institutions of higher education, such as universities, engineering schools, teachers' colleges, vocational training colleges, and art academies as new "comprehensive universities." The comprehensive university was to combine theoretical and applied work in new ways. One of the objectives of this legislation was to break down institutional barriers that impeded efficient recruitment of students from all social strata, a goal that all of the major parties and affected groups supported. It was thus not surprising that the original aim of the federal government had been to insist that all new universities would be organized along the 1971 guidelines. Existing universities were encouraged to merge with other institutions to form comprehensive universities. On this score the government encountered opposition. A number of states insisted that in many situations "cooperative" comprehensive universities evolving numerous arrangements between different institutions of higher learning would achieve the desired objective more efficiently and effectively than would "integrated" comprehensive universities uniting everything under one roof. The various hearings and debates in both the Bundestag and the Bundesrat were remarkable for the far-reaching consensus that was reached on the basic concept of the comprehensive university, supported for reasons of both economic efficiency and social equality, and the broad spectrum of opinions on how and when it should be implemented (Schmittner, 1971, pp. 9–14).

However, only a few years later the question of access assumed a dramatically different form (Karpen, 1976). Because state and federal governments were unable to increase their expenditures, universities could not expand to match the explosion in the number of students. Under these circumstances qualified students leaving secondary school were denied automatic university admission in a growing number of fields. Since the late 1960s the fields of medicine and related subjects had restricted admission (*numerus clausus*) and devised special selection procedures. Although they did not affect overall enrollment, restricted admission did affect the distribution of students across disciplines. The deep recession of 1974–75, growing concerns about the job prospects of university graduates, and a shift in the public mood toward conservatism consolidated the conclusion of various government agencies and planning bodies that it would be infeasible and unwise to expand the capacities of universities to meet current "social demand" in all fields. This conclusion was based also on demographic studies that forecast a sharp drop in student enrollment in the 1990s. Thus altered circumstances lowered plans for university expansion considerably after 1975.

Public policy might logically have moved toward an increasingly restrictive admissions policy based on a general extension of the *numerus clausus*. But instead, "higher education in the Federal Republic of Germany took a surprising turn in 1976/77 towards what was called 'Opening of Higher Education' " (Teichler, 1983, p. 8). All of the major parties, state governments, and interested groups reached a political compromise based on three main considerations. First, the Federal Constitutional Court had ruled against restricted university admission as a general policy in 1972. Second, restricted university admission intensified competition in secondary schools so much that the entire educational system threatened to deteriorate. Finally, higher education needed to become more open, many felt, to avoid inflicting intolerable disadvantages on age cohorts belonging to the demographic bulge. If universities refused to enroll growing numbers, academically tracked high-school students would turn to vocational training schools and apprenticeship programs, thus displacing other students leaving secondary school who had been the real target of the drive for greater equality. As a result of this shift in policy, university enrollments increased by 30 percent between 1977 and 1982, whereas staff and facilities increased only 5 percent. Universities and governments sharply reduced the number of academic disciplines with limited enrollment. Thus between 1977 and 1982 the growth in the number of applicants to restricted fields of study was only half as large as the growth in the number of qualified school graduates (Teichler, 1983, pp. 8–9).

Public discussion about questions of access during the transformation of West Germany's universities to a system of mass education never approached the intensity of conflict which characterized the reorganization of the universities' internal governing structure. The traditional university run only by the full professors (*Ordinarienuniversität*) was to be replaced by the new group university (*Gruppenuniversität*) enshrining the principles of "codetermination" of all groups of academic and non-academic employees as well as students (see Chapter 3). In fact, "the basic fiction of a 'corporate' German university, as a 'community of teachers and students' . . . was merely carried forward into the 'democratised' *Gruppenuniversität*—a university governed by representatives of the various constituent groups" (Hennis, 1982, p. 1). Student demonstrations and disruptions mobilized both the proponents and the opponents of reform on campuses throughout the Federal Republic. The radically anti-authoritarian political currents among West German students demanded a democratization of decisionmaking procedures as well as reforms in the curriculum to encompass empirical material and theories critical of established social arrangements and state institutions. New universities founded, for example, in Bielefeld, Constance, Bochum, Regensburg, and, finally, Bremen, expressed different phases in the evolution of university reform. In different ways they incorporated the concept of a group university into their charters. Existing universities also reformed their governing structures and system of internal administration to conform to the different legislations passed in each of the eleven states in the early 1970s. These changes, however, did not appear uniformly throughout the Federal Republic. Conservative opposition, especially of an organization representing senior faculty, succeeded in some states more than in others in influencing state legislation. In addition "there remained vast differences largely because the universities displayed an enormous capacity for inertia" (Gellert, 1984, p. 219).

Politicians and administrators called for federal legislation to harmonize different administrative practices adopted in the different states and to bring about an uniformly modern university system throughout the Federal Republic (see pp. 46–47, 76–80). After five years of intensive discussion in the media, Bundestag hearings, and debates, the Federal Framework Law for Universities (Hochschulrahmengesetz) was passed in 1976 (see Reading 7-5) (Teichler, 1972, 1974). In this arduous process the federal government was forced to make numerous political compromises with state governments that jealously guarded their constitutional power to formulate and implement all cultural policy. The 1976 law is too complex to be summarized fully (Gellert, 1984, pp. 219–20). Among other provisions it promised to (1) offer a differentiated set of traditional university courses side by side with a more practically inclined curriculum and provide mutual possibilities for transfer; (2) limit the length of university studies; (3) initiate a curriculum reform and streamline course offerings; (4) change the personnel structure of the university by leveling the sharp distinction between chaired professors and a range of middle-level researchers, and distinguishing instead simply between three different types of professors; (5) regularize the position of university president as a full-time administrator to be elected by the delegates of the new group university; and, finally, (6) establish firmly the right to participate in decisionmaking for the representatives of various university groups.

By the early 1980s disenchantment with university reform had become widespread in the Federal Republic. The deep recession of 1981–83 and rising unemployment required further cuts in expenditures for education. Overcrowding of universities became an increasingly serious problem as the number of university students swelled to 1.4 million by the mid-1980s. As a result, public discussion about fostering new centers of excellence—inside or outside the reformed university—intensified the greater skepticism that the CDU had always had about university reform (Teichler, 1983, pp. 9–18). When the new CDU/CSU-FDP government was elected in the spring of 1983, the CDU thus pushed for partial changes in the reform legislation (see Reading 7-8). Despite the strong opposition of the SPD and most education experts, the new government scrapped the grants program for high-school students which had been instituted in 1971. For eligible university students the program was restructured from grants to loans. Furthermore, the new government revised the University Framework Law. It strengthened the position of the professors holding chairs, abolished the lowest professorial rank (but not its holders who, as civil servants, enjoy life-long tenure), and replaced the independent university assistants with a different type of assistant (whose duties remain to be defined but will presumably include doing more work for full professors).

At the same time, important elements of continuity with the previous decade of reform transcend partisan differences. "On the one hand, the concern about a deterioration of the quality of higher education due to an intolerable 'over-load' is more widespread than political support for the Christian Democrats; on the other hand, the desire to avoid a revival of a strong 'numerus clausus' and its consequences has far more backers than supporters of the Social Democrats" (Teichler, 1983, p. 9). The new government is seeking to use the increased diversity of the reformed university system to increase competition among different institutions, to improve the quality of teaching and research, and thus perhaps to strengthen once again the university's autonomy from state interference.

Compared to the early 1970s, university reform has lost its political salience. Yet the Kohl government cannot avoid the issue. Some of the changes that have been effected by the reforms of the last two decades could not be rolled back even if the new coalition government were to hold to vastly more conservative persuasions. The new system of mass education cannot be dramatically shrunk. The new group university has lost a great deal of its precarious autonomy from the state. And the federal government must continue to struggle with the same questions of governance, quality, access, and autonomy that defeated many, though by no means all, of the aspirations of the reformers of the 1970s.

Process

The process of policy formulation and implementation with regard to university reform reflects the dependence of the federal government on other actors (Briese, 1972). The decentralization of the policy process is more evident in this policy sector than in any other previously analyzed. The Basic Law stipulates that cultural policy, which includes policy regarding universities, is primarily under the jurisdiction of West Germany's states. Furthermore, since questions of education affect both the staffing of state institutions and the pattern of social stratification, they have given rise to some of the most heated and prolonged political conflicts in the Federal Republic. The courts' numerous interventions have thus helped lower the political temperature.

A good example of the process of policy formulation is the operation of the Science Council (Wissenschaftsrat) (Berger, 1974) (see also pp. 78–79). Lacking any administrative powers, the Science Council was set up jointly by the federal government and the states in 1957. It became in fact a thinktank for some of the major reform proposals. Its working papers were typically an important benchmark of subsequent discussions. The volume of recommendations which it issued in 1960 was a landmark study. Well before any public discussion of an "educational catastrophe," it raised the issue of both the quantitative expansion and qualitative improvement that the West German university system would have to confront. In subsequent reports issued annually, the Science Council fleshed out different parts of the reform agenda: the structure of new universities (1962), rational planning procedures for expansion (1963), forecasting student enrollments (1964), university governance and the enlargement of the teaching staff (1965), curriculum reform (1966).

The German Educational Council (Deutscher Bildungsrat), founded in 1965, was created by joint agreement between federal and state governments in July 1965. Ostensibly a complement to the Science Council, it was charged to address reform issues at the primary and secondary school level. But questions of access to education at the secondary level had an immediate impact on the university. The council did much technical work, forecasting financial requirements, long-range physical planning, and the demand for manpower. These experts underestimated future enrollment in the 1970s and 1980s by about 30 percent. The margin of error was not a result of changes in demography, for forecasts were made for students already born. Instead, manpower specialists seriously underestimated the rapidity with which mass education replaced West Germany's elite university system. The enduring contribution of the Educational Council was rather to increase greatly the proportion of students leaving secondary school entitled to enroll in universities. That decision was both a response to and a reinforcement of the demographic pressures that ushered in the era of a system of mass education at the university level in West Germany.

But it would be a mistake to think that these parapublic institutions in fact shaped the policymaking process on questions of university reform. Because of the constitutionally mandated decentralization, partisan politics became a more important aspect of the policy process once university reform had become a major item on West Germany's political agenda in the 1960s. Thus in the 1970s the cultural ministers (KMK) have been handicapped by the fact that for any of their decisions to be binding in any one state, they must find unanimous agreement among all. On controversial issues that divided CDU- and SPD-led state governments in the 1970s, this condemned the KMK to relative inactivity.

Partisan politics is important for a second reason. Educational reform on questions such as the creation of comprehensive schools or universities signifies the shift from an elite to a mass system of education. Established patterns of social stratification are in turn profoundly affected. Inevitably this issue mobilizes political parties. This process of politicization can be illustrated easily by the difference in the ratification process of the Federal Law for Educational Assistance in 1969, on the one hand, and the ratification process for the University Framework Law between 1969 and 1976, on the other. A system of individual fellowships had been instituted in 1957 (Honnefer Modell). It proved workable only until the issue of university reform and expansion gained prominence. By 1962, however, SPD opposition was proposing legislation for a more comprehensive system of educational assistance. The veto of the Finance Ministry in 1964 and uncertainties about the division of federal and state responsibilities led to a four-year hiatus in which frequent debates in the Bundestag did not result in any legislative initiatives at the federal level. Meanwhile, CDU/CSU was gradually warming to the argument that stressed the economic importance of educational reform as expressed, for example, in the second annual report of the Council of Economic Experts. By the time the CDU/CSU, then heading the Great Coalition, introduced a bill in the Bundestag in 1968, the remaining controversies involved defining the extent and limits of the new "cooperative federalism" in West Germany's system of intergovernmental relations (see Chapter 1). As was true of the other major reform projects of the late 1960s, the Educational Assistance Act was carried in 1969 by a broad support of all of the major parties and groups at the federal level.

When the SPD-FDP coalition seized the reins of power in the fall of 1969, the reforms of the constitutional basis of West Germany's federal system had increased the extent of the federal government's activity on questions of university reform (Kloss, 1971). In light of diverging state legislation governing all aspects of the university, the federal government decided to push for the adoption of framework legislation governing the process of university reform (see Reading 7-5) (Merritt, 1979; Teichler, 1972, 1974). Before the federal government submitted its proposal to the Bundesrat in December 1970, Hans Leussink, a nonpartisan minister for education and science, had submitted his fourteen theses for public discussion; there had been numerous public hearings in the Bundestag focused on all of the important institutions in tertiary education; and a succession of modified ministerial proposals had been submitted for public discussion and Bundestag scrutiny. Even though the Bundesrat agreed to the government's proposal in principle, hopes for an early passage of the legislation were disappointed: the Bundesrat suggested about 100 alterations in the proposed bill on January 29, 1971.

It was hardly accidental that on the same day the CDU/CSU opposition introduced its own version of the bill in the Bundestag. It differed from the government's in important respects, including a rejection of the comprehensive university as the norm for further expansion, the distribution of power in the university, the relation between university and the state, guarantees for academic freedom, and the policy instruments for bringing about curriculum reform. Over the next five years public debate and partisan controversy dragged on. The first draft of the government's bill died in the Bundestag committee. A second version of the draft law passed the Bundestag in 1974 but was defeated by a single vote in the Bundesrat. After intensive negotiations a new compromise bill acceptable to both the Bundestag and Bundesrat was prepared. As the West Germans put it, the reform had been talked to death. Two ministers of education and science, Hans Leussink and Klaus von Dohnanyi, came and went. "By 1976, the passage of the Framework Law had become a political end in itself, rather than a means to a more effective system of higher learning" (Mushaben, 1981, p. 157). It was a law no one liked. The supporters of university reform saw it as an unnecessary legislative sanctioning of a number of court decisions that had derailed university reform in its early stages. A conservative observer of the West German university, Wilhelm Hennis, has argued that "the clear support given to this law by all the state governments controlled by the CDU, with the exception of Bavaria, is one of the most unintelligible actions of West German politicians" (Hennis, 1982, p. 28).

Such action does, however, make sense if viewed as a result of the contentious and slow process of policymaking on the basis of the lowest common denominator (see Reading 7-6). For it is distinctive of West German–style democracy that the politicization of university reform policies through partisan politics was circumscribed by the judicial intervention of an activist Constitutional Court as well as by numerous important rulings of administrative courts (Merritt, 1979; Mushaben, 1984). In two major cases concerning the rules governing access to the university and the question of parity codetermination of senior faculty, junior faculty, nonacademic staff, and students, the 1972 and 1973 decisions of the Constitutional Court removed two of the most controversial reform issues from party politics. Restrictions on university admissions policies in the 1970s meant students had to wait more than five years before entering medical and veterinary schools and more than seven years before entering dental schools (Teichler, 1982, p. 163). When Bavaria and the city-state of Hamburg moved to impose general restrictions on university admissions policies, they triggered judicial action that administrative courts referred to the Constitutional Court. In a landmark decision in 1972, the Court ruled this practice unconstitutional and insisted that the norm of equal access contradicted the administrative practice of limiting access to popular academic fields, such as medicine, and thus violated Article 12 of the Basic Law (see Reading 7-4).

Restricting access to particular fields of study, the Court argued, was constitutional only as a temporary measure to deal with temporary problems of overcrowding and only until legislatures had designed either nondiscriminatory admissions criteria or a lottery system. The Court hinted, furthermore, that a national office for the assignment of study places might be established. Such an office would be charged to administer the admission of students in fields where the number of applicants exceeded the number of study places (Carbone, 1974, pp. 3–4). By the fall of 1973 the eleven states had established a central office that used uniform standards to control university admissions policies in about a dozen disciplines. In another far-reaching decision, the Court again mandated further changes in the admissions procedure of the most desirable fields (Merritt, 1979, pp. 16–17).

Of comparable importance was the Court's ruling in 1973 in favor of 398 professors and associates who objected to the introduction of three-way parity in university decisionmaking as mandated by educational legislation in Lower Saxony. The Court ruled that parity power in university governance violated the constitutional rights that faculty enjoyed under Article 5 of the Basic Law. The Court stipulated that professors had to be guaranteed at least one-half of all seats in any body that regulated teaching and examinations and be assured of a clear majority in all bodies dealing with research and academic hiring and firing. Thus the Court "took in fact the first critical step in the standardization of university governance" (Mushaben, 1981, p. 154). It recognized in principle the need for group representation in academic decisionmaking while limiting the amount of power of each group according to the level of its academic qualification. In these two instances as well as other rulings concerning, for example, classroom capacities, teaching loads, and government supervision of personnel policy, court rulings on some of the most controversial issues in university reform greatly influenced state governments and the 1976 framework legislation. Judicial decisions thus narrowed the range of admissible solutions that party politicians could impose on the policy process. Although the affected groups and parties failed to resolve their disagreements within peak associations behind closed doors, court interpretations of Bundestag statutes tended to counteract the explicit politicization of the policy process so atypical of West German politics. In the words of an eminent German legal scholar, Thomas Oppermann, " 'Viewed as a whole, the constitutional trench warfare in Karlsruhe and elsewhere about the limits of the federal role in education is the unavoidable consequence of the unholy disintegration into two antagonistic camps of our German educational scene' " (quoted in Mushaben, 1981, p. 360).

On some of the issues of university reform the Court's intervention affected the policy process at the stage of not only formulation but also implementation. To the 1972 decision on university admissions policies (see Reading 7-4), for example, the state bureaucracy reacted by creating restrictive, uniform procedures determined by law and administrative regulations (Carbone, 1974; Karpen, 1978). Shortly after the Court's decision, the states agreed on a list of criteria for admission and, with considerable acrimony and court intervention, developed a scoring system to equate school grades from different states. An executive committee of the group of state education ministers was put in charge of university admissions policies. Since the 1970s, a central office in Dortmund with a staff of several hundred has decided on the fields with restricted admission and on what factors will shape admissions decisions. The rulings of this group gain the force of law by being adopted by the individual states. An academic advising committee of the executive committee has no decisionmaking power. The admissions process is routinized. Students apply to the central office, listing their field of study and indicating their preference among a list of universities. These data are fed into a computer that assigns the student to a particular campus based on a number of factors (grades, proximity, waiting time for admission, etc.). If a student does not get assigned a field of her choice, she has two options—reapplying in the next semester or switching to a field with unrestricted admission. To take the power to handpick next year's freshman class away from the university or to let a computer pick your next crop of graduate students would be considered outrageous in the United States. But in the bureaucratic and legalized environment in which West German universities operate, it is accepted as unavoidable by some and desirable by others.

In the implementation of the Educational Assistance Act of 1969, the federal government sought to create the same sort of legal and bureaucratic routine without any direct prompting by the Court. Lacking any adequate institutional mechanisms by which to implement the Educational Assistance Act, the federal government relied on an institution charged with disbursing student aid (Studentenwerke) to funnel scholarship funds to students (Bork and Klee, 1979–80, pp. 28–29). As a private social service organization embodying the principle of self-help, the student organization dates back to the aftermath of World War I. The third amendment to the Educational Assistance Act explicitly granted it the legal authority to administer such aid. Nationwide the funds thus administered increased from 54 million deutschmarks in 1971 to 154 million in 1977. As a result, almost all student organizations changed their legal form to become legally recognized parapublic institutions with student representation. The reason was simple. During the Bundestag deliberations surrounding the 1969 legislation, it had become clear that over the long term the state would not allow private institutions to be responsible for the implementation of legislation. "On the whole it must unfortunately be acknowledged that state influence on the activities of the *Studentenwerke* and on their decisions has increased with the transformation of these organizations into public institutions. It is useless to lament this development, although this increased state influence seems to be the price that has had to be paid for the relatively liberal expansion of social services on the part of the state" (Bork and Klee, 1979–80, p. 29).

But other questions that had been depoliticized less through the courts or the bureaucracy remained politically charged in the process of implementation. This was perhaps no more evident than in the case of the comprehensive universities established in the 1976 framework legislation as the norm for any further expansion of the university. By the time the law had passed, financial constraints had already forced federal and state governments to scale down greatly their projections for future expansion. Still, it is remarkable that only a few states implemented this provision of the law and that only half a dozen comprehensive universities are operating in the Federal Republic in the 1980s, compared to the fifty to eighty that had been mentioned in the reform discussion in the early 1970s.

Among the numerous factors that Aylâ Neusel and Ulrich Teichler identify (1982, pp. 176–79) as impediments to policy reform, one in particular stands out. The basic political consensus on the very concept of the comprehensive university began to erode as early as 1972. It is thus not surprising that comprehensive universities were not established in any states in which the CDU/CSU held power. Party differences within the context of the federal system thus were a very important factor in shaping the policy process. This is nicely illustrated in the case of the state of Baden-Württemberg. In the late 1960s a committee of that state's Ministry of Culture, headed by Ralf Dahrendorf (one of the founders of a new university at Constance and a champion of the notion of equal access to education) published its report on the comprehensive university which laid out the full agenda for reform policy. Yet at the same time, a second committee working for the same ministry produced a second and much more conservative report. "At the first public hearing in the State Parliament of Baden-Württemberg, called to learn the universities' attitudes, charges and countercharges filled the air, and Ralf Dahrendorf publicly resigned and joined the F.D.P., then the opposition party" (Wildenmann, 1971, p. 343). In the 1970s Baden-Württemberg might well have adopted a plan for comprehensive universities had it not been for the fear that such a move would soon lead to further radical changes.

Whereas in the 1970s mergers of different types of universities had been an important way to establish the handful of comprehensive universities, in the climate of economic recession which characterized the early 1980s, institutional mergers of universities are not the viable option in West Germany which they were in Britain. But since student enrollment has continued to increase, closing universities is not viable either. The federal government was forced to rescind the sharp financial cuts in university construction which it proposed in the summer of 1980. Between 1981 and 1984 federal outlays were to be reduced from 850 million to 530 million deutschmarks. Universities and states protested so strongly that the intended cuts were reduced by about one-half (Teichler, 1982, p. 168). But all decisions affecting jobs, and financial allocations for the universities are made by the education and finance ministers of each state rather than by academics. The West German case is instructive compared to Britain's not only because cuts have been less drastic but because of the absence of central regulatory bodies. "Hence 'savings measures' are applied piecemeal and frequently in isolation. . In spite of the reforms of the seventies an education minister and his civil servants still possess extensive powers of legal, administrative and financial control. . . . When exercising their powers they intervene directly and specifically and more often than not they usually seem to have only limited and immediate objectives in mind" (Kloss, 1985, p. 280). But the powers of the West German state are at the same also circumscribed. The civil service status of the German professoriate is equivalent to the tenure system in the United States. Although appointments are state-controlled, civil service status is a safeguard against unconstrained state intervention (Gellert, 1985, p. 290).

Consequences

To assess the successes and failures of West Germany's university reform policies is an impossible task. Ladislav Cerych's general conclusion (1980, p. 10) is surely applicable to West Germany. "Indeed the very nature of this [implementation] process makes it pointless to speak of success or failure with regard to these reforms. In fact, they have always been a mixture of both, a mixture of achieved, partially achieved and unachieved goals, of intended, unintended, sometimes positive, and sometimes negative, results." But we can distinguish clearly between incremental and large-scale changes. Many of the objectives of the reform which were discussed in the late 1960s and early 1970s were not achieved. Comprehensive universities, at best, are complementing rather than replacing the traditional universities; they account for only a very small proportion of the total student enrollment in the 1980s. Since they are governed by the same laws, new universities in Constance, Bremen, or Bochum do not differ drastically from their older peer institutions (Mushaben, 1981, pp. 136–45). The length of study has not been reduced greatly. Despite many painful and time-consuming efforts, progress in curriculum reform has been miniscule. Financial constraints have greatly slowed the expansion of university facilities since the mid-1970s. And a dramatic expansion in the number of university students has forced state authorities to impose restrictions on the constitutionally guaranteed right to university admission for all qualified students leaving secondary schools.

University reform policies have had a substantial effect on West German high schools (Heister, 1985, pp. 256–57). Greater flexibility and choice of subject matter introduced in the last three years of high school made it possible for students, seeking their highest grade point average, to select "easy" subjects. Furthermore, those with the highest average increasingly chose restricted fields of study at the university. The competitive pressure put on West German high school students has, by most accounts, been detrimental to the quality of their education. Employment problems for university students have increased greatly since the late 1970s, reflecting both a change in economic conditions and a halt in any further expansion of the West German education system. The traditional autonomy of the university has in the process been substantially reduced and state influence has increased. It is thus no surprise that in the public's esteem of different political institutions, the universities have ranked at the very bottom in the 1980s.

But it is easy to overlook the changes that have transformed the structure of West German higher education. The quantitative enlargement of the university system has been phenomenal (Gellert, 1985, pp. 284–85). Table 7-1 illustrates that between 1950 and 1980 the number of university students increased fivefold. University personnel increased by more than 400 percent. Between 1961 and 1981 public expenditure on higher education increased from 1.7 billion deutschmarks (0.5 percent of gross national product) to 18.6 billion deutschmarks (1.2 percent of gross national product) (Teichler and Sanyal, 1984b, p. 124). The quota of the respective age cohort of students leaving secondary school has quadrupled to more than 20 percent; a figure almost twice as large

TABLE 7-1   Students at Institutions of Higher Education by Type of Institution, 1950–80 (in thousands)[a]

Type of Institution	1950	1960	1970	1975	1980
Universities (including technical universities and special universities)	112	217	350	553	735
Comprehensive universities	N/A[b]	N/A[b]	N/A[b]	42	70
Teachers' colleges	10[c]	33	59	79	19
Theological seminaries	5	3	2	2	2
Art academies	5	8	11	15	18
Fachhochschulen	40[c]	68[c]	112[c]	146	202
Total	172[c]	329[c]	534[c]	837	1,044

Source: Adapted from Ulrich Teichler and B. C. Sanyal, "Higher Education and Employment in the Federal Republic," in R. Avakov, M. Buttgereit, B. C. Sanyal, U. Teichler, eds., *Higher Education and Employment in the USSR and in the Federal Republic of Germany* (Paris: *UNESCO*, International Institute, 1984), p. 101.

[a]Data include foreign students; figures are for winter semesters.
[b]N/A = not available.
[c]Approximate figures.

as, for example, that for Britain. In the early 1960s, Britain still led West Germany by a significant margin. Equally important, the cumulative effect of the reform discussions of the 1960s, the student movement, state legislation, the 1972 court decision, and the framework legislation of 1976 has been to transform the internal structure of the university. In the traditional university professors holding chairs had exercised almost unchecked powers. Junior faculty members, doctoral candidates, students, and staff had typically been totally dependent on the senior faculty. In the late 1960s student protestors, referring to the university's complicity with the Nazis, mocked their elders who were parading at a function of the University of Hamburg sporting their traditional robes, hats, and medals: "Under the academic robe, 1,000 years of mold" (*unter den Talaren—Muff aus 1000 Jahren*). The reforms of the 1970s have altered the governing structure of the university. The changes that the new CDU/CSU-FDP government has made in the University Framework Law of 1984 are by no means trivial. But they cannot and are not designed to restore the conditions prevailing in the early 1960s (see Reading 7-8).

The coincidence of stalemate and large-scale change is illustrated particularly well in the class composition of the university student body. Rallying under the banner of equal opportunity, liberals such as Dahrendorf succeeded in the 1960s in convincing substantial strata of the political elite and of the West German mass public that the university needed to be opened up especially to children of working-class background. Their proportion had increased slowly from 2.1 percent in 1928–29 to 4.1 percent in 1951–52 (Teichler, 1976, p. 88). One important attraction of the comprehensive university was to create more upward social channels to the university level and to provide closer links between practical and theoretical areas of study. The proportion of working class students increased from 4 percent in 1952, to 7 percent in 1967, 12 percent in 1973, and 16 percent in 1982 (Teichler, 1976, p. 88, 1984, p. 7). Based on these data, Ulrich Teichler thus concluded (1976, pp. 88–89) that "when one considers the relative chances for access to higher education of youth from the upper strata compared with that of lower-strata youth in different European countries, then the diminishing of inequality in the FRG in the 1960s appears to have taken place fairly rapidly." On the other hand, in comparison to the accomplishment of Britain, arguably the European society with the deepest status divisions, the West German accomplishment looks less impressive. In 1965 the chances of an English working-class child to attend university were three to four times as great as in West Germany. After fifteen years of dramatic expansion and reform in West Germany, the English lead had narrowed to about 2:1 (Rüschemeyer, 1982, p. 40). Characteristically, the concept of "democratization" means in the United States or Britain increasing equality of opportunity; in the Federal Republic, in the context of West German university reform policy, it refers to a mode of participation within universities (Teichler, 1976, p. 109).

University reform policies are linked directly to several of the policy sectors discussed earlier. The political discourse about "self-administration" of the university and the principle of "codetermination" of all groups in the university evoke the discussion of participation in the social insurance funds or industrial corporations. Because of their public character and financial dependence on the state, universities are peculiar parapublic institutions. But for better or for worse, efforts at changing the extent of the services universities render and, indeed, their very character have been discussed and acted upon in the language of parapublic institutions.

Concern over the economic competitiveness of West German exports was an important consideration for the support conservatives gave to university reform proposals in the 1960s. Similar concerns explain the renewed emphasis on policy regarding scientific research and development and regional development since the CDU/CSU-FDP coalition was elected to office in 1983 (see Reading 7-8). As in the United States in the 1980s, closer bonds are being forged in West Germany between universities and business. The federal government's political commitment to using universities to foster regional economic development is rising. For party politicians in particular, technology is increasingly replacing the university as a central focus of interest and concern (Gellert, 1985; Künzel, 1985). By the same token, policy for higher education is no longer viewed as much a part of social policy as it was in the 1960s and 1970s. The social mobility of working-class children and the issue of equal opportunity are not pressing policy concerns in the 1980s.

Social issues are, however, raised in discussions of the employment prospects of university graduates. Although the fear of the rise of a new academic "proletariat" has been largely dispelled, the unemployment rate among university graduates is beginning to converge with the national average. In 1985 more than 100,000 university graduates were jobless. Tight labor markets explain why tens of thousands of university students enroll in universities: not to study for their exams but to take advantage of the free coverage under the social insurance system which all students enjoy (see Reading 7-7). Although this widespread practice corrodes the academic atmosphere of the university, it is tolerated as the smallest evil by party politicians of all stripes. In most professions the glut of qualified personnel is reaching serious proportions (*Der Spiegel*, May 13, 1985, pp. 40–67; May 20, 1985, pp. 158–76, May 27, 1985, pp. 160–80; June 3, 1985, pp. 154–68; June 10, 1985, pp. 154–72; June 17, 1985, pp. 124–38). The share of university graduates finding jobs in the public sector declined from 60 percent in the early 1970s to 25 percent by the end of the decade (Teichler, 1982, p. 164). Foremost affected were schoolteachers. In 1984 25,000 qualified teachers registered for unemployment; 65,000 teachers have remained without teaching positions since the mid-1970s; and with low retirements expected for the years ahead, an additional 130,000 qualified teachers may be seeking employment for a declining number of teaching positions (Heister, 1985, pp. 258–59; Teichler, 1982, p. 164). But as a result of university reform, the smaller number still finding jobs in the public sector is often better qualified. State schools for public administration, for example, have become more like universities. Their graduates today have much better qualifications than they did a generation ago. Subsequent increases in promotions have led to a salary and grade inflation that has been a serious problem for the civil service (see Chapter 6).

Most important, perhaps, is the noticeable effect that university reform policies have had on West German politics. In the early 1970s Richard Merritt and his associates concluded (Merritt, Flerlage, and Merritt, 1971, pp. 359–60) that "although few would argue that such reform 'caused' the more extensive demands for change heard and partially implemented in the last two years, they certainly contributed to the social and political climate that made such demands 'thinkable.' " This argument seems apt for the reform of the 1970s as well. University reform policies were greatly accelerated by the political mobilization of students on West German campuses after 1967. Quickly defeated in their attempts to build an alliance with a conservative working class, student radicals paraphrasing Mao prepared for "a long march through the institutions of West Germany." The stranglehold of West German capitalism was to be broken at its weakest link, in universities and schools.

Although the hope of the extreme Left were disappointed, educational reform has unintentionally challenged West Germany's traditional political establishment. Academically trained, politicized elites have transformed the membership and leadership cadres of the traditional political parties and are producing new conflicts within as well as between parties. Although concentrated among the Greens, this new elite, many of whom are teachers, has established itself firmly in all major parties and constitutes a crucial voting bloc in the electorate. "Based on its experiences in the educational system, this new elite has the ability to let critical discourse become the dominant style of political conflict. Their desired practical goals, predominantly non-material, make consensus building difficult" (Feist and Liepelt, 1983, p. 77).

Why was nonincremental change possible in this case, in contrast to the others examined in Chapters 2–5? One reason is that West Germany's peak associations remained largely passive on this issue, "not because members chose to keep quiet, but because the political figures involved in promulgating the Federal Framework Law preferred to draw on other reserves of support" (Mushaben, 1981, p. 73). This was true in particular during the crucial, initial phases of reform in the late 1960s (Mushaben, 1981, pp. 97, 101, 104). Without the active support of the major producers, parapublic institutions were not policy actors but policy arenas. This is not to argue that social groups were inactive. Numerous groups affiliated directly with the university generated a large number of reform proposals that were mostly discredited or ignored by state officials. Instead, reform policies evolved at the intersection of three sets of interests: the universities aimed at enlarging their funding while avoiding comprehensive plans; the states wanted to maintain their control over education while shifting some of the fiscal burden to the federal level; and the government in Bonn hoped for long-term gains for the Federal Republic on an issue over which it had limited jurisdiction. This is a plausible reason why, between 1969 and 1986, West Germany had six ministers of education and science.

The courts, on the other hand, have occupied a central position in policymaking. Hans Weiler has written a number of instructive papers on the role of courts in education reform. In response to the reform protest of the late 1960s which greatly taxed West Germany's semi-sovereign state, the courts mandated certain kinds of procedures. According to Weiler (1981a, p. 35), they showed "a capacity for making legislative institutions do things which they don't seem to be able to do on their own political momentum"; he refers to this power as "compensatory legitimation." Judicial activism is for Weiler both a symptom of the legitimacy of the modern executive and tends to enhance the role of the Bundestag. In the area of education, including university reform, policy innovations were a response to social protest movements; yet they also anticipated more diffuse legitimacy problems of the modern state (Weiler, 1981b and 1982).

At the same time, the continuing preoccupation with university reform illustrates important continuities spanning these decades of reform. Internal university administration is limited to purely academic matters. Even questions of examination and curriculum now involve state officials. As a result of the developments of the last two decades, the climate of moderate state control of the 1950s and 1960s has changed dramatically in the 1970s. "We can now observe ministers in charge of education who proudly tell parliament how frequently they have appointed professors who were not the first choice of the university in question" (Teichler, 1982, p. 171). Politicized confrontations inside the university have drawn state governments deeply into academic politics. In the late 1970s a comparative study of how European universities were managed ranked the Federal Republic second from the bottom in its autonomy from state intervention (Bender, 1980). The links between the universities and the state have become tighter. University budgets must be approved in detail by state legislatures. State ministers control faculty appointments. University teachers are civil servants. And university graduates still find employment in the public sector in very large numbers.

Over the last two decades university reform policies have not resulted in steady, incremental policy change. Instead, the occurrence of one large-scale change, from an elitist system to a mass system, has coincided with stalemate on most other issues. The extraordinary swing in policy from an all-out expansion in enrollment in the late 1960s to restricted admission only a few years later illustrates that West German policymakers found themselves in a political environment atypical of the economic and social issues discussed in Chapters 2–5. By opening itself to new social movements, such as the student movement of the 1960s, the university lacked the inherent stability of the state bureaucracy discussed in Chapter 6. In contrast to the various administrative reform movements that never got off the ground, university reform acquired for a short time a momentum of its own. As the political consensus that supported reform evaporated quickly in the early 1970s, state institutions (education ministries in the states, the courts, and the federal legislature) imposed their own solutions on a policy sector that had resisted steady and consensual change.

The distinctiveness of West Germany's semisovereign state lies in its involvement in shaping social and economic developments. Government by coalition, cooperative federalism, and parapublic institutions—the three central institutional nodes of West Germany's policymaking network—did not confront this problem very effectively. For constitutional reasons, the states rather than the federal government were the prime players. Government by opposition and a tortuous process of bargaining between the SPD-dominated Bundestag and the CDU-dominated Bundesrat was the rule. A politicized and "uncooperative" federalism pitted the CDU/CSU against the SPD-FDP. And parapublic institutions that lacked the support of major producers were arenas rather than actors in the policy process. The result was direct state intervention and policymaking by the courts or the executive, rather than a centrist politics and incremental policy change. West Germany's disappointments with university reform policies are instructive precisely because they highlight indirectly the distinctive institutional characteristics of its semisovereign state.

Readings

7-1. WEST GERMANY'S EDUCATIONAL CATASTROPHE*

Georg Picht's invocation of an imminent educational catastrophe was published in a series of newspaper articles in 1963. Reissued in expanded form in 1964, it became the opening shot in a public debate about the reform of West German universities and its education system more generally. As these selections show, Picht's analysis focuses on the economic consequences of educational stagnation. In language designed to attract public attention, Picht criticizes politicians of all polit-

*Georg Picht, *Die deutsche Bildungskatastrophe: Analyse und Dokumentation* (Olten: Walter, 1967), pp. 16–17, 65, 83, 86–87.

ical persuasions. He advocates a dramatic expansion in the resources devoted to the expansion of the educational system and an enlargement in the jurisdiction of the federal government. In subsequent years West German governments responded to both demands.

The educational system is one of the basic pillars of any modern state. Nobody should know this better than the Germans. After all, schools and universities made possible Germany's rise in the nineteenth century. Before World War I, a modern school system and world-class scientists provided the foundation for Germany's political position, its economic prosperity, and the expansion of its industry. We are still living off that heritage. The economic and political elites who after 1945 made possible the so-called "economic miracle" attended school before 1914; today's elites were educated in the Weimar Republic. But now we have exhausted our rich legacy. International school statistics reveal that the Federal Republic ranks at the very bottom in Europe, right next to Yugoslavia, Ireland, and Portugal. Young scientists are emigrating in droves. They no longer find adequate working conditions at home. The situation in West German schools is worse. If we let things take their natural course, in a few years we will have to send our children back home for lack of both teachers and classrooms. We are confronted with an educational emergency that only a small handful of people comprehend.

Educational emergency means economic emergency. The economic growth that we have experienced to date will end quickly, if we lack the next generation of qualified scientists. Without science no system of economic production can remain competitive in this technological era. If the education system fails, the very fabric of our social existence is threatened. But West Germany's political leaders refuse to confront these unpleasant facts and preside, with a mixture of lethargy and complacency, over Germany's increasing backwardness in the international developments that are leading toward a new scientific civilization. . . .

Our school and university system has become so antiquated that it can no longer meet even its own requirements. This is an inescapable conclusion which emerges from a critical reading of the manpower projections of the Standing Conference of Ministers of Culture. The ministers have artfully disguised for the German public what can only be called a national emergency of the first order. We are not dealing with temporary bottlenecks in an unimportant sector of public life. Instead the very foundations of our social and economic order are threatened. In an immediate emergency citizens are entitled to expect their government to take action. Yet the ministers of culture to date have not proposed a program that promises to solve for West Germany the problems identified by their manpower projections. Admittedly the Bavarian government has announced a far-reaching school development plan. But the other states have to date not followed suit. Meanwhile the problems have become so acute that they can no longer be solved on a regional basis. . . .

It should be clear by now that the educational catastrophe staring in our face might undermine our entire constitutional order unless we take timely action. A political danger of such proportion cannot be met successfully with the unobtrusive instruments of every-day politics. What is needed instead is a far-reaching reorganization of the entire system of cultural administration. The highest organs of our federal state must intervene forcefully.

None of the necessary measures will be adopted unless we declare a national emergency for our educational system. Since we are dealing with a national emergency rather than regional bottlenecks, this declaration cannot be made by each of our eleven states. . . .

The emergency program must be complemented by financial plans. The funds necessary are so substantial that the German people will have to make the required sacrifices. In 1961 the Germans spent as much for cigarettes as for schools (5.9 billion [deutschmarks]). And in 1963 they spent 7.2 billion deutschmarks on tourism alone. The German people evidently can mobilize the funds necessary to save the economy from a catastrophic decline. Increases in the normal school and university budgets could conceivably be financed by the normal system of revenue sharing among the states. But the truly horrendous differences between different states can be surmounted only through a financial program that permits the creation of regional centers of excellence. Only if the government succeeds in finding new methods for financing education can we hope to preserve or restore the uniformity of living standards throughout the Federal Republic which the Basic Law mandates.

Each people has the education system it deserves. There is still time to soften the unmitigated impact of the educational catastrophe. Germany might still survive. But we need a dramatic reorientation in policy. The German people must be prepared to incur financial sacrifices and pay for the omissions of the last decades. Governments and legislatures must act—now. If they don't, then at least we shall know already today who is responsible for the third great collapse of Germany in the twentieth century.

7-2. RESOLUTION OF THE STANDING CONFERENCE OF MINISTERS OF CULTURE*

By 1968 political discussion had progressed to the point where the Standing Conference of Cultural Ministers issued general principles that were to inform a revised university law. These principles reflect a degree of consensus on questions of university reform among the CDU/CSU, the SPD, and the FDP which by the early 1970s had largely disappeared. Significantly, several of the issues addressed in 1968 stayed on the political agenda for the next two decades.

The "Guidelines for a Modern University Law and for a Structural Reform of the University System" of the Standing Conference of the Ministers of Culture of April 10, 1968 are informed by the following considerations:

(1) The educational system should be organized at all levels so that it guarantees de facto a free choice of whatever occupation and training suit individual talent and educational qualification.

(2) The educational system should be sufficiently differentiated so that individual aspirations for education match as much as possible the demands of business and society at large, including the requirements of the educational system.

(3) In their educational planning and policies, the states should be put in a position of having access to more sophisticated methods of forecasting and analyzing future demand. The development of such methods will require a close and successful cooperation between state and federal governments.

These considerations inform the following basic principles of educational reform:

(1) All universities should create an office of university president or some equivalent, thus increasing the working capacity and continuity of the central university administration. Academic committees and univer-

*Guntram von Schenck, *Das Hochschulrahmengesetz: Hochschulreform in der Gesellschaftskrise* (Bonn–Bad Godesberg: Neue Gesellschaft, 1976), pp. 114–15.

sity professors should have to do less administrative work. In adjusting the university more flexibly to the changing requirements of research and teaching, both the university administration of the state and the central administrative offices of the university should increase the scope of their jurisdictions.

(2) Endowed professorships and small institutes should be merged into larger departments, academic divisions, or faculties. These larger units should receive the resources necessary for carrying out teaching and research.

(3) Groups involved in teaching and research, including students, should be granted the right of codetermination. The principle of codetermination should not be applied mechanically but should be informed instead by the tasks to be performed by the different academic organizations. Codetermination should not impair the normal operation of such organizations.

(4) A reform of the faculty should include a more precise description of teaching obligations, an expansion of the junior faculty, and the incorporation, on a full-time or part-time basis, of academically trained persons in university teaching and examinations. The responsibilities of the junior faculty in teaching and research should be specified. To avoid excessive dependence on individual professors, junior faculty members should be affiliated with larger academic units. Academic promotion through research should become more regularized and uniform. Specifically, academic promotion should not involve considerations of the candidate's needs or his dependence on one sponsor. Academic promotion should not depend solely on the publication of a substantial book after the Ph.D. dissertation, as long as other publications or equivalent achievements bear witness to the candidate's academic qualifications.

(5) Vacant professorships should be advertised publicly, and the results should be evaluated by a university search committee. That committee should put together a list of preferred candidates and submit that list, together with all applications received, to the respective state ministry for culture. Negotiations with successful candidates should be restricted to questions of individual salaries.

(6) The reform of curriculum and examinations should be continued so that the time students spend at the university can be shortened. More specifically, on the basis of careful manpower projections, vocational guidance in high schools and academic advising in the universities should be strengthened. Rules governing examinations and courses of

study should specify the subjects that a student is expected to have mastered. Examinations should be public. To increase the efficiency of teaching, universities should encourage the organization of supervised study and research groups for students. Correspondence courses relying on public radio and television also should help to reduce the universities' load. The traditional semester system should be replaced by a full academic year. Additional courses and seminars offered during semester breaks should help increase the operating capacities of the university. These additional courses and seminars should be taught primarily by junior faculty. Student stipends should be granted for the full year for beginning as well as advanced students. After proper deliberations, shortened study courses should be introduced for specific academic titles.

(7) Limiting student access to the universities (*numerus clausus*) in overcrowded study courses should be permitted only as an emergency measure. State and university should cooperate in developing and implementing objective and uniform criteria limiting access.

7-3. REPORT ON EDUCATION*

The introductory pages of this report by the federal government lay out the overarching themes of university reform policies in 1970. These themes summarize the political discussions of the previous years and show an awareness of the problems that West German federalism subsequently created for policymaking in the 1970s.

1. Educational Policy as an All-State Task

In the Government Declaration by the Federal Chancellor of October 28, 1969, the Federal Government emphasized the social policy importance of educational and scientific policy. The Declaration said: "Education and training, science and research are at the top of the reforms to be carried out."

The decision to give priority to educational policy in overall policy was not only made because technical progress, economic growth and social security depend on the efficiency of the educational system and research. To a greater extent, education and science develop individual

*Report of the Federal Government on Education 1970: The Federal Government's Concept for Educational Policy (Bonn: Der Bundesminister für Bildung und Wissenschaft, 1970), pp. 9–13.

and cultural values that are a precondition for the essential humanization of a technological civilization and for the survival of the liberal, democratic social system.

The social policy aim of all educational reforms is the implementation of the right to education: its most important principle is not a privileged elite, but equality of opportunity through the individual promotion of talent; its essential criterion is not a levelling, but a differentiation of educational aims and qualitative improvements.

With these comprehensive social policy aims, educational policy will become a task that can be realized only within an all-state framework and only with close interaction among the various sections of social and economic policy. The complex process which takes place as a consequence of this interaction between scientific and technological development, economic and social structural change and personal autonomy, must be recognized, observed and influenced supraregionally, that is to say by the Federal Government and Länder [states] jointly. Extensive reforms in the educational system can only be realized with any hope of success if account is taken of the interrelation of planning and decision-making processes.

This is a test not only of co-operative, but also coordinated federalism. The Federal Government and Länder must also coordinate planning in educational policy, tackle overlapping tasks jointly, and where necessary, bring their own competencies into joint planning. The Federal Government, which is responsible for most of the social policy, cannot and may not leave ideas on educational policy out of consideration. Likewise, the Länder, which are responsible for broad areas of the educational system, cannot plan and make decisions independently within a regional framework. For their part, they are also bound by all-state connections, conditions and developments.

Finally, there is increasing international integration in the educational system. Consideration and account has [sic] to be taken of this more than before.

For these reasons, the Federal Government reaffirms its view that pending educational policy tasks and reforms can only be carried out jointly by the Federal, Länder and local governments.

It maintains the view that the desire for reforms in the Federal Republic may no longer dissipate and peter out in partial reforms, but that it is time to implement basic changes in the educational system, comprehensively, quickly and jointly.

The German educational system, which was established in the 19th century not according to democratic, but class and authoritarian state ideas on order and education, produced achievements acknowledged throughout the world under the social conditions and criteria pertaining at that time.

However, despite many partial reforms and individual corrections, this system no longer meets the demands of present social development. It neither contributes to implementing the right to education, nor does it fulfill the demands of modernization and democratization.

2. Principles for Reforming the Educational System

The following general aims must, therefore, be pursued in educational reform in the coming years.

1. The prime aim is a democratic, efficient and flexible educational system which is open to every citizen from pre-school education to further education for his personal, professional and political education.

2. The constitutional principle of equality of opportunity must be realized through an intensive and individual promotion of those being taught at all levels of the educational system. Education should help people to shape their own lives. The younger generation must experience the possibilities of greater flexibility and freedom, so that they can learn to choose usefully for themselves. Education should create a permanent basis for liberal co-existence through learning and experiencing democratic values and through an understanding of social development and its changes. Education should awaken joy in independent, creative work.

3. In order to achieve these aims, the division between the various kinds of schools and the various kinds of universities must be removed. With the development of an extensive, integrated and differentiated comprehensive school and comprehensive university system, a democratic and efficient educational system is to be established in the Federal Republic as has been similarly planned and developed in past decades in other democratic, industrial states.

4. As a result of the increasing importance of science in all walks of life and the increasingly rapid changes in professional and private life, the school of the future must provide everyone with a better and more thorough education, on which a qualified professional training can be built. Vocational education must be relevant to the interests and abilities of the individual and be developed as an integrated part of the educational system.

5. The university of the future must be reorganized through a reform of studies which takes account of the development of science and society both in content and in a didactic sense. It must be developed into an integrated comprehensive university. Its capacity will have to be more than doubled in the next ten years. Hierarchical structures and forms of organization have to be dismantled. The autonomy of the university must be strengthened. It must be the aim of this reform to give equal rights to all those working on the same tasks in teaching and research and to permit all university members to take part in the decision-making processes.

6. The willingness and motivation to practice lifelong learning must be implanted in the school and be constantly encouraged by appropriate possibilities in further education. It is therefore necessary to develop an independent fourth sector in the educational system, in which gaps in education and training can be filled and in which further training of all kinds can be pursued.

7. The reforms have to be introduced immediately. The permanent process of reform ahead of us demands systematic and coordinated educational planning, research and development.

At the start of the 1980s, considering the prices that will then be prevalent and in particular the salaries, the public authorities will have to spend at least three times as much as today on education and science. The share of the GNP spent on education and research, which today lies between 4% and 5%, including funds from industry, will increase to at least 8% according to current estimates.

If a plan period of more than ten years is to be considered, this conclusion can be drawn from the present situation: The restructuring of institutions, the training of additional teachers, the formulation of new curricula and the extension of existing educational institutions cannot, as shown by the experience of other countries, be implemented in a shorter period of time.

7-4. DECISION OF THE FEDERAL CONSTITUTIONAL COURT ABOUT ACCESS TO UNIVERSITIES (JULY 18, 1972)*

This decision of the Federal Constitutional Court set one of the most important parameters for the evolution of university reform policy in the

*Ulrich Karpen, ed., *Access to Higher Education and Its Restrictions under the Constitution* (Munich: Minerva, 1980), pp. 1–2, 14–16, 50–52 (selections).

1970s. The decision insists on the principle of equal access for individuals to education and severely curtails any discretionary power of the universities to select their students. In overruling parts of the university laws of Hamburg and Bavaria, the Court served notice that restricted access to higher education on constitutional grounds could not be tolerated. But the decision also opened the door to a bureaucratic formalism that symbolizes how substantive and procedural objectives become fused in the West German policy machinery.

3. Absolute numerus clausus for first-year students in a particular field of studies is only constitutional, if
a) it is ordered within the limits of absolute necessity and having completely exhausted the available educational and training capacity,
b) and if the choice and distribution of applicants takes place according to objective criteria with chance for each applicant qualified for higher education and under due consideration of individual choice in selecting his institution of higher education.
4. The essential decisions for the necessary requirement for the order of absolute numerus clausus and for the selection criteria to be applied must be determined by the legislature. The institutions of higher education can be authorized to regulate further particulars within certain limits.
5. § 17 of the "Hamburg University Law" of April 25th 1969 is incompatible with the federal constitution in as much as the legislature itself has failed to determine in the case of absolute numerus clausus the type and ranking order of selection criteria. . . .
6. Art. 3 § 2 of the "Bavarian Admission Law" of July 8th 1970 is incompatible with the constitution insofar as applicants with a legal residence in Bavaria, who are in possession of a school record from an institution in Bavaria, or neighboring states, are generally admitted to home-state universities even in the case of complete exhaustion of training capacity and to this purpose receive preferential treatment with regard to their ranking. . . .
7. The joint responsibility of Federal and State governments for the distribution of all available student space through an over-regional agency employing standardized selection criteria. . . .
1. The plaintiff in the Hamburg case, who in May 1969 passed his Abitur in Itzehoe with a grade point average of 3,25 after an unsuc-

cessful application for the winter semester 1969/70, re-applied to medical school for the summer semester 1970. After his application was refused for the second time due to insufficient student places and after being informed of his list ranking, the plaintiff, after unsuccessfully appealing the decision, brought a claim to the court to ascertain that this refusal was illegal. In the opinion of the plaintiff it is unconstitutional to retain the numerus clausus for so many years although doctors are urgently needed in various branches of the medical profession, and in previous years considerably more applicants were admitted and sufficient time has been available to expand training and educational capacity. . . .

2. The Administrative Court suspended the procedures under Art. 100 § 1 GG.

a) The Hamburg Administrative Court demands the decision of the Federal Constitutional Court on the question whether § 17 UniG is constitutional under Art. 12 § 1 GG. The provisions of the admission regulations are consistent with the statute. They remain within the frame of a "very broad authorization" in § 17 UniG and the judgement cannot be objected to. Whether the privileged position of applicants from Hamburg, the equal evaluation of all grades in the Abitur, the reserving of student places for foreigners and capacity calculation are valid can be left open, when considering the constitutionality of the numerus clausus as applied to the plaintiff, as the judgement depends entirely upon the fact whether § 17 UniG is consistent with Art. 12 § 1 GG. This question has to be answered in the negative.

Art. 12 § 1 GG does not limit itself to be merely a defensive right against measures which lead to the control of the possible choice of vocation or profession, but commits the state, in any case, when as in the medical profession, the state has the educational and training monopoly, to provide facilities which cover the demand. The introduction of the numerus clausus is therefore always constitutionally questionable. Admission restrictions might prove to be necessary in order to avoid a greater harm of overcrowding and the resulting breakdown of the educational and training apparatus. But the numerus clausus may never lose its character of being a temporary measure to becoming a constant institution which undermines the constitutional right of free vocational and professional choice. Since § 17 UniG makes possible an unlimited duration of the numerus clausus and the law itself does not include the obligation of the state to supply sufficient educational and training capacity, this regulation is unconstitutional due to the unlimited duration of the numerus clausus. . . .

1. The previously mentioned requirements for the order of admission restrictions belong to the core of admission procedures to higher education in the same manner as the regulation dealing with the selection of applicants. Its difficulties are characterized with respect to material law in that from a group of applicants, who are equally entitled to be admitted, there are those who have the advantage of being admitted and those that have the disadvantage of being rejected and are thereby hindered in beginning their study or even more may be excluded from the profession of their choice. In this connection there is no need to discuss the importance of the Abitur as a final examination of general education of whether this manner of qualifying for higher education should be reformed. Wherever the line is drawn for the matriculation requirements, in any case, the absolute numerus clausus presents the problem of selecting among applicants who fulfill all the individual requirements for enrollment.

Since this kind of selection means unequal treatment of those actually equally entitled to enrollment, the margin in setting the rules of selection, which normally the principle of equality leaves, is in this case not very large. That the regulation may not be arbitrary in the sense of being evidently unobjective, goes without saying. Here especially, those responsible are obliged, while constantly orientating [*sic*] themselves along the lines of equality, to find reasonably acceptable selection for those that are at a disadvantage. In particular the regulation must give a real chance to every applicant entitled for enrollment.

As far as formal legality is concerned, it is the responsibility of the legislature itself to establish the regulations for selection. If the legislature authorizes a delegation of its authority, it must as a minimum requirement regulate the selection criteria and their ranking order. The constitution permits the legislature to delegate its legislative power to others through explicit legal authorization. However, if the regulation interferes with the fundamental rights of Art. 12 § 1 GG and has as consequence an allocation of chances in life, then, in a constitutional parliamentary democracy the provision, that in the field of fundamental rights intervention is only legal by law or on the basis of a law means that the legislature must be responsible for the basic elements of the decision relating to this intervention.

7-5. HIGHER EDUCATION FRAMEWORK LAW (JANUARY 26, 1976)*

This reading excerpts some of the important points of the single most controversial piece of federal legislation on university reform passed in the 1970s. An English translation of the full bill runs fifty-five printed pages. The law is a ringing affirmation of state power over traditional notions of university autonomy.

Paragraph 2. Responsibilities

1. Institutions of higher education, in accordance with their position of responsibility, serve the encouragement and development of the sciences and the arts through research, teaching, and study. They prepare the students for professional endeavors requiring the application of scientific knowledge and scientific methods or the capacity for artistic expression. . . .

8. The various responsibilities of the individual institutions are determined by the state. Other responsibilities besides those enumerated in this law can be transferred to these institutions only when they are related to the responsibilities enumerated in Paragraph 2. . . .

Paragraph 5. Comprehensive Universities (Gesamthochschulen)

1. For the fulfillment of the goals in Paragraph 4, Subsection 3, the various types of higher educational institutions are to be fused into a new system of higher education. Institutions of higher education are to be expanded or combined into comprehensive universities (integrated Gesamthochschulen) or are to be joined by common boards while preserving their official independence (cooperative Gesamthochschulen). In cases in which comprehensive universities cannot or cannot yet be formed, they are to be linked through various joint bodies. . . .

Paragraph 8. Educational Reform

1. Institutions of higher education have the continuing responsibility of revising and further developing the content and structure of education in cooperation with the competent public authorities, with consideration

---

*"Higher Education Framework Law of January 26, 1976 (Federal Republic of Germany)," *Western European Education* 8, 3 (1976), pp. 60–115 (selections).

for developments in science and the arts, the requirements of professional application, and the necessary changes in the professional
world. . . .

Paragraph 9. Committees for Educational Reform

1. To further the reform of education and testing and to coordinate
and support the reforms made in individual institutions, educational reform committees shall be formed. The states shall form joint committees for educational reform with the same jurisdiction as this law.

2. Committees for educational reform shall be formed by the competent state authorities in cooperation with the respective institutions. For
courses of study that are based primarily on common branches of science or related fields of endeavor, joint committees for educational reform should be formed. In addition, it is to be guaranteed that the work
of the individual committees for educational reform is coordinated with
respect to organization and content.

3. Representatives of higher educational establishments and public
authorities as well as specialists in professional practice shall participate
in the proposed committees for educational reform. In courses of study
that are completed with an official examination, the representatives of
public authorities shall comprise more than one-half of the votes, in
committees for educational reform as defined in Subparagraph 1, Sentence 2, at least two-thirds of the votes.

4. The committees for educational reform are charged with formulating, within specified deadlines, recommendations for courses of study
and for the development of an offering of courses of study. . . .

6. The recommendations shall be presented to the competent state
authorities; before they are approved, the institutions of higher education are to have an opportunity to take a position regarding them.

7. The competent state authorities can, after consulting the institutions of higher education, demand that current study and testing programs of the institutions be made to conform to the recommendations,
or that study and testing programs be instituted in accordance with the
recommendations; instead of a change in current study and testing programs, they can also demand that special study and testing programs
(Paragraph 8, Subparagraph 2) be instituted in accordance with the
recommendations. . . .

Paragraph 27. General Requirements

1. Every German citizen, as defined by Article 116 of the Constitution, has the right to the higher education of his choice, when he exhibits the required qualification for that education. Hindrances to admission that reside in the student applicant personally, without being related to qualification, shall be dealt with by state law. . . .

Paragraph 38. Composition and Voting Rights

1. The nature and scope of participation as well as the numerical composition of university bodies, committees, and other boards are determined by their duties and by the qualifications, functions, responsibility, and concern of the members of the institution. The shares of the votes the groups (Subparagraph 2) have at their disposal in the central bodies of the institution of higher education and in the department are to be set by law.

2. Representation on the boards consists of one group each of
   (1) the professors;
   (2) the students;
   (3) the associates in science and the arts, as well as the higher education assistants;
   (4) other associates.

Representation by other members of the institution of higher education is regulated by state law. State law can provide for one common group to be formed of members described in Sentence 1, Item 3 jointly with the members described in Sentence 1, Item 4 when, because of their small number, formation of their own group is not justified.

3. In the central bodies of the institutions of higher education that are responsible for the functions described in Paragraph 63 and in the departments, all participant groups must be represented with a voice, according to the standards of Subparagraph 4; this does not apply to committees of these boards. The professors shall preside over the absolute majority of the votes on all boards with the authority to make decisions in matters connected with research, projects for the development of the arts, teaching, or the appointment of professors.

4. To the extent that they are represented on the board, the professors, the director of the institution or a member of the board of directors, the higher education assistants, the associates in science and the arts, the students, and those persons on a par with them in accordance

with Paragraph 36, Subparagraphs 2 and 3 shall participate by vote in decisions that are directly connected with research, projects for the development of the arts, teaching, or the appointment of professors. Other members of the institutional community belonging to the board have the right to vote on matters of research if they exercise appropriate functions at the institution and have acquired special experience in the field of the research; the same applies to their participation in teaching matters and in matters concerned with projects for the development of the arts. If members of the board do not have a voice as in Sentence 2, they participate in an advisory capacity.

5. Decisions directly connected with research, projects for the development of the arts, and the appointment of professors require not only the majority of the board, but also the majority of the professors on the board. If, in accordance herewith, there still is no resolution after the second vote, then agreement of the majority of the professors on the board will suffice for a decision. In the case of appointment suggestions, the majority of the board is authorized to submit its own suggestion as an additional appointment recommendation.

Paragraph 39. Elections

The representatives of the participant groups in the central institutional governing bodies and in the departments are elected in free, equal, and secret voting by the respective participant groups and usually according to the principles of personalized election by proportionate representation. By regulation of the voting process and the establishment of the time of the election, conditions are to be created for as high a voter participation as possible; for direct election to the central institutional governing bodies and the departments, all eligible voters are to be given the opportunity to vote by absentee ballot. . . .

Paragraph 72. Adjustment Deadlines

1. Within three years after this law goes into effect, state laws must be passed in accordance with the provisions of Chapters 1-5; Paragraph 48, Subparagraph 2, and Paragraph 51 are effective immediately.

7-6. THE INCOMPLETE QUEST FOR A UNIFORM UNIVERSITY LAW*

Published three years after the university law of 1976, the newspaper article below surveys how this legislation has been implemented by the eleven states. The article is a useful reminder of the decentralized character of policymaking on university policies even in areas where the federal government enjoys jurisdiction, as it did in this instance.

The federal framework law for universities passed three years ago intended to unify legal practices in the eleven states. This objective has been met only within limits. The individual states have adopted different regulations dealing with controversial issues such as a prescribed duration of university studies, maintenance of campus order, codetermination, and student self-administration. The trend to strengthen the position of the state administration at the expense of university autonomy is, however, uniform. In Baden-Württemberg the minister of culture enjoys both far-reaching legal and substantive control. And in the Saar the state has taken over from the university full supervision of university personnel.

Universities have not accepted the curtailment of their traditional rights without opposition. Debates in Baden-Württemberg and Bremen have shown that the universities are intent on using, to the fullest extent possible, whatever room for maneuver they retain. Court action will be a likely consequence of this strategy. Because some states allegedly favor the senior faculty too much, the Education Ministry in Bonn is considering filing lawsuits against Bavaria, Baden-Württemberg, and Schleswig-Holstein. Conversely, university professors in North Rhine-Westphalia are not excluding the possibility of litigation against the planned equalization of their position with that of professors at teacher training colleges. The rules governing codetermination in Bremen have already led to a constitutional complaint in Karlsruhe.

A prescribed duration of studies lasting eight semesters has been written into the law of every state. But this regulation is interpreted very liberally. When petitioned, most states grant an "extension" of two semesters which without great difficulties can prolong the period of study to 14 semesters (seven years) on account of internships, study abroad,

*Die Welt, February 7, 1979.

student self-government, and social or personal hardship. Bremen has the most liberal provision; an extension "should" not exceed two years. Baden-Württemberg is most restrictive; it denies students the right to be examined if they extend their studies.

CDU- and SPD-governed states follow different policies on questions of university codetermination. The CDU tends to interpret liberally the insistence of the Constitutional Court that professors be granted an absolute majority in all university bodies; and it tends to extend this provision also to university parliaments, whatever their names. In contrast, states governed by the SPD and the FDP continue to adhere to the rule of group parity in university parliaments: professors, students, senior administrative staff, and at times researchers divide the available seats.

Rules concerning the maintenance of campus order and security are often concealed behind regulations terminating student status. Most states punish with a compulsory leave of absence, lasting up to two years, all exhortations to, threats of, or engagement in violent action. Schleswig-Holstein's parliament voted down a proposed law that would have made the exhortation to or threat of violent action a criminal offense. In Bremen a student has to be found guilty of at least three infractions of rules prohibiting serious obstructions of other members of the university community; only then can he or she be expelled.

Student self-administration is also a controversial issue. With the exception of Baden-Württemberg and Bavaria, all states recognize student organizations as corporate groups of the university, with compulsory membership and their own budget. After many lawsuits, none of the states grants these corporate groups or their elected officials the right to choose positions publicly on issues of a general political nature. Student self-administration is treated most liberally in Hamburg and Hesse, which delegate to student groups the task of political education. In Bremen student self-administration is given the task of representing student interests "in the university and in the society at large . . . only in this sense does the student self-administration exercise a political mandate on behalf of its members."

In addition to these four controversial issues—a prescribed duration for university study, codetermination, maintenance of campus order, and student self-administration—other questions had also to be addressed in the wake of federal legislation. The creation of the office of a university president has strengthened the central administration of the university. In most states it has prevailed over the traditional system of annually elected university presidents. Only North Rhine-Westphalia and Bremen retain the old system. Berlin, Baden-Württemberg, and Lower Saxony leave open both possibilities. . . .

7-7. WEST GERMAN STUDENTS THROUGH AMERICAN EYES*

Looking at West German university life with American eyes highlights some of the differences in everyday university life between the two countries. This vivid and opinionated account of an American student illustrates some of the fundamental characteristics of university life which are not questioned by West German students. At the same time, this account also shows that mass education in the Federal Republic differs greatly from the system of mass education in other industrial states.

Last fall, a German student asked me a question I didn't understand. We were sitting together in a Heine section at the Free University here when she asked if I was going to demonstrate against the high cost of studying. Next spring, she informed me, the semester fee would be 30 Deutsche marks. Would I come afterward to her protest work group?

I didn't answer right away. I was too busy doing math in my head. Thirty Deutsche marks is $12. My sister was going to pay $1,965 for her spring semester studying literature at the University of Wisconsin. Something wasn't clear. The student left to meet her work group in the cafeteria. I left to buy some Heine poems in a bookstore. Demonstrating against a $12 fee seemed pretty silly.

But that was before I learned to figure things in terms of the German student's economy.

When German high-schoolers pass their *Abitur*— the rigorous prerequisite for higher education here—they graduate into an almost entirely subsidized existence. The title "university student" buys them the moral and legal right to be sustained by parents and state for the five years or more it usually takes to get their first degree. The state pays their tuition. Their parents must pay living expenses if they can afford to. If they can't, as is deemed the case with 30% to 35% of German

*Amity Shlaes, "Why Student Princes Live as Perpetual Paupers," *Wall Street Journal*, September 29, 1983, p. 30.

students' families, the state steps in again. One Berlin friend of mine gets a pretty typical government financial-aid packet: $260 plus rent supplement, plus discount at the public health service.

About $300 a month is something, but for my friend, and for most other 25-year-olds living in the Western world, it isn't quite enough. The only way you can get by on this sum in West Berlin is if you mooch. . . . The German student sees—he would have to be less than college material if he didn't—that it's smart to cling to his student status. Almost a quarter of the students enrolled in the Free University have been students for eight years, and their conception of reality is very often far more skewed than that of American professional students.

At fault in large measure for this stagnation is the West German government's financial-aid system. Students receiving any federal money at all—even as little as $160 a month—may earn only $2,120 a year. Thus, unless he wants to lose that $160, a student must live on $336 a month.

Nor does the antiquated and overloaded university system provide incentive to change. In the past 20 years, more and more grammar-school students were channeled into the college preparatory gymnasiums, and in turn into the universities; 500-year-old universities designed for small elites became anonymous "mass universities." Even the construction of new universities—such as those at Konstanz, Bochum, and Berlin—was inadequate to serve the rise in the number of students. In the 1970s alone, the number of students in Berlin rose 82%. The traditional German system of leaving the student's education up to the student—for his first two years at a university, a literature student does almost all his work on his own, with no paper deadlines and no tests—which worked well when universities were smaller, now often only provides opportunity for abuse.

Even greater, though, than the ripping off of German taxpayers here is the ripping off of German society. Reforms in the education system are imminent. The state of North Rhine-Westphalia plans to introduce a new three-year-only program, and tuition will in all likelihood be introduced soon nationally, but it will be too late for the generation now in its 20s. At 19, the *Abiturient,* or German college-tracked high-school graduate, knows more and explains it better than his American counterpart. Six years later, though, he lags behind. While the American is working and two years out of school, the German is, particularly if he is a humanities student, unsure of his profession and still muddling toward his first degree.

The official student line is that an "Americanization" of the German university system should be avoided at all costs, but I am not sure if all German students actually believe this. I watched a special about the American Bachelor of Arts program on German television with a German who got her degree here this spring. She was silent until the end, and then she turned around to talk about American college. "Lucky you," she said.

7-8. INTERVIEW WITH DOROTHEE WILMS, FEDERAL MINISTER FOR EDUCATION AND SCIENCE*

This interview with Minister Dorothee Wilms illustrates the changes in university policy which the CDU-led coalition government was proposing after its election victory in 1983. On a broad sepctrum of issues, Minister Wilms signals no drastic change in policy but a partial reorientation of policy. The emphasis on greater social and political equality has now been replaced by more emphasis on competition and technological advance. In the 1980s the policy agenda is evidently marked by more modest objectives than those of the reformers of the 1960s.

Zeit: Mrs. Minister, you have recently issued sixteen theses for a university policy of the 1990s. Why did you decide to do so at this time?
Wilms: I think we should address two problems. First, how do we cope with the great burden which has been placed on the universities? We want to give this generation of high-school graduates the chance to pursue university studies. That is, we want to keep the universities open. Second, we must throw the switches for future developments today. For we know already that the number of students will remain very high in the late 1980s and early 1990s.
Zeit: Is the federal government thus giving a signal that it will fully exploit its jurisdiction, in contrast to questions of secondary and vocational education where the federal government has returned many tasks to the states?

---

*"Lasst viele Blumen blühen: ZEIT-Gespräch mit dem Bundesminister für Bildung und Wissenschaft Dorothee Wilms," *Die Zeit,* December 30, 1983.

Wilms: I believe that the federal government must be involved in the shaping of university policy. It should provide general guidelines within which the individual states can pursue their specific university policies.

Zeit: Let us turn to a discussion of the sixteen theses. You have endorsed a higher profile of West German universities. Are you advocating that the German university system be made more similar to the American or French systems, with their elite and mass universities?

Wilms: No . . . [but] we should return to a situation where universities are distinguished by research priorities and a more autonomous profile. . . .

Zeit: You just mentioned the tradition of the universities. Since Humboldt we have had a tradition of preserving the unity of research and teaching. But in your theses you plead for a broader conception. Couldn't we eventually end up with two types of university professors: those who only teach and those who only do research?

Wilms: Basically I do not want to abandon the principle of the unity of research and teaching. But since we have different types of universities, the relative importance of research and teaching will unavoidably differ. . . .

Zeit: You favor more competition among the universities and thus demand for the universities more autonomy and less bureaucracy in the administration of their budget allocations and in the acquisition of funds from other sources. Don't we risk having entire universities become the playing fields for particular research groups and specific private interests?

Wilms: For starters the state must provide the basic university budget. But universities are complaining today about excessive bureaucratization in their financing systems. Here we need more flexibility. Moreover, universities, professors, research institutes and individual departments should be encouraged to raise funds from other sources that would be targeted quite specifically. . . . I believe that serious and respected researchers will make sure that they do not serve unduly any specific private interest.

Zeit: You are not convinced that codetermination in the university should be extended to include these financial questions?

Wilms: You should have a minimum of trust in the professionalism of the scientists laboring in these vineyards. And should such professional standards have disappeared, then it would indeed be very urgent to reintroduce them once again into our universities.

Zeit: In contrast to the university policy of the SPD-FDP coalition, you favor not more integration but differentiation in the university sector. You advocate that vocational training colleges acquire once again a more independent status while insisting at the same time that these colleges should be viewed as equivalent to universities. What do you mean by the term "equivalent"?

Wilms: . . . The graduates of different types of universities should have similar chances of advancement in their chosen careers. Entry salaries in the public sector and in private life should not be permitted to diverge too far. More important, graduates of vocational training colleges and other academies should have opportunities of social and professional advancement similar to those of the graduates of research universities. . . .

Zeit: In your theses you do not back comprehensive universities, even though equivalent advancement should be, and partly has been, achieved by this type of university.

Wilms: The original hopes in and aspirations for the comprehensive university have been disappointed. . . .

Zeit: Let us turn to issues of curriculum reform. This is a permanent question in West Germany's university policy. Do you have concrete ideas about what should be done? Should the universities take on a more central role?

Wilms: Many of the hopes which originally had been set in the commission for curriculum reform have been disappointed. This disappointment is very evident today. But I also think that it is a very great advantage that today we have a broad consensus that courses of study should not be extended to suit the individual student. It is urgent that we reduce, within the limits of reasonableness, the number of semesters studied. Young people should not delay unduly the start of their working life. And we need space so that we can train further those who would like to pursue a career in research and teaching. I anticipate that the Science Council will soon discuss these issues further and will offer food for thought about how to limit the duration of university studies.

Zeit: Mrs. Minister, your theses for "guidelines for a new university policy" are issued at a time when the universities have a very different concern: how to educate the "demographic bulge" of our society at a time of financial stringency. Shouldn't university teachers and students expect concrete help rather than new discussions about structural reforms?

Wilms: You should do the one and not stop doing the other. We must cope with the demographic bulge. This is foremost the task of the individual states which finance the universities. But the federal government is doing its share. We shall continue to help. In 1984 the federal allocation for university construction has been increased to 1.2 billion deutschmarks, and we are committing ourselves to this level of expenditure in our medium-term financial plans. This is a very substantial contribution in a time of empty coffers. I am delighted that my theses have found such a positive reception. Everywhere I encounter a willingness to pursue these issues further through discussion. I am therefore encouraged. But because of the pressing problems of today we should not forget those waiting for us in the future. We should not repeat the mistake of the past, to only think of today and never of tomorrow.

8 Policy in West Germany's Semisovereign State

When Chancellor Kohl took office in 1982, his program was to bring about the "Big Change" (*Die Wende*). But as the six policy case studies analyzed in this book show, the Kohl government has effected only moderate policy changes. Continuity with the policies of the Schmidt government is stronger in some areas (such as economic management, social welfare, migrant labor, and administrative reform) than in others (for example, industrial relations and university reform). But the Kohl government has not been able to match the substantial changes in policy brought about, for example, by the American, British, and French governments in the early 1980s. This continuity in policy is more surprising than that in Japan, which has not experienced any changes in the composition of its government since 1955. Furthermore, in contrast to Sweden's conservatives in 1976, the Kohl government did not have to deal with the hegemonic policies of four decades of Social Democratic rule. Changes in the partisan composition of the government are important in West Germany. Why then are these changes not translated into large-scale policy changes?

This formulation of the German Question differs from the one that students of German politics usually pose. It does not look backward (to the unconditional surrender of 1945, the Nazis' seizure of power in 1933, the start of World War I in 1914, or the unification of the German Empire in 1871) to examine the causes of Germany's tragic confrontation with modernity. Instead, it looks forward (from the election victories of the SPD-FDP coalition in 1969 and 1972 and the return of the CDU/CSU to power in 1982–83) to uncover the political structures that make incremental policy change such a plausible political response in the Federal Republic.

West Germany's semisovereign state is, in a word, the answer to this version of the German Question. Coalition governments, cooperative federalism, a wide range of parapublic institutions, and, as I argued in the chapter on administrative reform, the state bureaucracy itself are the domestic shackles that have tamed the power of the West German state. Since it also lives with powerful international constraints, the Federal Republic thus exemplifies what I have called the condition of semisovereignty.

It is easy to mistake incremental change for an incapacity to change. It is equally easy to misinterpret the West German pattern of policymaking simply as one more instance of bureaucratic inertia defeating forward-looking political leadership. There is a world of difference between incrementalism and immobilism. In his classic analysis of French bureaucracy, Michael Crozier argued (1967) that the French bureaucracy experiences systematic blockages. These blockages, Crozier suggests, account for the cycle of immobility and political upheavals which has characterized French politics since 1789. Posing the question of why West German politics does not resemble the French pattern leads us back to an analysis of the Federal Republic's semisovereign state. We can, similarly, grant that bureaucratic inertia is a factor operating in all advanced industrial states. But this leaves open the question of why some states, such as France, produce white elephants—for example, the Concorde—while West German policy moves cautiously over a couple of decades to develop new policy sectors as it did, for example, in response to issues concerning labor markets and the environment. We can answer this question not by pointing to a universal factor, such as bureaucratic inertia, but by appreciating instead the distinctive institutions of West Germany's semisovereign state which favor incrementalism over large-scale policy change.

It is, however, problematic to move from this characterization of West Germany to an evaluation of the "success" or "failure" of different policies. For several reasons, simple economic or social criteria of efficiency or effectiveness are typically misplaced. Policy choices have an effect on economic and social outcomes without determining them. A persuasive case can, for example, be made that the economic "success" of the Federal Republic may have had as much to do with luck—producing for the right international markets—as with the "rationality" of policy. Similarly, the "failure" of university reform policies may have been affected as much by long-term changes in West Germany's birth rate as by the "irrationality" of policy. Leaving aside questions of success and failure, we can view the policy choices in different sectors as the result of the institutional design of West Germany's semi-sovereign state. Within the constraints and opportunities that characterize the Federal Republic, incremental policy change, I have argued, is a politically logical choice.

The three nodes of the policy network have both a very large measure of institutional stability and good antennas for recognizing and responding to social change. The two major political parties, but especially the CDU/CSU, cut across wide segments of society. Yet marginal electoral swings matter in a centrist party system favoring government by coalition. West Germany's cooperative federalism is by no means free from blockages and rigidities. But the system of intergovernmental relations has expressed to some extent changes in the relative strength of political parties and, equally important, has not quashed new currents in local politics which express embryonic changes in society. West Germany's parapublic institutions, finally, include the major economic groups and social organizations. Social currents producing new institutions are somehow both selectively coopted and neglected by West Germany's policymaking institutions.

By focusing on the interaction between institutions and policy, I have slighted one explanatory factor (social interests) and neglected another (culture). I argued in Chapter 1 (see pp. 12–15) that the homogeneity of West German society was greatly enhanced by its defeat in World War II, partition, and the Occupation. I noted also that throughout the postwar years the "social capitalism" preferred by the Right and the "Keynesian capitalism" championed by the Left have overlapped substantially. Discussion of the policy agenda in the six case studies has reflected this important fact about West German politics. But a predominant or exclusive focus on social interests is too general for what is crucial in any analysis of policy and politics. It bypasses the policy process and thus fails to uncover how in the unending interaction between policy and politics, institutions are relegitimated.

There are three reasons for my neglect of a cultural explanation of policy and politics in the Federal Republic. First, assembling a group of West Germans around a table, one will find that in the first five minutes they all agree that culture is absolutely essential for understanding West German politics. But they will spend the rest of the hour deeply divided on whether West Germany has a culture of consensus or conflict. Second, cultural explanations explain too much. Because they focus on what is distinctive about West Germany in general, cultural explanations are too weak to sort out different outcomes in different policy sectors. Why, for example, was policy change not incremental only in the case of university reform? Finally, in the hands of the unskilled, cultural explanations easily degenerate into labeling phenomena rather than learning about them. One could, for example, argue that West German policy changes incrementally because this is what the West Germans like. Tautological reasoning will provide a ready answer for every outcome, but it does not lead to deeper understanding. By focusing on institutions, we can avoided styles of analysis that are either too general or too specific for the task at hand.

From this vantage point, fears about the erosion of West Germany's semisovereign state do not ring true. West Germany's political institutions can express political agreement on a mixture of "social capitalism" and "Keynesian capitalism" without either eliminating specific policy disagreements or suppressing new economic, social, and cultural developments. More to the point are worries about the oligopolistic style of politics which creates incremental policy changes. To include the major social organizations in policymaking is not necessarily equivalent to representing all social interests. The inability to quash or coopt new institutions can be seen, especially by established elites in old institutions, as a symbol of institutional failure rather than an act of political foresight. West Germany's semisovereign state is undeniably democratic. But as the evidence in the previous chapters shows, it is by no means clear that the West German variant of democracy follows the dictates of Anglo-Saxon liberalism. This is neither surprising nor alarming. The Allied Occupation left a deep imprint on West German politics. But its legacy accommodated itself to traditional German norms and institutional practices that helped create the semisovereign state. Unlike West Germany's authoritarian predecessors, the actions of this semisovereign state are not likely to pose a direct military threat to its neighbors in the future.

This concluding chapter first analyzes some of the challenges to the institutions that constrain large-scale policy changes, the most important of which are the Greens. In the second section it compares West German policy across the six issues previously analyzed and in the third compares West German politics to that of other states. The fourth section elaborates on my central theme, namely that West Germany's semisovereign state reflects a modification rather than an erosion of state power. To correctly interpret this modification in state power, we must view the state as a set of deeply rooted institutional relations rather than as an actor. Only then can we appreciate that lacking the power to impose its objectives in noisy political battles, West Germany's semi-sovereign state instead merges with social and political actors and thus diffuses its norms and procedures quietly. This condition of semi-sovereignty can be found as well in other industrial states. But I shall argue in the fifth and final section that its West German variant is distinguished by legal norms that diffuse conflict and thus reinforce the inclination for incremental policy change.

1. New Challenges

The institutions that create the context in which incremental policy change occurs in the Federal Republic have not been left unaffected by changes in their social and political environment. Since the legacy of the Weimar Republic and Nazi Germany was strong, established interpretations of West German politics have focused exclusively on potential threats from the extremes of the political spectrum. But it is now clear that neither the extreme Right nor the extreme Left have succeeded in building significant bases of social and institutional support. The changes that are affecting West German politics do not originate directly in the past. They reflect rather the political issues of the present (a growing tolerance for industrial strife, as I argue below) and the constraints and opportunities of the future (offered by the "new" politics of the Greens).

Some of these changes are relatively minor, such as the rise of an informal economy or of independent, decentralized self-help organizations in the area of social welfare. Other changes are global and affect capitalist democracies everywhere. In the 1970s and 1980s fears about the erosion of the "Keynesian compromise" have preoccupied other countries in addition to West Germany. Responding to small and large changes and pressing their claim for a new environmental policy, the Greens have articulated a new policy and asked for new participatory political institutions. They pose the most interesting political challenge that West Germany's semisovereign state faces today.

West German elites have developed a growing tolerance for change. This can be illustrated by comparing the reaction to the two most important strikes of the postwar period, the metal workers' strike of 1963 and the steel workers' strike of 1984 (Mangines, 1985). Although the post-war period of reconstruction had ended by 1963, labor markets remained tight with the number of unfilled jobs twice as large as the 200,000 unemployed. The strike was ostensibly fought over wages, with the employers offering a 4.5 percent increase and the union asking for 6.0 percent. On April 29 the first 100,000 metal workers walked off their jobs. The employers retaliated with lock-outs on May 1 and May 4. On May 7 the workers of North Rhine-Westphalia, West Germany's most populous state, voted in favor of strike action. On the same day Economics Minister Ludwig Erhard intervened as mediator. He and most other West Germans believed that a prolongation and further spread of industrial conflict would bring the economy to a total stand-still. Erhard summoned representatives of both sides to his office and demanded a settlement. Twelve hours later he had worked out an acceptable compromise, thus proving his mettle to the West German public.

In 1984 the West German economy was in the midst of its most severe and prolonged postwar depression. Unemployment had climbed above 2 million. The metal workers' union asked for a reduction in the workweek from 40 to 35 hours without a cut in pay. The idea was to spread less work among more workers, thus decreasing the number of unemployed. Business adamantly opposed this demand, which, it argued, would increase labor costs by 20 percent and destroy West Germany's international competitiveness. The first workers walked off their jobs on May 14, 1984. By the fourth week strike and lock-outs affected more than a quarter-million workers. On June 20 the conflict went to arbitration and six days later the chairperson of the arbitration board stepped forward with a proposal that was subsequently approved by both sides. The strike was immeasurably more costly than the one in 1963. The union reportedly lost half of its 200-million-dollar strike fund. West Germany's automobile producers lost millions of dollars each day. Yet compared to 1963, the West Germans did not view the strike in 1984 as a national catastrophe even though it lasted six times longer and was much more bitterly fought. The 1980s are thus not, as some West Germans argue, a return to the 1960s or 1950s. The "formed society" that Chancellor Erhard proposed (see Chapter 2) has not taken hold in the Federal Republic.

Some of the changes affecting West German institutions in the 1980s appear to be relatively minor. Economic recession and cutbacks in welfare spending, for example, have coincided with the spread of a shadow economy and local self-help organizations. Although little is known about its size and character, West Germany's "informal economy" is both a "cash" and an "alternative" economy. Some small producers seek to increase their income by circumventing the collection of state taxes; they insist on cash payments. Other producers want to increase work satisfaction by avoiding market exchanges: they engage in barter trade. In either of its variants, the informal economy challenges established institutions. But by all accounts it complements and energizes yet does not threaten an economy dominated by large corporations.

In the area of social welfare, new forms of social self-help organizations are being increasingly tried out. These include communes for teenagers, centers for old people, counseling services for drug users and the young, free clinics for the care and rehabilitation of the chronically ill, shelters for battered women, women's centers, and alternative schools. Although the available data are sketchy, current estimates put the number of such organizations between 5,000 and 28,000. Perhaps as much as 1 or 2 percent of the West German population participate in these self-help groups (Murswieck, 1986, pp. 191–204; Olk and Heinze, 1985, pp. 247–48). The purpose of many such groups is to provide the opportunity for cooperation in solving particular problems on the basis of voluntarism, shared responsibilities, and social solidarity. Some of these groups exist autonomously. Others seek financial support for their work and typically receive it not directly from the state but from one of the large welfare associations that disburse public funds. These self-help groups thus do not displace the traditional institutions of West Germany's welfare state. Instead they complement and add to the institutional capacities of the large-scale public and parapublic bureaucracies administering social policy (Bronke, Wenzel, and Leibfried, 1985; Windhoff-Héritier, 1982).

West Germans must cope with more fundamental challenges. For example, the 1980s have challenged the durability of the "Keynesian" compromise that has linked business and labor not only in the Federal Republic but in all of the major capitalist states since the end of World War II (Gourevitch, 1986). West Germany's unions are clearly on the defensive. Unemployment has stayed close to 2 million. Neither center-left nor center-right governments have apparently been able to do much about it. A conservative government seized power since 1982 and is pursuing policies aiming at greater deregulation and flexibility in the economy. As a result, solidarity among different groups of workers is becoming more fragile. Furthermore, the unions are having serious problems attracting young workers and organizing women and other nontraditional sectors of the working class. More generally, the unions have been slow to respond to changing values and priorities, and to cope with a growing skepticism toward technological progress and increasing awareness of environmental degradation. Finally, the unions watch uneasily as the SPD experiments with different models of cooperation with the Greens in state and local politics.

The growing number of problems which the labor movement must confront in the 1980s are evident. However, these problems point not to a breakdown of but to an adjustment in the relation between unions, business, and their allies in party politics. In 1986 the position of organized labor in the Federal Republic is arguably stronger than in the United States, Britain, France, or Japan. Only the Swedish labor movement holds a position of greater political strength. West Germany's labor laws may have constrained union militancy in times of prosperity, but they secure the unions' position in harder times. West German business, especially the big firms and the employers' associations, know that by sharply reducing the role of labor they would risk much more than they might gain. West German unions are, in the eyes of business, responsible for keeping order in the factories and preventing British-style industrial strife from spreading in the Federal Republic. Kohl's center-right coalition government does not wish to earn a reputation for having shattered West Germany's social peace. Instead, the government prefers to support piecemeal reforms.

West German politics is most visibly affected by the Greens, a hybrid between social movement and political party which is challenging West Germany's semisovereign state (Brand, 1982; Brand, Büsser, and Rucht, 1983; Capra and Spretnak, 1984; Nelkin and Pollak, 1980; Papadakis, 1984; Raschke, 1982, 1985). The Green's challenge is not restricted to specific issues such as environmental policy, nuclear power, or peace; it expresses a broader vision of politics which is at odds with West Germany's semisovereign state. In his analysis of the SPD's election victory of 1969, Heinz Hartmann argued (1970) that West Germany in the late 1960s was distinguished by the gap separating institutional immobility from attitudinal change. This argument dovetails with my analysis. In reaction to the pattern of politics and policy typical of West Germany, different social movements have been a constant feature since

1945 (Mushaben, 1985). In the 1950s rearmament and nuclear weapons became the focus of a movement that was still partially related to the SPD, at that time, the opposition. In the 1960s emergency legislation and the Great Coalition created its own extraparliamentary opposition and boosted the strength of the student movement. In the 1970s, the antinuclear movement began to challenge the leadership of all parties and producers on an issue of vital importance to West Germany's future. And in the 1980s the Greens, though small, have attracted a sufficient number of the voting public to have an important effect on the delicately balanced relations in West Germany's party system.

In the 1970s the number of people who at one time or another participated in civic action groups was probably larger than the combined membership of all the established political parties. By the end of the decade there were about 50,000 such groups (Mewes, 1983, pp. 53–54). Many of them organized around urban planning, highway construction, and broader environmental issues. They brought an unheard-of degree of democratization to West German local politics. In 1972 sixteen citizen groups founded a national umbrella organization that eventually claimed about 1,000 affiliates with a total of over 300,000 members. Dedicated to a program of decentralization, deconcentration, and simplification, these groups championed a participatory and non-hierarchical form of politics. But it was the ambitious nuclear energy program of the federal government, backed by all of the major producers, which finally triggered the emergence of a national social movement (Kitschelt, 1980). With the rise of this movement, many West Germans joined the European chorus protesting against the stationing of thousands of nuclear warheads on West German territory (Bredow, 1982). The first local and regional Green parties appeared in 1977. In 1979 in the city-state of Bremen a Green list overcame the 5 percent electoral barrier, thus gaining representation in a state parliament for the first time.

Activists organized Green parties not only in other Social Democratic urban areas but also in West Germany's more conservative, rural southwest (Kitschelt, 1986). Political independents and disenchanted former SPD supporters, as well as activists on the far Left, dominated what came to be a national party with primarily environmental concerns. They hoped to build a new progressive party that would create a bridge between ecology and socialism. But the decision to organize a national political party was more than the search of a few hundred political activists for a new organization. It should also be seen as a response to the logic of West Germany's semisovereign state. Through both mass demonstrations and court proceedings, environmental groups scored some impressive gains, slowing down, for example, the build-up of West Germany's nuclear industry and the expansion of West German airports. So far, however, the results of the Greens' efforts have fallen far short of the founders' initial optimistic expectations. Although party membership increased more than tenfold, from 3,000 in 1979 to 40,000 in 1984–85, only 1.87 percent of those voting for the Greens in the federal election of 1983 were also party members. This compares to an average of 5.3 percent for the other main parties (Kitschelt, 1986, pp. 146–47, 165–66).

Since 1980 the Greens have been wracked by dissent about their true mission (Bürklin, 1985; Feist and Liepelt, 1983; Kitschelt, 1985, 1986; Müller-Rommel, 1985). The "realists" have argued for policies that aim to share power with the SPD. The "fundamentalists" have decried such a strategy as dangerous opportunism. The party's Bundestag leadership as well as its delegates debating the issue at national conventions have remained deeply divided on this question. Between October 1985 and February 1987 one of the leaders of the realists joined the cabinet in the state of Hesse as a member of the coalition between the SPD and the Greens. The arithmetic and political impact of the Greens on West Germany's party system are great. In the 1980s the electorate has been split almost evenly between supporters of the "black-blue" coalition of the CDU/CSU-FDP and those who support the potential "red-green" coalition of the SPD and the Greens.

This combination of internal division and heterogeneity is, however, also a source of the Greens' political strength. If West Germany's other small party, the FDP, were to fall short of the 5 percent hurdle in a federal election, its supporters would probably move permanently into one of the other party camps. Yet should the Greens fail to win reelection to the Bundestag, they would survive in local politics as they have in a number of states where their electoral campaigns have been unsuccessful. For a social movement active in particular in local politics, "survival" is not defined simply in electoral terms. Survival consists rather in politicizing a range of issues neglected by the established parties and pressing a style of politics organized around the principle of direct participation rather than indirect representation. The environment, peace, or the issue of gender inequality attracts different social strata within a movement which are sufficiently broad and hetero-

geneous to resist being "organized" by any one party. The "dif-
fuseness" and the "lack of realism" that the established parties criticize
in the Greens reflect the grassroots strength the Greens enjoy in sectors
of West German society whose values have changed rapidly during the
last fifteen years.

The value change is of course not restricted to West Germany (Baker,
Dalton, and Hildebrandt, 1981; Barnes, Kaase and Allerbeck, 1979;
Conradt, 1980; Meulemann, 1983). What Ronald Inglehart has called
(1977, 1981) the "silent revolution" in the values of the electorate in
industrial democracies has had an undeniable effect in the Federal Republic. Traditional economic and religious issues are complemented by
new nonmaterial concerns and quality-of-life issues. The sources of
these changes are complex and not yet fully understood. Younger voters
respond to these new issues more readily than do older ones. Professional white-collar employees, especially teachers, are also strong supporters of the Greens. At this time, however, any inventory of the demographic and sociological profile of the "typical" Green supporter
remains incomplete. Furthermore, we do not know whether social
movements such as the Greens arise cyclically or are reactions to a
specific combination of economic and political events. Finally, value
changes are occurring constantly. For example, since the early 1980s (in
contrast to the 1970s), West German youths have become once again
very achievement-oriented and interested in traditional values. But it is
too early to tell how this "silent reaction" will transform West German
society, and how it will affect West Germany's political parties in the
next decade.

What is certain is that, for the time being, the Greens present the only
open challenge to the ·political arrangements of West Germany's semisovereign state. Unconventional in their political strategy and tactics,
they do not shy away from raising politically taboo subjects. For thirty-
five years none of the West German parties had pushed the Allied forces
in West Berlin to account for the annual appropriations voted them by
the Bundestag. With the sum reaching 1.4 billion deutschmarks in
1986, the Greens did—albeit unsuccessfully (*Der Spiegel,* Jan. 6,
1986, pp. 24–25). Similarly, the Greens were the harshest critics of the
financial scandals that have implicated all of the established parties in
the 1980s. At the risk of losing a larger share of their total income than
any of the other parties, the Greens filed an unsuccessful lawsuit with
the Constitutional Court charging that the 1984 Party Finance Law was

unconstitutional (*Der Spiegel,* March 17, 1986, pp. 53–57). It is thus not totally surprising that, to the consternation and outrage of many West Germans, in the winter of 1984 State Secretary Carl-Dieter Spranger directed West Germany's internal security police forces to forward to him whatever material they might have on any of the Green members of the Bundestag. The Greens and the established political elites operating in West Germany's semisovereign state are, as these examples show, separated by a wide gap.

Indeed, the political culture of the Greens is suspect to many segments of West Germany's political elite precisely because it appears to offer a real alternative to the policies and politics of the semisovereign state. This political culture is a reaction to West Germany's existing political arrangements. Green politics distances itself from the state, markets, and organized group hierarchies. A triumph of consciousness over institutions, it creates both new pressures and new opportunities for the institutions shaping policy and politics in West Germany. For example, established parties have finally responded with alacrity to the issue of environmental degradation which they had downplayed in the 1970s. But the new political culture creates divisions even within the established parties as well as between them and the Greens (Feist and Liepelt, 1983). In the wake of the nuclear disaster at Chernobyl in the spring of 1986, Chancellor Kohl went so far as to institute the new Ministry for the Environment. Administrative courts are revising some of the rulings that affect the grounds on which social groups are awarded standing in courts. West German firms have responded to new "alternative" consumers, for example, in the food they market, the newspapers and books they print, and in the clothes they design. The "new politics" of the Greens attracts a highly educated, new middle class reared under conditions of postwar affluence. But the issues of the new social movements clustered around the Greens often attract much broader though diffuse support. The rise of the Greens can be plausibly viewed as a reaction to the policy and politics of West Germany's semisovereign state. The response of some of West Germany's most important institutions, many informed observers argue, appears to confirm the possibility that "the Green movement will suffer from the typical German etatist bias to channel protest via centralized institutions" (von Beyme, 1986, p. 171).

2. Six Policy Cases Compared

I have developed one line of argument about the intersection of policy and politics in West Germany. The Federal Republic has a distinctive institutional configuration: a decentralized state and a centralized society are connected by political parties, an interlocking politics between different levels of government, and numerous parapublic institutions. This institutional structure creates particular capacities and incapacities in different policy sectors. Although I have traced policy developments only in six sectors, I have drawn in my analysis on a much larger number. Chapter 1, for example, presents some policy material on environment, safety, and health policies (pp. 31–34). Furthermore, the section on cooperative federalism (pp. 45–58) builds on the extensive research of West German scholars on a large number of policy sectors including manpower, vocational training, agriculture, regional development, urban renewal, social housing, transportation, university and hospital construction, environmental protection, and revenue sharing. As we found, each of the six case studies was like a Russian doll. Under closer scrutiny policy sectors break into segments that connect one policy problem to another. Although it would be foolish to claim that I have covered all important policy issues, I have not tried to make my case with a biased set of examples.

Foreign policy, however, is conspicuously absent from this book. Adenauer's Western policy in the early 1950s and Brandt's Eastern policy in the early 1970s were anything but incremental. Thus foreign policy might seem to refute the argument I have developed. I chose to exclude case material on foreign policy primarily because of the format of the series of which this book is a part. But had foreign policy been included, it would have offered important corroborating evidence for my main thesis. Both Adenauer and Brandt used foreign policies of integration with the West and accommodation to the East as a way of securing their position in power. Adenauer implemented his policy in the early years of the Federal Republic when West German institutions had not yet taken a firm hold. Indeed, one of the most careful studies of the foreign policy process in the early 1950s talks of the "vacuum" in which Adenauer executed foreign policy almost single-handedly (Baring, 1969, 1971). Brandt's Eastern policy, on the other hand, escaped the restrictions that, as I have argued, West German politics imposed on virtually all other ambitious reform policies of his government. In both cases, foreign policy promised substantial long-term political gains for a particular social alliance and coalition government. Such gains are much more difficult to achieve in the institutional framework shaping West Germany's domestic politics. Adenauer and Brandt succeeded because their foreign policy strategies exploited opportunities in the international state system which West Germany's domestic structures simply did not afford.

The compelling logic of West Germany's domestic politics is also illustrated by how the opposition reacted to the foreign policy successes of Adenauer and Brandt. Because it was realistic and wanted to enhance its electoral chances, the SPD embraced the policy of Western integration after 1959. When Brandt became foreign minister in 1966 and chancellor in 1969, continuity in the policy of Western integration was beyond doubt. Similarly, after its electoral defeat of 1972 the CDU/CSU gradually came to accept the premise of the Eastern policy. When the CDU/CSU returned to power in 1982–83, Chancellor Kohl continued the Eastern policy of the previous government. Indeed, Franz-Josef Strauss, leader of the CSU and one of the most conservative politicians in West Germany, negotiated two substantial loans with East Germany. This continuity in foreign policy across different governments supports my basic argument: incrementalism rather than large-scale policy change typifies West German politics.

The six areas examined here in depth—economic management, labor relations, migrant labor, social welfare, administrative reform, and university reform—are like the different windows of a house. Each window provides us with a different glimpse of the inside. Those who argue that the political logic of the problem is more important than the political logic of the country would expect the furnishings of each room to differ drastically in shape and color; after all, the living room serves a different purpose than the dining room or the bedroom. Those who argue that the political logic of the country is more important than the political logic of the problem, on the other hand, would expect a uniform style throughout the house because the same people live, eat, and sleep in the different rooms. Some, finally, might agree with my position. Even though the political logic of the country is more compelling than the political logic of the problem, that country logic does not explain all policy cases equally well; deviations and exceptions that do exist·must, however, be systematically accounted for. Although each house has a distinctive style, it also has a couple of rooms filled with odd pieces and comfortable junk. Needless to say, these are not the first rooms shown to the guests when they arrive.

How do the six case studies compare to one another? Table 8-1 summarizes some of the important characteristics of the different policy sectors. As the first four columns indicate, the institutional structures of the state are decentralized, while the structure of society is centralized. That parapublic institutions are active in all four policy sectors attests to their importance in the West German policymaking process.

In the four sectors of economic and social policy unavoidable tensions exist between institutional stability and policy stability. These are brought about by a system of coalition governments, cooperative federalism, and powerful parapublic institutions, on the one hand, and political and social change, on the other. Policymakers dealing with questions of economic management and industrial relations have a strong incentive to avoid partisan controversy. In the area of economic management this depoliticization is achieved by a system of checks and balances within the state executive as is illustrated, for example, by the important roles played by the Bundesbank and the Council of Economic Experts. The situation is more complex in the area of industrial relations. Since the early 1950s political controversy about the question of parity codetermination in corporate boardrooms has been greater than controversy about the system of factory councils in the plant. Business, the CDU/CSU, and the FDP strongly opposed parity codetermination. They viewed it as an attempt by the labor movement to enlarge its power base in the private economy. The institutionalization and subsequent amendment of the West German system of works councils was less con-

TABLE 8-1   Institutional Structures in Six Policy Sectors

	Economic Management	Industrial Relations	Social Welfare	Migrant Labor	Administrative Reform	University Reform
Decentralized State	Yes	Yes	Yes	Yes	Yes	Yes
Centralized Society	Yes	Yes	Yes	Yes	No	Yes/No
Parapublic Institutions	Yes	Yes	Yes	Yes	No	Yes/No
Party Conflict	No	Yes/No	No	No	No	Yes
Segmentation Tendencies	Yes	Yes	Yes	Yes	Yes/No	Yes
Incremental Policy Change	Yes	Yes	Yes	Yes	Yes	No

troversial because it reinforced, under the legal auspices of the state, one pillar of the system of parapublic institutions which linked all private and public actors. Continuity was also brought about by a far-reaching regulation of industrial relations through the system of codetermination as well as the mediation or adjudication of labor grievances by the labor courts.

The resultant tendency toward depoliticization is also evident in policies affecting social welfare and migrant workers. On these questions the state delegates important tasks to other parapublic institutions such as the social security funds, the Federal Employment Office, and religious as well as secular welfare associations. But depoliticization is fragile, especially in the harder economic times experienced by the Federal Republic in the 1970s and 1980s. Yet despite persistently high levels of unemployment, the steel workers' strike of 1984, cutbacks in welfare spending, and a mounting tide of "economic refugees" from Third World countries, West German institutions continue to downplay overt conflicts and to favor incremental policy change.

Policy innovation has occurred in two spurts in the Federal Republic. Until the mid-1950s many basic pieces of legislation were passed, some with bitter conflict—for example, codetermination in 1951–52—others in an atmosphere of relative political calm—for example, the pension reform of 1957. A second period of policy innovation coincided with the Great Coalition of the CDU/CSU and the SPD between 1966 and 1969. In the 1970s and early 1980s the intensity of partisan conflict between the CDU and the SPD was probably higher than it had been in the 1960s. Yet after its landslide victory in 1972, the SPD never delivered on its promised program of domestic reform. When the CDU assumed office after its electoral victory in 1983, continuities in policy were again much more striking than discontinuities. The structure of West Germany's semisovereign state favors an incremental policy even when the electoral mandate for change is as great as it was in 1972 and in 1983.

Social changes seriously test the capacities of West German institutions to deal with issues in increments. West Germans are increasingly talking about the rise of the "two-thirds society," a figure of speech that describes a situation in which economic, social, and political dualism is increasing (Goldthorpe, 1984). This situation is readily apparent in all six policy sectors. The government's commitment to a full-employment economy has been replaced by substantial structural unemployment. It is government policy to enhance flexibility in labor markets. Corporations rely increasingly on small subcontractors and part-time or marginal labor. This encourages a new form of plant syndicalism with most of the benefits accruing to a firm's permanent, native, full-time, and typically male labor force. In the 1970s the gap between welfare recipients and the rest of the West German population widened. In the harsher economic climate of the 1980s migrant workers especially from Turkey and Third World countries face increasing discrimination. To date, however, these various tendencies toward economic and social segmentation have not yet created divisions wide enough to overcome the proclivity of West German institutions for incremental change. Dualism coexists with the semisovereign state.

Table 8-1 illustrates that administrative and university reform policies were framed in institutional arenas that deviated significantly from economic and social issues as well as from one another. In administrative reform a decentralized state was a target of reform. The absence of centralized institutions in the private sector was irrelevant. Administrative reform of state institutions, we found, was largely sheltered from the direct influence of social forces. Parapublic institutions played no prominent role in this problem area. West Germany's state institutions resisted a number of attempts to bring about wholesale change. But they accommodated a number of incremental policy adjustments, such as the "system Globke." Administrative reform policies generated little partisan controversy beyond a very restricted political elite. Segmentation tendencies were noticeable only in the shift of welfare cuts from federal and state levels to local governments charged with the administration of welfare programs. In brief, although the institutional constraints differed from those evident in the other four economic and social issues, the West German penchant for incremental policy change was the same.

In light of the large-scale change that they effected, university reform policies, on the other hand, differed from the other five cases. The decentralization of the state impeded reform. Uncharacteristically for the Federal Republic, university reform policies were enacted at the urging of a large number of organized social interests. In contrast, for example, to the case of migrant labor, parapublic institutions involved in university reform lacked the strong backing of the major economic interest groups which they command in other policy sectors. Without such support, these institutions turned out to be political arenas rather than political actors. Party conflicts about the content and pace of reform were very important. With the dramatic expansion in the number of university graduates as well as a shrinking job market, tendencies toward social segmentation increased in the 1980s. But the key to our understanding of why only in this one case large-scale policy change proved possible lies in the default of two important institutional restraints. Neither coalition governments at the federal level nor parapublic institutions backed by major producers countered the social pressure for substantial change. Because of its tradition of autonomy under state auspices, the university proved to be relatively open to such pressure. As a consequence, in less than two decades, West Germany's university system was transformed from an elite system to a mass system.

Compared to the four other economic and social issues, several features make the university reform case anomalous. The context of policy differs. The last period of major university reform predated Germany's Industrial Revolution rather than coinciding with it, as was true of the other four issues. Since the Basic Law leaves all questions of cultural policy, including education, to the eleven states, the policy agenda was shaped by conflicting party objectives debated in public rather than by bargaining behind closed doors. Significantly, one of the greatest bones of contention was the idea of a comprehensive university. Although less controversial than the idea of comprehensive schools in secondary education, the proposal for a comprehensive university was opposed by conservative politicians because it appeared to alter the basic pattern of social stratification. In the policy process, groups of producers as well as several of the university-affiliated interest groups remained uncharacteristically uninvolved in policymaking. This lack of involvement contrasts sharply with the integrated network of groups and institutions which emerged in the mid-1950s to manage West Germany's policy toward research and development (R&D). The consequence of university policy differed, therefore, not only from the four economic and social issues but also from the stalled reform of secondary schools as well as the incremental evolution of R&D policy.

There is a final lesson to be learned from these six case studies. The political logic underlying West German institutions and the criterion of democratic participation do not necessarily converge. We could summarize the West German version of the democratic dilemma in policymaking by paraphrasing the song by Mick Jagger and the Rolling Stones, "You Can't Always Get What You Want." One might well argue that in the policy cases which deviate from West Germany's characteristic institutional structure, such as university reform, the West Germans are getting what they want but not what they need. In other cases, such as economic policy, the West Germans are getting what they need but not what they want. In some settings, political parties interacting with other institutions are part of a policy solution that does not match liberal norms of democratic participation. In other settings, political parties reinforce the policy problem despite and sometimes because they fulfill their mandate of democratic participation.

3. West German Politics in Comparative Perspective

Politics and policy in West Germany's semisovereign state bear more resemblance to some countries than to others. I have argued elsewhere (Katzenstein, 1984, 1985) that in the structural determinants of politics West Germany's greatest political affinities lie not with large or medium-sized countries, such as the United States, Japan, Britain, and France, but with Sweden and the other rich small European states: Norway, Denmark, the Netherlands, Belgium, Austria, and Switzerland. Like the Federal Republic, these states favor incremental policymaking and deliberate experimentation over programs for large-scale change. The small European states typify the politics of democratic corporatism in five ways. First, their open international economies create a perception of vulnerability that is conducive to political compromises and finds expression in a system of social partnership between business and labor. Second, like other major interest groups, business and labor have centralized organizations and represent different social and economic constituencies. Third, in the process of bargaining, political elites in small states avoid stalemate by seeking links with other actors across diverse issues. Fourth, ideologically moderate political parties play an important role in corporatist politics. Elections act as periodic shocks for a system that otherwise might easily degenerate into a cozy cartel of large interest groups. Finally, the historical origins of democratic corporatism lie in the 1930s and 1940s. Traditions of political accommodation, the Great Depression, the fear of Nazism, and World War II pushed political elites in the small European states to institutionalize a consensual politics and a preference for incremental policy change.

In many ways policy and politics in the Federal Republic resemble this pattern. Reduced in size since 1945, West Germany is still experiencing great international vulnerability. Little needs to be said about the military vulnerability of a country that has lived at the center of the Cold War. West Germany is, however, also very vulnerable to shocks in the international economy. Its main manufacturing sectors—automobiles, chemicals, electrical equipment, and machinery—sell one-half to two-thirds of their total production abroad. Second, West Germany has a fully developed system of social partnership to which, despite the changes of the 1970s and 1980s, its ideological and political commitment remains strong. Third, its system of groups is mostly centralized and, as in the small European states, broadly representative of social and economic interests. Indeed, in many instances West German law provides a legal framework for centralized bargaining between interest groups, state bureaucracies, and political parties. Fourth, ideological moderation distinguishes the major parties in West Germany. Finally, as in the small European states, the transformation in West German politics brought about by the cataclysmic changes of the 1930s and 1940s built on historical traditions favoring corporatist-style accommodations.

Among the small European states, furthermore, there exist two types of corporatism, liberal and social. Switzerland and Austria, respectively, represent each of these types (Katzenstein, 1984, 1985, pp. 125–29). Switzerland's powerful, internationally oriented business community collaborates with a less powerful and relatively decentralized labor movement. The Swiss state is small and its power, except during times of crisis, is remarkably weak. Switzerland's referendum democracy undercuts the vitality of its political parties. Moreover, a strong federal system creates a relatively decentralized politics. In Austria a strong and united labor movement collaborates with a business community that is largely nationalized. The Austrian state is large. Political parties play a central role in national politics, the focus for which is Vienna. Significantly, the Federal Republic shares important traits with both of its Central European neighbors. Its business community is strong and oriented toward world markets, like that of Switzerland. And a relatively strong federalism makes for a decentralized politics. As in Austria, unions and political parties are relatively strong. Finally, West Germany shares with both Switzerland and Austria a penchant for political stability through incremental policy change. If we consider Switzerland and Austria to be exemplars of liberal and social corporatism, respectively, we may call West Germany a third, statist variant of democractic corporatism.

Although the case for characterizing West German politics as a variant of corporatism is strong, it is not fully compelling. For reasons of size alone, for example, policy networks in West Germany are much less tight than in Switzerland, Austria, and the other small European states. In federal politics, except for the duration of the Great Coalition (1966– 69), policy bargaining across different issues has been more difficult. West German–style corporatism is thus more fragile. More important, in democratic corporatism actors endowed with differential power resources and bargaining skills tend to narrow political inequalities. In both Switzerland and Austria this has had effects on state power utterly uncharacteristic of West German politics (Katzenstein, 1984, pp. 133– 61). In times of crisis the Swiss grant the federal executive extraordinary powers for defining and implementing policy. Beneath the liberal veil of Switzerland's corporatism, the concentrated power of the state can be brought to bear on pressing economic and social problems. Since 1949 West German politics simply has not shown any similar trust in state power. West Germany has instead experienced prolonged political battles over the adoption of emergency legislation, passed finally by the Great Coalition in 1968. Conversely, Austria's political parties have penetrated the state bureaucracy so fully that partisan patronage has robbed the state of almost all vestiges of autonomy. Patronage politics occurs in some of West German states and in local politics but is largely absent in national politics. Thus neither Switzerland's artificial enhancement of state power nor Austria's deliberate neutralization resembles the taming of the power of West Germany's semisovereign state.

A comparison with Britain and France, the two other medium-sized welfare states in Western Europe, also helps to identify the specific institutional features of West Germany's semisovereign state (Ashford, 1981, 1982). In the movie *The Mouse That Roared* Peter Sellers conveyed the message that it pays to lose a war and then rebuild, as did the West Germans, with the aid of the victors. Mancur Olson has developed a similar argument. He claims (1982) that the shock of losing a war disrupts the tight grip of special interest groups on the body politic. Reduced institutional sclerosis in the wake of a lost war is for Olson the precondition for West Germany's success and Britain's failure. My institutional analysis of the policy and politics of West Germany does not, however, support Olson's claim. A set of varied institutions links state and society and represents diverse interests in the Federal Republic. Centralized and powerful interest groups are represented directly in the political parties and in Bundestag committees dealing with matters of special concern to them. The force of habit as well as of law assure these groups of privileged access to the state bureaucracy. West Germany's parapublic institutions typically delegate political authority and limit political participation. These institutional arrangements have created a political context that is supportive of rather than inimical to incremental policy change. Compared to the major policy departures that appear probable in Britain and France, West Germany's incremental approach is less prone to errors.

My emphasis on the condition of semisovereignty gains support from comparisons between West Germany and the world's two large capitalist states, the United States and Japan. In the United States the federal government turns over responsibility for the articulation of its objectives in many instances to the market. It often relies on litigation to enforce its will. The market is a structure that the state controls only with difficulty. Because of the arms'-length relation between the public and the private sector, litigation is in fact the only instrument that the United States government commands fully (Vogel, 1986). The autonomous ability of the American state to formulate many of its objectives is thus small, its ability to implement policy, brittle.

In Japan bureaucrats and politicians articulate state objectives in full awareness of but without subordinating them to the dictates of the market. Litigation is of minimal importance because varied and close relations with important social groups give the state many instruments for achieving its objectives. Compared to the United States, the Japanese state formulates its policy objectives more autonomously and implements policy more effectively. In contrast to West Germany, political legalism is considered illegitimate in the United States and unnecessary in Japan. Litigation is an accepted political tactic in America, but the legalization of politics through judicial norms and state institutions is not. Japan typically relies on extralegal methods of containing conflict. When these methods break down, political legalism offers no oil for calming political waters.

I have shown in this book that in West Germany the state bureaucracy operates through a policy network that permits political leaders and bureaucrats to hammer out policies together with the leaders of the major private-sector institutions and political parties. Parapublic institutions rather than unregulated markets or an interventionist state often harbor the secret to the convergence of limited power and incremental policy change which characterizes West Germany's semisovereign state.

4. West Germany's Semisovereign State

West Germans use many terms to refer to their state: lawful state (*Rechtsstaat*), federal state (*Bundesstaat*), welfare state (*Wohlfahrts-staat, Sozialstaat*), party-run state (*Parteienstaat*). Legal theorists searching for one basic principle of constitutional law may find this situation perplexing. Students of state institutions on the other hand can infer from this abundance of terms that nobody in the Federal Republic disputes the existence of the state. Whatever term West Germans may use to label the state, most of them agree that the authoritarian state (*Obrigkeitsstaat*) that characterized Germany in the past is no longer the central institution organizing West German politics.

The term "semisovereignty," which I have used to characterize the West German state, is distinguished by three institutional nodes—coalition governments, intergovernmental relations, and parapublic institutions—that instill political caution and a preference for incremental policy change. These nodes date back to different historical eras. The principle of territorial "self-administration" emerged between the seventeenth and nineteenth centuries; it still shapes West Germany's system of cooperative federalism. Drawing on established traditions, the representation of interest groups in the system of parapublic institutions spread in the late nineteenth century. Although political parties formed in the nineteenth century, they did not become fully accepted as institutions of democratic governance until after 1945. Defeat in World War II, the Occupation, and partition have left West Germany with a special international status. Its politics is deeply penetrated by international forces. West Germany's external sovereignty remains distinctively incomplete. Relying on policy material for empirical evidence, I have argued that a similar condition obtains in West Germany's domestic politics. With the distinction between state and society blurred, social forces have gained wide access to state institutions while making themselves available as conduits for the diffusion of state norms and political practices.

In interpreting contemporary West German politics, how should we conceive of this fusion of state and society so typical of the condition of semisovereignty? Take, for example, Josef Stingl, former head of the Federal Employment Office in Nuremberg. Formally he exercised his power under the control of the Labor Ministry. Yet during the 1970s

Stingl enjoyed virtual immunity from government interference. In the words of a senior civil servant, " 'any criticism from the federal government would have generated an uproar in defense of the principle of self-administration. . . . About Stingl I will not make any public statements; otherwise I find myself attacked as if I had criticized the Pope' " (*Der Spiegel,* April 3, 1978, pp. 65–68). But this is only one side of the coin. The other side is the fact that private groups participating in West Germany's parapublic institutions and thus in policymaking are often considered "public." In the area of social welfare, for example, "people tend to regard all institutions as state-run. Social policy makers may differentiate between public and voluntary agencies. But in the general view of things . . . this distinction is relatively unimportant" (Bauer, 1978, p. 9).

This example encapsulates what I take to be a general point. It is implausible to view the West German state as an actor that imposes its will on civil society. It is more useful instead to conceive of the state as a structure of relationships within and between each of the three nodes that together create a propensity for incremental policy change. The ability of the West German state to impose its objectives on other actors is thus weak. But because it has drawn so many "private" actors into its political orbit, it is at the same time strong. Semisovereignty is not, however, a condition unique to West German politics. Rather, I would argue, this condition is diffused more broadly among industrial states. For reasons of history and international politics, West Germany stands out among the large and medium-sized capitalist states (such as the United States, Britain, Japan, and France) as an exemplar of semisovereignty. History has endowed West Germany with a generous dose of state tradition; and international politics has rendered traditional pillars of state power, such as the military, largely irrelevant. As a result, the power of the West German state has not been broken but transformed. It affords us a particularly clear view of the contemporary state.

If we were to think of the West German state as an actor, we would stress its impotence. But in this book I have conceived of it instead as a set of institutional relations linking the public and the private sector which impinges on politics. I have therefore emphasized its omnipresence (Evans, Rueschemeyer, and Skocpol, 1985). This omnipresence of the semisovereign state, I argue below, shapes virtually all aspects of West German politics. Unsurprisingly, we can discern the semisovereign state at its very core, in the changing mission of West Germany's police forces. But it is also reflected at the periphery, in the character of oppositional social movements and the Social Democratic Left. Finally, West Germany's semisovereign state has indelibly fused with the political parties that have played on the center stage of West German politics since 1945.

Police

Monopoly over the internal means of violence is, as Max Weber noted long ago, an essential, defining characteristic of the modern state. West Germany is no exception to this generalization (Busch et al., 1985; Funk et al., 1984; Landfried, 1985; Linnan, 1984; Thomaneck, 1985; Werkentin, 1984). After 1945 West Germany was compelled to "de-police" many policy sectors. Thus the traditionally strong role of the administrative police has diminished sharply. Administrative functions for maintaining order (such as issuing passports and identity cards), enforcing regulations (concerning prices, trade, commerce, building permits, roads, hunting, fishing) and supervising health, veterinary, and other civil matters are now left to other parts of the state bureaucracy (Thomaneck, 1985, p. 154). The maintenance of law and order thus has become the exclusive task of the West German police. In fact, however, the division of labor between the police and other state agencies is not so simple. The police are called into action in crisis situations that the welfare bureaucracy cannot handle on its own, such as the collection of fines, the forcible transferral of individuals into mental institutions, or the arrest of juvenile delinquents. Although individually these instances are exceptional in the daily life of any one state agency, together they amount to a substantial share of the total work of the police (Funk et al., 1984, pp. 188–89).

But there exists a second and more significant overlap between the police and other state agencies. The traditional task of the police was to defend public order against immediate and present danger. In the 1960s and 1970s this task increasingly was redefined to prevent threats to public order from arising in the first place. This change in mission coincided with various "crises" of public order in West Germany: student demonstrations and the extraparliamentary opposition in the late 1960s, waves of terrorist attacks in the 1970s, and antinuclear demonstrations in the late 1970s and 1980s. But the new mission also appears to be one additional manifestation of the redefinition of the state as a social service institution. In the mid-1980s a decade-long debate about a new, comprehensive police law remained inconclusive. But through various piecemeal reforms the police has de facto been given its new, preventive task.

The student demonstrations of the late 1960s initiated a process in which the police force reoriented itself away from its preparation for extreme situations approximating civil war to the more mundane task of day-to-day supervision and control of mass demonstrations. As a result, security forces reorganized themselves, changed their equipment and training, and adjusted their strategy and tactics. For a more "efficient" and "adequate" monitoring of reality, the police force now relies on computerized data archives that contain vast amounts of information about individuals (Busch et al., 1985, pp. 115–46). In 1978, for example, the criminal police stored information on 200,000 suspects and 700,000 fingerprints. The databank included information on situations the police considered to be potential security risks, such as twenty- to thirty-year-old people sharing apartments. A West German news magazine estimates that all of the security services combined store information on several million individuals, or about 20 percent of the West German adult population (Funk et al., 1984, pp. 181, 185–86). Since only fragmentary information about the extent of surveillance is part of the public record, such estimates are notoriously unreliable. But there can be little doubt that the computer revolution has vastly increased the quantity of readily stored information accessible to the police. Indeed, in the 1970s West German criminologists were at the forefront of developing entirely new methods of police investigation. These methods involved the construction of elaborate statistical profiles of probable suspects which could be matched against data on real individuals. The doctrine of preventing security risks before they arise endangers traditional civil liberties. In his novel *The Lost Honor of Katharina Blum* (1975), subsequently made into a movie, Nobel Prize winner Heinrich Böll has painted a grim picture of the potentially grave consequences of these developments for West German democracy.

Like all other states, West Germany's semisovereign state has not relinquished its monopoly over the application of domestic coercion. The "depolicing" of many sectors of society after 1945 and the move to a doctrine of preventive police intervention in the 1970s do not necessarily mean that coercion has somehow become less necessary in West Germany's semisovereign state. The total personnel of all police forces increased from 165,000 in 1965 to 217,000 in 1978, and relative to total public expenditures, the cost of internal security has remained a relatively constant 3–4 percent since 1951 (Funk et al., 1984, p. 180; Landfried, 1985, p. 212).

The Greens and the SPD

West Germany's ecology movement has also been profoundly shaped by West Germany's semisovereign state (Greve, 1984; Nelkin and Pollak, 1980). Since this social movement found itself excluded from the deliberations of government bureaucrats, as in other countries West German ecologists turned to the courts. Federal legislation passed in 1976 facilitated this political strategy. It provided a rationale for courts to delay the construction of nuclear power plants for reasons of safety and inadequate sites for nuclear waste disposal. However, compared, for example, to the United States, the legal strategy of West German ecologists was seriously constrained by the more limited access they could gain to the court system in the 1970s. In contrast to the United States, class action suits were not possible in the Federal Republic. Standing in court was granted only to claimants with a direct and tangible interest, such as property or individual freedom. Abstract principles or intangibles such as general health, a clean environment, or the safety of future generations did not constitute sufficient grounds for pressing legal action. By forming their own political party, ecological groups hoped to increase through electoral politics the attention and leverage that West Germany's bureaucracy and legal system had accorded them only in part. The ideology of the Greens incorporates key elements of the ideology of German statism which, at the same time, it seeks to transcend (Kvistad, 1985). In line with this older ideology, the Greens view politics as a source of public morality, a problem-solving process for achieving consensus, and an object of suspicion if left to political parties. The Greens, to be sure, are trying to articulate a conception of grassroots political action which breaks radically with West Germany's semisovereign state. But in the process of doing so they also illustrate the omnipresence of that state.

The presence of West Germany's semisovereign state is also well illustrated where, at first glance, it may seem least apparent, among the Social Democrats. In the 1970s, for example, the SPD became a strong supporter of the policy of domestic security (Dyson, 1975; Kvistad, 1984, 1985; Landfried, 1985). Forty years after the Nazis eradicated from the state bureaucracy and the professions what they regarded as subversive elements, an SPD government dedicated to the extension of democracy joined hands with the CDU/CSU opposition in its support for the legalized screening of civil service applicants. This erosion of civil liberties in West Germany in the 1970s began as a defense against the alleged "long march" of left-wing radicals and reformers through West Germany's educational institutions. It accelerated in response to the terrorist pressure of the Baader-Meinhof group and subsequent generations of Red Army cadres.

Admittedly, the Federal Republic remained a *Rechtsstaat*. At the height of the terrorist wave, for example, the debate about preventive detention was brief, conducted in low voices, and restricted to conservative circles. No West German state government has tried to suppress the Communist party, an action for which ample legal grounds have existed ever since the Constitutional Court ruled on the issue in 1956. Indeed, compared to West Germany's Communist witch-hunt in the 1950s, civil liberties were more secure in the 1970s. But West Germany lacks a strong liberal tradition and an informal elite consensus that, as in other countries, discriminates informally against the employment of political radicals in the public sector. Instead, West Germany's political elite relies on a legalistic formalization of administrative procedures for dealing with difficult political issues. In any case, the 1970s are noteworthy not for the courageous defense of liberal norms of privacy but for the speed with which administrative regulations were tightened in the interest of internal security. This restrictive policy was inaugurated and supervised neither by authoritarian landowners, nor aggressive generals, nor antisemitic Nazis. Instead, well-intentioned SPD reformers implemented a policy at both federal and state levels which permitted state officials to scrutinize the private lives of hundreds of thousands of citizens. The SPD's support of this decision may have been defensive (based on worry over the party's public image of being trustworthy of governing state institutions), offensive (based on a strong state mentality in social and economic affairs which is supportive also of state strength in security affairs), or otherwise motivated (Schmidt, 1980, pp. 75–77, 112–24). Whatever its motive, when the SPD saw state security endangered, it rushed to defend state institutions.

Political Parties

The presence of West Germany's semisovereign state is also felt throughout the party system. West German parties are institutions that both represent social interests in state institutions and mediate state influence throughout society (Dyson, 1977, 1979). To put it boldly, semi-sovereignty is reflected in the conjoining of the party-run state with statist parties. This pervasive trait of West German politics characterizes the relation between political parties and a number of different institutions and political arrangements: the Constitutional Court, the Bundesrat, the civil service, the system of party finance, and the character of West Germany's political class.

The autonomous and powerful position of West Germany's Constitutional Court is open to party influence at one point, the initial appointment of the judges. Half of the members of the Court are elected by the Bundestag, half by the Bundesrat. Party representation on the Bundestag's prestigious judicial selection committee is proportionate to party strength. Unlike all other Bundestag committees, it derives its legitimacy from the Basic Law. The other half of the members of the Court are elected by the Bundesrat as a whole, with a two-thirds vote required for successful election. In reality the parties in the Bundestag and the Bundesrat negotiate with one another beforehand about the selection of their preferred candidates. The politicization of the appointment process has been a source of intense controversy in the past. But the opposition party is assured of a number of appointments; the rigorous selection criteria exclude underqualified candidates; the judges are selected for twelve-year, nonrenewable terms; and retirement at the age of sixty-eight is mandatory. These provisions limit the possibility of politicization. For example, seven of the sixteen judges on the Court retired in 1986 and 1987. But American-style charges of Kohl "packing" the court were not heard.

At the same time, however, the Court ultimately controls the political parties. Article 21 of the Basic Law grants West Germany's political parties a constitutional right to "participate in forming the political will of the people." Yet this constitutional rule, unique among the advanced industrial states, remains subject to the Court's approval. The Court is the guardian of the democratic character of political parties. "Antidemocratic" organizations can be outlawed. This happened in the 1950s when the Court outlawed both a neo-Nazi party and the Communist party because they were deemed "antidemocratic." These rulings warned other groups to stay within the bounds of legitimate opposition. But they also illustrated the final and decisive power that the Constitutional Court held over the party system.

The Bundesrat similarly illustrates that West Germany is not only a party-run state but also endowed with statist parties. When the SPD-

FDP coalition was elected in 1969, the CDU/CSU opposition relied on the Bundesrat, which it controlled, to oppose or modify the domestic reforms of the new government in areas such as foreign policy, marriage and divorce, sexual offense and abortion, urban development and land use, taxation and university reform (Schmidt, 1978). The SPD-FDP government dominating the Bundestag was increasingly forced to bargain with the opposition in the Conference Committee, which consisted of eleven members each of the Bundestag and the Bundesrat. Committee members operated in secret and are released from the instruction of the individual state governments, on the one hand, and the shackles of party discipline, on the other. Institutional decentralization encouraged a fusion of power. Between 1972 and 1974, for example, that committee ruled on a record number of ninety-six occasions—more than in the entire period of 1949–72 (Pulzer, 1978, p. 202). This pattern of opposition politics acted as a brake on the SPD-FDP program of domestic reforms. By 1976, after a string of election victories in various states, the CDU/CSU majority in the Bundesrat had increased from one to eleven votes, thus forcing the federal government to compromise on many of its legislative programs. Ten years later the situation was almost reversed. A CDU/CSU-FDP coalition government in Lower Saxony was reelected with a slender one-vote majority in the state parliament. Had the SPD instead been able to form a government, the majority in the Bundesrat would have swung from the CDU/CSU to the SPD. As the government's major opposition, the SPD was planning to use those tactics used by the CDU/CSU in the 1970s. By subordinating diverse territorial interests to political considerations, the dynamics of party competition in Bonn have politicized a federal institution and its administrative political style. In the clash between two conceptions of state power—federalism (*Bundesstaatsprinzip*) in Article 20(i) of the Basic Law, the party-run state (*Parteienstaatsprinzip*) in Article 21(i)—the party-run state prevailed. In the early years of the Federal Republic, Chancellor Adenauer had insisted that the CDU break the coalition governments with the SPD which existed in several states. Similarly, after 1969 the CDU/CSU sought to coordinate state-level party organizations and strategies and to frame political campaigns at the state level in terms of the political situation in Bonn. Party competition thus has penetrated West German federalism.

At the same time, as Gerhard Lehmbruch has argued (1976, 1978) persuasively, political parties have also been colonized by West Germany's system of cooperative federalism. Even though, as government and opposition, parties are supposedly representing different constituencies and interests, the growing policy interdependence among different levels of government has forced upon them a bargaining process common to coalition partners. In contrast to Britain, West German federalism can grant the opposition institutional levers that may compel the government to negotiate. The Conference Committee "serves to correct the competitive features of the party system and to restore a pattern of (reluctant) cooperation" (Lehmbruch, 1978, p. 162). The resulting policies often look as if they have been formulated by a large coalition. Similarly, the interdependent interests among constituencies in West Germany's cooperative federalism lead to a loss of democratic control against which the political parties have been helpless (Scharpf, 1985). Such interdependence reinforces a pattern of cooperation in a charged political atmosphere.

Like the Court and the Bundesrat, West Germany's civil service also mirrors the conjoining of the party-run state and statist parties. Since the late 1960s the political parties have overtly penetrated the top echelons of the West German civil service. Increasing party competition has changed the composition and self-conception of the senior civil service. When the SPD-FDP government took over in 1969, two developments coincided. The first postwar generation of senior civil servants was retiring; and the SPD reformers were intent on removing "political" officials, state secretaries, and division heads who had served under a CDU-led government for up to two decades. Thus in 1969 eleven state secretaries and eight division heads were replaced immediately, and eventually one-fifth of all division heads in the federal bureaucracy turned over. The infusion of new blood, including a number of "outside" appointments who were to assist the new government in a variety of planning bodies (see Chapter 6), led to a substantial change in the self-conception of the West German senior civil service. In the 1970s a number of sociological studies have illustrated that West German senior bureaucrats regard themselves as being not above politics but an integral part of politics (Mayntz, 1980). "There is emerging a new type of politically conscious official who is less detached and procedure-oriented and more problem-and-program oriented, more open and flexible for new problem-solving strategies . . . the traditional isolation and autonomy of the higher public service has disappeared" (Dyson, 1977, pp. 29, 34). Following the footsteps of his Social Democratic predecessors,

Chancellor Kohl confirmed this political evolution by replacing many of the leading officials in the chancellory after winning the election of 1983.

However, the reverse process has also taken place. The lower echelons of the civil service have penetrated political parties. Parties have in fact embraced civil servants as their preferred candidates. In 1978, for example, the proportion of civil servants in the Bundestag was 46 percent; and the corresponding figure exceeded 50 percent in five of the eleven states (Dyson, 1979, p. 383). Judging by these figures, the notion of a separation of powers has been undercut. Since the occupational category "civil servant" is broad, the situation is complex. Teachers, for example, have civil service status. Like other public-sector employees, they have been drawn into party politics in large numbers since the mid-1960s. Many of them view themselves not as representatives but as critics of the state. Thus the relations between state and party are symbiotic and complex.

West Germany's system of party finance also illustrates the semi-sovereignty of the West German state. The appetite of West Germany's political parties for financial subsidies from the private sector has been insatiable. By the fall of 1985 two former FDP economics ministers, Count Otto von Lambsdorff and Hans Fridrichs, were tried for having accepted illegal subsidies. The files of federal prosecutors contain the names of hundreds of politicians from all major parties who are suspected of having solicited or accepted illegal contributions from many of West Germany's major corporations which then failed to declare these funds on their tax returns. One study reports that as of 1984 prosecutors had uncovered more than 700 instances of illegal tax maneuvers and disguised contributions to all of the major political parties. The list of names of top politicians and businesspeople reads like a *Who's Who* of the Federal Republic (Lösche, 1984, p. 20).

But private corruption is complemented by state subsidies that have been legislated since 1967. In the late 1960s the West German state allocated to the parties 9 million deutschmarks, the equivalent of 4 percent of all state subsidies, 10 percent of the combined income of the Catholic and Protestant churches, or the entire income of the trade union movement (von Beyme, 1983, p. 62; Lösche, 1984; Nassmacher, 1981, p. 372, 1984). A decade later the amount had increased fivefold, three times faster than the general rate of inflation. The Basic Law also grants the political parties an important role in organizing the political education of citizens. Each of the four major parties has organized a foundation which has been generously subsidized by the federal and state governments, as are parliamentary party groups. In 1979 these subsidies alone amounted to about 110 million deutschmarks, compared to 9 million in 1967. The figure for campaign reimbursement was almost twice as large (199 million deutschmarks). A substantial share of the funds comes from the budget of the Ministry of Economic Cooperation which finances party-run aid programs in the Third World. All in all, about one-half of the total income of the political parties comes from the state.

Last, in a curious way West Germany's new political class also reflects the conjoining of the party-run state and statist parties. The "place at the top" of West German society is no longer empty, as Ralf Dahrendorf argued (1979) in his celebrated book, first published in the mid-1960s. But it is easier to identify West Germany's new political class by what it is not than by what it is. West Germany's political class is not formed by an upper class sustained by economic success and social prestige, as in the United States, or by tradition and inherited wealth, as in Britain. In contrast to its counterparts in France and Japan, West Germany's political class is not staffed by politically visible elite bureaucrats who conceive of themselves as endowed with the ability to articulate long-term state interests. West Germany's political class consists instead of officials who are sustained neither by capitalist riches nor the state's power. They administer a "cartel" of big, publicly subsidized party bureaucracies. They play a complex game of electoral conflict and policy cooperation which connects mass participation and the representation of societal interests with collaboration among elites and the governance of state institutions. The ambiguity of the position of West Germany's political class stems from the fact that it accomplishes two things at once. Representing the "party-run state," it is an agent of politicization. Representing the "statist parties," it is an agent of depoliticization. The scope for politics is simultaneously widened and narrowed. Political controversy is diffused together with mechanisms for consensus formation. "Once policies have been adopted there is a strong pressure to maintain them, not only on the part of the government but also as an implied constraint on the opposition. In consequence, the political system is geared to making only gradual changes of course in any field of policy and putting stress on the virtue of continuity" (Smith, 1981, p. 174).

Like other industrial states, West Germany faces the crucial dilemma of democratic participation in public policy. The dilemma is revealed in the tensions between the popular mandate of a democratic politics and the constraints that West Germany's semisovereign state imposes on political actors. West Germany's semisovereign state has afforded its political class the opportunity both to represent constituent interests and to shield policymaking in the 1970s and 1980s from a declining social and political consensus. A strong CDU Chancellor Adenauer in the 1950s and a re-form-minded SPD coalition government headed by Chancellor Brandt in the early 1970s captured only the visible parts of West German politics. Its invisible part is the very substantial agreement that has been created and maintained by West Germany's semisovereign state. There is thus less to the partisan conflict between West Germany's parties than meets the eye. In the 1970s SPD Chancellor Schmidt, representative of the West German synthesis of both "reds" and "experts," followed relatively conservative and cautious policies. This may help explain why CDU Chancellor Kohl, despite much talk about a fundamental reorientation of policy in the 1980s, is with few exceptions following the broad outlines of the political strategies of the SPD government.

5. Legal Norms and Public Policy

The West German variant of semisovereignty is distinguished by the strong effect that legal norms have on the formulation and implementation of policy and possibly on public attitudes more generally. A sharp increase in the number of norms articulated each year has created an intensive debate among specialists. In 1982, for example, the Bundestag and state parliaments passed 330 laws, while federal and state bureaucracies issued 880 decrees (*Verordnungen*) and 5,000 administrative regulations (*Verwaltungsvorschriften*). The courts published 20,000 rulings. Legal scholars published 24,000 books, monographs, and articles (Hopt, 1984, p. 231). In West Germany law is the embodiment of the state. Both shape and reflect political reality.

West Germans prefer technical criteria in decisionmaking and legal methods of conflict resolution. They think of state and society as separate but intimately related spheres. State interest in their eyes is more than the sum total of individual or group preferences. Public sentiments favoring both a separate state and close cooperation between state and society are made compatible by a persistent faith in state "neutrality" which approximates what I have called here semisovereignty. The consensus ideology of a social welfare state informs both the behavior of.

the main "social partners" and of the "cooperative state" (Ritter, 1979). The common good is anchored in a process of reaching a consensus that bridges state and society rather than in the imposition of policy goals by state officials on antagonistic social actors. The state provides an integrative concept and a normative order legitimating policy choice (Dyson, 1980, pp. 3, 51–52).

Even when ideological conflict increases, as it did in the 1970s, West German policy operates in this normative framework codified in legal terms (Dyson, 1982; Scharpf, 1970). The rule of law (*Rechtsstaat*) offers a rationale for linking public policy not to constitutional norms but to legislation duly passed by the Bundestag. West Germans do not view the state merely as an agency that enforces the law. It is instead a concept imbued with connotations of "right" and "law" which logically as well as normatively precedes any particular type of political regime such as democracy or authoritarianism. In contrast to Britain, which conceives only of the functionally operating parts of the state—Crown, Parliament, Whitehall—West Germans attach special significance to a holistic conception of the state (Smith, 1976, p. 400). The intellectual style typical of West German policymaking is didactic, dispassionate, and marked by a careful search for the best policy options (*Sachlichkeit*).

The growing number of norms codified in legal terms signifies the far-reaching power of the state bureaucracy. Increasingly legislation is becoming the process of altering existing laws rather than creating new ones. Of the fifty-one laws passed by Parliament in 1978 only seventeen were still in force in 1981 (Ellwein and Hesse, 1985, p. 120). The Bundestag is preoccupied with the task of making legislative changes that the bureaucracy suggests it needs to effectively implement policy. Since the federal government in most instances lacks its own administrative agencies, an increasing specificity in legislation has become the government's preferred approach to influencing policy. West Germans expect that the exercise of state power will be predictable, inconspicuous and deliberative.

West Germany's Basic Law and its legal ethos express the notion of a nonpolitical and impartial bureaucracy implementing parliamentary legislation (Greve 1986, pp. 260–66; Scharpf, 1970). Compared to those in the United States, administrative agencies are given very little discretion in the Federal Republic. Consequently, a much larger number of political decisions are frozen into law. Yet comprehensive and complex legislative objectives are typically not easily translated into legal rules. The systematic cooptation of groups in parapublic institutions or similar political arrangements is the West German answer to this predicament. State bureaucrats thus rely on the information and expertise of relevant social sectors. In this process of political exchange, affected groups trade their advance commitment to live by a particular set of rules regarding policy implementation against the assurance that their political demands will be heeded in the process of policy formulation. Parapublic institutions provide a convenient way to make this exchange.

West Germany's incremental approach to policy is thus the result of the fusion of political and judicial styles of public policy (Blair, 1978). In setting norms, the law defines the state conceived here broadly as a network linking the public and the private sphere; but the law also derives from the state conceived more narrowly as an actor, one or several of the branches of government (Johnson, 1978; Schram, 1971). Half of all West German lawyers are judges and other career civil servants, as compared to one-fifth in the United States; and one-fifth of all West German judges sit on administrative courts (Rueschemeyer, 1973). Like the United States, West Germany's federal government lacks, with few exceptions, an administrative infrastructure at state and local levels. Uniformly applied law is therefore an essential device for dealing with social problems. "Some of the actions of German judges—especially in political matters—would leave the most activist American jurist open-mouthed. In a landmark case on the constitutionality of government subvention of election campaigns, for example, the justices not only threw out the formula fixed in the law; they straightforwardly 'suggested' one of their own which *would* be constitutional" (Rogowski, 1970, pp. vii-2–vii-3).

But the pervasiveness of West Germany's legal norms derives from two additional sources. It reflects the fact that the law is the main instrument of elites to articulate their objectives and project their power. In addition, law is part of the tradition of a rule-based culture that applies rather than interprets law, that is inquisitorial rather than adversarial, and that seeks to diffuse political conflict and unburden the political process by pushing into the legal arena messy political questions such as the reform of industrial relations or higher education (see Chapters 3 and 7). Between 1970 and 1978 the number of lawsuits filed in West Germany's civil, administrative, and finance courts increased by a factor of three, about three times faster than the case load in the U.S. district courts and district courts of appeal (Mushaben, 1981, pp. 435–

36). It is thus not surprising that the West Germans continue to accord so much respect to judges and bankers whose actions, judged eminently political in other countries, have the effect of depoliticizing some of the most important issues on the public agenda (Dyson, 1979). "Under serious institutional restrictions," Klaus von Beyme thus argues (1985, p. 21), "the autonomy of the Federal Bank or the Constitutional Court is not limited by the fact that governments and parties influence the selection of their leading figures. The weight of appointment is smaller than the gravity of the office." In short, the pervasiveness of legal norms in West Germany's semisovereign state shapes the substance and the style of policy and makes the preference for incremental policy change so compelling.

West German politics is marked by what Charles Maier has called "incomplete" and "insufficient" statehood. "The West Germans should understand that this situation brings more opportunities than liabilities. . . . Indeed all of us—not merely Germans—could learn a useful lesson by learning how to live without a state" (Maier, 1982, pp. 188, 197). The three nodes of West Germany's policy network open the state to the influence of parties, subordinate levels of government, and interest groups. But in fusing state and society, these nodes are also conduits in the formulation and implementation of policy. Since it links tightly most of the major organized political actors, thus multiplying potential sources of veto, West Germany's semisovereign state is not well equipped to initiate bold policy change. But by its very structure, West Germany's semisovereign state is well suited to bring about steady, incremental policy change.

Since the middle of the nineteenth century, dynamic changes inside Germany have exploded in two world wars. The condition of semisovereignty which the Federal Republic has experienced after 1945 in foreign affairs is also matched by its domestic political arrangements. State power has not disappeared. But its exercise has been constrained in ways that are reflected in West German policy and politics. It is possible to argue that during the last forty years West German policy has transformed David into Goliath. But it is a Goliath tied down by distinctive domestic institutions and political arrangements. Germany's authoritarian state projected its power with ferocity in both foreign and domestic affairs before 1945. But since 1945 the power of West Germany's semisovereign state has been tamed.

References

General

Ackermann, Paul. 1970. *Der Deutsche Bauernverband im politischen Kräftespiel der Bundesrepublik: Die Einflussnahme des DBV auf die Entscheidung über den europäischen Getreidepreis.* Tübingen: J.C.B. Mohr.

Albertin, Breitand von, et al. 1980. *Politischer Liberalismus in der Bundesrepublik.* Göttingen: Vandenhoeck and Ruprecht.

Altenstetter, Christa. 1974. *Health Policy-Making and Administration in West Germany and the United States.* Beverly Hills: Sage Publications.

———. 1978. "Health Policy Implementation and Corporate Participation in West Germany." In Charles R. Foster, ed., *Comparative Public Policy and Citizen Participation: Energy, Education, Health and Urban Issues in the U.S. and Germany,* pp. 173–93. New York: Pergamon Press.

———. 1980. "Hospital Planning in France and the Federal Republic of Germany." *Journal of Health Politics, Policy and Law* 5(2):309–32.

———. 1982a. "Implementation of National Health Insurance Seen from the Perspective of General Sickness Funds (AOKs) in the Federal Republic of Germany, 1955-1975," P/82-1. Berlin, Wissenschaftszentrum Berlin.

———. 1982b. "Organizational Processes in a Three-Tiered Membership Organization of Health Insurance Funds Seen from Below: Experiences from Germany," P/82-3. Berlin, Wissenschaftszentrum Berlin.

———. 1982c. "Ziele, Instrumente und Widersprüchlichkeiten der deutschen Krankenhauspolitik, vergleichend dargestellt am Beispiel der Implementation der Bundespflegesatzverordnung," P/82-2. Berlin, Wissenschaftszentrum Berlin.

Andrlik, Erich. 1981. "The Farmers and the State: Agricultural Interests in West German Politics." *West European Politics* 4(1):104–19.

Ashford, Douglas E. 1981. *Policy and Politics in Britain: The Limits of Consensus.* Philadelphia: Temple University Press.

————. 1982. *Policy and Politics in France: Living with Uncertainty.* Philadelphia: Temple University Press.

Averyt, William F. 1976. "Agricultural Interest Groups in the European Community: The *Comité des Organisations Professionnel les Agricoles.*" Ph.d. diss., Yale University.

Badaracco, Joseph L. 1985. *Loading the Dice: How Institutional Arrangements Shape Business-Government Relations.* Boston: Harvard Business School.

Baker, Kendall; Dalton, Russell J.; and Hildebrandt, Kai. 1981. *Germany Transformed: Political Culture and the New Politics.* Cambridge, Mass.: Harvard University Press.

Baring, Arnulf. 1969. *Aussenpolitik in Adenauers Kanzlerdemokratie: Bonns Beitrag zur Europäischen Verteidigungsgemeinschaft.* Munich: Oldenbourg.

————. 1971. "The Institutions of German Foreign Policy." In Karl Kaiser and Roger Morgan, eds., *Britain and West Germany: Changing Societies and the Future of Foreign Policy,* pp. 151–70. London: Oxford University Press.

Barnes, Samuel; Kaase, Max; and Allerbeck, Klaus. 1979. *Political Action: Mass Participation in Five Western Democracies.* Beverly Hills: Sage Publications.

Bauer, Rudolph. 1978. *Wohlfahrtsverbände in der Bundesrepublik: Materialien und Analysen zu Organisation, Programmatik und Praxis. Ein Handbuch.* Weinheim: Beltz.

Benz, Arthur. 1985. *Föderalismus als dynamisches System: Zentralisierung und Dezentralisierung im föderativen Staat.* Opladen: Westdeutscher Verlag.

Berger, Rolf. 1974. *Zur Stellung des Wissenschaftsrats bei der wissenschaftspolitischen Beratung von Bund und Ländern.* Baden-Baden: Nomos.

Berghahn, Volker. 1985. *Unternehmer und Politik in der Bundesrepublik.* Frankfurt: Suhrkamp.

Beyme, Klaus von. 1983. *The Political System of the Federal Republic of Germany.* Gower: Aldershot.

————. 1984. "Politische Kybernetik? Politik und wissenschaftliche Information der Politiker in modernen Industriegesellschaften." *Journal für Sozialforschung* 24(1):3–16.

————. 1985. "Policy-Making in the Federal Republic of Germany: A Systematic Introduction." In Klaus von Beyme and Manfred G. Schmidt, eds., *Policy and Politics in the Federal Republic of Germany,* pp. 1–26. New York: St. Martin's Press.

————. 1986. "The Role of Deputies in West Germany." In Ezra N. Suleiman, ed., *Parliaments and Parliamentarians in Democratic Politics,* pp. 154–75. New York: Holmes and Meier.

Beyme, Klaus von, and Schmidt, Manfred G., eds. 1985. *Policy and Politics in the Federal Republic of Germany.* New York: St. Martin's Press.

Blackbourn, David, and Eley, Geoff. 1985. *The Peculiarities of German Histo-*

ry: Bourgeois Society and Politics in Nineteenth-Century Germany. Oxford: Oxford University Press.

Blair, P. M. 1981. *Federalism and Judicial Review in West Germany.* Oxford: Oxford University Press.

Blair, Philip. 1978. "Law and Politics in Germany." *Political Studies* 26(3):348–62.

Blankenburg, Erhard, and Rogowski, Rolf. 1984. "West German Labor Courts and the British Tribunal System: A Socio-Legal Comparison." *Disputes Processing Research Program.* Working papers 1984-10. Madison: University of Wisconsin Law School.

Blankenburg, Erhard; Rogowski, Rolf; and Schönholz, Siegfried. 1978. "Phenomena of Legalization: Observations in a German Labour Court," Dp/78-20. Berlin, International Institute of Management.

Blankenburg, Erhard; Schmid, Günther; and Treiber, Hubert. 1975. "Legitimitäts- und Implementierungsprobleme 'aktiver Arbeitsmarktpolitik'," I/75-66. Berlin, International Institute of Management.

Blankenburg, Erhard, and Schönholz, Siegfried. 1979. *Zur Soziologie des Arbeitsgerichtsverfahrens: Die Verrechtlichung von Arbeitskonflikten.* Neuwied: Luchterhand.

Böll, Heinrich. 1975. *The Lost Honor of Katharina Blum: How Violence Develops and Where It Ends.* New York: McGraw-Hill.

Bogs, Harald. 1977. "Strukturprobleme der Selbstverwaltung einer modernen Sozialversicherung." In Harald Bogs, Christian von Ferber, and Infas, *Soziale Selbstverwaltung: Aufgaben und Funktion der Selbstverwaltung in der Sozialversicherung,* pp. 11–96. Bonn: Verlag der Ortskrankenkassen.

Brand, Karl-Werner. 1982. *Neue Soziale Bewegungen: Entstehung, Funktion und Perspektive neuer Protestpotentiale.* Opladen: Westdeutscher Verlag.

Brand, Karl-Werner; Büsser, Detlev; and Rucht, Dieter. 1983. *Aufbruch in eine andere Gesellschaft: Neue soziale Bewegungen in der Bundesrepublik.* Frankfurt: Campus.

Braunthal, Gerard. 1965. *The Federation of German Industry in Politics.* Ithaca: Cornell University Press.

———. 1983. *The West German Social Democrats, 1969-1982: Profile of a Party in Power.* Boulder: Westview Press.

Brecht, Arnold, and Glaser, Comstock. 1940. *The Art and Technique of Administration in German Ministries.* Cambridge, Mass.: Harvard Universtiy Press.

Bredow, Wilfried von. 1982. "The Peace Movement in the Federal Republic of Germany: Composition and Objectives." *Armed Forces and Society* 9(1):33–48.

Breuer, Rüdiger. 1977. "Selbstverwaltung und Mitverwaltung Beteiligter im Widerstreit verfassungsrechtlicher Postulate." *Die Verwaltung* 10(1):1–29.

Brickman, Ronald; Jasanoff, Sheila; and Ilgen, Thomas. 1985. *Controlling*

Chemicals: The Politics of Regulation in Europe and the United States.
Ithaca: Cornell University Press.

Briese, Volker. 1972. *Zentralisierung der Kulturpolitik in der Bundesrepublik Deutschland: Reformen zwischen Ökonomie und Ideologie.* Research Report 2. Constance: Center for Educational Research.

Bronke, Karl; Wenzel, Gerd; and Leibfried, Stephan. 1985. "Soziale Dienste zwischen Herrschaft und öffentlicher Produktion—zur Doppelstruktur kommunaler Sozialverwaltung." In Thomas Olk and Hans-Uwe Otto, eds., *Gesellschaftliche Perspektiven der Sozialarbeit 4: Lokale Sozialpolitik und Selbsthilfe,* pp. 23–54. Neuwied: Luchterhand.

Broughton, David, and Kirchner, Emil. 1984. *The FDP in Transition—Again?* Colchester, England: University of Essex.

Bruche, Gert, and Reissert, Bernd. 1985. *Die Finanzierung der Arbeitsmarktpolitik: System, Effektivität, Reformansätze.* Frankfurt: Campus.

Bruder, Wolfgang, and Ellwein, Thomas, eds. 1979. *Raumordnung und staatliche Steuerungsfähigkeit.* Special issue 10 of *Politische Vierteljahresschrift.* Opladen: Westdeutscher Verlag.

Bulmer, Simon, and Paterson, William. 1987. *The Federal Republic of Germany and the European Community.* London: Allen and Unwin.

Bürklin, Wilhelm P. 1985. "The German Greens: The Post-Industrial Non-Established and the Party System." *International Political Science Review* 6(4):463–81.

Busch, Heiner; Funk, Albrecht; Kauss, Udo; Narr, Wolf-Dieter; and Werkentin, Falco. 1985. *Die Polizei in der Bundesrepublik.* Frankfurt: Campus.

Calleo, David. 1978. *The German Problem Reconsidered: Germany and the World Order, 1870 to the Present.* Cambridge: Cambridge University Press.

Cameron, David R., and Hofferbert, Richard I. 1974. "The Impact of Federalism on Educational Finance: A Comparative Analysis." *European Journal of Political Research* 2(3):225–58.

Capra, Fritjof, and Spretnak, Charlene. 1984. *Green Politics: The Global Promise.* New York: Dutton.

Carl-Sime, Carol. 1979. "Bavaria, the CSU and the West German Party System." *West European Politics* 2(1):89–107.

Conradt, David P. 1980. "Changing German Political Culture." In Gabriel A. Almond and Sidney Verba, eds., *The Civic Culture Revisited,* pp. 212–72. Boston: Little, Brown.

———. 1982. *The German Polity.* 2nd ed. New York: Longman.

Crozier, Michael. 1967. *The Bureaucratic Phenomenon.* Chicago: University of Chicago Press.

Dahrendorf, Ralf. 1979. *Society and Democracy in Germany.* New York: Norton.

Dietzel, Gottfried T. W. 1978. "Sachverständigenräte als neue Staatsorgane?" *Der Staat* 17(4):582–90.

Döring, Herbert, and Smith, Gordon, eds. 1982. *Party Government and Political Culture in Western Germany.* New York: St. Martin's Press.

Dohse, Knuth. 1981. *Ansländische Arbeiter und bürgerlicher Staat: Genese und Funktion von staatlicher Ausländerpolitik und Ausländerrecht. Vom Kaiserreich bis zur Bundesrepublik Deutschland.* Königstein/Ts.: Anton Hain.

Doubrawa, Kurt. 1969. *Selbstverwaltung, Aufsicht und Dienstrecht der Sozialversicherungsträger.* 2nd ed. Stuttgart: Kohlhammer.

Drummond, Gordon D. 1982. *The German Social Democrats in Opposition, 1949-1960: The Case against Rearmament.* Norman: University of Oklahoma Press.

Dunn, James A., Jr. 1981. *Miles to Go: European and American Transportation Policies.* Cambridge, Mass.: MIT Press.

Duwendang, Dieter, ed. 1973. *Macht und Ohnmacht der Bundesbank.* Frankfurt: Athenäum.

Dyson, Kenneth F. 1974. "The German Federal Chancellor's Office." *Political Quarterly* 45(3):364–71.

———. 1975. "Left-Wing Political Extremism and the Problem of Tolerance in Western Germany." *Government and Opposition* 10, (3):306–31.

———. 1977. *Party, State, and Bureaucracy in Western Germany.* Beverly Hills: Sage Publications.

———. 1979. "The Ambiguous Politics of Western Germany: Politicization in a 'State' Society." *European Journal of Political Research* 7:375–96.

———. 1980. *The State Tradition in Western Europe.* New York: Oxford University Press.

———. 1982. "West Germany: The Search for a Rationalist Consensus." In Jeremy Richardson, ed., *Policy Styles in Western Europe,* pp. 17–46. London: Allen and Unwin.

Edinger, Lewis J. 1986. *West German Politics.* New York: Columbia University Press.

Eley, Geoff. 1986. *From Unification to Nazism: Reinterpreting the German Past.* Boston: Allen and Unwin.

Ellwein, Thomas, and Hesse, Joachim Jens. 1985. "Plädoyer für eine Fortsetzung der Verwaltungsvereinfachung und für eine Verstetigung der verwaltungspolitischen Diskussion." In Thomas Ellwein and Joachim Jens Hesse, eds., *Verwaltungsvereinfachung und Verwaltungspolitik,* pp. 119–32. Baden-Baden: Nomos.

Emerson, Rupert. 1928. *State and Sovereignty in Modern Germany.* New Haven: Yale University Press.

Evans, Peter B; Rueschemeyer, Dietrich; and Skocpol, Theda, eds., 1985. *Bringing the State Back In.* Cambridge: Cambridge University Press.

Faber, Heiko. 1969. *Wirtschaftsplanung und Bundesbankautonomie.* Baden-Baden: Nomos.

Feist, Ursula, and Liepelt, Klaus. 1983. "New Elites in Old Parties: Observations on a Side Effect of German Educational Reform." *International Political Science Review* 4(1):71–83.

Ferber, Christian von. 1977. "Soziale Selbstverwaltung—Fiktion oder Chance? Gutachten erstattet im Auftrag des Bundesministeriums für Arbeit und Sozialordnung." In Harald Bogs, Christian von Ferber, and Infas, *Soziale Selbstverwaltung: Aufgaben und Funktion der Selbstverwaltung in der Sozialversicherung,* pp. 99–199. Bonn: Verlag der Ortskrankenkassen.

Fischer, Erwin. 1971. *Trennung von Staat und Kirche: Die Gefährdung der Religionsfreiheit in der Bundesrepublik.* Frankfurt: Adolf Metzner.

Fried, Robert C. 1976. "Party and Policy in West German Cities." *American Political Science Review* 70(1):11–24.

Frye, Charles E. 1965. "Parties and Pressure Groups in Weimar and Bonn." *World Politics* 17(4):632–55.

"Die Fünf Weisen und der reine Sachverstand." 1977. *Leviathan* 2:157–62.

Fürst, Dietrich, and Hesse, Joachim Jens. 1981. *Landesplanung.* Düsseldorf: Werner.

Fürst, Dietrich; Hesse, Joachim Jens; Richter, Hartmut. 1984. *Stadt und Staat: Verdichtungsräume im Prozess der föderalstaatlichen Problemverarbeitung.* Baden-Baden: Nomos.

Funk, Albrecht; Haupt, Heinz G.; Narr, Wolf-Dieter; and Werkentin, Falco. 1984. *Verrechtlichung und Verdrängung: Die Bürokratie und ihre Klientel.* Opladen: Westdeutscher Verlag.

Garlichs, Dietrich, and Hull, Chris. 1978. "Central Control and Information Dependence: Highway Planning in the Federal Republic of Germany." In Kenneth Hanf and Fritz W. Scharpf, eds., *Interorganizational Policy Making: Limits to Coordination and Central Control,* pp. 143–65. Beverly Hills: Sage Publications.

Goldthorpe, John H. 1984. "The End of Convergence: Corporatist and Dualist Tendencies in Modern Western Societies." In John H. Goldthorpe, ed., *Order and Conflict in Contemporary Capitalism,* pp. 315–43. Oxford: Clarendon Press.

Gourevitch, Peter. 1986. *Politics in Hard Times: Comparative Responses to International Economic Crises.* Ithaca: Cornell University Press.

Greve, Michael S. 1984. "Public Interest Politics: Environmentalism in West Germany and the United States." Unpublished paper, Dept. of Government, Cornell University.

———. 1986. "Environmentalism in West Germany and the United States." Unpublished manuscript, Dept. of Government, Cornell University.

Groser, Manfred. 1983a. "Ökonomie parastaatlicher Institutionen." In *Jahrbuch für Neue Politische Ökonomie,* 2:239–53. Tübingen: J.C.B. Mohr (Paul Siebeck).

———. 1983b. "Die Organisation von Wirtschaftsinteressen in der chemischen Industrie der Bundesrepublik Deutschland." Berlin, International Institute for Management.

————. 1985. "Die Repräsentation regionaler Wirtschaftsinteressen—die Rolle der Industrie- und Handelskammern." Paper read at the meeting of the German Political Science Association, Berlin, June 7.

Gunlicks, Arthur B. 1985. "Financing Local Governments in the German Federal System." Paper read at the annual meeting of the American Political Science Association, New Orleans, August 29–September 1.

Hancher, Leigh, and Ruete, Matthias. 1985. "Legal Administrative Culture as Policy Determinants: Licensing and the Drug Industry." Paper read at the ESRC Conference on Government and Industry Relations in Major OECD Countries, Trinity Hall, Cambridge, December 11–13.

Hanf, Kenneth, and Scharpf, Fritz, W., eds. 1978. *Interorganizational Policy Making: Limits to Coordination and Central Control.* Beverly Hills: Sage Publications.

Hanrieder, Wolfram F. 1967. *West German Foreign Policy, 1949-1963: International Pressure and Domestic Response.* Stanford: Stanford University Press.

Hartmann, Heinz. 1970. "Institutional Immobility and Attitudinal Change in West Germany." *Comparative Politics* 2(4):579–91.

Hartwich, Hans-Hermann. 1970. *Sozialstaatspostulat und gesellschaftlicher Status Quo.* Cologne: Westdeutscher Verlag.

Haungs, Peter. 1983. "Die Christlich Demokratische Union Deutschlands (CDU) und die Christlich Soziale Union in Bayern (CSU)." In Hans-Joachim Veen, ed., *Christlich-demokratische und konservative Parteien in Westeuropa,* 1:9–194. Paderborn: Schöningh.

Heclo, Hugh, and Madsen, Henrik. 1987. *Policy and Politics in Sweden: A Study in Welfare State Hegemony.* Philadelphia: Temple University Press.

Heffter, Heinrich. 1950. *Die deutsche Selbstverwaltung im 19. Jahrhundert: Geschichte der Ideen und Institutionen.* Stuttgart: Koehler.

Heidenheimer, Arnold J. 1985. "Comparative Policy at the Cross Roads: The Past Decade in Perspective." Paper read at the 13th World Congress, International Political Science Association, Paris, July 15–20.

————. 1986. "Politics, Policy and Policey as Concepts in English and Continental Languages: An Attempt to Explain Divergences." *Review of Politics* 48(1):3–30.

Heinze, Rolf G. 1976. "Zur Politisch-Sozialen Funktion des Deutschen Bauernverbandes (DBV)." Master's thesis, Dept. of Sociology, University of Bielefeld.

————. 1981. *Verbändepolitik und "Neokorporatismus": Zur politischen Soziologie organisierter Interessen.* Opladen: Westdeutscher Verlag.

Heinze, Rolf G., and Olk, Thomas. 1981. "Die Wohlfahrtsverbände im System sozialer Dienstleistungsproduktion: Zur Entstehung der bundesrepublikanischen Verbändewohlfahrt." *Kölner Zeitschrift für Soziologie und Sozialpsychologie* 33(1):94–114.

———. 1984. "Wohlfahrtsverbände." In Hanns Eyferth, Hans-Uwe Otto, and Hans Thiersch, eds., *Handbuch zur Sozialarbeit/Sozialpädagogik*, pp. 1262–77. Neuwied: Luchterhand.

Hesse, Joachim Jens, ed. 1978. *Politikverflechtung im föderativen Staat: Studien zum Planungs- und Finanzierungsverbund zwischen Bund, Ländern und Gemeinden.* Baden-Baden: Nomos.

———, ed. 1982. *Politikwissenschaft und Verwaltungswissenschaft.* Special issue 13 of *Politische Vierteljahresschrift.* Opladen: Westdeutscher Verlag.

———, ed. 1985. *Erneuerung der Politik "von unten"? Stadtpolitik und kommunale Selbstverwaltung im Umbruch.* Baden-Baden: Nomos.

Hesse, Joachim Jens; Ganseforth, Heinrich; Fürst, Dietrich; and Ritter, Ernst-Hasso, eds. 1983. *Staat und Gemeinden zwischen Konflikt und Kooperation.* Baden-Baden: Nomos.

Hilbert, Josef. 1984. "Verbände im produzierenden Ernährungsgewerbe der Bundesrepublik Deutschland: Eine Studie zu Strukturen, Problemen und Wirkungen der 'Organisation von Wirtschaftsinteressen'." Unpublished manuscript, Dept. of Sociology, University of Bielefeld.

Hoffmann, Albert, and Tennstedt, Florian. 1980. "Im Warenkorb der Sozialhilfe ist Menschenwürde nicht enthalten." *Frankfurter Rundschau*, April 22, p. 10.

Hoffman, George W., ed. 1981. *Federalism and Regional Development: Case Studies on the Experience in the United States and the Federal Republic of Germany.* Austin: University of Texas Press.

Hopt, Klaus J. 1984. "Wettbewerbsbeschränkungen und Verrechtlichung." In Friedrich Kübler, ed., *Verrechtlichung von Wirtschaft, Arbeit und sozialer Solidarität: Vergleichende Analysen*, pp. 229–87. Baden-Baden: Nomos.

Huber, Ernst Rudolf. 1958. *Selbstverwaltung der Wirtschaft.* Stuttgart: Kohlhammer.

Hucke, Jochen. 1982. "Implementing Envronmental Regulations in the Federal Republic of Germany." *Policy Studies Journal* 11(1):130–40.

———. 1985. "Environmental Policy: The Development of a New Policy Area." In Klaus von Beyme and Manfred G. Schmidt, eds., *Policy and Politics in the Federal Republic of Germany*, pp. 156–75. New York: St. Martin's Press.

Hunter, J.S.H. 1973. *Revenue Sharing in the Federal Republic of Germany.* Canberra: Australian National University Centre for Research on Federal Financial Relations.

Inglehart, Ronald. 1977. *The Silent Revolution: Changing Values and Political Styles among Western Publics.* Princeton: Princeton University Press.

————. 1981. "Postmaterialism in an Environment of Insecurity." *American Political Science Review* 75(4):880–900.

Infas. 1977. "Die Selbstverwaltung." In Harald Bogs, Christian von Ferber, and Infas, *Soziale Selbstverwaltung: Aufgaben und Funktion der Selbstverwaltung in der Sozialversicherung*, pp. 207–55. Bonn: Verlag der Ortskrankenkassen.

Irving, Ronald E. 1979. *The Christian Democratic Parties of Western Europe*. London: Allen and Unwin.

Jacob, Herbert. 1963. *German Administration since Bismarck: Central Authority vs. Local Authority*. New Haven: Yale University Press.

Johnson, Nevil. 1973. *Government in the Federal Republic of Germany: The Executive at Work*. Oxford: Pergamon Press.

————. 1978. "Law as the Articulation of the State in Western Germany: A German Tradition Seen from a British Perspective." *Western European Politics* 1(2):177–92.

Kahn, Herman, and Redepenning, Michael. 1982. *Die Zukunft Deutschlands: Niedergang oder neuer Aufstieg der Bundesrepublik*. Stuttgart: Poller.

Katzenstein, Peter J. 1984. *Corporatism and Change: Austria, Switzerland and the Politics of Industry*. Ithaca: Cornell University Press.

————. 1985. *Small States in World Markets: Industrial Policy in Europe*. Ithaca: Cornell University Press.

Kirberger, Wolfgang. 1978. *Staatsentlastung durch private Verbände: Die finanzpolitische Bedeutung der Mitwirkung privater Verbände bei der Erfüllung Öffentlicher Aufgaben*. Baden-Baden: Nomos.

Kirchheimer, Otto. 1957. "The Waning of Opposition in Parliamentary Regimes." *Social Research* 24(2):127–56.

————. 1966. "Germany: The Vanishing Opposition." In Robert A. Dahl, ed., *Political Oppositions in Western Democracies*, pp. 237–59. New Haven: Yale University Press.

Kitschelt, Herbert. 1980. *Kernenergiepolitik: Arena eines gesellschaftlichen Konflikts*. Frankfurt: Campus.

————. 1985. "Between Movement and Party: Structure and Process in Belgian and West German Ecology Parties." Paper read at the 5th International Conference of Europeanists, Washington D.C., October 18–20.

————. 1986. "The Logic of Party Formation: The Structure and Formation of the Belgian and West German Ecology Parties." Unpublished, Dept. of Political Science, Duke University.

Knott, Jack H. 1981. *Managing the German Economy: Budgetary Politics in a Federal State*. Lexington, Mass.: D. C. Heath.

König, Klaus; Oertzen, Hans Joachim von; and Wagener, Frido, eds. 1983. *Public Administration in the Federal Republic of Germany*. Deventer: Kluwer.

Könneker, Wilhelm. 1973. *Die Deutsche Bundesbank.* 2nd ed. Frankfurt: Knapp.

Körnich, Jörn-Heiko. 1978. *Das arbeitsgerichtliche Beschlussverfahren in Betriebsverfassungssachen.* Berlin: Duncker and Humblot.

Kommers, Donald P. 1976. *Judicial Politics in West Germany: A Study of the Federal Constitutional Court.* Beverly Hills: Sage Publications.

Konukiewitz, Manfred, and Wollmann, Hellmut. 1982. "Physical Planning in a Federal System: The Case of West Germany." In David H. McKay, ed., *Planning and Politics in Western Europe,* pp. 71–110. London: Macmillan.

———. 1985. "Urban Innovation—A Response to Deficiencies of the Intervention and Welfare State?" In Terry N. Clark, ed., *Research in Urban Policy,* 1:327–39. Greenwich, Conn.: JAI Press.

Krautkrämer, Uta. 1978. "Labour Market Administration in the Federal Republic of Germany," IIM/78-14b. Berlin, International Institute of Management.

Kvistad, Gregg O. 1984. "Radicals and the German State: Hegel, Marx and the Political Demands on German Civil Servants." Ph.D. diss., University of California, Berkeley.

———. 1985. "Between State and Society: Green Political Ideology in the Mid-Eighties." Paper read at the annual meeting of the American Political Science Association, New Orleans, August 29–September 1.

Lampe, Ortrun. 1971. *Die Unabhängigkeit der Deutschen Bundesbank: Eine verfassungsrechtliche und verwaltungsrechtliche Untersuchung.* 2nd ed. Munich: C. H. Beck'sche Verlagsbuchhandlung.

Landfried, Christine. 1984. *Bundesverfassungsgericht und Gesetzgeber: Wirkungen der Verfassungsrechtsprechung auf parlamentarische Willensbildung und soziale Realität.* Baden-Baden: Nomos.

———. 1985. "Legal Policy and Internal Security." In Klaus von Beyme and Manfred G. Schmidt, eds., *Policy and Politics in the Federal Republic of Germany,* pp. 198–221. New York: St. Martin's Press.

Landsberger, Henry A. 1981. *The Control of Cost in the Federal Republic of Germany: Lessons for America?* International Health Planning Series 3. Washington, D.C.: U.S. Department of Health and Human Services.

Laufer, Heinz. 1974. *Der Föderalismus der Bundesrepublik Deutschland.* Stuttgart: Kohlhammer.

Layton-Henry, Zig, ed. 1982. *Conservative Politics in Western Europe.* New York: St. Martin's Press.

Lehmbruch, Gerhard. 1968. "The Ambiguous Coalition in West Germany." *Government and Opposition* 3(2):181–204.

———. 1976. *Parteienwettbewerb im Bundesstaat.* Stuttgart: Kohlhammer.

———. 1978. "Party and Federation in Germany: A Developmental Dilemma." *Government and Opposition* 13(2):151–77.

Leichter, Howard M. 1979. *A Comparative Approach to Policy Analysis: Health Care Policy in Four Nations.* Cambridge: Cambridge University Press.

Leopold, Dieter. 1974. *Die Selbstverwaltung in der Sozialversicherung.* 2nd ed. Bonn: Asgard-Verlag.

Linnan, David K. 1984. "Police Discretion in a Continental European Administrative State: The Police of Baden-Württemberg in the Federal Republic of Germany." *Law and Contemporary Problems* 47(4):185–223.

Lösche, Peter. 1984. *Wovon leben die Parteien? Über das Geld in der Politik.* Frankfurt: Fischer.

Loewenberg, Gerhard. 1967. *Parliament in the German Political System.* Ithaca: Cornell University Press.

MacMillan, Keith, and Turner, Ian. 1985. "Government-Industry Relations in the Pharmaceutical Industry." Unpublished paper, The Management College, Henly, England.

Maier, Charles S. 1982. "*Bonn Ist Doch Weimar:* Informal Reflections on the Historical Legacy of the Federal Republic." In Andrei S. Markovits, ed., *The Political Economy of West Germany: Modell Deutschland,* pp. 188–98. New York: Praeger.

Mangines, Brian. 1985. "Collective Bargaining in West Germany: The Union's Challenge." Unpublished paper, Dept. of Government, Cornell University.

Mangun, William R. 1979. "West European Institutional Arrangements for Environmental Policy Implementation—Especially Air and Water Pollution Control." *Environmental Conservation* 6(3):201–11.

Markovits, Andrei S. 1986. *The Politics of the West German Trade Unions: Strategies of Class and Interest Representation in Growth and Crisis.* Cambridge: Cambridge University Press.

———, ed. 1982. *The Political Economy of West Germany: Modell Deutschland.* New York: Praeger.

Markovits, Andrei S., and Allen, Christopher S. 1984. "Trade Unions and the Economic Crisis: The West German Case." In Peter Gourevitch, Andrew Martin, George Ross, and Stephen Bornstein, *Unions and Economic Crisis: Britain, West Germany and Sweden,* pp. 89–188. London: Allen and Unwin.

Massing, O. 1974. "The Federal Constitutional Court as an Instrument of Social Control: Propaedeutic Sketches for a Critical Functional Form-Analysis of Constitutional Jurisdiction." In Klaus von Beyme, ed., *German Political Studies,* 1:215–52. Beverly Hills: Sage Publications.

Mayntz, Renate. 1978. "Intergovernmental Implementation of Environmental Policy." In Kenneth Hanf and Fritz W. Scharpf, eds., *Interorganizational Policy Making: Limits to Coordination and Central Control,* pp. 201–14. Beverly Hills: Sage Publications.

———. 1980. "Executive Leadership in Germany: Dispersion of Power or

'Kanzlerdemokratie'?" In Richard Rose and Ezra N. Suleiman, eds., *Presidents and Prime Ministers*, pp. 139–70. Washington, D.C.: American Enterprise Institute.

————. 1984. "German Federal Bureaucrats: A Functional Elite between Politics and Administration." In Ezra N. Suleiman, ed., *Bureaucrats and Policy Making: A Comparative Overview*, pp. 174–205. New York: Holmes and Meier.

Mayntz, Renate, and Scharpf, Fritz W. 1975. *Policy-Making in the German Federal Bureaucracy*. Amsterdam: Elsevier.

Merkl, Peter H. 1959. "Executive-Legislative Federalism in West Germany." *American Political Science Review* 53(3):732–41.

Meulemann, Heiner. 1983. "Value Change in West Germany, 1950-1980: Integrating the Empirical Evidence." *Social Science Information* 22(4-5):777–800.

Mewes, Horst. 1983. "The West German Green Party." *New German Critique* 28:51–85.

Mintzel, Alf. 1978. "The Christian Social Union in Bavaria: Analytical Notes on Its Development, Role and Political Success." In Max Kaase and Klaus von Beyme, eds., *Elections and Parties, German Political Studies*, 3:191–225. Beverly Hills: Sage Publications.

Montgomery, John. 1957. *Forced to be Free: The Artificial Revolution in Germany and Japan*. Chicago: Chicago University Press.

Müller, Edda. 1986. *Innenwelt der Umweltpolitik: Sozial-liberale Umweltpolitik-(ohn)macht durch Organisation?* Opladen: Westdeutscher Verlag.

Müller, Heinz. 1969. *Die Politik der deutschen Zentralbank 1948-1967: Eine Analyse der Ziele und Mittel*. Tübingen: J.C.B. Mohr (Paul Siebeck).

Müller-Groeling, Hubertus. n.d. "The Planning and Advisory System in West Germany." Unpublished manuscript, Weltwirtschaftsinstitut, Kiel.

Müller-Rommel, Ferdinand. 1982. *Innerparteiliche Gruppierungen in der SPD: Eine empirische Studie über informell-organisierte Gruppierungen von 1969-1980*. Opladen: Westdeutscher Verlag.

————. 1985. "New Social Movements and Smaller Parties: A Comparative Perspective." *West European Politics* 8(1):41–54.

Murswieck, Axel. 1986. "Public Policies in Disarray: Political and Legal Restraints in Public Policy-Making." *International Social Science Journal* 38(2):191–204.

————. 1983. *Die staatliche Kontrolle der Arzneimittelsicherheit in der Bundesrepublik und den USA*. Opladen: Westdeutscher Verlag.

————. 1985. "Health Policy-Making." In Klaus von Beyme and Manfred G. Schmidt, eds., *Policy and Politics in the Federal Republic of Germany*, pp. 82–106. New York: St. Martin's Press.

Mushaben, Joyce Marie. 1981. "The State vs. the University: Juridicalization and the Politics of Higher Education at the Free University of Berlin, 1969-1979." Ph.d. diss., Indiana University, Bloomington.

———. 1985. "Cycles of Peace Protest in West Germany: Experiences from Three Decades." *West European Politics* 8(1):24–40.

Nassmacher, Karl-Heinz. 1981. "Öffentliche Parteifinanzierung in westlichen Demokratien." *Journal für Sozialforschung* 21(4):351–74.

———. 1984. "Recent Developments in Public Subsidies and Reporting Procedures: The Examples of Austria, Italy, Sweden, and West Germany." Paper read at the International Political Science Association Round Table on Political Finance, Oxford, England, March 26.

Nelkin, Dorothy, and Pollak, Michael. 1980. *The Atom Besieged: Extra-Parliamentary Dissent in France and Germany.* Cambridge, Mass.: MIT Press.

Nelles, Wilfried, and Oppermann, Reinhard, eds. 1980. *Partizipation und Politik: Beiträge zur Theorie und Praxis politischer Partizipation.* Göttingen: Schwartz.

Norman, Peter, and Gumbel, Peter, 1984. "West German Central Bank Gets Good Marks for Restoring Country's Economic Well-Being." *Wall Street Journal,* December 31, p. 12.

Norpoth, Helmut. 1982. "The German Federal Republic: Coalition Government at the Brink of Majority Rule." In Eric C. Browne and John Dreijmanis, eds., *Government Coalitions in Western Democracies,* pp. 7–32. New York: Longman.

Nussbaum, Bruce. 1983. *The World after Oil: The Shifting Axis of Power and Wealth.* New York: Simon and Schuster.

Offe, Claus. 1975. *Berufsbildungsreform: Eine Fallstudie über Reformpolitik.* Frankfurt: Suhrkamp.

Olk, Thomas, and Heinze, Rolf G. 1985. "Selbsthilfe im Sozialsektor." In Olk and Hans-Uwe Otto, eds., *Gesellschaftliche Perspektiven der Sozialarbeit 4: Lokale Sozialpolitik und Selbsthilfe,* pp. 233–67. Neuwied: Luchterhand.

Olson, Mancur. 1982. *The Rise and Decline of Nations: Economic Growth, Stagflation, and Social Rigidity.* New Haven: Yale University Press.

Orthbandt, Eberhardt. 1980. *Der Deutsche Verein in der Geschichte der deutschen Fürsorge.* Frankfurt: Selbstverlag des Deutschen Vereins.

Otte, George, and Zuelch, Ruediger. 1977. "Party and Policy in West German Cities: A German View." *American Political Science Review* 71(2):592–95.

Papadakis, Elim. 1984. *The Green Movement in West Germany.* New York: St. Martin's Press.

Paterson, William E. 1981. "Political Leadership in the Federal Republic: The Federal Chancellor." Paper read at ECPR Conference, Patterns of Executive Arrangement across the World.

———, and Smith, Gordon, eds. 1981. *The West German Model: Perspectives on a Stable State.* London: Frank Cass.

Pinney, Edward L. 1963. *Federalism, Bureaucracy, and Party Politics in West-*

ern Germany: The Role of the Bundesrat. Chapel Hill: University of North Carolina Press.

Pridham, Geoffrey. 1977. *Christian Democracy in Western Germany: The CDU/CSU in Government and Opposition, 1945-1976.* New York: St. Martin's Press.

Pulzer, Peter. 1978. "Responsible Party Government and Stable Coalition. The Case of the Federal Republic of Germany." *Political Studies* 26(2):181–208.

Ramm, Thilo. 1971. "Labor Courts and Grievance Settlement in West Germany." In Benjamin Aaron, ed., *Labor Courts and Grievance Settlement in Western Europe,* pp. 83–157. Berkeley: University of California Press.

Raschke, Joachim. 1985. *Soziale Bewegungen. Ein historisch-systematischer Grundriss.* Frankfurt: Campus.

———, ed. 1982. *Bürger und Parteien: Ansichten und Analysen einer schwierigen Beziehung* Opladen: Westdeutscher Verlag.

Reissert, Bernd, and Schaefer, Günther F. 1985. "Centre-Periphery Relations in the Federal Republic of Germany." In Yves Mény and Vincent Wright, eds., *Centre-Periphery Relations in Western Europe,* pp. 104–24. London: Allen and Unwin.

Rinken, Alfred. 1971. *Das Öffentliche als verfassungstheoretisches Problem dargestellt am Rechtsstatus der Wohlfahrtsverbände.* Berlin: Duncker and Humblot.

Ritter, Ernst-Hasso. 1979. "Der kooperative Staat." *Archiv des Öffentlichen Rechts.* 104(3):389–413.

Roberts, Charles C. 1979. "Economic Theory and Policy Making in West Germany: The Role of the Council of Economic Experts." *Cambridge Journal of Economics* 3(1):83–89.

Rogowski, Ronald L. 1970. "Social Structure and Stable Rule: The German Case." Ph.d. diss., Princeton University.

Rose, Richard. 1982. "The Role of Laws in Comparative Perspective." *Studies in Public Policy* 106. Centre for the Study of Public Policy, University of Strathclyde.

Rueschemeyer, Dietrich. 1973. *Lawyers and Their Society: A Comparative Study of the Legal Profession in Germany and in the United States.* Cambridge, Mass.: Harvard University Press.

Safran, William. 1967. *Veto-Group Politics: The Case of Health Insurance Reform in West Germany.* San Francisco: Chandler.

Scharpf, Fritz W. 1970. *Die politischen Kosten des Rechtsstaats.* Tübingen: J.C.B. Mohr (Paul Siebeck).

———. 1985. "The Joint-Decision Trap: Lessons from German and European Integration," IIM/LMP 85-1. Berlin, Wissenschaftszentrum.

Scharpf, Fritz W.; Reissert, Bernd; and Schnabel, Fritz. 1976. *Politikverflechtung: Theorie und Empirie des kooperativen Föderalismus in der Bundesrepublik.* Kronberg, Ts.: Scriptor.

————. 1978. "Policy Effectiveness and Conflict Avoidance in Intergovernmental Policy Formation." In Kenneth Hanf and Fritz W. Scharpf, eds., *Interorganizational Policy Making: Limits to Coordination and Central Control*, pp. 57–112. Beverly Hills: Sage Publications.

————, eds. 1977. *Politikverflechtung II: Kritik und Berichte aus der Praxis.* Kronberg, Ts.: Athenäum.

Schattschneider, Elmer E. 1960. *The Semisovereign People: A Realist's View of Democracy in America.* New York: Holt, Rinehart and Winston.

Schlotter, Peter. 1985. "Military Policy and External Security." In Klaus von Beyme and Manfred G. Schmidt, eds., *Policy and Politics in the Federal Republic of Germany*, pp. 222–42. New York: St. Martin's Press.

Schmidt, Manfred G. 1978. "The Politics of Domestic Reform in the Federal Republic of Germany." *Politics and Society* 8(2):165–200.

————. 1980. *CDU und SPD an der Regierung: Ein Vergleich ihrer Politik in den Ländern.* Frankfurt: Campus.

————. 1983. "Two Logics of Coalition Policy: The West German Case." In Vernon Bogdanor, ed., *Coalition Government in Western Europe*, pp. 38–58. London: Heinemann.

————. 1985. "Allerweltsparteien in Westeuropa? Ein Beitrag zu Kirchheimers These vom Wandel des westeuropäischen Parteiensystems." *Leviathan* 13(3):376–97.

Schmitter, Philippe C. 1979. "Still the Century of Corporatism?" In Philippe C. Schmitter and Gerhard Lehmbruch, eds., *Trends toward Corporatist Intermediation*, pp. 7–52. Beverly Hills: Sage Publications.

Schnitzer, Martin. 1972. *East and West Germany: A Comparative Economic Analysis.* New York: Praeger.

Schönbohm, Rudolf. 1979. *CDU: Porträt einer Partei.* Munich: Olzog.

Schram, Glenn. 1971. "Ideology and Politics: The *Rechtsstaat* Idea in West Germany." *Journal of Politics* 33(1):133–57.

Schreckenberger, Waldemar. 1983. "Intergovernmental Relations." In Klaus König, Hans Joachim von Oertzen, and Frido Wagener, eds., *Public Administration in the Federal Republic of Germany*, pp. 65–82. Deventer: Kluwer.

Schwarz, Hans-Peter. 1985. *Die gezähmten Deutschen. Von der Machtbesessenheit zur Machtvergessenheit.* Stuttgart: Deutsche-Verlags-Anstalt.

Schweigler, Gebhard L. 1975. *National Consciousness in Divided Germany.* Beverly Hills: Sage Publications.

————. 1984. *West German Foreign Policy: The Domestic Setting.* New York: Praeger.

Seffen, Achim. 1973. *Die Selbstverwaltung in der Sozialversicherung.* Cologne: Deutscher Instituts-Verlag.

Simon, Walter. 1976. *Macht und Herrschaft der Unternehmerverbände BDI, BDA und DIHT.* Cologne: Pahl-Rugenstein.

Smith, Gordon. 1976. "West Germany and the Politics of Centrality." *Government and Opposition* 11(4):387–407.

———. 1979. *Democracy in Western Germany: Parties and Politics in the Federal Republic.* New York: Holmes and Meier.

———. 1981. "Does West German Democracy Have an 'Efficient Secret'?" In William E. Paterson and Gordon Smith, eds., *The West German Model: Perspectives on a Stable State,* pp. 166–76. London: Frank Cass.

Spahn, Heinz-Peter. 1979. *Die Stabilitätspolitik des Sachverständigenrates: Zur Abhängigkeit ökonomischer Paradigmenwechsel von wirtschaftspolitischen Handlungsimperativen.* Frankfurt: Campus.

Spahn, P. Bernd. 1978. *Principles of Federal Policy Coordination in the Federal Republic of Germany: Basic Issues and Annotated Legislation.* Canberra: The Australian University, Centre for Research on Federal Financial Relations.

Spotts, Frederic. 1973. *The Churches and Politics in Germany.* Middletown, Conn.: Wesleyan University Press.

Standfest, Erich. 1977. "Soziale Selbstverwaltung. Zum Problem der Partizipation in der Sozialpolitik." In Christian von Ferber and Franz-Xaver Kaufmann, eds., *Soziologie und Sozialpolitik,* special issue 19 of *Kölner Zeitschrift für Soziologie und Sozialpsychologie,* pp. 424–37. Opladen: Westdeutscher Verlag.

Stone, Deborah A. 1979. "Health Care Cost Containment in West Germany." *Journal of Health Politics, Policy and Law* 4(2):176–99.

———. 1980. *The Limits of Professional Power. National Health Care in the Federal Republic of Germany.* Chicago: Chicago University Press.

Streeck, Wolfgang. 1982. "Organizational Consequences of Neo-Corporatist Co-operation in West German Labour Unions." In Gerhard Lehmbruch and Philippe C. Schmitter, eds., *Patterns of Corporatist Policy-Making,* pp. 29–82. Beverly Hills: Sage Publications.

———. 1983a. "Die Reform der beruflichen Bildung in der westdeutschen Bauwirtschaft 1969-1982. Eine Fallstudie über Verbände als Träger öffentlicher Politik," IIM/LMP 83-23. Berlin, Wissenschaftszentrum Berlin.

———. 1983b. "Between Pluralism and Corporatism: German Business Associations and the State." *Journal of Public Policy* 3(3):265–84.

Süllow, Bernd. 1982. *Die Selbstverwaltung in der Sozialversicherung als korporatistische Einrichtung.* Frankfurt: Peter Lang.

Tennstedt, Florian. 1976. "Sozialgeschichte und Sozialversicherung." In Maria Blohmke et al., eds., *Handbuch der Sozialmedizin,* 3:385–492. Stuttgart: Enke.

———. 1977. *Soziale Selbstverwaltung: Geschichte der Selbstverwaltung in der Krankenversicherung. Band 2.* Bonn: Verlag der Ortskrankenkassen.

———. 1981. "Fürsorgegeschichte und Vereinsgeschichte: 100 Jahre Deutscher

Verein in der Geschichte der deutschen Fürsorge." *Zeitschrift für Sozialreform* 27(2):72–100.

Thränhardt, Dietrich. 1981. "Kommunaler Korporatismus: Deutsche Traditionen und moderne Tendenzen." In Dietrich Thränhardt and Herbert Uppendahl, eds., *Alternativen lokaler Demokratie: Kommunalverfassung als politisches Problem*, pp. 5–23. Königstein Ts.: Anton Hain.

Thomaneck, Jürgen. 1985. "Police and Public Order in the Federal Republic of Germany." In John Roach and Jürgen Thomaneck, eds., *Police and Public Order in Europe*, pp. 143–84. London: Croom Helm.

Twain, Mark. [1880] 1961. "The Awful German Language." In Charles Neider, ed., *The Complete Humorous Sketches and Tales of Mark Twain*. Garden City, N.Y.: Hanover House.

Verheugen, Günter. 1984. *Der Ausverkauf: Macht und Verfall der FDP*. Reinbek: Rowohlt.

Vogel, David. 1986. *National Styles of Regulation: Environmental Policy in Great Britain and the United States*. Ithaca: Cornell University Press.

Wadbrook, William P. 1972. *West German Balance-of-Payments Policy. The Prelude to European Monetary Integration*. New York: Praeger.

Walter, Norbert. 1976. "No 'advise and consent' for Council of Economic Experts." *German Tribune*, October 3, pp. 6–7.

Waterkamp, Rainer. 1974. *Politische Leitung und Systemveränderung: Zum Problemlösungsprozess durch Planungs- und Informationssysteme*. Cologne: Europäische Verlagsanstalt.

Watkins, Carolyn. 1984. "Interest Group Influence in Bureaucratic Decision Processes: The Implementation of Clean Air Policy in the U.S. and the F.R.G." Paper read at the annual meeting of the American Political Science Association, Washington, D.C., August 30–September 2.

Webber, Douglas. 1983. "A Relationship or 'Critical Partnership'? Capital and the Social-Liberal Coalition in West Germany." *West European Politics* 6(2):61–86.

Weber, Hajo. 1984. "Intermediäre Organisation: Zur Organisation von Wirtschaftsinteressen zwischen Markt, Staat und Gewerkschaften." Ph.D. diss., University of Bielefeld.

Wegner, Klaus. 1981. *Im Blickpunkt: Sachverständigenrat und Konjunktur- und Wachstumspolitik der Bundesregierung seit 1964*. Frankfurt: Fischer.

Weiler, Hans N. 1982. "Protest and Reform in West Germany: Cycles of Causation in Education and Energy Policy?" Paper read at the Conference of Europeanists of the Council for European Studies, Washington D.C., April 29–May 1.

Werkentin, Falco. 1984. *Die Restauration der deutschen Polizei: Innere Rüstung von 1945 bis zur Notstandsgesetzgebung*. Frankfurt: Campus.

Wiesenthal, Helmut. 1981. *Die Konzertierte Aktion im Gesundheitswesen: Ein*

Beispiel für Theorie und Politik des modernen Korporatismus. Frankfurt: Campus.

Willey, Richard J. 1974. "Trade Unions and Political Parties in the Federal Republic of Germany." *Industrial and Labor Relations Review* 28(1):38–59.

Windhoff-Héritier, Adrienne. 1982. "Selbsthilfe-Organisationen: Eine Lösung für die Sozialpolitik der mageren Jahre?" *Soziale Welt* 33(1):49–65.

Wolfe, Robert, ed. 1984. *Americans as Proconsuls: United States Military Government in Germany and Japan, 1944-1952.* Carbondale: Southern Illinois University Press.

WSI-Studie No. 35. 1978. *Sozialpolitik und Selbstverwaltung: Zur Demokratisierung des Sozialstaats.* Cologne: Bund Verlag.

Wunderlich, Frieda. 1946. *German Labor Courts.* Chapel Hill: University of North Carolina Press.

Yago, Glenn. 1984. *The Decline of Transit: Urban Transportation in German and U.S. Cities, 1900-1970.* Cambridge: Cambridge University Press.

Zimmermann, Horst. 1981. *Studies in Comparative Federalism: West Germany.* Washington, D.C.: Advisory Commission on Intergovernmental Relations.

Zinn, Karl-Georg. 1978. "Politik und Sachverständigenmeinung—Sachverständigenrat und Council of Economic Advisers im Vergleich." *Gewerkschaftliche Monatshefte* 29(3):179–88.

Economic Management

Abelshauser, Werner. 1983. *Wirtschaftsgeschichte der Bundesrepublik Deutschland 1945-1980.* Frankfurt: Suhrkamp.

———. 1984. "The First Post-Liberal Nation: Stages in the Development of Modern Corporatism in Germany." *European History Quarterly* 14:285–318.

Anderson, Douglas D. 1980. "Germany (B): The Uncertain Stride of a Reluctant Giant," Case 1-380-121. Boston: Harvard Business School.

Arndt, Hans-Joachim. 1966. *West Germany: Politics of Non-Planning.* Syracuse: Syracuse University Press.

Braunthal, Gerard. 1965. "The Struggle for Cartel Legislation." In James B. Christoph, ed., *Cases in Comparative Politics,* pp. 241–55. Boston: Little, Brown.

Deubner, Christian. 1984. "Change and Internationalization in Industry: Toward a Sectoral Interpretation of West German Politics." *International Organization* 38(3):501–35.

Dyson, Kenneth. 1984. "The Politics of Corporate Crises in West Germany." *West European Politics* 7(1):24–47.

———. 1986. "The State, Banks, and Industry: The West German Case." In

Andrew Cox, ed., *State, Finance, and Industry: A Comparative Analysis of Post-War Trends in Six Advanced Industrial Economies*. New York: St. Martin's Press.

Esser, Josef; Fach, Wolfgang; and Dyson, Kenneth. 1984. "'Social Market' and Modernization Policy: West Germany." In Dyson and Stephen Wilks, eds., *Industrial Crisis: A Comparative Study of the State and Industry*, pp. 102–27. New York: St. Martin's Press.

Friedrich, Carl-Joachim. 1955. "The Political Thought of Neo-Liberalism." *American Political Science Review* 40(2):509–25.

Gerschenkron, Alexander. 1962. *Economic Backwardness in Historical Perspective*. Cambridge, Mass.: Harvard University Press.

Hankel, Wilhelm. 1977. "West Germany." In Wilfrid L. Kohl, ed., *Economic Foreign Policies of Industrial States*, pp. 105–24. Lexington, Mass.: D. C. Heath.

Hardach, Karl. 1980. *The Political Economy of Germany in the Twentieth Century*. Berkeley: University of California Press.

Hardes, Heinz-Dieter. 1974. *Einkommenspolitik in der BRD: Stabilität und Gruppeninteressen—Der Fall Konzertierte Aktion*. Frankfurt: Herder and Herder.

Hartrich, Edwin. 1980. *The Fourth and Richest Reich*. New York: Macmillan.

Hirsch, Joachim. 1968. *Parlament und Verwaltung: Haushaltsplanung und Haushaltskontrolle in der Bundesrepublik Deutschland*. Stuttgart: Kohlhammer.

Hofman, Gunter. 1980. "Die Handschrift des Kanzlers." *Die Zeit*, August 8.

Horn, Ernst-Jürgen. 1982. *Management of Industrial Change in Germany*. University of Sussex: Sussex European Research Centre.

Johnson, Chalmers. 1982. *MITI and the Japanese Miracle: The Growth of Industrial Policy, 1925–1975*. Stanford: Stanford University Press.

Johnson, Nevil, and Cochrane, Allan. 1981. *Economic Policy-Making by Local Authorities in Britain and Western Germany*. London: Allen and Unwin.

Kloten Norbert; Ketterer, Karl-Heinz; and Vollmer, Rainer. 1985. "West Germany's Stabilization Performance." In Leon N. Lindberg and Charles S. Maier, eds., *The Politics of Inflation and Economic Stagnation: Theoretical Approaches and International Case Studies*, pp. 353–402. Washington, D.C.: Brookings Institution.

Knott, Jack H. 1981. *Managing the German Economy*. Lexington, Mass.: D. C. Heath.

Kreile, Michael. 1978. "West Germany: The Dynamics of Expansion." In Peter J. Katzenstein, ed., *Between Power and Plenty: Foreign Economic Policies of Advanced Industrial States*, pp. 191–224. Madison: University of Wisconsin Press.

Küster, Georg H. 1974. "Germany." In Raymond Vernon, ed., *Big Business and the State: Changing Relations in Western Europe*, pp. 64–86. Cambridge, Mass.: Harvard University Press.

MacLennan, Malcolm; Forsyth, Murray; and Denton, Geoffrey. 1968. *Economic Planning and Policies in Britain, France and Germany*. New York: Praeger.

Markovits, Andrei S., ed. 1982. *The Political Economy of West Germany: Modell Deutschland*. New York: Praeger.

Molitor, Regina, ed. 1973. *Zehn Jahre Sachverständigenrat zur Begutachtung der gesamtwirtschaftlichen Entwicklung: Eine kritische Bestandsaufnahme*. Frankfurt: Athenäum.

Narr-Lindner, Gudrun. 1984. *Grenzen monetärer Steuerung: Die Restriktionspolitik der Bundesbank 1964–1974*. Frankfurt: Campus.

Neumann, Wolfgang, and Uterwedde, Henrik. 1986. *Industriepolitik: Ein deutsch-französischer Vergleich*. Opladen: Leske and Budrich.

Pempel, T. J. 1982. *Policy and Politics in Japan: Creative Conservatism*. Philadelphia: Temple University Press.

Reuss, Frederick, G. 1963. *Fiscal Policy for Growth without Inflation: The German Experiment*. Baltimore: Johns Hopkins University Press.

Riemer, Jeremiah M. 1983. "Crisis and Intervention in the West German Economy: A Political Analysis of Changes in the Policy Machinery during the 1960's and 1970's." Ph.D. diss., Cornell University.

Schäfer, Günther F. 1974. "Public Corporation and Public Policy: The Case of Germany." Unpublished paper.

Scharpf, Fritz W. 1984. "Economic and Institutional Constraints of Full-Employment Strategies: Sweden, Austria, and West Germany, 1973-1982." In John H. Goldthorpe, ed., *Order and Conflict in Contemporary Capitalism*, pp. 257–90. Oxford: Clarendon Press.

Schlesinger, Helmut. 1976. "Neuere Erfahrungen der Geldpolitik in der Bundesrepublik Deutschland." *Kredit und Kapital* 9(4):433–54.

Schmidt, Manfred G. 1982. *Wohlfahrtsstaatliche Politik unter bügerlichen und sozialdemokratischen Regierungen: Ein internationaler Vergleich*. Frankfurt: Campus.

———. 1985. "Budgetary Policy: A Comparative Perspective on Policy Outputs and Outcomes." In Klaus von Beyme and Manfred G. Schmidt, eds., *Policy and Politics in the Federal Republic of Germany*, pp. 27–55. New York: St. Martin's Press.

Skuka, Dario. 1984. "Selected Comparative Economic Statistics for Seven Major Industrial Countries, 1970-1983." Report 84-619E. Washington D.C.: Library of Congress, Congressional Research Service.

Seitenzahl, Rolf. 1974. *Einkommenspolitik durch Konzertierte Aktion und Orientierungsdaten*. Cologne: Bund.

Shonfield, Andrew. 1965. *Modern Capitalism: The Changing Balance of Public and Private Power.* London: Oxford University Press.

Sturm, Roland. 1985a. "Budgetary Politics in the Federal Republic of Germany." *West European Politics* 8(3):56–63.

———. 1985b. "Entscheidungsstrukturen und Entscheidungsprozesse in der Haushaltspolitik: Zum Selbstverständnis des Haushaltsausschusses des Deutschen Bundestages." *Politische Vierteljahresschrift* 26(3):247–69.

U.S. Congress. Joint Economic Committee. 1976. "Achieving the Goals of the Employment Act of 1946—Thirtieth Anniversary Review." In volume 4, *Economic Planning.* Paper No. 1, *Economic Planning in Five Western European Countries: An Overview.* Washington, D.C.: U.S. Government Printing Office.

———. 1981. *Monetary Policy, Selective Credit Policy, and Industrial Policy in France, Britain, West Germany, and Sweden.* Washington, D.C.: U.S. Government Printing Office.

Wadbrook, William P. 1972. *West German Balance-of-Payments Policy: The Prelude to European Monetary Integration.* New York: Praeger.

Wallich, Henry C. 1955. *Mainsprings of German Revival.* New Haven: Yale University Press.

Webber, Douglas. 1985. "The Framework of Government-Industry Relations and Industrial Policy Making in the Federal Republic of Germany." Unpublished paper, School of Social Science, University of Sussex.

Zweig, Konrad. 1980. *The Origins of the German Social Market Economy: The Leading Ideas and Their Intellectual Roots.* London: Adam Smith Institute.

Industrial Relations

Alexis, Marion. 1983. "Neo-Corporatism and Industrial Relations: The Case of German Trade Unions." *West European Politics* 6(1):75–92.

Bamberg, Ulrich, et al. 1984. *Praxis der Unternehmensmitbestimmung nach dem Mitbestimmungsgesetz 76: Eine Problemstudie.* Düsseldorf: Hans-Böckler-Stiftung.

Baring, Arnulf. 1969. *Aussenpolitik in Adenauers Kanzlerdemokratie: Bonns Beitrag zur Europäischen Verteidigungsgemeinschaft.* Munich: Oldenbourg.

Bergmann, Joachim, and Müller-Jentsch, Walther. 1975. "The Federal Republic of Germany: Cooperative Unionism and Dual Bargaining System Challenged." In Solomon Barkin, ed., *Worker Militancy and Its Consequences, 1965-75: New Directions in Western Industrial Relations,* pp. 235–76. New York: Praeger.

Blankenburg, Erhard; Rogowski, Ralf; and Schönholz, Siegfried. 1978. "Phenomena of Legalization: Observations in a German Labour Court," IIM dp/78-20. Berlin, Wissenschaftszentrum Berlin.

Blumenthal, Werner M. 1956. *Codetermination in the German Steel Industry.*

Research Paper No. 94. Princeton, N.J.: Princeton University Industrial Relations Section.

Braunthal, Gerard. 1976. "Codetermination in West Germany." In James B. Christoph and Bernard Brown, eds., *Cases in Comparative Politics*, 3rd ed., pp. 215–47. Boston: Little, Brown.

Bunn, Ronald, F. 1958. "Codetermination and the Federation of German Employers' Associations." *Midwest Journal of Political Science* 2(3):278–97.

Dorscht, Axel. 1985. "Economic Development and Changing State-Labour Relations in the Federal Republic of Germany." *Occasional Papers No. 12*. Dept. of Political Science, Carleton University, Ottawa.

Embassy of the Federal Republic, Press Office. 1974. *German Press Review*, October 23.

Fogarty, Michael P. 1965. *Company and Corporation—One Law*. London: Chapman.

Fürstenberg, Friedrich. 1969. "Workers' Participation in Management in the Federal Republic of Germany (No. 4)." *Bulletin of the International Institute for Labor Studies*, no. 6:94–148.

Hancock, M. Donald. 1977. "The Political Role of Organized Labor in West Germany: In Pursuit of Codetermination and Full Employment." Paper read at the annual meeting of the American Political Science Association, Washington, D.C., September 1–4.

Hartmann, Heinz. 1970. "Codetermination in West Germany." *Industrial Relations* 9(2):137–47.

———. 1975. "Codetermination Today and Tomorrow." *British Journal of Industrial Relations* 13(1):54–64.

Hassencamp, Alfred, and Bieneck, Hans-Jürgen. 1983. "Technical and Organisational Changes and Design of Working Conditions in the Federal Republic of Germany." *Labour and Society* 8(1):39–56.

Helm, Jutta A. 1984. "Codetermination in West Germany: What Difference Has It Made?" Paper read at the annual meeting of the American Political Science Association, Washington, D.C., August 30–September 2.

Jacobi, Otto; Jessop, Bob; Kastendick, Hans; and Regini, Marino, eds. 1986. *Economic Crisis, Trade Unions and the State*. London: Croom Helm.

Kerr, Clark. 1954. "The Trade Union Movement and the Redistribution of Power in Postwar Germany." *Quarterly Journal of Economics* 68(4):535–64.

Kurth, E. A. 1954. "Codetermination in Germany—Peace at Last?" *Social Order* 4:19–28.

Markovits, Andrei S. 1986. *The Politics of the West German Trade Unions: Strategies of Class and Interest Representation in Growth and Crisis*. Cambridge: Cambridge University Press.

Markovits, Andrei S., and Allen, Christopher S. 1980. "Power and Dissent:

The Trade Unions in the Federal Republic of Germany Re-Examined." *West European Politics* 3(1):68–86.

―――. 1984. "Trade Unions and the Economic Crisis: The West German Case." In Peter Gourevitch, Andrew Martin, George Ross, and Stephen Bornstein, *Unions and Economic Crisis: Britain, West Germany and Sweden*, pp. 89–188. London: Allen and Unwin.

McPherson, William. 1955. "Codetermination in Practice." *Industrial and Labor Relations Review* 8(4):499–519.

Mitbestimmungskommission. 1970. *Mitbestimmung im Unternehmen: Bericht der Sachverständigenkommission zur Auswertung der bisherigen Erfahrungen bei der Mitbestimmung*. Drucksache VI/334. Bonn: Deutscher Bundestag.

Moses, John A. 1982. *Trade Unionism in Germany from Bismarck to Hitler, 1869-1933*. 2 vols. London: George Prior.

Narr-Lindner, Gudrun. 1984. *Grenzen monetärer Steuerung: Die Restrikstionspolitik der Bundesbank 1964–1974*. Frankfurt: Campus.

Riemer, Jeremiah M. 1975. "Bringing Union Politics into the Factory: Three Strategies for *Betriebsnahe Tarifpolitik* in West Germany." Unpublished paper, Dept. of Government, Cornell University.

Shigeyoshi, Tokunaga, and Bergmann, Joachim. 1984. *Industrial Relations in Transition: The Cases of Japan and the Federal Republic of Germany*. Tokyo: Tokyo University Press.

Shuchman, Abraham. 1957. *Codetermination: Labor's Middle Way in Germany*. Washington, D.C.: Public Affairs Press.

Solyom-Fekete, William. 1976. *Co-Determination Rights of Employees in the Federal Republic of Germany*. Washington, D.C.: Library of Congress.

Spieker, Wolfgang, and Strohauer, Heinrich. 1982. *30 Jahre Management gegen die Montan-Mitbestimmung: Tatsachen und Deutungen des Konflikts Mannesmann/IG Metall 1980/81*. Cologne: Bund.

Spiro, Herbert. 1958. *The Politics of German Codetermination*. Cambridge, Mass.: Harvard University Press.

Streeck, Wolfgang. 1981. *Gewerkschaftliche Organisationsprobleme in der sozialstaatlichen Demokratie*. Königstein/Ts.: Athenäum.

―――. 1984. "Codetermination: The Fourth Decade." In B. Wilpert and A. Sorge, eds., *International Perspectives on Organizational Democracy*, pp. 391–422. New York: Wiley.

Sturmthal, Adolf F. 1964. *Workers Councils: A Study of Workplace Organization on Both Sides of the Iron Curtain*. Cambridge, Mass.: Harvard University Press.

Teague, Burton. 1971. "Can Workers Participate in Management—Successfully? The German Experience." *Conference Board Record* 8:48–52.

Thimm, Alfred L. 1981. "How Far Should German Codetermination Go?" *Challenge* 11(7–8):13–22.

Wiedemann, Herbert. 1980. "Codetermination by Workers in German Enterprises." *American Journal of Comparative Law* 28(1):79–92.

Wilpert, Bernhard. 1975. "Research on Industrial Democracy: The German Case." *Industrial Relations Journal* 6(1):53–64.

Wilson, Arlene. 1982. "Wage and Price Policy in West Germany." In U.S. Congress, Joint Economic Committee, *Wage and Price Policies in Australia, Austria, Canada, Japan, the Netherlands, and West Germany*, pp. 48–56. Washington, D.C.: U.S. Government Printing Office.

Social Welfare

Adamy, Wilhelm, and Naegele, Gerhard. 1985. "Armenpolitik in der Krise. Bestandsaufnahme und Entwicklungstrends." In Stephan Leibfried and Florian Tennstedt, eds., *Politik der Armut und die Spaltung des Sozialstaats*, pp. 94–121. Frankfurt: Suhrkamp.

Adamy, Wilhelm, and Steffen, Johannes. 1984. "Zwischenbilanz von Sozialmontage und Umverteilungspolitik seit 1982." Unpublished paper, Seminar für Sozialpolitik, Cologne University.

Alber, Jens. 1980. "Der Wohlfahrtsstaat in der Krise? Eine Bilanz nach drei Jahrzehnten Sozialpolitik in der Bundesrepublik." *Zeitschrift für Soziologie* 9(4):313–42.

———. 1982. *Vom Armenhaus zum Wohlfahrtsstaat: Analysen zur Entwicklung der Sozialversicherung in Westeuropa*. Frankfurt: Campus.

———. 1984. "Versorgungsklassen im Wohlfahrtsstaat: Überlegungen und Daten zur Situation in der Bundesrepublik." *Kölner Zeitschrift für Soziologie und Sozialpsychologic* 36(2):225–51.

———. 1985. "How the West German Welfare State Passed through the Recent Years of Economic Crisis." Paper read at the 13th World Congress of the International Political Science Association, Paris, July 15–20.

Blankenburg, Erhard; Schmid, Günther; and Treiber, Hubert. 1975. "Legitimitäts- und Implementierungsprobleme 'Aktiver Arbeitsmarktpolitik'," I/75-66. Berlin, International Institute of Management.

Bosch, Gerhard, and Sengenberger, Werner. 1984. "Employment Policy, the State and the Unions in the Federal Republic of Germany." Country report prepared for the 6th annual conference of the International Working Party on Labour Market Segmentation, Budapest, July 24–28.

Bruche, Gerd, and Reissert, Bernd. 1985. *Die Finanzierung der Arbeitsmarktpolitik: System, Effektivität, Reformansätze*. Frankfurt: Campus.

Faust, Anselm. 1981. "State and Unemployment in Germany 1890-1918 (Labour Exchanges, Job Creation and Unemployment Insurance)." In W. J.

Mommsen, ed., *The Emergence of the Welfare State in Britain and Germany: 1850-1950*, pp. 150–63. London: Croom Helm.

Ferber, Christian von. 1967. *Sozialpolitik in der Wohlstandsgesellschaft: Was stimmt nicht mit der deutschen Sozialpolitik?* Hamburg: Christian Wegner.

————, and Kaufmann, Franz-Xaver, eds. 1977. *Soziologie und Sozialpolitik.* Special issue 19 of *Kölner Zeitschrift für Soziologie und Sozialpsychologie.* Opladen: Westdeutscher Verlag.

Flora, Peter, and Heidenheimer, Arnold, eds. 1981. *The Development of Welfare States in Europe and America.* New Brunswick: Transaction Books.

Galperin, Peter. 1985. "Sozialhilfe und Bedarfsprinzip. Zum Streit um die Konkretisierung der Bedarfsdeckung." In Stephan Leibfried and Florian Tennstedt, eds., *Politik der Armut und die Spaltung des Sozialstaats*, pp. 153–68. Frankfurt: Suhrkamp.

Geissler, Heiner. 1976. *Die Neue Soziale Frage: Analysen und Dokumente.* Freiburg: Herder.

Glaser, William. 1978. *Health Insurance Bargaining: Foreign Lessons for Americans.* New York: Gardner Press, 1978.

Groth, Klaus-Martin. 1977. "Die Krise der Sozialversicherungen: Zur gegenwärtigen Lage der Sozialversicherungen im Rahmen der 'Finanzkrise' des Staates." *Kritische Justiz* 1:1–10.

Hartmann, Helmut. 1985. "Armut trotz Sozialhilfe. Zur Nichtinanspruchnahme von Sozialhilfe in der Bundesrepublik." In Stephan Leibfried and Florian Tennstedt, eds., *Politik der Armut und die Spaltung des Sozialstaats*, pp. 169–89. Frankfurt: Suhrkamp.

Hartwich, Hans-Hermann. 1970. *Sozialstaatspostulat und gesellschaftlicher Status Quo.* Cologne: Westdeutscher Verlag.

Heclo, Hugh. 1974. *Modern Social Politics in Britain and Sweden.* New Haven, Conn.: Yale University Press.

Heidenheimer, Arnold, J. 1980. "Unions and Welfare State Development in Britain and Germany: An Interpretation of Metamorphoses in the Period 1910-1950," IIVG/ dp/80-209. Berlin, International Institute of Comparative Social Research.

————. 1981a. "Education and Social Security Entitlements in Europe and America." In Peter Flora and Arnold J. Heidenheimer, eds., *The Development of Welfare States in Europe and America*, pp. 269–304. New Brunswick: Transaction Books.

————. 1981b. "The Indexation of Pension Entitlements: The West German Initiative in Comparative Perspective." Paper read at Western Societies Program conference, Post-Keynesian Politics: Remaking the Welfare State, Cornell University, September 17–19.

Hockerts, Hans Günter. 1980. *Sozialpolitische Entscheidungen im Nachkriegs-*

deutschland: Alliierte und deutsche Sozialversicherungspolitik 1945 bis 1957. Stuttgart: Klett-Cotta.

———. 1981. "German Post-war Social Policies against the Background of the Beveridge Plan. Some Observations Preparatory to a Comparative Analysis." In W. J. Mommsen, ed., *The Emergence of the Welfare State in Britain and Germany: 1850-1950,* pp. 315–39. London: Croom Helm.

Johannesson, Jan, and Schmid, Günther. 1980. "The Development of Labour Market Policy in Sweden and Germany: Competing or Convergent Models to Combat Unemployment?" *European Journal of Political Research* 8:387–406.

Kaim-Caudle, P. R. 1973. *Comparative Social Policy and Social Security: A Ten-Country Study.* New York: Dunellen.

Krautkrämer, Uta. 1978. "Labour Market Administration in the Federal Republic of Germany," IIM/78-14b. Berlin, International Institute for Management.

Leibfried, Stephan. 1976. "Armutspotential und Sozialhilfe in der Bundesrepublik: Zum Prozess des Filterns von Ansprüchen auf Sozialhilfe." *Kritische Justiz* 4:377–93.

———. 1978. "Public Assistance in the United States and the Federal Republic of Germany: Does Social Democracy Make a Difference?" *Comparative Politics* 11(1):59–76.

Leibfried, Stephan, and Tennstedt, Florian. 1985a. "Armenpolitik und Arbeiterpolitik. Zur Entwicklung und Krise der traditionellen Sozialpolitik der Verteilungsformen." In Leibfried and Tennstedt, eds., *Politik der Armut und die Spaltung des Sozialstaats,* pp. 64–93. Frankfurt: Suhrkamp.

———, eds. 1985b. *Politik der Armut und die Spaltung des Sozialstaats.* Frankfurt: Suhrkamp.

Machtan, Lothar. 1985. "Zur Entstehungs- und Wirkungsgeschichte sozialstaatlicher Intervention (im späten 19. und frühen 20. Jahrhundert). Einige Neuerscheinungen auf dem Gebiet der historischen Sozialpolitikforschung." In H.-G. Haupt et al., *Proletarische Lebenslagen und Sozialpolitik,* pp. 361–80. Bremen: Forschungsschwerpunkt Reproduktionsrisiken.

Markham, James M. 1984. "Europe Too Feels the Social Program Pinch." *New York Times,* February 19, p. E3.

Michalsky, Helga. 1985. "The Politics of Social Policy." In Klaus von Beyme and Manfred G. Schmidt, eds., *Policy and Politics in the Federal Republic of Germany,* pp. 56–81. New York: St. Martin's Press.

Mommsen, W. J., ed. 1981. *The Emergence of the Welfare State in Britain and Germany: 1850-1950.* London: Croom Helm.

National Industrial Conference Board. 1932. *Unemployment Insurance and Relief in Germany.* New York: National Industrial Conference Board.

Offe, Claus. 1975. *Berufsausbildungsreform: Eine Fallstudie der Reformpolitik.* Frankfurt: Suhrkamp.

Organization for Economic Co-operation and Development. 1978. *Public Expenditure on Income Maintenance Programmes.* Paris: OECD.

Rimlinger, Gaston V. 1967. "The Economics of Postwar German Social Policy." *Industrial Relations* 6(2):184–204.

————. 1971. *Welfare Policy and Industrialization in Europe, America, and Russia.* New York: John Wiley.

Safran, W. 1967. *Veto-Group Politics. The Case of Health Insurance Reform in West Germany.* San Francisco: Chandler.

Scharpf, Fritz, et al. 1982. *Implementationsprobleme offensiver Arbeitsmarktpolitik: Das Sonderprogramm der Bundesregierung für Regionen mit besonderen Beschäftigungsproblemen.* Frankfurt: Campus.

Schmid, Günther. 1985. "Labour Market Policy under the Social-Liberal Coalition." In Klaus von Beyme and Manfred G. Schmidt, eds., *Policy and Politics in the Federal Republic of Germany,* pp. 107–31. New York: St. Martin's Press.

Schmidt, Manfred G. 1982. *Wohlfahrtsstaatliche Politik unter bürgerlichen und sozialdemokratischen Regierungen: Ein internationaler Vergleich.* Frankfurt: Campus.

Tampke, Jürgen. 1981. "Bismarck's Social Legislation: A Genuine Breakthrough?" In W. J. Mommsen, ed., *The Emergence of the Welfare State in Britain and Germany: 1850-1950,* pp. 71–83. London: Croom Helm.

Tennstedt, Florian. 1976. "Sozialgeschichte der Sozialversicherung." In Maria Blohmke et al., eds., *Handbuch der Sozialmedizin,* 3:325–492. Stuttgart: Enke.

————. 1981. *Sozialgeschichte der Sozialpolitik in Deutschland: Vom 18. Jahrhundert bis zum Ersten Weltkrieg.* Göttingen: Vandenhoeck and Ruprecht.

————. 1983. *Vom Proleten zum Industriearbeiter: Arbeiterbewegung und Sozialpolitik in Deutschland, 1800-1914.* Colgone: Bund Verlag.

Walker, Robert; Lawson, Roger; and Townsend, Peter, eds. 1984. *Responses to Poverty: Lessons from Europe.* Rutherford, N.J.: Fairleigh Dickinson University Press.

Webber, Douglas. 1983. "Combatting and Acquiescing in Unemployment? Crisis Management in Sweden and West Germany." *West European Politics* 6(1):23–43.

Weisbrod, Bernd. 1981. "The Crisis of German Unemployment Insurance in 1928/29 and Its Political Repercussions." In W. J. Mommsen, ed., *The Emergence of the Welfare State in Britain and Germany: 1850-1950.* London: Croom Helm.

Zacher, Hans. 1980. *Sozialpolitik und Verfassung im ersten Jahrzehnt der Bundesrepublik Deutschland*. Berlin: Schweitzer.

———. 1982. "Social Market Economy, Social Policy, and the Law." *Zeitschrift für die Gesamte Staatswissenschaft* 138(3):367–88.

Zöllner, Detlev. 1982. "Germany." In Peter A. Köhler and Hans F. Zacher, eds., *The Evolution of Social Insurance 1891-1981*, pp. 1–92. London: Pinter.

Migrant Workers

Andersen, Uwe. 1984. "Political Participation of Immigrants in Germany." European Consortium for Political Research, 12th Joint Session of Workshops, Salzburg, April 13–18.

Bade, Klaus J. 1984a. "Einführung: Vom Export der Sozialen Frage zur importierten Sozialen Frage: Deutschland im transnationalen Wanderungsgeschehen seit der Mitte des 19. Jahrhunderts." In Bade, ed., *Auswanderer, Wanderarbeiter, Gastarbeiter: Bevölkerung, Arbeitsmarkt und Wanderung in Deutschland seit der Mitte des 19. Jahrhunderts*, 1:9–72. Ostfildern: Scripta Mercaturae.

———. 1984b. "Einführung." In Bade, ed., *Auswanderer, Wanderarbeiter, Gastarbeiter: Bevölkerung, Arbeitsmarkt und Wanderung in Deutschland seit der Mitte des 19. Jahrhunderts*, 2:621–24. Ostfildern: Scripta Mercaturae.

Baker, David P.; Lenhardt, Gero; and Meyer, John. 1985. "Effects of Immigrant Workers on Educational Stratification in Germany." *Sociology of Education* 58(4):213–27.

Barkin, Solomon. 1966. "Trade Union Policies and Programmes for National Internal Rural Migrants and Foreign Workers." *International Migration* 4(1):3–19.

Berger, John. 1975. *A Seventh Man: Migrant Workers in Europe*. New York: Viking Press.

Böhning, Wolf R. 1970. "Foreign Workers in Post-War Germany." *New Atlantis* 2(1):12–38.

Castles, Stephen, and Kosack, Godula. 1974. "Immigrant Workers and Trade Unions in the German Federal Republic." *Radical America* 8(6):55–77.

———. 1985. *Immigrant Workers and Class Structure in Western Europe*. London: Oxford University Press.

Dohse, Knut. 1981a. *Ausländische Arbeiter und bürgerlicher Staat: Genese und Funktion von staatlicher Ausländerpolitik und Ausländerrecht. Vom Kaiserreich bis zur Bundesrepublik Deutschland*. Königstein/Ts.: Anton Hain.

———. 1981b. "Ausländerpolitik und betriebliche Ausländerdiskriminierung," IIVG/pre 81-220. Berlin, Wissenschaftszentrum Berlin.

————. 1985. "Arbeitsplatzentwicklung und staatliche Regelungsmechanismen." Berlin, Science Center.

Ferencz, Benjamin B. 1979. *Less than Slaves: Jewish Forced Labor and the Quest for Compensation.* Cambridge, Mass.: Harvard University Press.

Freeman, Gary P. 1979. *Immigrant Labor and Racial Conflict in Industrial Societies: The French and British Experience 1945-1975.* Princeton: Princeton University Press.

Gupte, Pranay. 1984. "Germany's Guest Workers." *New York Times,* August 14, section 6, pp. 86–101.

Homze, Edward L. 1967. *Foreign Labor in Nazi Germany.* Princeton: Princeton University Press.

Hoskin, Marilyn. 1985. "Public Opinion and the Foreign Worker: Traditional and Non-traditional Bases in West Germany." *Comparative Politics* 17(2):193–210.

Huber, Bertold, and Unger, Klaus. 1982. "Politische und rechtliche Determinanten der Ausländerbeschäftigung in der Bundesrepublik Deutschland." In Hans-Joachim Hoffman-Nowotny and Karl-Otto Hondrich, eds., *Ausländer in der Bundesrepublik Deutschland und in der Schweiz: Segregation und Integration. Eine vergleichende Untersuchung,* pp. 124–94. Frankfurt: Campus.

International Labour Office. 1959. *International Migration 1945-1957.* Pp. 7–42. Geneva: International Labour Office.

Kindleberger, Charles P. 1967. *Europe's Post-War Growth: The Role of Labor Supply.* Cambridge, Mass.: Harvard University Press.

Klauder, Wolfgang. 1984. "Arbeitsmarktperspektiven unter besonderer Berücksichtigung der Ausländerbeschäftigung." In Klaus J. Bade, ed., *Auswanderer, Wanderarbeiter, Gastarbeiter: Bevölkerung, Arbeitsmarkt und Wanderung in Deutschland seit der Mitte des 19.Jahrhunderts,* 2:696–730. Ostfildern: Scripta Mercaturae.

Lohrmann, Reinhard, and Manfrass, Klaus, eds. 1974. *Ausländerbeschäftigung und internationale Politik: Zur Analyse transnationaler Sozialprozesse.* Munich: Oldenbourg.

Markovits, Andrei S., and Kazarinov, Samantha. 1978. "Class Conflict, Capitalism, and Social Democracy." *Comparative Politics* 10(3):373–91.

Mehrländer, Ursula. 1978. "Bundesrepublik Deutschland." In Ernst Gehmacher, Daniel Kubat, and Ursula Mehrländer, eds., *Ausländerpolitik im Konflikt: Arbeitskräfte oder Einwanderer? Konzepte der Aufnahme- und Entsendeländer,* pp. 115–37. Bonn: Neue Gesellschaft.

Miller, Mark J. 1981. *Foreign Workers in Western Europe: An Emerging Political Force.* New York: Praeger.

Reimann, Horst, and Reimann, Helga. 1979. "Federal Republic of Germany."

In Ronald E. Krane, ed., *International Labor Migration in Europe*, pp. 63–87. New York: Praeger.

Rist, Ray C. 1978. *Guestworkers in Germany: The Prospects for Pluralism*. New York: Praeger.

Schiller, Günter. 1975. "Channelling Migration: A Review of Policy with Special References to the Federal Republic of Germany." *International Labor Review* 3(4):335–55.

Sievering, Ulrich O., ed. 1981. *Integration ohne Partizipation? Ausländerwahlrecht in der Bundesrepublik Deutschland zwischen (verfassungs-) rechtlicher Möglichkeit und politischer Notwendigkeit*. Frankfurt: Haag and Herchen.

Spaich, Herbert. 1981. *Fremde in Deutschland: Unbequeme Kapitel unserer Geschichte*. Weinheim: Beltz.

Thränhardt, Dietrich. 1984. "Patterns of Organization of Different Ethnic Minorities in Germany." European Consortium for Political Research, 12th Joint Session of Workshops, Salzburg, April 13–18.

Viviano, Frank, and Browning, Frank. 1983. "Immigration: The American Problem Comes to Europe." *TransAtlantic Perspectives* 9(August):3–7.

Wallraff, Günter. 1985. *Ganz Unten*. Cologne: Kiepenheuer and Witsch.

Weber, R. 1965. "The Employment of Aliens in Germany." *International Migration* 3(1–2):35–46.

Zuleeg, Manfred. 1985. "Politik der Armut und Ausländer." In Stephan Leibfried and Florian Tennstedt, eds., *Politik der Armut und die Spaltung des Sozialstaats*, pp. 295–308. Frankfurt: Suhrkamp.

Administrative Reform

Albertin, Lothar. 1980. "Local Territorial Reform in the Context of West German Social Development." Paper read at the Conference of Europeanists, Council for European Studies, Washington, D.C., October 23–25.

———. 1982. "Reforms in Local Governmental Institutions in the Federal Republic of Germany." Paper read at the International Conference, Local Institutions in National Development: Strategies and Consequences of Local-National Linkages in the Industrial Democracies, Bellagio, Italy, March 15–19.

Armstrong, John A. 1973. *The European Administrative Elite*. Princeton: Princeton University Press.

Cole, Taylor. 1952. "The Democratization of the German Civil Service." *Journal of Politics* 14(1):3–18.

Dyson, Kenneth H.F. 1973. "Planning and the Federal Chancellor's Office in West German Federal Government." *Political Studies* 21(3):348–62.

———. 1974. "Anti-Communism in the Federal Republic of Germany: The Case of the 'Berufsverbot'." *Parliamentary Affairs* 28(1):51–67.

————. 1975a. "Improving Policy-Making in Bonn: Why the Central Planners Failed." *Journal of Management Studies* 12(2):157–74.

————. 1975b. "Left-Wing Political Extremism and the Problem of Tolerance in Western Germany." *Government and Opposition* 10(3):306–31.

Edinger, Lewis. 1960. "Post-Totalitarian Leadership." *American Political Science Review* 54(1):58–82.

Ellwein, Thomas, and Hesse, Joachim Jens. 1985. *Verwaltungsvereinfachung und Verwaltungspolitik*. Baden-Baden: Nomos.

Faude, Alfred. 1975. "Bemühungen um eine Reform von Bundesregierung und Bundesverwaltung." In C. A. Andrae, D. J. Prins, and Alexander Van der Bellen, eds., *Reform Movements in Public Administration*, II/74-2. Berlin, International Institute of Management.

Frisch, Peter. 1977. *Extremistenbeschluss*. Leverkusen: Heggen.

Gillis, John R. 1971. *The Prussian Bureaucracy in Crisis*. Stanford: Stanford University Press.

Grottian, Peter. 1974. *Strukturprobleme staatlicher Planung: Eine empirische Studie zum Planungsbewusstsein der Bonner Ministerialbürokratie und zur staatlichen Planung der Unternehmenskonzentration und des Wettbewerbs (GWB)*. Hamburg: Hoffmann and Campe.

Gunlicks, Arthur B. 1977a. "Comparative Local Government Reform: United States and Germany." Paper read at the annual meeting of the American Political Science Association, Washington, D.C., September 1–4.

————. 1977b. "Restructuring Service Delivery Systems in West Germany." In Vincent Ostrom and Frances Pennell Bish, eds., *Comparing Urban Service Delivery Systems: Structure and Performance*, pp. 173–96. Beverly Hills: Sage Publications.

————. 1981. "The Reorganization of Local Governments in the Federal Republic of Germany." In Gunlicks, ed., *Local Government Reform and Reorganization: An International Perspective*, pp. 169–81. Port Washington, N.Y.: Kennikat Press.

————. 1984. "Administrative Centralization and Decentralization in the Making and Remaking of Modern Germany." *Review of Politics* 46(3):323–45.

————. 1986. *Local Government in the German Federal System*. Durham, N.C.: Duke University Press.

Hanf, Kenneth I. 1968. "The Higher Civil Service in West Germany: Administrative Leadership and the Policy Process." Ph.D. diss., University of California, Berkeley.

————. 1973. "Administrative Developments in East and West Germany: Stirrings of Reform." *Political Studies* 21(1):35–44.

Herz, John H. 1957. "Political Views of the West German Civil Service." In Hans Speier and Phillips Davison, eds., *West German Leadership and Foreign Policy*, pp. 96–135. Evanston, Ill.: Row, Peterson.

Hesse, Joachim Jens, ed. 1982. *Politikwissenschaft und Verwaltungswissenschaft*. Special issue 13 of *Politische Vierteljahresschrift*. Opladen: Westdeutscher Verlag.

Hirsch, Joachim. 1980. *Die Sicherheitsstaat: Das 'Modell Deutschland' seine Krise und die neuen sozialen Bewegungen*. Frankfurt: Europäische Verlagsanstalt.

Hochschwender, Karl Albert. 1962. "The Politics of Civil Service Reform in West Germany." Ph.D. diss., Yale University.

Katzenstein, Peter J. 1969. "Chancellery and Chancellor Democracy." Unpublished paper, Harvard University.

Keller, Berndt. 1984. "Beamtenlobbies: Verbandsmacht und Interessendurchsetzung in der BRD." *Journal für Sozialforschung* 24(2):163–83.

Komitee für Grundrechte und Demokratie. 1982. *Ohne Zweifel für den Staat: Die Praxis zehn Jahre nach dem Radikalenerlass*. Reinbek: Rowohlt.

Kvistad, Gregg O. 1984. "Radicals and the German State: Hegel, Marx and the Political Demands on German Civil Servants." Ph.D. diss., University of California, Berkeley.

———. 1986. "Radicals and the State: The Political Demands on West German Civil Servants." Paper read at the annual meeting of the American Political Science Association, Washington, D.C., August 28–31.

Landfried, Christine. 1985. "Legal Policy and Internal Security." In Klaus von Beyme and Manfred G. Schmidt, eds., *Policy and Politics in the Federal Republic of Germany*, pp. 198–221. New York: St. Martin's Press.

Lehmbruch, Gerhard. 1977. "Verfassungspolitische Alternativen der Politikverflechtung. Bemerkungen zur Strategie der Verfassungsreform." Unpublished paper, University of Tübingen.

Lompe, Klaus. 1970. "The Role of Scientific Planning in the Governmental Process: The West German Experience." *American Journal of Economics and Sociology* 29(4):369–87.

Mayntz, Renate. 1984. "German Federal Bureaucrats: A Functional Elite between Politics and Administration." In Ezra N. Suleiman, ed., *Bureaucrats and Policy Making: A Comparative Overview*, pp. 174–205. New York: Holmes and Meier.

Mayntz, Renate, and Scharpf, Fritz. 1975. *Policy-Making in the German Federal Bureaucracy*. Amsterdam: Elsevier.

———, eds. 1973. *Planungsorganisation: Die Diskussion um die Reform von Regierung und Verwaltung des Bundes*. Munich: Piper.

McDermott, Raymond C. 1981. "The Functions of Local Levels of Government in West Germany and Their Internal Organization: Some Reflections on the Problems of Administrative Reform." In Arthur B. Gunlicks, ed., *Local Government Reform and Reorganization: An International Perspective*, pp. 182–201. Port Washington, N.Y.: Kennikat Press.

Miko, Francis T. 1976. "The Civil Service in the Federal Republic of Germany." In *History of Civil Service Merit Systems of the U.S. and Selected Foreign Countries*, pp. 391–410. Washington, D.C.: Library of Congress, Congressional Research Service.

Montgomery, John D. 1957. *Forced to Be Free: The Artificial Revolution in Germany and Japan*. Chicago: University of Chicago Press.

Murswieck, Axel. 1975. *Regierungsreform durch Planungsorganisation: Eine empirische Untersuchung im Bereich der Bundesregierung*. Opladen: West-deutscher Verlag.

Putnam, Robert D. 1973. "The Political Attitudes of Senior Civil Servants in Western Europe: A Preliminary Report." *British Journal of Political Science* 3(3):257–90.

————. 1975. "The Political Attitudes of Senior Civil Servants in Britain, Germany, and Italy." In Mattei Dogan, ed., *The Mandarins of Western Europe*, pp. 87–127. New York: Wiley.

Rosenberg, Hans. 1958. *Bureaucracy, Aristocracy and Autocracy: The Prussian Experience, 1660-1815*. Boston: Beacon Press.

Scharpf, Fritz W. 1973. *Planung als politischer Prozess: Aufsätze zur Theorie der planenden Demokratie*. Frankfurt: Suhrkamp.

————. 1974. *Politische Durchsetzbarkeit innerer Reformen*. Göttingen: Schwarz.

Schatz, Heribert. 1976. "The Development of Political Planning in the Federal Republic of Germany." In Klaus von Beyme et al., eds., *German Political Systems: Theory and Practice in the Two Germanies*, pp. 41–68. Beverly Hills: Sage Publications.

Schmid, Günther, and Treiber, Hubert. 1975. *Bürokratie und Politik: Zur Struktur und Funktion der Ministerialbürokratie in der Bundesrepublik Deutschland*. Munich: Wilhelm Fink.

Schmidt, Manfred G. 1980. *CDU und SPD an der Regierung: Ein Vergleich ihrer Politik in den Ländern*. Frankfurt: Campus.

Seiler, Dietmar. 1984. "Federal Republic of Germany: Planning in Federal Government and Federal Administration." *Indian Journal of Public Administration* 30(3):827–37.

Shefter, Martin. 1977. "Party and Patronage: Germany, England, and Italy." *Politics and Society* 7(4):403–51.

Steinkemper, Bärbel. 1974. *Klassische und politische Bürokraten in der Ministerialverwaltung der Bundesrepublik Deutschland*. Cologne: Heymanns.

Steinkemper, Hans Günther. 1980. *Amtsträger im Grenzbereich zwischen Regierung und Verwaltung: Ein Beitrag zur Problematik der Institution des politischen Beamten in der Bundesexekutive*. Frankfurt: Peter D. Lang.

Waterkamp, Rainer. 1974. *Politische Leitung und Systemveränderung: Zum*

Problemlösungsprozess durch Planungs- und Informationssysteme. Frankfurt: Europäische Verlagsanstalt.

University Reform

Ben-David, Joseph. 1971. *The Scientist's Role in Society: A Comparative Study.* Englewood Cliffs: Prentice-Hall.

Bender, Ignaz. 1980. "Die deutschen Universitäten an der kurzen Leine des Staates." *Deutsche Universitätszeitung* 19:587–90.

Berger, Rolf. 1974. *Zur Stellung des Wissenschaftsrats bei der wissenschaftspolitischen Beratung von Bund und Ländern.* Baden-Baden: Nomos.

Bork, Uwe, and Klee, Manfred. 1979–80. "*Studentenwerke*—Their Work and Their History." *Western European Education* 11(3–4):21–33.

Briese, Volker. 1972. *Zentralisierung der Kulturpolitik in der Bundesrepublik Deutschland: Reformen zwischen Ökonomie und Ideologie.* Constance: University of Constance, Center for Educational Research.

Carbone, Robert. 1974. "West German Universities—The Problem of Too Many Students." Research Paper No. 3. University of Maryland, Comparative Education Center.

Cerych, Ladislav. 1980. "Retreat from Ambitious Goals?" *European Journal of Education* 15(1):5–13.

Dahrendorf, Ralf. 1965. *Bildung ist Bürgerrecht: Plädoyer für eine aktive Bildungspolitik.* Hamburg: Nannen.

Fallon, Daniel. 1980. *The German University: A Heroic Ideal in Conflict with the Modern World.* Boulder: Colorado Associated University Press.

Feist, Ursula, and Liepelt, Klaus. 1983. "New Elites in Old Parties: Observations on a Side Effect of German Educational Reform." *International Political Science Review* 4(1):71–83.

Fuhrig, Wolf-Dieter. 1966. "State and University in the Federal Republic of Germany." Ph.d. diss., Columbia University.

Gellert, Claudius. 1984. "Politics and Higher Education in the Federal Republic of Germany." *European Journal of Education* 19(2):217–32.

———. 1985. "State Interventionism and Institutional Autonomy: University Development and State Interference in England and West Germany." *Oxford Review of Education* 11(3):283–93.

Giles, Geoffrey J. 1976. "University Government in Nazi Germany: The Example of Hamburg." *Yale Higher Education Program Working Paper,* no. 15. New Haven: Yale University, Institution for Social and Policy Studies.

Graaff, John H. van de. 1975. "Legislating German University Structure: The Politics of Tradition in Hesse, 1960-1966." *Yale Higher Education Program Working Paper,* no. 1. New Haven: Yale University, Institution for Social and Policy Studies.

————. 1978. "Federal Republic of Germany." In van de Graaff, Burton R. Clark, Dorotea Furth, Dietrich Goldschmidt, and Donald F. Wheeler, *Academic Power: Patterns of Authority in Seven National Systems of Higher Education*, pp. 15–36. New York: Praeger.

Hahn, Walter. 1963. "Higher Education in West Germany: Reform Movements and Trends." *Comparative Education Review* 7(1):51–60.

Heister, Matthias M. 1985. "Notes on Current Planning for Higher Education in the Federal Republic of Germany." *Oxford Review of Education* 11(3):255–61.

Hennis, Wilhelm. 1982. "Germany: Legislators and the Universities." In Hans Daalder and Edward Shils, eds., *Universities, Politicians and Bureaucrats*, pp. 1–30. Cambridge: Cambridge University Press.

Karpen, Ulrich. 1976. "University Admission Criteria: Some German-American Comparative Observations." *International Review of Education* 22(2):203–21.

————. 1978. "Constitutional Problems Concerning Admission to Institutions of Higher Education—Questions Relevant to a German-American Comparison." *International Review of Education* 24(1):3–20.

Kloss, Günther. 1968. "University Reform in West Germany: The Burden of Tradition." *Minerva* 6(3):323–53.

————. 1971. "The Growth of Federal Power in the West German University System." *Minerva* 9(4):510–27.

————. 1985. "The Academic Restructuring of British and German Universities and Greater Efficiency: A Comparative Perspective." *Oxford Review of Education* 11(3):271–82.

Künzel, Klaus. 1985. "Regional Development and Continuing Education: A Case for a Fresh Look at University Evolution in West Germany?" *Oxford Review of Education* 11(3):305–15.

Merritt, Richard L. 1979. "The Courts, the Universities and the Right of Admission in the Federal German Republic." *Minerva* 1:1–32.

Merritt, Richard L.; Flerlage, Ellen P.; and Merritt, Anna J. 1971. "Political Man in Postwar West German Education." *Comparative Education Review* 15(3):346–61.

Mushaben, Joyce Marie. 1981. "The State vs. the University: Juridicalization and the Politics of Higher Education at the Free University of Berlin, 1969-1979." Ph.d. diss., Indiana University.

————. 1984. "Reform in Three Phases: Judicial Action and the German Federal Framework Law for Higher Education of 1976." *Higher Education* 13:423–38.

Neusel, Aylâ, and Teichler, Ulrich. 1982. "Gesamthochschulen in der Bundesrepublik Deutschland—Geschichte, Implementationsprozess und

Zukunftsperspektiven." In Harry Hermanns, Teichler, and Henry Wasser, eds., *Integrierte Hochschulmodelle: Erfahrungen aus drei Ländern*, pp. 168–86. Frankfurt: Campus.

Picht, Georg. 1964. *Die deutsche Bildungskatastrophe: Analyse und Dokumentation.* Olten: Walter.

Ringer, Fritz K. 1967. "Higher Education in Germany in the Nineteenth Century." *Journal of Contemporary History* 2(3):123–38.

———. 1969. *The Decline of the German Mandarins: The German Academic Community 1890-1933.* Cambridge, Mass.: Harvard University Press.

Rüschemeyer, Dietrich. 1982. "Bildung und Ungleichheit: Zur Politik der Hochschulexpansion in der Bundesrepublik." *Frankfurter Hefte* 1:37–45.

Schelsky, Helmut. 1963. *Einsamkeit und Freiheit: Idee und Gestalt der deutschen Universität und ihrer Reformen.* Hamburg: Rowohlt.

Schmittner, Konrad. 1971. "Der Kampf um das Hochschulrahmengesetz des Bundes." *Konstanzer Blätter für Hochschulfragen* 9(31):5–18.

Teichler, Ulrich. 1972. "University Reform and Skeleton Legislation on Higher Education in the Federal Republic of Germany: Key Points and Problems in the Reform Efforts." *Western European Education* 4(3):224–38.

———. 1974. "University Reform and Skeleton Legislation on Higher Education in the Federal Republic of Germany: Breakdown of the Skeleton Legislation on Higher Education." *Western European Education* 5(4):34–55.

———. 1976. "Problems of West German Universities on the Way to Mass Higher Education." *Western European Education* 8(1–2):81–120.

———. 1982. "Recent Developments in Higher Education in the Federal Republic of Germany." *European Journal of Education* 17(2):161–76.

———. 1983. "Quantitative and Structural Development of Higher Education in the Federal Republic of Germany: Trends, Issues and Policies." Paper read at the 4th International Conference of Europeanists, Washington, D.C., October 13–15.

———. 1984. "Zum Funktionswandel der Hochschulen im Zuge ihrer Expansion." *Pädagogik und Schule in Ost und West* 32(1):4–13.

Teichler, Ulrich, and Sanyal, B. C. 1984. "Higher Education and Employment in the Federal Republic." In R. Avakov, M. Buttgereit, Sanyal, and Teichler, eds., *Higher Education and Employment in the USSR and in the Federal Republic of Germany*, pp. 89–184. Paris: UNESCO, International Institute for Educational Planning.

Weiler, Hans N. 1981a. "Equal Protection, Legitimacy, and the Legalization of Education: The Role of the Federal Constitutional Court in West Germany." Unpublished paper, Stanford University.

———. 1981b. "Compensatory Legitimation in Educational Policy: Legalization, Expertise, and Participation in Comparative Perspective." Paper read at the 10th European Conference on Comparative Education, Geneva, September 20–23.

———. 1982. "Protest and Reform in West Germany: Cycles of Causation in Education and Energy Policy?" Paper read at the Conference of Europeanists of the Council for European Studies, Washington, D.C., April 29–May 1.

Wildenmann, Rudolf. 1971. "Higher Education in Transition: The Case of the Universities in the Federal Republic of Germany." In Stephen D. Kertesz, ed., *The Task of Universities in a Changing World*, pp. 336–52. Notre Dame: University of Notre Dame Press.

Index